# The Man Who Understood Democracy

# The Man Who Understood Democracy

## THE LIFE OF
## ALEXIS DE TOCQUEVILLE

Olivier Zunz

PRINCETON UNIVERSITY PRESS
PRINCETON & OXFORD

Published by Princeton University Press
41 William Street, Princeton, New Jersey 08540
99 Banbury Road, Oxford OX2 6JX

press.princeton.edu

All Rights Reserved

Library of Congress Cataloging-in-Publication Data

Names: Zunz, Olivier, author.
Title: The man who understood democracy : the life of Alexis de Tocqueville / Olivier Zunz.
Description: Princeton : Princeton University Press, [2022] | Includes bibliographical references and index.
Identifiers: LCCN 2021041198 (print) | LCCN 2021041199 (ebook) | ISBN 9780691173979 (hardback) | ISBN 9780691235455 (ebook)
Subjects: LCSH: Tocqueville, Alexis de, 1805–1859—Political and social views. | Aristocracy (Social class)—France. | Democracy—Philosophy. | Political scientists—France—Biography. | Political scientists—United States—Biography. | BISAC: BIOGRAPHY & AUTOBIOGRAPHY / Philosophers | POLITICAL SCIENCE / Political Ideologies / Democracy
Classification: LCC JC229.T8 Z86 2022 (print) | LCC JC229.T8 (ebook) | DDC 306.2092 [B]—dc23/eng/20211128
LC record available at https://lccn.loc.gov/2021041198
LC ebook record available at https://lccn.loc.gov/2021041199

British Library Cataloging-in-Publication Data is available

Editorial: Priya Nelson, Barbara Shi
Jacket Design: Pamela L. Schnitter
Production: Danielle Amatucci
Publicity: James Schneider, Kate Farquhar-Thomson
Copyeditor: Joyce Li

Jacket image: Alexis Charles Henri Clérel, comte de Tocqueville (1805–1859). CPA Media Pte Ltd / Alamy Stock Photo

This book has been composed in Arno

Printed on acid-free paper. ∞

Printed in the United States of America

10  9  8  7  6  5  4  3  2  1

To the memory of my friend Michel de Certeau (1925–86),
who taught me that "l'histoire n'est jamais sûre."

# CONTENTS

*Color plates follow page 176*

# Prologue

"IS IT ANY WONDER that titles should fall in France? Is it not a greater wonder that they should be kept up anywhere? What are they? . . . When we think or speak of a Judge or a General, we associate with it the ideas of office and character; we think of gravity in one and bravery in the other"; but for "a Duke or a Count," one cannot say whether these words "mean strength or weakness, wisdom or folly, a child or a man, or the rider or the horse." So wrote Thomas Paine in 1791 during the French Revolution.[1] Alexis de Tocqueville, born in 1805, a scion of the highest ranks of the French nobility, agreed. He became the only member of his family to choose democracy over aristocracy. He always declined to use his own title of count, and he was annoyed when others so addressed him. Although he recognized he had aristocratic "instincts," he was a democrat "by reason" and worked hard to advance the great modern shift from aristocracy to democracy.[2] In an aristocracy, Tocqueville noted, "families maintain the same station for centuries, and often in the same place . . . link[ing] all citizens together in a long chain from peasant to king." Tocqueville opted instead for democracy, which "breaks the chain," "severs the links," and invites individual citizens to achieve their potential on their own.[3]

The measure of any form of government, Tocqueville believed, was liberty and equality. In an aristocracy, only privileged aristocrats could enjoy liberty—at the expense of the liberty of others. In Tocqueville's democracy, by contrast, all citizens have the liberty to act within an agreed-upon legal framework. Tocqueville viewed equality as the engine of liberty, and although he recognized the need to repair social injustice, he saw equality not as a means of leveling but of uplifting. He believed that the pursuits of liberty and equality were intimately linked; he even imagined "an extreme point at which liberty and equality touch and become one."[4]

The transformation from aristocracy to democracy was not without its costs, either for Tocqueville or society at large. Tocqueville's own family was decimated during the Revolutionary Terror that engulfed France between 1793 and 1794. Tocqueville's parents, Hervé de Tocqueville and Louise-Madeleine Le Peletier de Rosanbo, married in March 1793, only two months after Louis XVI had been beheaded. This alliance between a young army officer from Normandy, born to an ancient family of the military nobility (the nobility of the sword), and the daughter of a family that had risen through the highest echelons of royal administration (the so-called *grande robe*) might have fueled controversy only a few years earlier. But the wedding took place when the time for negotiating rivalries between different castes of French nobles was gone. Every noble in France was now suspected of conspiring against the Revolution—a crime whose penalty was death.

The bride's father, the marquis de Rosanbo, was an important man before the Revolution. He was a principal magistrate of the highest appeals court of the time, *président à mortier* of the "*parlement*" in Paris. The bride's grandfather, Chrétien-Guillaume de Lamoignon de Malesherbes, was even more important. As director of the book trade (la librairie) under Louis XV, Malesherbes had protected the philosophes, and as Louis XVI's minister he had promoted liberal reforms. He was one of two lawyers who defended the king at his revolutionary trial. Tocqueville admired his great-grandfather (whom he called his "grandfather") for "having pleaded the cause of liberty, a principle so dear to him, in the court of his no-less beloved royalty, and for having advocated for equality of rights despite being among those already privileged."[5] But Malesherbes's liberal views secured his family no protection.

The revolutionaries arrested all the adult members of the Malesherbes-Rosanbo-Tocqueville family—ten in total—at the château of Malesherbes in the Loiret over the course of a few days in December 1793, transporting them to various jails in Paris to await summary trial and execution. Alexis's maternal grandfather, Rosanbo, was first to be guillotined, on April 20. Two days later, on April 22, his grandmother, Marguerite, went to the scaffold, followed by Aline-Thérèse de Rosanbo, his aunt, and her husband, Jean-Baptiste de Chateaubriand (older brother of the great Romantic writer). Malesherbes was beheaded last on that day, after the executioners made him watch his daughter and grandchildren's heads fall from the guillotine in front of him.

The remaining family members—Tocqueville's parents, Aunt Guillemette and her husband, Charles Le Peletier d'Aunay, and Uncle Louis Le Peletier de Rosanbo—were in jail awaiting their turn when Robespierre's own fall and execution on 10 Thermidor Year II of the French First Republic (July 27, 1794) put an end to the slaughter. They remained imprisoned for another three months before finally being freed in October.

Louise-Madeleine, already prone to depression in her youth, never recovered her sense of well-being. Tocqueville's parents spent ten months of the first eighteen months of their married life in jail. They mourned the execution of their closest family, and on release, they found themselves caring for the survivors. On the day Jean-Baptiste de Chateaubriand was taken from prison to the guillotine, Hervé de Tocqueville promised him that, should he himself survive the Terror, he would adopt his brother-in-law's two young sons, Christian and Geoffroy, the only family members still in hiding at Malesherbes.

Eleven years later, in 1805, Louise-Madeleine gave birth to Alexis, her third biological child. She was disappointed that the baby was yet another boy, so keen had been her hopes for a daughter. Her husband attempted to console her with an optimistic prediction. Hervé recalled in his *Mémoires* that on first sight of the baby, he thought, "This child was born with so singularly expressive a figure that I told his mother he would become a man of distinction, adding with a laugh that he could one day become Emperor."[6] The first half of his prophecy came to pass. The boy would enter the canon of great political philosophers. But far from becoming an emperor, he would dedicate his life to ending despotism.

Great thinkers do not always have a life worthy of detailed telling. We often understand them better in conversation with other great minds across the ages rather than with their contemporaries. In this respect, however, Alexis de Tocqueville stands apart. His early life was shaped by the aftermath of the Revolutionary Terror in France, and he died two years before the start of the American Civil War. He was witness to a profound transformation of society and was as passionate about participating in politics as he was about studying the subject.

Tocqueville's fateful decision to journey to America, at age twenty-five, in 1831, showed remarkable initiative. There, he observed the palpable reality of a functioning democracy, and America remained central to Tocqueville's thought and action throughout his life, long after the trip and in almost inverse proportion to its brevity. He realized the extent to which the principle of equality gave "a certain direction to the public spirit and a certain shape to laws, establishe[d] new maxims for governing, and foster[ed] distinctive habits in the governed."[7] These observations would form the foundation for his most enduring work, *Democracy in America*.

Upon his return to France, Tocqueville pursued both his intellectual and political ambitions. As soon as possible after reaching the legal age to run for elected office, he campaigned to represent the area around his ancestral estate in Normandy in the French Chamber of Deputies. He participated in the great controversies of the July Monarchy on suffrage extension, the separation of church and state, and the colonization of Algeria. He was notably invested in the abolition of slavery in the French Caribbean, prison reform and the rehabilitation of criminals, and welfare reform. His political career climaxed in 1849 under the Second Republic in the aftermath of the 1848 Revolution, as drafter of its constitution, then briefly as foreign minister. Tocqueville continuously bridged the worlds of letters and politics, engaging in debates of literary academies, publishing polemics in the press (he briefly directed a newspaper), and participating in conversations in Parisian salons.

This biography tells how Tocqueville developed his ideas in the context of the charged political events of his lifetime. Fortunately, Tocqueville left an ample written record: speeches, draft speeches, a volume of memoirs on the Revolution of 1848 and his role in the Second Republic. Add to these the journals of his extensive travels not just to America but also to England, Switzerland, Sicily, and Algeria, as well as his notes on India, and his wide-ranging correspondence with some of the best minds of his generation. It is in this correspondence that Tocqueville's emotions and personal judgments come through. He often drafted and redrafted his thoughts about past and current events, developing a subtle analysis. Tocqueville corresponded not only with a galaxy of intellectuals and politicians in France, the United States, England, and Germany but also with family members, close friends he had made in his teenage years, and, of course, constituents. His many correspondents cherished his frequent letters, written with vibrancy in his barely decipherable handwriting. His gift for enduring friendships, sustained by daily correspondence over a lifetime, is a boon to the biographer.

Throughout his political career, Tocqueville remained firmly focused on current affairs, the future of democracy, and the need for political and social reform. Only after Louis Napoléon Bonaparte put an end to a short republican experiment and restored an authoritarian regime did Tocqueville retire from politics and turn his sustained attention to the Ancien Régime, and to the intensely complex drama of the French Revolution that ended the prominence and indeed the lives of Malesherbes and other members of his mother's family. But it was in mourning not for his family but for the recent demise of democracy in France that Tocqueville wrote his second masterpiece, published as *The Ancien Régime and the Revolution*. He intended it as the first installment of a larger work on the cycles of revolution and reaction that had become the curse of French history.

Confronted with many ambiguities in Tocqueville's thought, readers have often questioned the depth and sincerity of this scion of aristocracy's support for democracy. Tocqueville often vacillated between democratic ideas and more conservative views informed by his aristocratic heritage, though he may not have fully realized how conflicted he was. In reading him, one comes to appreciate the power of his conclusions because he persists in making them in the face of misgivings. He shared his doubts with readers by presenting opposite sides of many issues, tilting the balance only slightly one way or the other.

Tocqueville also assumed contradictory positions: He encouraged entrepreneurship while decrying materialism; he promoted the equality of all people but championed colonial domination; he wanted to reconcile democracy and religion—yet was unsure about his own faith. The list goes on. His need to resolve the opposing poles of his thought is one reason for his almost obsessive revisions. Although his edits did not necessarily clarify his thoughts, they did make his prose more pleasurable, something that was very important to him.

Readers then and now, especially of *Democracy in America*, have pointed to these real inconsistencies. Some contemporaries even turned the book into an indictment of democracy, to Tocqueville's dismay. For foreign readers, the potential for misreading a text that was already hard to grasp was compounded by translation. The correspondence between Tocqueville and his British translator Henry Reeve highlights these issues. In one letter, Tocqueville reproached Reeve for making him too much a foe of monarchy; in another, too much one of democracy.[8]

The upshot was that Tocqueville pleased no faction. Shortly before *Democracy in America* was published, Tocqueville confided to his cousin Camille d'Orglandes, "I do not hide what may be troubling about my position. It is not likely to enlist the active sympathy of anyone. Some will find that at bottom I do not like democracy and treat it rather severely. Others will think that I am incautiously encouraging its spread."[9] Even when Tocqueville took a stand against his elders, he remained ambiguous. To his uncle Louis de Rosanbo, a survivor of the Revolutionary Terror, who admonished his nephew for not being loyal to the Legitimist cause in the Chamber, Tocqueville wrote affectionately, "Let me continue to believe that my venerable ancestor [Malesherbes] continues to judge me worthy of him, which is all I have ever sought to be."[10]

For all the equivocation and sincere doubts that Tocqueville shared with family, friends, and readers, he nevertheless remained true to a set of basic unshakable convictions. He expressed them with perfect clarity in a brief note he sent to Chateaubriand that accompanied an advance copy of *Democracy in America*. This was, he wrote, a work in which he had joined heart and mind: "I've shown in this work a feeling carved deeply into my heart: the love of liberty. I've expressed an idea that obsesses my mind: the irresistible march of democracy."[11]

In other words, what has kept Tocqueville's work alive, read, and discussed are not his equivocations but his convictions, the force of which also drive this biography. Tocqueville's deepest belief was that democracy is a powerful, yet demanding, political form. What makes Tocqueville's work still relevant is that he defined democracy as an act of will on the part of every citizen—a project constantly in need of revitalization and of the strength provided by stable institutions. Democracy can never be taken for granted. Once the aristocratic chain connecting all parts of society is broken, democracy's need for vigilance, redefinition, and reinforcement is constant if it is to ensure the common good on which it must, in the end, depend.

# 1

# Learning to Doubt

## A Protected Childhood Spent in Paris and Verneuil

Go back in time. Examine the babe when still in its mother's arms.
See the external world reflected for the first time in the still-dark mirror of his intelligence. Contemplate the first models to make an impression on him. Listen to the words that first awaken his dormant
powers of thought. Take note, finally, of the first battles he is obliged
to fight. Only then will you understand where the prejudices, habits,
and passions that will dominate his life come from. In a manner of
speaking, the whole man already lies swaddled in his cradle.[1]

Alexis de Tocqueville made these observations in *Democracy in America*
to explain his rationale for studying America's "point of departure."
Of course, the beginning is also where the biographer must start. For
the young Tocqueville, that external world was dominated by figures
from the highest military and administrative nobility of the Ancien Régime, survivors of the Revolutionary Terror, loyal to the exiled Bourbons, and dead set against the liberal views Tocqueville himself would
eventually embrace. Presaging this divergence, Tocqueville displayed
considerable independence of mind at an early age, and he repeatedly
flouted expectations. At the same time, he developed the habit of casting doubt on much of what he did and saw.

Born in Paris on July 29, 1805, the third son of Hervé and Louise-
Madeleine de Tocqueville, Alexis spent the first nine years of his life

between the Faubourg Saint-Germain in Paris, where the family resided in winter, and the château of Verneuil-sur-Seine. These were comfortable homes; Hervé de Tocqueville had been skillful in recovering much of the family fortune after the Terror. A third residence, the Norman manor at Tocqueville, had remained uninhabited since the French Revolution, but the land was farmed profitably. On the Malesherbes-Rosanbo side, Louise-Madeleine owned an estate in Lannion in Brittany and inherited a share of her great-aunt Madame de Sénozan's domain of Verneuil. Since Malesherbes's sister had also been guillotined, the great Romantic writer Chateaubriand (who was the younger brother of Tocqueville's guillotined uncle) labeled Verneuil an "inheritance from the scaffold."[2]

Hervé de Tocqueville tactfully negotiated, over several years, agreements with the Malesherbes and Rosanbo heirs and creditors to acquire the property in full, a transfer made more complicated by the events of the Revolution. Some heirs had lost their property to the state by leaving France during the Terror.[3] In the bid to recover these estates, it helped that a few family members had concluded that Napoleon had saved France from chaos and rallied to him, notably Félix Le Peletier d'Aunay, Louise-Madeleine's first cousin, and Louis-Mathieu Molé, a more distant cousin. Chateaubriand also rallied to Napoleon, albeit temporarily. Hervé de Tocqueville and his brother-in-law, Louis de Rosanbo, although fiercely loyal to the Bourbons, successfully solicited and obtained an audience with Josephine de Beauharnais, the First Consul's wife, and succeeded in having Madame de Montboissier (Malesherbes's youngest daughter) struck from the list of émigrés.[4] In the end, by the time Alexis was born, the Tocquevilles owned Verneuil in full. Hervé de Tocqueville was an able proprietor, turning in a profit from two large farms, Verneuil and Mouillard, and collecting income from forestry, fishing, a large dovecote, and the rent from 103 small-time tenants.[5]

At Verneuil, Hervé de Tocqueville became a local official. The Seine-et-Oise prefect appointed him mayor in 1803.[6] It was common under Napoleon for local nobles to serve in these minor posts, regardless of political loyalties, as long as they supported the national conscription of 400,000 men a year.[7] The elder Tocqueville proved to be an able administrator. He responded forcefully when wounded returning soldiers carried typhus into the town, having every house hosting soldiers fumigated with vinegar.[8] He was knowledgeable and solicitous, with a demonstrated commitment to charity.

By all accounts, Alexis had a protected and happy childhood at Verneuil. His parents created an atmosphere of conviviality, and there was frequent entertainment. Despite suffering from underlying depression, Louise-Madeleine was a warm mother to her three sons and two adopted Chateaubriand nephews.

The family played parlor games and had literary evenings during which they read plays and recited poetry. Alexis remembered listening to readings of translations of popular English novels, even weeping over the fate of the unhappy Lady Clementina in Samuel Richardson's *Sir Charles Grandison*.[9] Chateaubriand, who had purchased La Vallée aux Loups, an estate some forty kilometers away, visited occasionally to spend time with his two nephews and to join in such evenings. Once, he greeted Hervé de Tocqueville disguised as an old woman.[10] Chateaubriand remembered in his *Mémoires d'outre-tombe* that Alexis, "the last famous person I would see ignored in his infancy," was nevertheless "more spoiled at Verneuil than I was at Combourg."[11]

There were serious moments, too. Alexis remembered a family celebration during which his mother sang in her languorous voice a famous song mourning the king. It was only about the king. There was no mention of close family members who had suffered the same fate; elders did not want to inflict recollections of their personal tragedies on the children.[12]

Even so protected, young Tocqueville was taught the importance of service to God and nation. Abbé Christian Lesueur, who had tutored the father, also instructed the children (who gave him the nickname Bébé). A nonjuring or refractory priest with Jansenist leanings, Lesueur developed a special relationship with the youngest and most talented child.[13] Alexis always loved his tutor even though he complained later in life that his teaching method had been less than perfect. Alexis once reminisced with his cousin Eugénie de Grancey that Bébé "had the singular idea to teach me how to write before knowing how to spell."[14] As a result, for the rest of his life, Tocqueville was never totally sure of his spelling. Bébé also insisted that there was only one law, and that was "the Gospel: its holy and charitable law, a law that brings happiness to all faithful Catholics."[15] Nation was next. Tocqueville recalled being repeatedly told in childhood that his paternal grandmother, Catherine Antoinette de Damas-Crux,

> was a saintly woman [who], after having impressed upon her young son all the duties of private life, never forgot to add: "But what is more, my child, remember that a man's first duty is to his country. For one's country, no sacrifice is too burdensome, and its fate must be kept foremost in one's mind. God requires man to commit, as needed, his time, his treasure, and even his life in service of the State and its king."[16]

Tocqueville dutifully conveyed the same message to his nephew Hubert years later: "One must first belong to one's country before one belongs to a party."[17]

Supporting the country, however, became a lot easier with the return of the Bourbons and the Restoration of the king when European armies finally defeated the emperor. There was hope when already on March 12, 1814, a detachment of Wellington's army occupied Bordeaux. By March 31, Russian, Prussian, and Austrian armies had retaken Paris. The Tocqueville family joined demonstrations taking place in Paris on the first days of April calling for the restoration of Louis XVIII, Louis XVI's younger brother, to the throne of France. At age nine, Alexis was old enough to be an enthusiastic participant hoping for his family's return to prominence. He joyfully reported to Bébé that he shouted "Vive, le roi!" along with the demonstrators.[18] His mother may have joined other wives in distributing Chateaubriand's tract, *De Buonaparte et des Bourbons, et de la nécessité de se rallier à nos princes légitimes pour le bonheur de la France et celui de l'Europe.* Napoleon formally abdicated on April 11, and Louis XVIII entered occupied Paris, after a twenty-three-year exile, on May 3.

## The Prefect's Son

Under the Bourbons, those nobles who had remained loyal to the crown regrouped and sought to recover prominent positions and prerogatives. Émigrés came back and demanded return of confiscated property. It was the hour of the Legitimists. The Tocqueville-Rosanbo family did well, as would be expected for loyal heirs of the great Malesherbes, who had defended Louis XVI at his trial at the cost of his own life, and those of several of his children. Hervé de Tocqueville began a career as prefect in several *départements* as early as mid-June 1814. He had been prefect for only a few months in Maine-et-Loire (Angers) when Napoleon returned from exile on Elba and seized power again. But the emperor's dramatic return did not last. Waterloo marked the limit of Napoleon's Hundred Days and the Bourbon monarchy was restored for a second time in July 1815, again under foreign authority, a humiliation that the Republican and Bonapartist opposition never forgave.

The Malesherbes-Rosanbos-Tocquevilles remained favored in the second restoration. Uncle Louis de Rosanbo was made peer of France (Chambre des pairs), and Hervé de Tocqueville was immediately reappointed prefect, this time in the Oise, and he and Louise-Madeleine moved to Beauvais. He then was appointed to a third post in the Côte d'Or, and they moved again to Dijon. After Tocqueville was appointed to a fourth prefecture in the Moselle at Metz in March 1817, Louise-Madeleine had had enough and decided to stay in Paris with their youngest son.

Alexis was eleven years old by then. His two brothers, Hippolyte and Édouard, had started their military careers; twenty-year-old Hippolyte was a sous-lieutenant in the Royal Guard and sixteen-year-old Édouard was already a Garde du Corps in a company.[19] Besides Bébé, Alexis had the frequent company of his cousin Louis de Kergorlay, one year his senior and the scion of another Legitimist family. The Tocquevilles and the Kergorlays lived a few blocks from one another in Paris on the rue Saint-Dominique. The two children became friends for life. Alexis also made regular trips to Metz to visit his father. He would often stay long enough that Hervé de Tocqueville arranged for a teacher from the local Collège Royal to tutor the child.[20]

At his father's request, and to Bébé's and young Louis de Kergorlay's dismay, Alexis moved to Metz in 1820, at the formative age of fourteen. For over three years, until the summer of 1823 after he turned eighteen, Alexis lived with his father in a whole new environment, and these years proved critical in Alexis's development.

It was obvious to Alexis that he was the son of one of the most important men in the city. As a prefect during the Restoration, Hervé de Tocqueville's goal was to support the returned Bourbons by replacing Napoleon's appointees in the ranks of the local administration, suppressing liberal and Bonapartist opposition, and favoring royalists but preventing outright hostility between bourgeois and nobles. One easy way for the prefect to influence local politics was to appoint mayors in the various communes of the Moselle. He also oversaw the hiring of schoolteachers and of the National Guard. Most importantly, the prefect authorized group meetings and delivered permits to assemble only to associations that posed no political threats to the regime. Finally, as the Bourbons had returned under the authority of foreign armies, Hervé had to negotiate with military occupiers in the Moselle and meet their needs.[21] The elder Tocqueville's deft handling of tasks that were both political and administrative would not be lost on his observant son. He became a reliable source on administrative matters and their entanglement with politics early in Alexis's career as he tried to identify the balance between equality and liberty in a democracy.

Hervé de Tocqueville was an "Ultra" or, some said, a "pure" royalist who tolerated little political dissent in the several departments where he served. Early in the Restoration, however, appeasement was the political order of the day.[22] Louis XVIII sought to unify the country even as he insisted on the divine source of his authority. Disputes among the Ultras and those who advocated reconciliation, the so-called Doctrinaires, defined Restoration politics in the years to come.

Pierre-Paul Royer-Collard, leader of the Doctrinaires, was key to implementing a national policy of reconciliation. Alexis de Tocqueville, who later came to know Royer-Collard well, portrayed him as a firm believer in the possibility of reconciling the spirit of the age inherited from the French Revolution (abolishing feudal privileges, guaranteeing equality before the law, ensuring the dignity and freedom of the individual) with "the old [royal] family." He sought to do so without approving of the revolutionary soul, which he thought, in agreement with the Ultras, was tainted by the spirit of adventure, violence, tyranny, and demagoguery.[23]

François Guizot, a young history professor and close associate of Royer-Collard, was appointed Secrétaire général of the Interior Ministry, a junior but influential position. Guizot would become both a major historian and formidable statesman; he was also, like Royer-Collard, a significant presence in the young Tocqueville's life. One of his first initiatives as Secrétaire général was to order what we would nowadays call a public opinion survey, pioneering a new role for local administrators. The Bourbons had been in exile, and thus out of power, for so many years that they had to rediscover France. In September 1814, Guizot instructed all prefects to inquire about the "hearts and minds of the masses, their general opinions, the general mentality and assumptions of each profession and each rank, and how they shaped public affairs in the département, especially regarding those opinions that are resistant to the authorities."[24] Guizot would eventually think of "governance of the public mind" as "the great challenge of modern society."[25]

Governing the minds of men could obviously be an instrument of repression as easily as one of reconciliation. In the early years of the Restoration, influential police minister Élie-Louis Decazes, a young man whom Louis XVIII treated as a protégé, pushed the king toward the national reunification Royer-Collard and others were calling for. Decazes was cautious about wielding repressive power, unlike Hervé de Tocqueville, and conflict between the two men sporadically erupted, accounting in part for the prefect's reassignments from one département to another. The last of these took place in Metz, in January 1820, before Alexis joined his father. Decazes judged Hervé de Tocqueville's censorship of local theater excessively heavy-handed and reminded the "Ultra" prefect that it was best to limit censorship to clear "cases of attacks on royal majesty and legitimate authority," and that there was no need to go further.[26]

Their differences ended the following month when, on February 14, Louis Pierre Louvel, a Bonapartist worker, assassinated the duc de Berry, son of Louis XVIII's autocratic younger brother, the comte d'Artois. Because Louis was childless, Louvel believed that killing the duc de Berry would put an end to the Bourbon dynasty, which had so shamelessly reassumed power under the swords of foreigners. No one knew at the time that the duchesse de Berry was expecting a child, the future comte de Chambord.

This dramatic political assassination instantly changed the direction of Restoration politics, as the Ultras came to dominate the government and put an end to Decazes's liberal reforms. By the time Alexis rejoined his father, the Ultras had the upper hand and were taking no chances with Republican and Bonapartist opposition while also neutralizing the liberal Monarchist camp. Because Louvel had lived in Metz in 1814, when Prussian, Russian, and Hessian troops attacked that city at the end of the Napoleonic wars, Hervé de Tocqueville played a significant role in the investigation of the assassination.[27] He gained additional influence when Chateaubriand became foreign minister in 1822, and he communicated directly with his relative in the cabinet. Chateaubriand orchestrated the French invasion of Spain in 1823, which aimed at restoring Ferdinand VII to power against liberal forces and giving the Bourbons the military prestige they lacked. Hervé de Tocqueville closely followed the reaction to the expedition in his department and appraised the minister of the local population's response, especially its fear of a return to absolutism.[28]

## Young Alexis's Experimentation

Amid the roiling changes of Restoration politics, Alexis enrolled full time at the Collège Royal of Metz in November 1821. He attended it for two full years, pursuing the curriculum in rhetoric and philosophy, and receiving his baccalaureate in 1823. He read classical Latin texts (Horace, Cicero, Tacitus, and Quintilian) as well as the seventeenth-century French tragedies of Racine.[29] Alexis performed brilliantly, collecting accolades and prizes. From afar, Bébé advised his pupil to spend time with the great Catholic preachers Bossuet and Louis Bourdaloue, but this was advice Alexis would follow only much later.[30] At the time, he much preferred the maxims of lighter moralists such as La Bruyère and La Rochefoucauld.[31] Alexis mingled with a few other boys, especially Eugène Stöffels and his younger brother Charles, who were of modest origins but conservative leanings, as well as another student named

Mathieu Henrion—all the while maintaining a regular correspondence with his childhood friend Louis de Kergorlay. In their company, Alexis in no way challenged his father's politics. The prefect took a special liking to the young Henrion, the most openly conservative of the group.

This seemed all too easy: a brilliant student, the son of the most powerful local civil servant, breezing through the last two years of high school before moving on to study law. In fact, at Metz, teenaged Alexis was ready for significant experimentation with other aspects of life. He remembered his youthful fearlessness in a letter of advice he later wrote to Alexis Stöffels, his namesake and son of his childhood friend Eugène. "You never succeed, particularly when you are young, unless you have a bit of the devil in you. At your age I would have leaped between the towers of Notre Dame if what I was looking for was on the other side."[32]

The pious Catholic student of Bébé ventured into his father's library at age sixteen, in 1821, before matriculating at the Collège Royal. There, Alexis had a dramatic encounter with religious doubt—his first major existential crisis. Tocqueville never specified exactly what he read, but the library contained much agnostic eighteenth-century philosophy. Alexis must have conveyed enough of his experience to Louis for the latter to be alarmed to see his friend "burying himself in doubt, becoming a sad Pyrrhonian, dark and heavy with thought."[33] Lesueur also learned that Alexis was no longer receiving the sacrament and anxiously begged his protégé to "repair this atrocious evil."[34]

Religious doubt caused the young Tocqueville great pain. He later explained his feelings to Charles Stöffels, writing him from Philadelphia in 1831.

When I first started to think, I found the world full of self-evident truths. One merely needed to look carefully to see them. But as soon as I applied myself to consider the objects of thought, I could discern only inextricable doubt. I cannot tell you, my dear Charles, in what horrible situation such a discovery put me. It was the most unhappy time of my life. I can only compare myself to a man seized with vertigo who senses the floor giving way under him and the walls about to crumble. Even today it is with a sense of horror that I remember those days. I can truly say that doubt and I were locked in hand-to-hand combat, and I have rarely done so since with more despair.[35]

At fifty-one, still trying to regain his faith, Tocqueville related the full incident to Sofia Swetchine, a new friend and Parisian society figure leading an effort to promote a Catholic Church that would be more receptive to representative government. Tocqueville described to her the solitary visits to his father's library as if they had happened the day before. He recalled that his

> life up to then had flowed in an interior full of faith which had not even allowed doubt to penetrate my soul. Then doubt entered, or rather rushed in with unprecedented violence, not merely the doubt of this or that, but universal doubt. . . . From time to time, these impressions of my first youth (I was 16 years old then) possess me again; then I see the intellectual world turn again and I remain lost and bewildered in this universal movement which overturns or shakes all the truths on which I have built my beliefs and actions. Here is a sad and frightening illness. . . . Happy those who have never known it, or who no longer know it![36]

Metz was also where Alexis had his first relationships with women. There is some evidence that at age sixteen, Alexis fathered a child with a servant, perhaps conceived in a cabin the young man had built as a retreat on the grounds of the prefecture.[37] Nothing is known of the child save her name, Louise Charlotte Meyer.[38] Tocqueville's later interest in welfare measures in Normandy to help single mothers and rescue abandoned children may well have been motivated by this experience, though he never reflected on it in any of his writings.

Alexis also began an enduring relationship with Rosalie Malye, daughter of the prefecture's archivist.[39] The love affair lasted several years, but ultimately her different social class made an alliance unthinkable. It was not unthinkable, however, to defend Rosalie's honor, if indeed such was the reason for a duel Alexis fought with a schoolmate. An alarmed Louis, whom Alexis had informed of the matter, wrote from Paris, "Did you imagine I would receive this news calmly?"[40] All we know for sure is that Alexis was severely wounded, and that father and son made sure neither Louise-Madeleine nor Bébé would learn the cause of the injury.[41]

## Time to Choose an "État"

Although childhood tutor Bébé and childhood friend Louis expressed similar feelings of loss when young Alexis departed for Metz, they differed sharply in their views about Alexis's choice of career after high school. Louis de Kergorlay relentlessly pushed his friend to join his older brothers and now himself in the army, thus following in the tradition of the nobility of the sword. Bébé, aware of Alexis's fragile physical constitution and intellectual talents, vigorously protested and called on Alexis's older brother Édouard to counsel him:

> You must convince Alexis not to join the military, my little Édouard. You know the drawbacks of such a path, and on this point, he will listen to his brothers rather than to his father. It is that peculiar Louis de Kergorlay who put the idea in his head. The two have plans to meet, and I intend to plead with "Mr. Loulou" to leave us alone and to mind his own business. What a shame it would be to suffocate his talent, growing daily in distinction, under a helmet.[42]

Tocqueville eventually chose the law but only after some significant soul-searching, which he later related to his nephew Hubert. Tocqueville rejected not only the army but also any consideration of a career in public administration such as the one his father had pursued. Although remaining a devoted son and respecting his father's mastery of administrative affairs, he had made up his mind he could never subject himself to the mix of authority and submission such a job required. He told Hubert:

> I have always had, no matter the regime (I make no exception), a repugnance for bureaucracy. . . . I noticed that, to get ahead, one needed to be pliable and obsequious to those who give you orders, and duplicitous or violent towards those who take orders from you. In

France, the administrative state does not conduct itself with the general welfare in mind, but only in the interests of those who govern. And no one can hope to rise in the ranks without subordinating his interests to those of others. . . . And though many things I encountered in my judicial career displeased me, I embraced what seemed to me the only career in civil service that gave me any independence from the transient groups that cycle through power in our country, the only one where one can both be civil servant and oneself.[43]

By being "oneself," Tocqueville meant being an independent agent responsible for his actions.

Tocqueville would not always be so sanguine about the law. At the time, however, he returned to Paris, after a brief excursion to Switzerland, to enter law school; he lived again with his mother.[44] Kergorlay, for his part, was admitted at the École Polytechnique, the military academy, in 1824, so the two friends were reunited, studying in Paris for two years.

Tocqueville did not leave Metz completely behind. He stayed in touch with the Stöffelses, and he maintained an epistolary relationship with Rosalie, who visited him once in Paris.[45] Kergorlay meanwhile was using all his powers of persuasion to convince Tocqueville that the time had come to break off a relationship that had no future. But this languishing love affair was seemingly the only source of drama of these two years in Paris, for nothing could be more intellectually deadening than the law school Tocqueville entered in late 1823.

Earlier in the Restoration, under the leadership of Royer-Collard, who served as president of the Commission for Public Education, the Doctrinaires led a liberal experiment to reform the university, the national education apparatus created by Napoleon. They wanted to create a university capable of educating young people of different political persuasions and religious commitments, which entailed broadening the scope of the curricula of the various schools. Under the Consulate and the Empire, one learned in law school only Roman law, civil code, and the penal code. Royer-Collard added instruction in natural law, international law, commercial law, and administrative law. He also initiated a

curriculum in both Roman and French legal history and a course for
future lawyers in political philosophy. In other words, he sought to make
law school a school of moral and political sciences. He pursued equivalent reforms in other parts of the university.[46] The greater openness
brought with it unexpected student rebellion against the regime. In 1822,
Kergorlay reported to Tocqueville that "Jacobin" law students were
physically attacking Royalists, and there were similar incidents among
medical students.[47]

By the time Tocqueville began his studies, the Ultras dominated the
university, directed, under Charles X, to serve only throne and altar. Already in late 1819, Royer-Collard had resigned his position as head of the
university, under the weight of Ultra attacks and opposition to his reforms. An archconservative bishop *in partibus*,[48] Mgr. Denis-Luc Frayssinous, replaced Royer-Collard and put an end to the liberal experiment.
Young philosopher Victor Cousin, Royer-Collard's assistant at the Sorbonne, who taught in his place (as *"suppléant"*), was dismissed, not for
expressing political opinions in his 1818 lectures *Du vrai, du beau, du bien*,
but for teaching a philosophy that appealed to young people who loved
to think freely. Before his stint in the Interior Ministry, Guizot, who had
been appointed to a history professorship at the exceptionally young age
of twenty-five, had assisted Royer-Collard in devising reforms. Forced
out of the Interior Ministry after Decazes's fall, he had resumed teaching.
He too was dismissed.[49] If the university were to serve only church and
king, there was no room for professors who, through the study of philosophy or history, were pushing knowledge into new areas. Half of the
existing history chairs were eliminated between 1822 and 1828. Under
Mgr. Frayssinous's tenure as minister of cults and instruction, between
1820 and 1830, one-tenth of teaching personnel in Paris were fired or retired for political and religious reasons.[50]

The teaching of law was now reduced to the very minimum: statutory
law, positive law, penal code, and procedural practices.[51] There were no
controversies over points of theory that could stimulate original thinking. Not surprisingly, Tocqueville's heart was not in it. Tocqueville
ended up submitting two short, strictly factual theses, one in French on
a technical point of law concerning the annulment of obligations,[52] and

one in Latin, a brief commentary on a part of the pandects (Roman civil law), to satisfy graduation requirements.

It was unclear what would come next for Tocqueville now that he had completed a dull and uninspiring legal training. To mark the end of his studies, he went with his brother Édouard to Rome and Sicily in December 1826 and January 1827. In addition to being a refreshing distraction, the trip turned out to be an opportunity for Tocqueville to demonstrate his budding talents as a social observer and writer. From the fragments of the Sicilian diary that have survived, one sees Tocqueville's efforts to develop his prose which, ever his own harshest critic, he found to be mediocre. He wrote a dramatic rendering of a dangerous tempest during a sea crossing, a well-crafted account of two brothers' hike up to the crater of Mount Etna, as well as concise descriptions of the places they visited (Palermo, Agrigento, Syracuse, Catania, Messina, Milazzo). All along, he displayed a good grasp of mythology and ancient history, and he noted the ways Sicilians resisted Neapolitan absolutism and aspired to independence.[53]

These diaries also show the first manifestations of Tocqueville's aptitude for deciphering processes of social domination, in this case, by observing how the land was developed. He attributed the absence of villages in Sicily to the fact that only the nobility and religious communities owned land. The only places on the island where peasants could cultivate their own land were the fertile but dangerous parcels surrounding the island's volcanoes. In discussing the Neapolitan constitution with Édouard a few years later, though, Tocqueville felt he had failed at the time of their trip to connect constitutional issues with the social trends he was observing.[54]

## Apprentice Prosecutor at Versailles

Tocqueville was still in Sicily with his brother when he learned that his father had secured a position for him as an apprentice prosecutor at the Versailles court. Hervé de Tocqueville had gained additional influence when the comte d'Artois, Louis XVIII's brother, became Charles X in 1824. He was now a member of the King's Chamber, which gave him the privilege of accompanying the king to mass on Sunday and watching the king play whist after supper.[55] He was also appointed to the coveted position of Seine-et-Oise prefect, with its seat at Versailles. Alexis's British friend Richard Monckton Milnes once noted that "by making good use of his *Conseil général* (General Council), which is a kind of Parliament to him, [a prefect] may change the character of a whole province."[56] Hervé de Tocqueville's *Conseil général* was almost a family reunion. There sat his brother-in-law Rosanbo, and his wife's two cousins, Le Peletier d'Aunay and Molé.[57] It was a simple matter for the prefect to visit the minister of justice and get his son a job.

Alexis was not sure what this (unpaid) position as *juge auditeur* (apprentice judge) would entail. He seemed for a moment to have no special direction or even wishes. He had concluded his Sicilian diary by asking only one grace from God, "that he would one day make me want to do something that is worth the struggle."[58] At first, Tocqueville found he had landed at the Versailles courthouse in the company of "*cuistres*," priggish and pedantic young nobles from Legitimist families, who, as he told Kergorlay, "reason poorly and speak well."[59] Fortunately, not all fit that mold. The first exception was Gustave de Beaumont, Tocqueville's senior by three years, with whom he roomed. The pair experienced that sense of connection that Tocqueville described as "a new friendship that seemed old from the start."[60] This was especially true as Tocqueville was now feeling the first effects of fragile health. He relied on Beaumont for help during recurring disabling episodes of a stomach ailment that required much mental energy to overcome.[61]

Another new friend was Ernest de Chabrol, nephew of Prime Minister Joseph de Villèle's navy minister, with whom Tocqueville shared an apartment when Beaumont left Versailles after his promotion to Paris in the summer of 1829. At the same time, Tocqueville became friendly with Ernest de Blosseville, who preferred literature over law.[62] Outside the courthouse, Tocqueville befriended Louis Bouchitté, a young philosopher teaching at the local Collège Royal.[63] Once Tocqueville had given his friendship, he rarely withdrew it. The man who would one day develop the theory of associations was himself content with only a few friends. Tocqueville wrote to Kergorlay at the time that

friendship, "once born, should not weaken with age, or even change in
its essential nature I don't think. Especially not for those who know its
price, and ceaselessly tend to it, careful not to break that which supports
it: trust, in matters both large and small."[64]

Tocqueville had a hard time finding his post as apprentice prosecutor
interesting. He even told Kergorlay he was disgusted by "the turns of
phrase and customs of the legal profession."[65] But he overcame this initial rejection and reported on several important cases with a direct bearing on the enhanced status of the nobility in the Restoration. His role
as *juge auditeur* was to conduct and report on the investigations that
preceded a trial, assembling the facts, and interrogating the witnesses.
Tocqueville cut his teeth on a complicated case involving a debt an émigré had incurred before the state confiscated his property during the
Revolutionary Terror. The creditor was trying to collect the debt years
later. Tocqueville, who sided with the defendant in presenting the case
and more generally with the monarchist cause, conducted intensive
background work. He studied the laws and edicts of the First Republic
on confiscated wealth, as well as the subsequent legislation during the
Consulate and Empire regarding restitution. Finally, he exposed state
confiscation of émigré property as monstrous abuse.[66]

It was a tradition at the courthouse to ask a junior member to give a
lecture to his colleagues at the opening of the session. When the assignment fell on Tocqueville, he chose to talk about dueling, presumably
because the civil code ignored the topic. Despite being injured in his
first encounter, Tocqueville seems to have retained the romantic notion
of duels as the embodiment of virtue and honor. With the help of a fresh
reading of Montesquieu's writings, Tocqueville argued that if crime
there was, both parties were equally guilty. He also warned that the
decline of dueling would lead to more murders.[67]

Tocqueville, however, was not committed to a one-sided defense of
aristocratic values. He also saw the abuses of reactionary government.
During a popular rebellion at Saint-Germain-en-Laye, a group of young
workers was arrested for disturbing the peace while inebriated and
shouting slogans against the monarchy. All were eventually condemned
to severe prison sentences. Tocqueville tried unsuccessfully to assemble

facts that reflected the minimal seriousness of their actions, which he viewed as being motivated less by antimonarchist sentiment than by the precariousness of the economic situation and the high price of bread.[68] He was not to be confused with the fictional Restoration prosecutor whom Balzac portrayed in *Le cabinet des antiques,* a man who dreamed of boosting his career by uncovering yet another conspiracy against the absolute monarchy.[69]

The young magistrates lived their bachelor lives together in Versailles. For Tocqueville, this entailed a drawn-out final act with Rosalie. It so happened that Kergorlay, upon graduating from Polytechnique, entered artillery school at Metz. In effect, the two friends traded places. At Metz, Kergorlay now saw Eugène Stöffels regularly. After having persuaded Tocqueville to end his relationship with Rosalie, he served as a go-between with Rosalie and her sister. And after Rosalie's unhappy marriage to a François Begin in 1828, Kergorlay conveyed to Tocqueville her request that he continue to write her.[70] Tocqueville obliged, using invisible ink made from lemon juice. But soon, Kergorlay and Tocqueville conspired to use their family connections to obtain for Rosalie a respectable position in the postal service and this ended the romance in the most unromantic way.[71]

Meanwhile, at Versailles, Tocqueville met an eligible English woman named Mary Mottley. Mottley, born on August 20, 1799, was almost six years older than Tocqueville and lived in a nearby apartment with the aunt who had raised her. She came from a middle-class family from Portsmouth, where her father worked as an agent for the local Royal Hospital.[72] A portrait attributed to artist Candide Blaize from around 1830 depicts her as small-featured, with luminous eyes. She enjoyed Tocqueville's conversation. As their relationship progressed, Tocqueville found himself speaking to her candidly and unselfconsciously.[73]

## Reawakening of the Intellect

Work at the courthouse left significant time for other pursuits and in Beaumont, Tocqueville found a kindred soul who was similarly eager for intellectual stimulation. Guizot had resumed his lectures at the

Sorbonne, with immense success, and the two friends attended them assiduously. Both were avid readers and read widely. Beaumont delved into economics with Jean-Baptiste Say's *Treatise*,[74] Tocqueville into history with Prosper de Barante's *Histoire des ducs de Bourgogne*, and John Lingard's multivolume history of England, occasionally locking himself up "like a monk" just to read undisturbed.[75]

Tocqueville visited the uninhabited Château de Tocqueville, on his own and for the first time in his life, in early October 1828. There, he sat down to write a synopsis of English history in a lengthy letter to Beaumont. Tocqueville covered the period from the arrival of Angles and Saxons in the fifth century and their unification early in the ninth century and ended with the reign of the Tudors. This fast-moving account of England's extraordinarily complex dynastic history was even more astonishing because it was told from memory. Tocqueville acknowledged holes in his narrative and apologized to Beaumont for anachronisms as well as what he called "reveries" and flights of "imagination." The impetus for this outpouring seemed to be that he was only "one league away and within sight of the port where William sailed for England." When evoking his ancestor Guillaume Clérel's or Clarel's participation in the 1066 battle of Hastings and subsequent conquest of England, he admitted that he "succumbed to pride" and "juvenile enthusiasm."[76]

There was great deal of the partisan in this retelling. As Tocqueville reviewed key episodes of the Hundred Years' War, he expressed pain at the devastation of the French nobility at Crecy and Agincourt. "All these events became engraved in my memory and I became animated by that unreflective and instinctual hate towards the English that sometimes comes over me." Indeed, Tocqueville took special pleasure at narrating the worst moments of British monarchical tyranny that forced the English people to change religion four times, or "the tyranny of Henry VIII, who never let a woman's honor get in the way of his passions, nor ever set aside his anger to spare a man's life."[77]

Nonetheless, one can see in this account an insight that would provide the foundation of Tocqueville's historical thinking for the rest of his life. Contrary to the situation in France where, over centuries, the alliance of king and people weakened the aristocracy, Tocqueville argued in his reading of British history that the British aristocracy had succeeded in forming alliances with the "democratic classes" (as he told Beaumont, he would resort to anachronisms) to keep the prince at bay.[78] Tocqueville could have added that Charles X's systematic strengthening of the old nobility against the bourgeoisie that was unfolding under his own eyes (and that would ultimately bring the Bourbons' final demise) was an oddity in centuries of French history.

When he wrote this interminable letter on English history, Tocqueville had not yet attended Guizot's Saturday lectures at the Sorbonne, but he had already read some transcriptions. Like Guizot, he wanted to convey some "*idées mères*" in the letter—or core commitments that shape political cultures, and that Guizot defined as "common to the greater number of the members of the society" and exercising "a certain empire over their wills and actions."[79] Tocqueville attended the lectures himself in the 1829–30 cycle. During the summer of 1829, Tocqueville also read "the greatest part" of Guizot's works, including *Mémoires relatifs à l'histoire de France*, published in 1826–27, and probably also Guizot's narrative history and memoirs of the English revolution, published in 1823–25. Tocqueville described Guizot's work to Beaumont as "prodigious in its deconstruction of ideas and propriety of words, truly *prodigious.*"[80]

Tocqueville found that he had an immense affinity with Guizot's thought. First and foremost, he agreed with Guizot on the importance of history. In his lecture notes, Tocqueville underscored Guizot's pronouncement that "a people with no memory of its past is like a mature man who has lost all recollections of his youth."[81] Some key insights Tocqueville adopted and made his own. First was Guizot's idea of a "social state." Again, Tocqueville marked this passage in his notes: "A given social formation imprints on the human spirit a certain direction: it provides it with a body of general ideas . . . which shape its development by sheer force of momentum."[82] Tocqueville also heard Guizot theorizing about the negative side of equality—that is, equality in powerlessness. In Guizot's lectures, the third estate destroyed the feudal nobility and supported absolutism "so that at least all would be equal under one master." Tocqueville underlined this remark in his notes.[83]

Guizot awakened in Tocqueville the desire to analyze the immensely complex interplay of politics and society and in the process raised Tocqueville's political consciousness.

Tocqueville found in Guizot's "high stage of civilization" an early formulation of what would become, in the second volume of *Democracy in America*, Tocqueville's own theory of soft despotism. Borrowing directly from Guizot, Tocqueville wrote to Charles Stöffels:

> [In the case of a society] that has achieved a high degree of civilization, the social body has taken charge of everything: the individual has to take responsibility only for being born; for all else, society places him in the arms of its wet nurse, supervises his education, opens before him the paths of fortune. Society supports him on his way, brushes aside the dangers from his head. He advances in peace under the eyes of this second providence. This tutelary power that protected him during his life watches over the burying of his ashes as well: that is the fate of civilized man. Individual energy is almost extinguished.[84]

Guizot had been talking about an advanced state of civilization, not democracy. At the time of Guizot's lectures, Tocqueville was not yet thinking of democracy either. Moreover, Tocqueville was not yet prepared to counter Guizot's endorsement of "modern centralization" that, in Guizot's view, made it possible for one people to become "unified and compact in all its parts . . . acting for one goal, stirred by the same ideas, agitated by the same passions, finally marching as one man to overcome the same obstacles."[85] The critique of this idealized centralization would prove to be one of Tocqueville's most important contributions to political theory, but that still lay in the future.

The year 1829 was one of reactionary political change in the nation. Charles X appointed the prince de Polignac as his prime minister and with him orchestrated a sharp turn toward absolutism. There was widespread opposition to the move even from conservatives. Chateaubriand resigned as ambassador to Rome.[86] At the courthouse, Tocqueville expressed deep concern to his friend and colleague Blosseville. He predicted that if the king would now rule with ordinances, "royal authority would be playing with both its present and its future."[87] Tocqueville believed, however, that the king and Polignac would fail. In writing to his brother Édouard and his wife Alexandrine, who were on their honeymoon in Naples, Alexis predicted significant resistance to any such attempt:

> The day the king rules by ordinances the courts will no longer enforce them. I should know. Nobody wants the reign of executive decrees in France—that is a clear line in the sand. They serve the interests of no one. Judicial bodies would lose their importance, the peers would be without rank, men of talent would give up their hopes and dreams, the people would be without protection, and most military officers without hope for advancement. What to do against such a combined mass of wills?

Tocqueville also reported, "People's spirits are profoundly calm. There is little agitation in France. We are waiting."[88]

There was no need to wait for long. On May 16, 1830, Charles X dissolved the Chamber that had challenged him. Badly in need of military glory to quiet domestic opposition, he initiated the conquest of Algeria. For some time, the king had been reviving talks of invading Algeria, nominally under Ottoman rule but led by an independent dey freely exercising piracy in the Mediterranean Sea. Three years earlier, in 1827, the French consul had refused to acknowledge a debt France had incurred during Napoleon's Egypt expedition. Legend has it that the dey hit the French diplomat with a fly whisk three times in the face. The insult gave the French an excuse to blockade Algeria. Now Charles X launched a military campaign to consolidate his power. The fleet sailed from Toulon on May 25, 1830, with 103 warships, 350 transport ships, 83 artillery guns, 27,000 sailors, and 37,000 soldiers.[89] Tocqueville noted, "On our side we will need immense results, for the preparations have been prodigious, and if the ends don't justify the means, this administration is finished." On a personal level, Tocqueville was "mortally concerned," for Kergorlay was scheduled to be among the first artillery combatants (but at the last minute, Kergorlay's combat position was moved to the second battalion, not the first). Tocqueville also worried because his brother Hippolyte had volunteered for the expedition (although in the end did not go).[90]

News of the victory in Algiers arrived too late on July 5 to serve the government's bet. The previous day, elections to the Chamber had returned a large majority against the king. But with his Algerian victory, Charles X felt empowered to issue the four infamous ordinances that proved the undoing of his regime. In effect, the ordinances destroyed freedom of the press and reduced the size of the Chamber of Deputies by half. The property qualifications removed three-quarters of the electors from electoral rolls, and both Chambers were deprived of the right to amend bills. A new Chamber would be convened on September 28.[91]

Charles X signed the ordinances on July 25 and published them the following day. The king obviously expected unquestioning obedience from his subjects since he chose to go hunting that day in Rambouillet. His minister of war, Louis de Bourmont, was also away, while his interior minister, the comte de Peyronnet, was sitting for his statue.[92]

Tocqueville's Versailles colleague Blosseville saw the first signs of a revolution as he passed through Paris on July 28: shopkeepers were already removing their shop signs ornamented with fleurs de lis.[93] Tricolor flags and barricades followed with surprising speed. On July 29, Tocqueville wrote to Mary, with whom he had by then developed a close relationship, "Civil war has begun."[94] Tocqueville felt his first duty was to protect his parents who were Ultras. So he joined them and accompanied them to Saint-Germain-en-Laye where they could stay safely with Édouard's new in-laws, baron and baronne Ollivier.

Although in awe of Guizot the historian, Tocqueville had not participated in the work of Aide Toi Le Ciel T'Aidera (Heaven Helps Those Who Help Themselves), the association Guizot had led to mobilize and enlarge the electorate. Tocqueville watched from afar as a radicalized Guizot who, elected to the Chamber only a few months before, was designated by his colleagues to draft a formal protest against the ordinances. On July 29, the Chamber called back the National Guard that Charles X had disbanded in 1827, and it put the marquis de Lafayette in charge of restoring order. Tocqueville joined the National Guard and was given a rifle, but he did not confront the popular insurgency.[95]

After three days of bloody insurrection (Les Trois Glorieuses), the king withdrew the ordinances on the 30th and the duc d'Orléans accepted the Chamber's invitation to serve as lieutenant-general of the kingdom. On that day, Tocqueville, disturbed and ashamed of the government, confided in Mary, "I did not think it possible to so vividly experience feelings of this kind amidst the horrors that surround me. . . . I cannot convey to you the jumbled sensations of despair that fill my heart." And he unequivocally laid the blame on the king: "As to the Bourbons, they have behaved as cowards and aren't worth a thousandth part of the blood that has been spilled for their quarrel."[96] This is the first piece of evidence we have that Tocqueville had now begun seriously to question his loyalty to the Bourbons, if not yet to the idea of monarchy writ large.

The king fled Saint-Cloud on July 31, formally abdicating in favor of his grandson two days later. His first idea was to go to Versailles. Tocqueville spotted the king's party at the Porte de Saint-Cloud; Tocqueville's uncle Louis de Rosanbo was among them.[97] Blosseville remembered that when Tocqueville returned to Versailles, he reported "in terms blending pain and humiliation" that the end had come. Small signs spoke volumes. Tocqueville was shocked to see the escutcheons on the doors of the royal carriages covered with dirt, yet at Trianon, on the grounds of the Palace of Versailles, another reality endured: the chambermaid panicked when the king arrived before fresh butter could be procured for his lunch.[98] Facing a cold reception on the part of the local population, the royal party rapidly moved on to Rambouillet, on its way to exile.

Tocqueville realized in the weeks following the Revolution that he had no future at the courthouse and that he did not want one in any case. Still, unlike Kergorlay who resigned his commission, Tocqueville took his father's advice, kept his options open, and swore an oath to the new constitutional monarchy of Louis Philippe.[99] On August 17, Tocqueville wrote to Mary, "My conscience is clear, but I would rank this day among the worst of my life."[100] But when former Metz classmate and arch-Legitimist Henrion (who would later write a hagiographic account of the life of Mgr. Frayssinous, the man responsible for dismantling the university) mounted an attack on Tocqueville for having sworn the oath, Tocqueville defended his actions. Henrion invoked Malesherbes's memory at the king's trial and expressed his admiration for Louis Le Peletier de Rosanbo, going so far as to convey the message by way of Tocqueville's mother, Rosanbo's sister. Tocqueville angrily fired back that he felt his great-grandfather "would have acted exactly as I have done had he been in my place. Just as I have the presumption of hoping that I would have done as he did, were I in his shoes."[101]

Tocqueville had routinely defied expectations in his youth, and he defied them again now. He refused to take sides between Orleanists, who promoted a genuine constitutional monarchy, and Legitimists, who resisted it. He looked for a way he could maintain his independence of judgment and perhaps, in the best of scenarios, make a unique contribution to the welfare of France. Tocqueville decided to leave France for America to study what a republic looked like.

Tocqueville gave his reason for leaving most succinctly to Charles Stöffels: "My position in France is bad in every respect." Although esteemed by his courthouse peers who recognized his deep intelligence,[102] Tocqueville had never received a promotion or even a paid position, and this despite the fact that Hervé de Tocqueville, whom the king had made a peer of France, had made a point in September 1829 to see the minister of justice to obtain a better position for his son.[103] When the following month, Beaumont was promoted from Versailles to Paris, it was Chabrol, not Tocqueville, who was chosen to replace Beaumont. Tocqueville learned of this while traveling in Switzerland with Kergorlay. Recognizing his lack of oratory skills, he accepted the news as bravely as he could.[104] He remained Chabrol's friend and would room with him for the rest of his tenure at Versailles.

Tocqueville neither expected nor wanted better treatment from the new regime. As he explained to Charles Stöffels:

> I do not wish for advancement, because to do so would be to tie myself to men whose intentions I find suspect. So, my role would be that of an obscure assistant judge, confined to a narrow sphere and with no way to make my reputation. If I attempt to oppose the government from within the justice ministry, I will be denied even the honor of dismissal.

With no confidence in the new July Monarchy, as it was called, Tocqueville had to figure a way out.

> Now suppose that, without quitting the magistracy or giving up my seniority, I go to America. One will have formed a precise idea of the nature of a vast republic and of why it is feasible in one place and not feasible in another. Public administration will have been systematically examined in all its aspects. Upon returning to France one will of course feel stronger than one felt upon leaving. If the moment is ripe, a publication of some sort might alert the public to one's existence and draw the attention of the parties.

Then came the strategy to carry out the plan:

> Beaumont and I will request a leave of eighteen months along with a mission to go to America to examine the state of the penitentiary system. . . . The issue is in no way political and has to do solely with the well-being of society in general. Of course, this is a pretext, but a very honorable pretext, which will make us seem particularly worthy of the government's interest, whatever the government happens to be, and will ensure that our request is looked upon kindly. . . . In order to obtain this mission we have drafted a memorandum, which I believe is well crafted.[105]

How Tocqueville settled on this plan is unclear, but there was a widespread sense in Restoration intellectual circles that the Old World could learn from the grand American "experiment" of democratic governance.[106] George Washington was revered in France as a virtuous general who lived humbly, fought only when necessary, and relinquished his power at the end of his term—a kind of anti-Napoleon. Nobody drew the contrast better than Chateaubriand in his *Voyage en Amérique*, published in 1827 and widely excerpted in the French press. "Washington and Buonaparte both emerged from the republic's bosom; both were the children of freedom," Chateaubriand remarked but added, "Washington remained loyal to freedom, but Buonaparte betrayed it."[107] Praise for America came just as much from the opposition to the Restoration regime as from its proponents. One such voice was Arnold

Scheffer's. Scheffer was a member of the Charbonnerie, a secret society intent on dethroning the Bourbons. Scheffer attacked French repressive laws while praising Americans' First Amendment rights in his 1825 *Histoire des États-Unis de l'Amérique septentrionale*.[108] Tocqueville would later turn to Scheffer, in the 1840s, for assistance in launching a political newspaper (see chapter 9).

To propose to study prisons to secure support for a journey to America was an inspired decision. The topic was in the air. During the early days of the Restoration, with the king's encouragement, Minister Decazes had founded a Royal Society for the Improvement of Prisons. The Society enlisted the most influential men of its time in the project of reforming France's chaotic prison system and produced the first national investigation of prisons in 1819, along with a law to introduce basic reforms.[109] Charles Lucas, a young lawyer who would later be called father of "penitentiary science," won the Montyon Prize of the French Academy in 1830 for a three-volume investigation of prisons in the United States and five European countries. He took his work to the Chambers of Deputies and Peers, strongly urging them to introduce a coherent penitentiary system in France, and the approving legislators responded by having Lucas made an inspector general of prisons.[110] Camille de Montalivet, the newly appointed interior minister, was himself the son of a prison reformer and aware of the rising pressure to act.[111]

Tocqueville's and Beaumont's interest in prison reform was also a natural extension of their prosecutorial responsibilities—and they gathered information to support their proposal. Their friend Blosseville had gone to Geneva and shared with them his observations on the experimental Swiss "cellular" system.[112] This led them to study other reform efforts, mainly by English theorists such as John Howard, who argued that prisons could reform prisoners by restricting their communication with one another, and Jeremy Bentham, who became so famous in France for his panopticon scheme for surveillance that he was made an honorary French citizen in 1792.[113]

From the courthouse at Versailles, Tocqueville and Beaumont made several visits to Poissy, the central prison of the département. They learned the rules and observed the inmates. When they reported that

Sunday meals at Poissy, where inmates could spend freely their *"pécule"* (earnings from their prison wages), resembled "a feast given by Satan to his friends," this rang true with reformers. In other words, Tocqueville and Beaumont had gathered enough information to write a proposal seeking leave to see US penitentiaries in person. They each wrote a draft independently and then combined their texts.[114] In the proposal, they depicted themselves as sincere reformers who wanted not only to punish criminals but also to rehabilitate them. They argued that firsthand observations were the most effective way to determine how Americans had seemingly achieved rehabilitation of criminals at moderate costs (and in some instances, profit).

It was a compelling, masterfully written proposal, and it worked, with some help from cousin Le Peletier d'Aunay, several times vice-president of the Chamber. Interior Minister Montalivet granted the assignment and Minister of Justice Félix Barthe the leave of absence. The assignment was unpaid, but the Tocqueville and Beaumont families came through, the Tocquevilles with 5,000 francs and the Beaumonts with 2,000, which the two promised to spend wisely. Then came the rush to prepare for departure, including collecting letters of introduction. Lafayette did not respond to a request for a letter, but it seems as though a member of his household alerted novelist James Fenimore Cooper. Prison reformer Charles Lucas was not enthusiastic about encouraging potential rivals but nevertheless provided Tocqueville and Beaumont a note for American secretary of state Edward Livingston, whose work on prisons for the Louisiana legislature he had translated; he also furnished them with a letter to James J. Barclay, a prominent member of the Philadelphia Society for Alleviating the Miseries of the Public Prisons, who could help arrange visits to sites such as the Eastern State Penitentiary. Former minister to the United States Hyde de Neuville wrote a letter of introduction to fellow diplomat William Short (who had begun his career as Jefferson's private secretary); the duc de Montebello provided one to Henry Gilpin, a noted Philadelphia Quaker who practiced law. Ex-consul David Bailie Warden, the baron de Gérando, and Chateaubriand likely provided letters as well. Tocqueville and Beaumont collected as many as seventy letters in total. The two friends also decided to do some preparatory reading. They acquired a number of guides, including Volney's two-volume *Tableau du climat et du sol des Etats-Unis d'Amérique* (1803) and, in translation, James Fenimore Cooper's *Lettres sur les mœurs et les institutions des États-Unis de l'Amérique du Nord* (1828), the book Lafayette had suggested Cooper should write.[115]

On April 2, 1831, they sailed from Le Havre. As Tocqueville reported to Eugène Stöffels, "The ship became our universe." They were "out of sight of land for 35 days." They socialized with other crossers but spent much time "in deep solitude."[116] They worked on their English, read American history, studied Jean-Baptiste Say, and sketched out an itinerary.

Thus began a new chapter not just in their lives but also in the history of democracy, although at the time it was impossible to tell what the outcome of the trip would be and Tocqueville had no clear sense of it. Writing from Switzerland in October 1829, Tocqueville had told Beaumont, "Some good historical work might still come of our joint endeavors." But he added, perhaps as a reflection of the awakened political consciousness he owed to Guizot, "it is the politician that we must build up in ourselves."[117] The time for that had not yet come. But Tocqueville had intuited that leaving France behind and exploring American democracy might someday make it possible.

# 2

# "Everything about the Americans Is Extraordinary"

As we study the penitentiary system, we will see America. While visiting its prisons, we will visit its inhabitants, its cities, its institutions, and its mores. We will come to know the workings of its republican government. That government is not known in Europe. People talk about it endlessly and make false comparisons with countries that in no way resemble the United States. Wouldn't it be good to have a book that gave an exact idea of the American people, that broadly set forth its history, that boldly portrayed its character, that analyzed its social state and rectified any number of erroneous opinions?[1]

Gustave de Beaumont wrote these words to his father on the packet boat to America. He and Tocqueville explored much of the expanding American territory to find out whether the American model was at least in part applicable to France. They followed a circuitous route. After landing in Newport, Rhode Island, and traveling by steamboat to New York, they went up the Hudson River and along the Mohawk Valley to the Great Lakes. They then navigated the lakes, journeyed north through the future state of Michigan, and reached the frontier of settlement in Wisconsin. Reversing course, they traveled through Canada on their way to New England. After time in Boston, Hartford, Connecticut, and other cities, they traveled south to Philadelphia and Baltimore. Next, they cut west through Pennsylvania as far as the Ohio River, which they followed downstream. With free states to the north and slave states to the south, they reached the Mississippi and traveled to New Orleans. They returned by coach to Washington, DC, tracing their way through the South and then finally returning to New York and sailing for home. Along the way, they talked to about 200 informants, transcribed information they considered "invaluable" in notebooks, and instructed family members and such friends as Tocqueville's cousin Louis de Kergorlay, classmate Eugène Stöffels, and colleague Ernest de Chabrol to keep their letters.[2]

If they had preconceived ideas, these were challenged upon entering a country where the social revolution of Jacksonian democracy was transforming the constitutional principles that the founding generation had established. "I am tempted to burn my books to make sure I apply only new ideas to such a new social state," declared Tocqueville.[3] As they traveled, Tocqueville and Beaumont recorded similar scenes, agreeing on the specifics of what they saw but eventually judging America differently. Of the two, Beaumont was most shocked by the brutal race relations pervading society. He eventually wrote a novel on race, his 1835 *Marie, or Slavery in the United States.* Tocqueville, although critical, focused on the larger democratic promise of America. He returned to France with his famous pronouncement that "a world totally new demands a new political science," and he provided it in what would become his most famous work, *Democracy in America.*[4] Nine and a half months in America remained a well of inspiration for the rest of his life.

When they arrived at Newport, Tocqueville and Beaumont were overwhelmed with impressions that signaled they were in a very different world from the one that they had left. One was the intermingling of religion and commerce, which they suspected extended to the nation as a whole. Tocqueville and Beaumont, who had read James Fenimore Cooper's *Notions of the Americans*, expected undemanding customs officers to inspect their trunks only perfunctorily but were taken aback when asked to swear on the Bible that they owed no duty.[5] After submitting to this remarkable ceremony, they were also surprised to count five banks vying for a modest local clientele on the main street of this "spotless" little town.[6] These commercial buildings appeared to them

Saint Thomas de Montmagny
Quebec
*Saint Lawrence River*
Montreal
*Lake Champlain*
Whitehall
*Niagara Falls*
Boston
Albany
Buffalo
Hartford
Journey of
May–Oct. 1831
Erie
Journey of
Oct. 1831–Feb. 1832
New York
Pittsburgh
Philadelphia
Baltimore
Washington, DC
Norfolk
Fayetteville
Columbia

Arrive Newport, RI,
May 9, 1831

Depart NY City,
Feb. 20, 1832

# Tocqueville and
# Beaumont's Journey

·········· Travel by water
- - - - - - Travel by land

0        100        200        300 miles

0    100    200    300 kilometers

emblematic of the American landscape—just as much as the "remarkable architectural specimen" of the nearby church steeple that Beaumont rushed to sketch.[7]

The next day, on the steamboat from Newport to New York City, Tocqueville and Beaumont felt an entirely new sensation they had not anticipated, an "incredible contempt for distances." They attributed this sensation only to the technology that allowed them to move through the majestic landscape, not yet realizing that legal changes had also made interstate travel easier and faster.[8] Only seven years earlier had the Supreme Court declared that steamboat commerce could not be interrupted at state lines. Under Justice John Marshall's guidance, the court ended state monopolies granted to steamboat companies and eliminated state boundaries in navigation, thus greatly facilitating the national "intercourse" the travelers were discovering.[9]

## New York City

The two travelers reached New York City, the preeminent mercantile and financial center of the nation and its most productive manufacturing center, on May 11. They certainly did not expect the city to look like a European capital but were surprised by the absence of clear landmarks. They looked in vain for "a dome, a steeple, or a major building."[10] They were stunned that columns fronting a few Greek revival public buildings, which resembled marble from a distance, were merely painted wood.[11] At first, they saw only monotonous brick houses, with no "cornices, balustrades, or coach entrances," lining poorly paved streets (although with sidewalks which, they noted in fairness, were still rare in Paris).[12]

Using the broken English they had practiced during the sea voyage, the two travelers rented modest accommodations in a so-called boarding house, or *pension*, at 66 Broadway for a seven-week stay. Fortunately, Americans they had befriended during five weeks at sea did not leave them to their own devices for long. They sought out the two young Frenchmen and introduced them to their many acquaintances in the city's political, commercial, and social elites. One such friend was Peter Schermerhorn, who had been returning home with his family after two years in Europe. In New York, Schermerhorn had built a large shipping business and invested heavily in real estate. Among his connections were the prominent Livingston and Fish families. Robert Livingston had negotiated the Louisiana Purchase with Talleyrand and formed a business partnership with famed steamboat inventor Robert Fulton. Preserved Fish had made a fortune in shipping by initiating regular transatlantic crossings.[13] Most helpful in connecting with city officials who could assist with the prison investigation was Charles Palmer, an Englishman and former Member of Parliament who had also crossed the ocean with them and who made his considerable political connections available. These included Mayor Walter Bowne, city recorder Richard Riker, and several aldermen and magistrates.[14] Nathaniel Prime, the city's most important banker and first president of the New York Stock Exchange, to whom Tocqueville and Beaumont had taken a letter of credit, also brought the two into his circle.[15]

Rumor that the French government had sent two commissioners to investigate the unique American penitentiary system circulated rapidly, and local newspapers reported on their arrival and purpose. Tocqueville and Beaumont had no need to ask the French consul, baron Durant de Saint André, whom they deemed "utterly ungifted for observation" anyway, to open doors for them.[16] As it turned out, they also had little need for the letters of recommendation they had carefully collected before leaving France. Meeting people was easy. A resident of the Broadway boarding house, Judge J. O. Morse, introduced them to New York governor Enos Throop, who was in town for a meeting of the Tammany Society, the local political organization affiliated with the Democratic Party.[17] The two young Frenchmen thus enjoyed a short informal encounter with the man the state legislature had just elected to replace Martin Van Buren, whom President Andrew Jackson had appointed secretary of state.

City officials were drawn from the local mercantile society, whose social pretensions Tocqueville and Beaumont were learning. These wealthy New Yorkers were the first "proud champions of equality" Tocqueville and Beaumont met. Although they bore no resemblance to French nobility, Tocqueville and Beaumont found they were equally conscious of their high status and conspicuous position in local life. They liked to address each other as "honorable esquire," and some even traveled in carriages bearing coats of arms.[18] In New York, they controlled Tammany Hall. As one of the Livingstons explained, "The people are by no means unwilling to vote for the wealthiest and best-educated among them."[19] Yet class conflict was lurking in the background. Mayor Bowne had recently ordered the watch to disperse all crowds on New Year's Eve to prevent a riotous and cacophonic procession from harassing wealthy revelers like himself.[20] Tension within Tammany was mounting between the elites still in charge and a growing number of craftsmen and workingmen, who were excluded from political power in the city's administration. If they were aware of these tensions, Tocqueville and Beaumont totally ignored them during their stay.

On May 25, Mayor Bowne arranged for an initial tour of the city's penal institutions followed by dinner with city officials. Tocqueville and Beaumont welcomed the former but dreaded the latter. Having reluctantly taken an oath of loyalty to France's new constitutional monarchy, they worried their hosts would embarrass them with toasts to marquis de Lafayette. Had not the same New Yorkers given a hero's welcome to Lafayette a few years before, including a memorable public ball at Castle Garden[21] and more recently celebrated the Trois Glorieuses—the three days of the July 1830 Revolution that put an end to the Bourbon monarchy? The fear proved unwarranted, but Tocqueville and Beaumont felt obligated to drink their glass down "with the utmost solemnity" at every toast uttered that evening, in a ritual Tocqueville described as "the world's most lugubrious exercise in gaiety."[22]

Having been granted universal access to correctional facilities, Tocqueville and Beaumont could focus during their stay in New York City on the main reform program, which was to separate prisoners into categories that best fit their crimes and conditions. For too long, murderers and petty thieves had shared the same crowded rooms in promiscuous prisons; men and women were not always separated. Children were routinely thrown into the mix, as were beggars and mentally ill persons who needed relief or treatment, not criminal imprisonment. Tocqueville and Beaumont devoted their attention to some of the new institutions that came out of this reform effort. They examined the records of a pioneering, privately funded school for young delinquents and foundlings, where director Nathaniel C. Hart inculcated in children's hearts the "two remarkably simple precepts" of "never lie" and "do the best you can."[23] They twice inspected a prison designed by architect John Haviland, which was under construction (with convict labor) on Blackwell's Island. The new building was meant to remove prisoners sentenced to short terms from the congested old Bridewell municipal jail, where indicted and convicted prisoners were thrown together indiscriminately.[24] They visited Bloomingdale Insane Asylum, also privately funded, and the poor house.[25] They then left the city for the entire first week of June to observe Sing Sing Penitentiary, up the North River, now known as the Hudson. There, they boasted of sharing the life of the inmates "save for sleeping in a cell and being whipped with a rope."[26] Completed three years earlier, also with convict labor, Sing Sing operated according to the Auburn system of inmates working in groups during the day, in total silence enforced by the whips of very few guards, followed by solitary confinement at night. The system was designed to prevent dangerous criminals from communicating among themselves. That silence, discipline, and work could be successfully imposed was open to question. A minister at Sing Sing "compared the warden to a man who has tamed a tiger but who might one day find himself devoured by it."[27]

While in New York, Tocqueville and Beaumont navigated between the city's penal institutions and mansions of the elite. Some days, they managed to set aside a few hours for reading at the Athenaeum, an institution founded in 1824 for the cultivation of literature and science. The prison investigation grounded their visit in daily exposure to the fault lines of a democracy, personal failure, forms of social exclusion, means of punishment and rehabilitation. Unfortunately, the time they spent in high society would provide few interpretive clues—although it would lead to additional contacts. When the evening came, they dropped their official mission, put on kid gloves, and attended high society balls. They had not anticipated these invitations. Tocqueville asked his brother Édouard urgently to send gloves, silk stockings, and silk ties, which were very expensive locally.[28] They went to five balls and banquets in seven days! On June 9, they were at the home of Colonel Nicholas Fish, George Washington's comrade in arms and the president of the New York branch of the hereditary Cincinnati Society.[29] On June 10, they went to a dance at banker James Gore King's home. He was the son of Massachusetts's delegate to the Continental Congress, Rufus King, a partner in the banking firm Prime, Ward, and King, and eventually president of the Erie Railroad. On June 15, they had dinner at the Schermerhorns', at their country home overlooking the East River. The young Miss Edwards, who had tutored them in English on the boat, was there along with other transatlantic travelers. Two days later, the party was at the luxurious neighboring country home of banker Nathaniel Prime to celebrate his daughter Mathilda's wedding. Mathilda played piano while Beaumont accompanied her on the flute. They also went to a banquet at the fashionable home of lawyer Robert Emmet, son of the famous Irish barrister.[30]

Not all was to their taste at these parties. As at city hall, the Frenchmen feared possible toasts to the "health of republics" they could not (yet) join. "Culinary arts" were "in their infancy: vegetables and fish before the meat, oysters for dessert—in a word, utter barbarity."[31] American music was "the most barbarous in the world," women singing "with a certain cooing in the throat . . . which has nothing in common with the laws of harmony."[32]

They also recognized they had much to learn about American women, who did not fit their stereotypes. The two young Frenchmen were surprised to find young women remarkably unsheltered. At Prime's estate, Beaumont was attracted by the beautiful Julia Fulton, the steamboat inventor's daughter, and even managed a "moonlight stroll" with her.[33] Tocqueville reported to Chabrol, "We are beginning to eye the women with an impudence that ill becomes representatives of the penitentiary system. But our virtue is still holding up!"[34] If they were interested in the booming sex trade of the city, not unknown to some of their patrician male acquaintances like John R. Livingston, they left no account.[35] Tocqueville had been embroiled in affairs at an early age, but he seemed to be preoccupied by Mary Mottley, the young English woman he had met in Versailles. While in the United States, he maintained some correspondence with her, courtesy of Chabrol.

Despite the prison investigation, Tocqueville's observations of New York society and governance remained preliminary. He needed interpretive guidance, and that meant both developing an analytical strategy and solidifying his knowledge of French administrative history to draw comparisons. He instructed Chabrol to find François Guizot's lectures at the Versailles apartment they shared and send them.[36] He asked him to explain the division of labor within French ministries and "decipher" the word *centralization*. He queried Ernest de Blosseville on administrative courts that had no equivalent in the United States;[37] he would later turn to his father, again regarding centralization.

If rereading Guizot's lectures was a useful exercise, it must have been only for Tocqueville to measure the distance that now separated him from Guizot's ideas on stages of civilization or his praise of mixed regimes.[38] America exploded these categories. Even though Tocqueville later told Camille d'Orglandes that he had thought of democracy since his student years, he was unprepared for the America he was seeing and had to think hard about how to investigate it.[39]

Tocqueville was still far from the elaborate interpretation of the American judiciary he would expound in *Democracy in America*. The best Tocqueville could do regarding the New York courts was to deplore that "the prosecutor speaks with his hands in his pockets, the judge chews tobacco, and the defense attorney picks his teeth while examining witnesses."[40] Tocqueville had the good fortune of meeting James Kent, "the American Blackstone," as Beaumont called him, who had presided over the Court of Chancery, the highest New York State court, as chancellor of New York. Yet he failed to provoke an important conversation. To be sure, Kent was already an older man, his views no longer in agreement with liberalizing economic jurisprudence.[41] But the encounter later proved its worth, when Tocqueville took the time to read on a Mississippi steamboat the four-volume *Commentaries on American Law* Kent had given him and grapple with fundamental differences between Roman codification, in which he was trained, and American jurisprudence, which was rooted in British common law.

Tocqueville was no better prepared as he conducted an interview with Swiss-born statesman Albert Gallatin, though this time the two could converse in French. Gallatin explained that Tocqueville would not find villages in America resembling those in Europe, for only towns existed; he talked about the prominence of lawyers in American society and the crucial role of the judiciary in keeping democracy "on an even keel."[42] He suggested that young people had few sexual restraints before marriage, especially in rural areas, but then adhered to marital fidelity. Tocqueville asked no question on the large contributions Gallatin made to territorial expansion as both treasury secretary and secretary of state in Thomas Jefferson's administration. He was seemingly unaware of Gallatin's influential report on canals and roads and equally ignorant of his study of Cherokee language. They did not talk about education either, though Gallatin had worked at reforming Columbia and served as first president of the council of New York University in 1830.

Still battling the crisis of faith that had overcome him during his teen-aged years, Tocqueville was deeply curious about the place of religion in democracy. Tocqueville sought out the local Catholic clergy on arrival in New York because he was anxious to reassure his mother that he attended mass.[43] But his extended conversations with local Catholic priests were misleading. Tocqueville reported without questioning it New York Irish priest John Power's assertion that only American Catholics, although they comprised less than 2 percent of the population in 1831, experienced true "faith." Therefore, only American Catholics could grow the "empire of authority" in the country while Protestant churches cared much more about morality than faith.[44] Hostage as he was to New York City high society networks, Tocqueville did not recognize the many signs of evangelical Protestantism in the popular neighborhoods where tract and Bible societies improvised revivals. The American Bible Society distributed 481,000 Bibles to ordinary, faith-seeking people in 1831.[45] Tocqueville reported on remarkably high levels of church attendance (streets around churches were closed to carriage traffic on Sunday),[46] but he attributed the commitment to the undemanding character of American religious observance. He totally missed that Protestant denominational fragmentation rose out of an urgent desire for more authentic experiences of faith and repentance. He was equally unaware of a small but vocal abolitionist movement but noted instead that religion and politics lived in peace in "two entirely different worlds."[47] He confidently asserted to Kergorlay upon leaving the city that he had not seen the sign of any "dissident movement" in Protestant churches.[48] Although Tocqueville ended up affirming in *Democracy in America* that the spirit of religion and the spirit of liberty strengthened each other in Protestant America in a way that was inconceivable in Catholic France, he developed only a partial understanding of American Protestantism.

Moreover, for all his connections with high society shipping magnates, Tocqueville failed to grasp the importance of New York as a great maritime center connecting international trade to the American interior. Of the trades, the wharves, the shops, the social life of ordinary people, he left no notes. And yet this was the very activity of middling sorts that generated the immense energy Tocqueville had felt ever since his first steamboat ride. He could declare that "incredible material bustle . . . increased man's strength without denaturing his reason," but he could not yet explain why this was the case.[49] Only raw "interest" came to mind as the secret of American energy. Tocqueville told Chabrol that Americans had raised an impulse he could not define, but which he called "interest," to the level of a "social theory."[50] This pursuit of "interest" generated "perpetual instability in people's desires, a constant need for change, an absolute absence of ancient traditions and ancient mores, a commercial and mercantile spirit that is applied to everything, even where it is least appropriate," but also a kind of happiness unknown in France. That was New York, "at least to judge by outward appearances."[51] These were first impressions that needed much deepening.

When they were ready to go north at the end of June, Tocqueville and Beaumont had integrated local society easily, experiencing only minor embarrassments, such as missing dinner at the Livingstons' estate near Sing Sing because they were confused about the time they were expected.[52] They had asked many questions, filled out some notebooks of conversations (and in the case of Beaumont, sketchbooks). But their only detailed notes were on prisons; other inquiries were preliminary. Despite City Recorder Riker providing many documents, Tocqueville left no notes on the workings of the local government, even though this would become a major theme of *Democracy in America*. And despite his conversation with Gallatin, he had not yet focused his attention on the relationship between the Union and the states that later also occupied a large portion of *Democracy in America*. For the moment, he could only say "government here seems to me in the infancy of the art."[53]

Tocqueville left New York, however, with some pertinent observations that already provided some foundation for *Democracy in America*. "What strikes me is that the vast majority of people share certain *common opinions*. . . . I have yet to find anyone of any rank who entertained the idea that a republic was not the best possible form of government or that the people might not have the right to choose whatever government they want." Tocqueville observed that even elites believed this:

> A second idea strikes me as similar in character: the vast majority of people have *faith* in human wisdom and common sense, and faith in the doctrine of human perfectibility. . . . No one denies that the majority might be mistaken, yet everyone believes that in the long run it is necessarily right, and that it is not only the sole legal judge of its own interests but also the most reliable and infallible judge.[54]

Tocqueville also admired the extreme respect that people seemed to have for the law, the principal reason for this, he concluded, being that the people make the law themselves and can therefore change it.

On first contact with Americans, Tocqueville concurred with Beaumont that "you'd have to be really blind to want to compare this country with Europe and adapt what works in one place for use in the other."[55] But upon leaving New York City, Tocqueville was speculating that France and the United States would ultimately follow the same path. "We are driven in this direction by an irresistible force. . . . Wealth will tend to be distributed more and more equally, the upper class will dissolve into the middle, and the middle class will grow vast and impose its equality on all. . . . Democracy is now something that a government can seek to *regulate* but not to halt." It was not easy to come to this conclusion, an aristocratic Tocqueville, still ambivalent toward democracy, assured Kergorlay.[56]

## Crossing New York State

Tocqueville and Beaumont booked passage on the steamship *North America* on June 28 and headed up the Hudson River to Albany. The trip did not go quite as planned. They had not gotten far before temporary interruption in service left the travelers stranded in the small town of Yonkers. The delay became an opportunity for Tocqueville to relax with his rifle, waging "a war to the death on the birds of America" while Beaumont sketched views of the Hudson. They had hoped to visit West Point, but when service resumed, the captain was determined to make up for lost time. So they missed the opportunity to see the military academy with its serious engineering training and possibly discover something important about science and engineering in America. As it turned out, the *North America* was not only trying to get back on schedule but also racing another steamboat, a dangerous pursuit given the frequency of boiler explosions. The *North America* celebrated victory with "rockets fired into the sky" launched from the deck in the middle of the night.[57] They reached Albany at five in the morning on July 2.

Tocqueville and Beaumont arrived in time for the July 4 celebrations, with a letter of introduction to Congressman Churchill Cambreleng, a member of the Albany Regency, the Jacksonian political machine founded by Martin Van Buren. With its mix of patronage and political influence, the Regency served the interests of small farmers and pioneers clearing land to the west and north, not those of the old Federalist oligarchy. It simultaneously embraced an ambitious program of canal building.[58]

Cambreleng, a former business associate of John Jacob Astor, received the two commissioners "most handsomely" and introduced them to other members of the state Democratic Party. Secretary of State Azariah Flagg (Beaumont rendered his title as Interior Minister for New York State), and Lieutenant Governor Edward P. Livingston (Governor Throop was not available) invited their French visitors to march with city officials in the procession.[59]

Tocqueville and Beaumont had briefly mistaken steamboat fireworks as early celebrations of the Fourth of July. But now they were in the thick

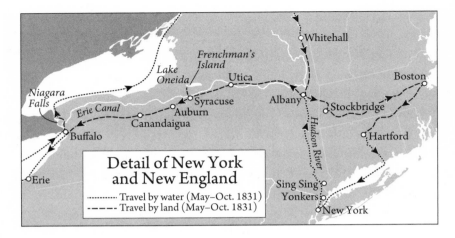

Detail of New York and New England

........... Travel by water (May–Oct. 1831)
- - - - - Travel by land (May–Oct. 1831)

of true commemoration, and there could be no better display of national values and civic pride. "The militia, civilian authorities, and representatives of every association that exists in the city gathered and marched in a procession to a church, where the Declaration of Independence was read, and a speech was delivered."

They saw once again evidence of the high place commerce played in the nation's hierarchy of values. Beaumont reported that

> representatives of all the industrial and commercial trades carried banners bearing the names of their organizations. It would be easy to ridicule banners with inscriptions such as "Butchers' Association," "Apprentices' Association," etc. But when you think about it, you realize that it is only natural that a nation that owes its prosperity to trade and industry should honor such symbols.

Beaumont seems to have forgotten that in the French processions of the Ancien Régime, the various guilds were represented along with the nobility, clergy, and bourgeoisie. In Albany, he was focusing on the peculiarly American mixture of commerce and religion they had detected on arrival at Newport, which was now on formal display. Religion pervaded American life. "The Declaration of Independence was read in the Methodist Church. . . . The reading was preceded by a prayer offered by a Protestant minister. I mention this," Beaumont wrote, "because it is typical of this country, where nothing is ever done without the aid of religion."[60]

Tocqueville was genuinely moved by the reading of the Declaration of Independence. Calling it the "*déclaration des droits*," he was conscious of witnessing a "truly beautiful sight . . . in this remembrance by an entire people of their nation's inception; in this union of the present generation with a generation that has passed away but whose generous passions everyone briefly shared—in all this there was something deeply felt and truly grand."[61]

But for all its effect, the July 4 focus on national unity masked deep political divisions that Tocqueville failed to divine. Tocqueville and Beaumont paid no more attention to local politics and the workings of local government in Albany than they had in New York City. Beaumont could say of Secretary of State Flagg that he "looks like a clerk and wears blue stockings; the rest of his attire is equally negligent,"[62] but he did not discuss or evidently appreciate his role as an ally of President Jackson in his war on the Second Bank of the United States.[63] Nor did Tocqueville and Beaumont comment on the Albany Regency, which was managing local growth by granting corporate charters and franchises through special acts of the legislature, through its monopoly over the sale of a twenty-million-acre public domain, and its ability to provide preferential credit and loans for farmers, transportation companies, and cotton, woolen, and iron manufacturers. They did not record that the state Democratic machine was facing opposition not only from its main political opponent, the National Republicans, but also from workingmen and hard money Democrats denouncing the state's banking policy as favoring monopolies.

These blind spots would affect Tocqueville's later thinking. In *Democracy in America*, Tocqueville argued that American freedom of association made secret societies pointless. He did not realize when talking to the Albany Jacksonians that they were prominent Masons, who had turned the secret meetings of the ostensibly beneficent society (that had included Washington) into a mechanism for monopoly control of appointments. The headlines about the assassination of an estranged Mason, William Morgan, who had threatened to reveal Masonic secrets, might have led him to pay closer attention. So might the subsequent growth in the antimasonry party in western New York, which reached a peak in 1831. At this point in his travels, Tocqueville did not know enough to heed these developments.[64]

Tocqueville and Beaumont were still viewing the United States through a French lens, which led them to underestimate its economic dynamism. They mistook Albany for an ordinary provincial town rather than a center of regional and national expansion. Beaumont compared it to Amiens, a French provincial "marketplace."[65] He noted in passing that the construction of the Mohawk and Hudson Railroad between Albany and Schenectady, one of the earliest railway lines in the United States, would contribute to the growth stimulated by the opening of the Erie Canal in 1825 and the other waterways, but this was a huge understatement. Tocqueville and Beaumont were crossing the most vital economic region of the country without realizing it. They mentioned that they had reached the Erie Canal but not that it was the greatest engineering accomplishment of the decade. They did not know, and no local politician seems to have told them, that the canal had been completed without public monies from the state any more than from the federal government. Instead, investors had paid the cost of the big dig in its entirety, so confident were they of its future revenues.[66]

The issue of possibly raising state taxes for extending the canal network came up briefly in a second conversation with Governor Throop in his home near Auburn. Again, all Tocqueville and Beaumont could say after visiting with the governor was that he was a very plain fellow, lived in a small house, farmed by himself, and was a clumsy shot. Elam Lynds, the former warden of Auburn prison, with whom they talked a few days later, reinforced the view that "men of great talent would not accept such a job. They would rather be in business or commerce, where you can make *more money*. There in a nutshell is the American character," mused Beaumont.[67]

After a few days, Tocqueville and Beaumont left Albany. The two friends disagreed on what they had seen. Tocqueville found inspiration in the July 4 celebrations, which he saw as embodying the kind of unity that a democracy could generate.[68] Beaumont came out of the same ceremony instead "increasingly aware of the impossibility of establishing [American] political institutions in France."[69] The project of jointly reporting on American governance was beginning to crumble.

The two friends were still in agreement about the importance of their prison investigation and headed west to Syracuse to see Lynds and then to nearby Auburn to visit the prison he had directed. They contemplated a detour north to Saratoga Springs, then as now a popular tourist destination, but opted to move west and hopefully see the wilderness and lay their eyes on Indians. No more kid gloves and upper-class parties but sturdy coaches and backaches. They entered the Mohawk Valley, traveling by coach along the Erie Canal, but without exploring the booming towns that lined the waterway. Utica was the first stop, then Lake Oneida, Syracuse, and Auburn.

At the time of their trip, these canal towns were in the midst of the Second Great Awakening. Tocqueville and Beaumont had already ignored this revival of evangelical Protestantism while in New York City and missed it again while upstate.[70] They stopped near Albany at a community of Shakers and dismissed the service as a series of "grotesque dances" and a "terrifying exercise" by a fringe community, founded "on the most antisocial principle that one can imagine: the sharing of all property."[71] By way of comparison, Beaumont could only think of the French Saint-Simonians preaching collective labor and free love.

This was a significant misinterpretation. Itinerant preachers had been promoting a full-scale Arminian revival along the Mohawk Valley for some time. They converted canal workers, promoted temperance, enforced the Sabbath, and boycotted boat lines operating on Sundays. Charles Grandison Finney, a self-declared Presbyterian, who admitted not having read the Westminster confession, had brought Utica to religious delirium only a few years earlier and had just brought Rochester residents to their knees. Mormon Joseph Smith also made converts in the region. Either no one informed our travelers about the revival, or they did not appreciate its significance. This was unfortunate, for evangelical Protestantism was the opposite of what they believed Protestantism to be. Denominational fragmentation meant a search for purity, not tolerance of minor differences as Tocqueville imagined. He never mastered this key distinction.[72]

While traveling between New York and Albany, Tocqueville and Beaumont had been fascinated with the speed of steamboats and the bustling economy they epitomized. But once they reached Albany, Tocqueville and Beaumont seemed to feel they were on the edge of the frontier and gave themselves over to a romanticized vision of America's virgin landscapes which they brought with them from France. They had their eyes not on the canal and locks that occupied the local population but on the river majestically flowing "between vertical stone walls of prodigious height."[73] They looked for traces of what nature was like before white pioneers fond of using rifle and muskets, as Cooper described them, killed wolves and other "ravenous beasts" such as bears and the occasional panther, and turned the landscape to their use.[74]

Reaching Oneida, Tocqueville and Beaumont encountered Native Americans, but they did not resemble the mythic figures described by Jean-Jacques Rousseau, Chateaubriand, and Cooper. The Frenchmen spotted "two Indian women walking barefoot on the road." It was a shock. "Their hair was black and dirty, their complexion coppery, and their faces quite ugly."[75] Where on earth, they wondered, had Chateaubriand met the beautiful Atala of his American novel? They felt that, despite a certain dignity, Native Americans were now "debased and degraded." Tocqueville despaired that "an ancient people, the first and legitimate ruler of the American continent, is melting away like snow on a sunny day and vanishing from the face of the earth, before our very eyes."[76]

And what of nature? Tocqueville's expectations were influenced by his memories of a children's book written by the popular German writer Joachim-Heinrich Campe, which was based on an account of the lives of Charles and Émilie de Wattines, aristocrats who fled the French Revolution and lived in exile on a deserted island in Oneida Lake. Tocqueville had read it in a French translation he had found among his older brother Hippolyte's books.[77] Ever since, he had fantasized that one could find "domestic happiness, the charms of marriage, and love itself" only on this tiny island. Tocqueville at times jokingly concluded conversations with friends with the assertion that "there is no happiness in the world except on the shores of Lake Oneida."[78] On July 8, they arrived at Fort Brewerton on the west side of the lake and crossed over to the island. They found traces of the log house and some vines and "a few items all but crumbled to dust" to mark where two unfortunate compatriots had once attempted to forget "revolutions, parties, cities, family, rank, and fortune," as Tocqueville noted. Having made the pilgrimage, they departed Frenchman Island "with a pang in our hearts" and traveled to Syracuse for their meeting with Captain Lynds.[79]

Lynds held a captain's commission in a New York regiment during the War of 1812. He took charge of Auburn State Prison South Wing when it was opened in 1817 and became warden of the entire prison in 1821. In 1825, Lynds brought Auburn inmates to Mount Pleasant to build Sing Sing, serving as warden there for five years. He now owned a hardware store in Syracuse. Tocqueville and Beaumont met the former warden first in his Syracuse home and then again in Auburn, where they established their quarters for almost a week "in a splendid hotel" in the small town of 2,000 people, where, as they noted, "twenty years ago, people hunted . . . for deer and bear."[80] Auburn had grown because of its proximity to the Erie Canal, and cheap prison labor had attracted industry.

Perhaps unsurprisingly, they found "the father of the present penitentiary system" to be "a man of utterly common appearance, his speech is similarly vulgar, his spelling is also quite poor," but they were impressed with his reasoning.[81] Prison reformers intent on isolating criminals had secured passage in 1819 and 1821 of laws requiring construction of solitary cells (in effect cages), and Lynds introduced the silent system in 1823.[82] Inmates were taken out of their cages during the day, marched in lockstep to the contractors' shops, where they worked under strict rules of silence, infractions being punished by the generous use of the whip. In a letter to the French minister of the interior, Casimir Perier, Tocqueville and Beaumont dutifully explained the Auburn routine, pointing to similarities and small differences with that of Sing Sing. Lynds's silent system was to ensure that dangerous inmates could not plot more criminal activity. "The only disciplinary measure here is whipping. The number of strokes is unlimited, and the decision is made by the guards at the moment of the infraction, without any need to seek the permission of the warden."[83] Tocqueville and Beaumont could have added that Lynds regarded whipping "as both the most effective and the most humane punishment, because it does not damage the prisoners' health and forces them to lead basically healthy lives."[84] Lynds, however, was opposed to full-time solitary confinement as "often ineffective and almost always dangerous." He also emphasized that inmates worked for "outside entrepreneurs" without compensation.[85] Administrators and philanthropists alike argued that pay would constitute a sort of bonus for crime, and Lynds himself defended the restriction by explaining that inmates "acquired the habit of constant work" while at the same time covering the cost of their incarceration. Although the habit of work might be considered a step toward rehabilitation, this was not Lynds's concern. The broader education that well-intentioned reformers advised was, in his view, a waste of time, for "prisons are full of coarse men . . . who have a very hard time grasping ideas or even responding to intellectual stimuli."[86] Lynds mentioned one of these foolish reformers by name: Edward Livingston, Jackson's secretary of state, who had spent most of his career in Louisiana and worked on prison reform.[87] Livingston would become one of Tocqueville's most valuable American guides.[88]

At Auburn, the two commissioners also interviewed the penitentiary's young Presbyterian chaplain, Reverend B. C. Smith, who, contrary to Lynds, believed in the potential of the prison system to reform the individual.[89] Smith visited prisoners' cells every night and ran Sunday classes.

Tocqueville and Beaumont were ready by now to leave the region, having learned more about the prison system but not being much more enlightened about the political system than they had been when leaving Albany. Fortunately, their meeting with attorney and state legislator John C. Spencer in Canandaigua, thirty-five miles to the west, provided the introduction to American governance that they lacked. Spencer was the first American informant who profoundly influenced the two travelers by teaching them some basic American constitutional principles.

Tocqueville, who had not read those figures of the Enlightenment, such as Condorcet, who had studied the American Constitution, was in real need of some tutoring.

Spencer's two beautiful daughters, Mary and Catherine, helped make the visit especially enjoyable. "We were more inclined to look at the daughters than at the father's books," Tocqueville wrote his sister-in-law Émilie. "They have among other charms, four blue eyes (that is, two each)" such as "you have never seen on the other side of the water."[90] Nevertheless, Spencer engaged the two young men in serious conversation. Like all other informants, Spencer was remarkably careful to avoid current controversies, as if intent on conveying only a positive image of the country. He explained that freedom of the press in America was balanced by the heavy fines to which newspapers were subjected if convicted of printing libelous statements. He revealed he had successfully prosecuted a libel case involving the Masons but not that he had written a tract exposing Masonic practices, which put him at odds with politicians of the Albany Regency and his neighbor, Governor Throop.[91]

Spencer went carefully over the state constitution he had helped revise. He shared his detailed knowledge of the judiciary, how civil law was "based entirely on precedents," not codification, and how this explained lawyers' disregard for theory. He argued that American Protestantism supported liberty and free institutions better than Catholicism could. Most importantly, he stressed the "axiomatic" adoption of legislative bicameralism throughout America even though House and Senate were "composed of the same elements and dominated by the same spirit." For "every bill must surmount two hurdles, time passes between the two debates and brings into play common sense and moderation."[92] A stimulated Tocqueville began to inquire of the ways American institutions affected social practices.

In addition to this crash course on American constitutional and legal principles, Spencer worked on restoring Tocqueville and Beaumont's respect for Native Americans. He told them of his own encounter with Red Jacket, a Native American who, at least in the telling, fit Tocqueville's stereotype of "savages" gifted with "the proud virtues that the spirit of liberty fosters."[93] Red Jacket was among the few Native Americans who sided with the United States during the War of 1812, eyeing, as a reward, Grand Island on the Niagara River to use as a hunting ground. Spencer remembered him as a man of "great eloquence," whose influence on his compatriots, whom he could defend successfully in American courts, was "immense." To a missionary trying to convince his people, the Senecas, to trade the Great Spirit for the Bible, Red Jacket suggested that "if his teaching prevents the white men from stealing our land and our livestock, as they do every day, then my father can come back to us, and you will find us more ready to receive your message."[94]

The two commissioners departed for Buffalo, where they would embark on the Great Lakes for Detroit. Although the town of about 12,000 had won the local competition to become a western terminus for the Erie Canal, Tocqueville and Beaumont did not retrace their steps to Syracuse to travel along the canal, choosing instead to move forward by horseback along barely passable roads. Had they taken the canal, they would have passed through Rochester and might have encountered the preaching of evangelist Charles Grandison Finney and registered this most important part of American religious life.

In Buffalo, the proud spirit of Red Jacket had all but disappeared. Now they witnessed white America's true racial cruelty in an encounter that shocked them profoundly. A group of Native Americans "had come to Buffalo looking for money owed them in exchange for land surrendered to the United States." Tocqueville noted they "resembled the dregs of the populace of a large European city. Yet they were still savages." They spotted a young Indian man lying drunk beside the road. Only "a few muffled moans escaped from his throat." They feared for his life and pleaded with some settlers to come to the rescue only to hear residents say, "What is the life of an Indian worth?" "The true owners of the continent are those who know how to take advantage of its riches." Tocqueville concluded, "Pleased with this argument, the American goes off to church, where he listens to a minister of the Gospel tell him that all men are brothers and that the Almighty who shaped each of them from the same mold made it the duty of all to help one another."[95]

## The Great Lakes

The steamboat *Ohio* took our travelers across Lake Erie to Detroit, stopping first at Cleveland. In Detroit, they entered a borderland that had for over a century been the scene of territorial disputes among American, French, and British populations. Regardless of which party emerged as the victor, the true losers were the Native American tribes who constantly lost ground amid changing allegiances (a history that Francis Parkman later brilliantly narrated). Much of the War of 1812 took place on the Great Lakes. While passing Middle Sister Island in the western part of the lake, Tocqueville noted that it was there that Commodore Matthew Perry had narrowly defeated the British in 1813, prior to invading Canada.[96] But Tocqueville was only marginally interested in that history, eager as he was to pass through the borderland and reach the end of human settlement. Paradoxically, it was in these sparsely populated parts of America that Tocqueville confronted, and took the measure of, America's racial and religious diversity. Only in the wilderness did he think seriously of Americans in the plural and the resulting encounter of cultures.

On the steamboat from Buffalo, they had conversed with John Tanner, a white man who had been captured as a child by Ojibwa Indians and lived with them for thirty years. Tanner was eking out a living as an interpreter in Sault Ste. Marie for explorer Henry Rowe Schoolcraft and for the local Baptist Mission, not unexpectedly experiencing much difficulty in returning to white society.[97] With only an approximate notion of English grammar, he had written his memoirs of life in captivity, which a local doctor edited and had printed. Tanner gave a copy to the two travelers as a primer for what they were keen to see, and this included significant descriptions of his life as a hunter and a trapper, a catalog of Indian totems he knew, reflections on Indians' knowledge of astronomy, their musical and poetic talents, and much more. Tocqueville's friend Blosseville later translated this important testimonial into French.[98]

In Detroit, Tocqueville showed little curiosity about the heirs of the French community that had built the original fort and fur-trading outpost early in the eighteenth century. If the population was still partly French, the city no longer bore physical marks of its origins: it had been totally rebuilt with a new plan after a massive fire in 1804. Tocqueville and Beaumont viewed it as the entry point to a part of the country "almost entirely unpopulated" only twenty years earlier and as a stepping-off point for the wilderness.[99] "How could we return to France without an image in our heads of a savage or a virgin forest?" Tocqueville wrote his cousin Eugénie.[100]

Tocqueville and Beaumont therefore wasted no time in seeking out John Biddle, the register of the land office, for advice on traveling through the wilderness.[101] Biddle had served as commander of the fort of Detroit in the War of 1812 and Indian agent at Green Bay, Wisconsin, before being elected mayor of Detroit and a delegate from the Michigan Territory to the US Congress. He naturally assumed the travelers wanted tips on where to buy land and turn a profit, rather than evade human settlement. So he explained to them the land acquisition process. This proved to be of unexpected interest. Surveying before settlement as directed by the great Land Ordinances of the 1780s had greatly facilitated western expansion.[102] Surveyors divided the territory into a grid consisting of numbered ranges, townships, and sections. Individual settlers and land companies could inquire about purchases at US government land offices throughout the territories and identify tracts by using the grid. "Quite a clever system," Beaumont thought.[103] Tocqueville was impressed as well. He mused, "An American thinks nothing of hacking his way through a nearly impenetrable forest, crossing a swift river, braving a pestilential swamp, or sleeping in the damp forest if there is a chance of making a dollar."[104] He noted that "since the last thaw, from May when the lake became navigable until July 1, approximately 5,000 "new settlers" arrived in Michigan.[105] Thinking about how the French Revolution had wreaked havoc on French society, Tocqueville wrote to Chabrol, "How can one even imagine a revolution in a land where man has such opportunities to satisfy his needs and passions, and how can the political institutions of such a people be compared to those of any other?"[106]

Had the two travelers wanted to investigate how pioneers settled the wilderness, they would have followed Biddle's advice, but they did exactly the opposite. Having learned where newcomers could acquire surveyed land, they set their course toward the "impenetrable forest" where they would find "nothing but wild animals and Indians."[107] On their way, they stopped at the small settlement of Pontiac, halfway between Detroit and the Flint River, where they found "twenty very neat and quite pretty houses, well-stocked stores, a clear stream, and a square clearing."[108] Early Pontiac settlers had even erected a common school. Major Oliver Williams, from Massachusetts, who had arrived around 1819 and lived with his wife, Mary, in a log cabin outside Pontiac, reassured them they could rely on Indians for guidance and pointed toward a still well-marked path to Flint. Another couple in Pontiac, Major Joseph Todd and his wife, gave them shelter, one on a bed, the other on the floor, and the next morning, found two Indian guides for them.[109]

The guides resembled the Native Americans Tocqueville had expected to meet all along, "to whom one reacts with an involuntary feeling of terror" until "the same man smiles and his whole face takes on a simple, kindly expression."[110] Beaumont described the guides as "running and leaping like deer."[111] "We followed as best we could, though even at a brisk trot our horses had a hard time keeping up." Past the Flint River, the party trekked through the dense "eternal forest all around": "fifteen leagues of wilderness" to Saginaw (close to Lake Huron) along "a narrow trail barely visible to the eye" in "a silence so deep, a stillness so complete, that a kind of religious terror grips the soul." They arrived in Saginaw after braving heat, thunder, mosquitoes, and constant fear of fatal rattlesnake bites. Evidently, the Native Americans had a remedy, but it would work only if applied in time.[112]

But even in this sparsely populated territory, the impact of European colonization could not be escaped. While on the Saginaw River, they were dumbfounded to encounter a Native American who addressed them in French. "Had my horse spoken to me," noted Tocqueville, "I don't think I would have been more surprised." With his almost impenetrable Norman accent, this "half breed" or "*bois brûlé*" was the offspring

of a French-Canadian fur trader and an Indian mother. He went on singing an old French love song, "Entre Paris et Saint Denis / Il était une
fille. . . ."[113]

They had reached the frontier. Saginaw Township, settled a few
months before in 1830, was merely a "seed recently sprouted in the wilderness." It was inhabited by only about thirty residents, Americans,
French Canadians (Tocqueville always says Canadians), Indians, and
*bois brûlés*, who lived on "whatever the wilderness can provide."[114]

Paradoxically, it was only when confronted with this embryo of a
society that Tocqueville seemingly became conscious of the ethnic and
racial fault lines of American society at large. This was an important
turning point in his view of America and helped inform his interests and
observations on the rest of this journey. He could not help but see that
"no common bond united them." But Tocqueville had no concept or
vocabulary to express his emerging thoughts. He could only turn to
stereotypes: The American was "cold, tenacious, and pitiless in arguments"; the French displayed a "carefree attitude towards life."[115]

Furthermore, in contrast to the religious latitude he thought was the
rule (against much contrary evidence he had been blind to), he found
the first residents of tiny Saginaw religiously intolerant. In Detroit, he had
met an influential French-born Sulpician priest, Gabriel Richard, publisher of the territory's first newspaper. That Father Richard could be
elected by an increasingly Protestant population to represent Michigan
Territory in Congress, Tocqueville interpreted as one more sign of remarkable religious tolerance.[116] Now, to Tocqueville's amazement, the
wilderness belied this. "Six different religions or sects vie for the faith of
this nascent society." "The Lutheran condemns the Calvinist to eternal
flames, the Calvinist condemns the Unitarian, and the Catholic re-
proves them all" while "in his primitive faith," Tocqueville speculated,
"the Indian confines himself to . . . dreaming of evergreen forests safe
forever from the pioneer's axe." Most bizarre was the "child of two races,"
who was naturally confused. Praying "at two altars. He believes in the
Redeemer and in the amulets of the medicine man."[117]

On July 29, as the travelers were retracing their steps through the
dense forest to return to Detroit, Tocqueville turned twenty-six. He

could not help recalling that was also the one-year anniversary of the three-day revolution in Paris, which had instituted a constitutional monarchy and triggered Tocqueville's desire to leave the Versailles courthouse, travel to America, and determine whether he could ever live in a democracy. "The shouts and smoke of combat, the roar of the cannon, the volleys of musket fire, the terrible clang of the tocsin—the memory of that terrible day seemed suddenly to erupt in flames out of the past and come to life before my eyes. It was but a sudden flash, a fleeting dream." The contrast with the wilderness felt overwhelming. "When I looked up and glanced around me, the apparition had already vanished." He had been looking forward to the wilderness, but now "the silence of the forest seemed more chilling, its shadows darker, or its solitude more complete."[118]

Tocqueville and Beaumont were back in Detroit on August 1. They very much wanted to keep exploring the region's mix of peoples and cultures when an opportunity to join a trip along the Great Lakes arose. They seized it and left again with 200 other passengers on the steamboat *Superior*. This was not the company they preferred. Beaumont uncharitably described the tourists as businessmen "incapable of intellectual work of any kind" with wives who once were pretty but "can never get it through their heads that they no longer are."[119] They went up the Saint Clair River, passed Fort Gratiot at entrance of Lake Huron, another fort of the War of 1812, where they were detained for a day because of contrary winds and lack of wood. With the Saginaw expedition fresh in mind, Tocqueville took the opportunity to write down his impressions, using a board on his knees as table. The result was *Quinze jours dans le désert* (Two weeks in the wilderness), a riveting account of their trip through the Michigan forest, which remained unpublished during Tocqueville's lifetime.[120]

The *Superior* then entered Lake Huron and threaded its way carefully through many islands, including Saint Joseph Island where the British had built a fort (destroyed in the War of 1812), and on to Sault Ste. Marie, a mission founded by French Jesuit "black robes" in 1668. As the cruise reached Sault Ste. Marie on August 5, Beaumont played Rossini on the deck with his English horn while the tourists were tossing brandy to

Indians in canoes.[121] Among the passengers was a Father Mullon, who
had founded a Catholic mission at Mackinac Island in 1829.[122] He
brought some of these Indians on board to baptize them while explaining
to Tocqueville and Beaumont that converted Indians became the most
fervent of all Catholics. At the same time, Tocqueville was observing
other Indians displaying the "most terrifying" spectacle of a war dance.[123]

As the steamboat could not go further up Saint Marys River, some of
the passengers (including women) went on a perilous canoe expedition
to Pointe aux Pins on Lake Superior. When they returned, it was time
to go back down the river toward Mackinac Island, situated at the entrance of Lake Michigan, where the British had relocated a fort the
French had once built on the mainland.[124]

The island was a center of the missionary movement, where Catholics and Protestants vied for the conversion of Native Americans. The
visit was another occasion for Tocqueville to reflect on the simultaneous but conflicting manifestations of American religious tolerance and
intolerance. On the boat, Episcopalian passengers had seemed content
to listen to a sermon by a Presbyterian minister, which prompted Beaumont to note, "This may be tolerance, but I would sooner die than call
it faith." But on the island, Protestant tolerance vanished when faced
with Catholic rivalry in proselytizing among Native Americans. Ministers exchanged harsh words. Father Mullon called Presbyterians "as
nasty as snakes" as he debated his opponent over the infallibility of the
church and priestly authority.[125]

From Mackinac, Tocqueville and Beaumont went on an excursion to
Green Bay, Wisconsin, where Biddle had once been the Indian agent
and where the military maintained Fort Howard. Major Lamard, who
ran the fort, saw local Indians in "contempt" of civilization. Why "cultivate a field," he despaired, "when all the game needed for survival can
easily be had with a rifle"?[126] Tocqueville almost drowned while swim-
ming in the wide Fox River. No Frenchman had ever traveled this far.

Traveling the Great Lakes, then, the two travelers were able to observe Native Americans in their exchanges with missionaries, fur traders, and the US military, while living on land they still largely controlled,
albeit not for much longer. These Indians fit their preconceptions and

they felt reassured to find them. At Green Bay, Beaumont encountered a young female Indian to whom he gave a painting of a woodpecker in exchange for a necklace of pearl and shells.[127] Tocqueville also penned a description of a

> Sauvage pharo. European hat, black feather curled around. Tin ring around the top. Three voltigeur feathers at the peak. Immense earrings. Pierced nose with a ring through it. Black tie. Blue blouse. Large necklace of pieces of tin with animals engraved on them, rings of tin around the legs, red garters with hundreds of small glass pearls. Embroidered moccasins. A red cloak over his shoulders. Opinion of an old Canadian that they are more handsome in their savage costume, entirely naked but for a belt and headdress of feathers. Long braids often hanging to the feet. Entire body painted.[128]

He also sketched a portrait of the man on the back of a manuscript page of "Two Weeks in the Wilderness."

Having so recorded a man, he penned for his sister-in-law Émilie a description of a woman he named after Chateaubriand's heroine—a portrait that indulged the expectations of its intended recipient:

> Atala is an Indian woman the color of dark café au lait, whose stiff, shiny hair hangs like drumsticks all the way down her back. She often has a big fat hooked nose, a broad mouth armed with sparkling teeth, and two black eyes that look in broad daylight the way a cat's eyes look at night. Make no mistake: for all her natural beauty, she does not neglect to make herself up. Not at all. To begin with, she draws a black ring around her eyes, then a nice red stripe underneath, then a blue one, and then a green one, until her face looks like a rainbow. From her ears she hangs what looks like a set of Chinese gongs that must weigh half a pound. The most fashionable of these ladies also wear a large tin ring in their nostrils, a ring that hangs down over the mouth to produce a most pleasing effect. They also wear necklaces made of large disks on which images of wild animals are engraved. Their clothing consists of a sort of canvas tunic, which comes down to just below the knees, and they usually wrap themselves in a

blanket, which at night they lie down on. The portrait is not yet complete: the fashion in the forests is to go pigeon-toed. I don't know if this is more unnatural than having the toes turned outward, but our European eyes have a hard time adjusting to this type of beauty. Can you believe that in order to achieve it, the feet of young Indian girls are bound? By the time they're twenty, the toes of their two feet touch when they walk. This garners a great deal of praise and is reputed to be quite fashionable. All that I know is that I would not want to play the role of Chactas [Atala's lover in Chateaubriand's novel] with one of these women for all the gold in the world.[129]

The *Superior* returned to Detroit on August 14. They had seen what they wanted, but they were not done with their discovery of the fate of Native Americans.

## Canada: Land of the Vanquished

What better way could there be to reflect on what they had learned so far than to cross the Canadian border? Not only was comparison Tocqueville's favorite investigative tool, but they were eager to discover how the French population abandoned by France since 1763 had fared under British rule.

The *Superior* took the travelers back to Buffalo. They rented a carriage and spent two days exploring Niagara Falls with some of the tourists who had been part of the Great Lakes cruise. "Niagara in Indian means 'thunder of waters,'" Tocqueville told his mother. Chateaubriand had sketched the waterfall as "the torrent from the Flood," but even he could not find adequate words for a scene that surpassed "any idea that the imagination can conceive in advance."[130] Yet Tocqueville could still see plainly that the United States was a country in which nature had been largely domesticated. Niagara had already become a site for international tourism. Tocqueville ventured the thought that all Americans needed was another "ten years before they build a sawmill or a flour mill at the base of the cataract."[131] Leaving both site and prediction behind,

Tocqueville and Beaumont took a steamboat across Lake Ontario and down the Saint Lawrence River to Montreal and Quebec City.

Tocqueville was not sure what he would find in Canada. Beaumont noted that England "holds on to the colony because it is of great political utility, especially for the timber that it supplies for the construction of British ships,"[132] but what of the French who lived there? Tocqueville's judgment was immediate. Street signs, he felt, do not lie: Even where "the population is exclusively French, when you come to an inn or shop, its sign is in English." They were entering a "conquered nation" inhabited by a "vanquished people."[133] Although the French Canadians "truly constitute a distinct nation," the English "control all foreign trade and dominate all domestic trade," and they "are constantly seizing control of land that Canadians believed to be reserved for their race."[134]

In forming his judgment, Tocqueville engaged mostly moderate local elites who resented British domination but did not resist it. Absent among his informants were Louis-Joseph Papineau and other radical leaders who encouraged rebellion. In New York, Father John Power had given Tocqueville a letter of introduction to Father Joseph-Vincent Quiblier, from Paris, superior of the Montreal seminary. They also met John Neilson, born in Canada of Scottish parentage, one of the few British Canadians allied with the French, speaking French "as easily as his own tongue,"[135] publisher of *La Gazette de Québec* / *The Quebec Gazette*, once a member of, but no longer allied with, Papineau's *Patriote* party. They talked to Dominique and Charles Mondelet, two brothers, both lawyers and moderate reformers; and they befriended two members of the Taschereau family, a journalist and a lawyer.

All these informants spoke with one voice; they insisted that French Canadians were a happy people. For their part, Tocqueville and Beaumont were pleased with the hospitality they received. "Since I have been in America, I have seen laughter only in Canada," Beaumont wrote to his father.[136] At dinner at the Taschereaus, everyone had to sing a song when dessert was served. "One is sure to find good cheer and cordiality whenever one is with Canadians." After their visit of Montreal and Quebec, Neilson took them north along the bank of the Saint Lawrence to the village of Saint Thomas de Montmagny, sixty miles northeast of Quebec, with a magnificent waterfall, where they saw "the houses are *all* well-built. All give out an air of prosperity and cleanliness. The churches are richly decorated but in very good taste."[137]

Tocqueville and Beaumont, however, suspected a much less happy reality behind the appearance of comfort. Although Tocqueville and Beaumont appreciated the hospitality shown to them, they were surprised by the dated French they heard and felt the people lacked spark. "I have yet to meet a man of talent!" noted Tocqueville.[138] Lower Canada seemed frozen in time. Tocqueville did not recognize the French he knew but a language that perhaps resembled that of his ancestors. "You'll find your beloved Lower Normand here," he told Émilie.[139] "The old France is in Canada; the New France is where we live."[140]

The travelers noted troubling remnants of feudalism even though their Canadian interlocutors went out of their way to portray these as minimal and irrelevant. Still, forty-two years after the "Night of August 4 [1789]," when the French formally abolished feudal rights in the early days of the French Revolution, one could see in Quebec "land divided into *seigneuries*, or estates, and each tenant required to pay dues to the lord. The dues are minimal: for example, 5 or 6 francs for 90 acres."[141] They also noted that the "lord" had a special pew in the church. To be sure, he was "lord" in name only and enjoyed no privilege of any kind. Neilson insisted that the overall cost to the peasant for using the seigneur's mill was less than the expenses incurred by US farmers, and fortunately nobody collected the old *taille* (tallage), the vague memory of which still sent "shivers down the [peasants'] spines."[142]

Informants also minimized the impact of a Catholic Church that in fact remained all-powerful. Father Quiblier was quick to reassure Tocqueville and Beaumont that the population willingly paid the tithe to the church, and the Mondelets insisted that priests were on the side of liberty. Indeed, Beaumont noted how strange it was "to see good country priests . . . preaching liberalism and speaking like demagogues."[143] The truth was that the Church was not really on the side of freedom. Priests defended the oppressed because they could only preach to the oppressed. But they taught them to respect authority and to accept the idea that the best life was the afterlife. In Canada, Tocqueville blamed the Catholic Church for discouraging individualism and education, thus forestalling the political potential of a broad electoral base.

Tocqueville's journey allowed him to compare the situation of Americans with that of French Canadians. From the Great Lakes, Tocqueville wrote his father that the vast stretch of land he had covered so far "will someday be one of the richest and most powerful in the world. You don't have to be a prophet to see this. Nature has laid the groundwork with fertile land and shipping routes unlike any other in the world. Nothing is lacking but civilized men, and they are knocking at the door."[144] Canada was another story. The French could never achieve liberty there. When leaving Canada for New England, Tocqueville concluded sadly that "the most irreparable harm a people can suffer is to be conquered."[145]

# 3

# A Crash Course in Democracy

## New England

Having visited Quebec, Tocqueville saw the United States in sharper relief when he and Beaumont arrived in Boston. The contrast between French Canadians, who seemed resigned to powerlessness, and New Englanders, who proudly believed in their own intellectual superiority, had the effect of deepening his understanding of American institutions, habits, and mores. Human intelligence needs such juxtaposition and comparison for sound judgment, Tocqueville later reflected, for "by a singular disability of our minds, we fail to adequately see things as they are, despite seeing them clearly and in broad daylight, without placing other objects beside them."[1]

Tocqueville and Beaumont, then, entered Boston on September 9. They immediately liked the city. Beaumont described it on arrival as "a city of 60,000" on an "island [actually a peninsula] accessible from all directions via roadways that cross the water." They were impressed by its "magnificent harbor," its "hilly terrain" where many private homes are designed with "taste and elegance," and a State House "worthy of note." Boston felt familiar in a number of ways: "there are a few who write," and they have "handsome libraries, all literary."[2] They settled comfortably at the recently completed Tremont House, a hotel offering "magnificent" service.[3]

Grief and worry briefly interrupted the travelers' cheerful mood. Tocqueville learned on arrival of the death of his beloved childhood tutor, Abbé Lesueur. He had lost the person who had first taught him "how to distinguish between good and evil," he wrote Cousin Eugénie.[4] And turning back to the task at hand, the two friends worried that Yankee reticence would prevent their contacts from being forthcoming about the American system and character.[5]

This fear turned out to be unwarranted. Tocqueville and Beaumont had extensive conversations on American constitutional principles and politics with "a number of distinguished men."[6] Tocqueville recognized the Boston elite as kindred spirits who, like him, believed that "if a people is to be republican, it must be level-headed, religious, and highly educated."[7] Moreover, Tocqueville discovered that his hosts worried about social change as much as he did. Former Federalists among them disdained Jacksonian democracy but were conscious of New England's declining national influence. Tocqueville, who had crossed the ocean in part to determine whether he could ever live in a democracy, was equally apprehensive of growing popular sovereignty.

The first occasion to meet members of Boston's elite presented itself almost immediately at a public parade headed for Faneuil Hall in support of a Polish uprising against Russian domination.[8] Tocqueville and Beaumont were introduced to two older gentlemen, Josiah Quincy and Harrison Gray Otis, among the marchers.[9] Both had begun their careers as stalwarts of the Federalist Party, defending New England maritime interests during the War of 1812. Now Quincy was president of Harvard College and Otis mayor of Boston. The mayor invited the two young men to a reception at the elegant home on Beacon Hill architect Charles Bulfinch had designed for him, and their experience there set the tone for the stay.[10]

At the mayor's home, Tocqueville met with two young men who were to become lifelong friends and correspondents. The first was George Ticknor, the brightest student in his Harvard cohort, who, upon graduation, had joined the college faculty and was working to raise its academic standards.[11] The other was Francis Lieber, a German refugee, who had fought at Waterloo but then sought in Boston a hospitable place for his liberal views. Lieber was editing an *Encyclopedia Americana* and was on his way to an academic career that included posts in South Carolina and at Columbia University in New York, where he would be the first faculty member to hold a chair in political science. President Lincoln would entrust him with writing the rules of military engagement for the Union army to limit war atrocities—the famous Lieber code.[12] Lieber became Tocqueville's lifelong correspondent and collaborator. At the party, they also met local officials and elegant ladies. Just in case Tocqueville and Beaumont might have forgotten they were in the mayor's home, the sheriff was among the guests, an office holder whose duties included that of executioner. For that reason alone, he would have been shunned by polite society in France, but in Boston nobody seemed to mind.[13]

One invitation led to another. A few days later, Tocqueville and Beaumont were sitting at wealthy David Sears's table in another Beacon Hill mansion. Among the dinner guests was Massachusetts senator Daniel Webster, who had become, with former president John Quincy Adams and Kentucky senator Henry Clay, a leader of the National Republican party in opposition to President Jackson.[14] As its spokesman in the US Senate, the famous orator insisted that the federal government should guide the people of the United States as a whole and not be "a creature of the State legislatures."[15] Tocqueville and Beaumont might have learned more that evening about the National Republican program of local economic improvement under federal leadership, with its protective tariff and central national bank supporting federal investments in roads and canals. Clay designated it the American system. Disappointingly, Webster could not be troubled to pay much attention to two young French visitors.

Fortunately, Tocqueville fared much better with John Quincy Adams, now a congressman, whom he met at a subsequent dinner at the home of Alexander Everett, former ambassador to the Netherlands and Spain. Most opportunely, Tocqueville was seated at dinner next to Adams, enabling him to converse freely with one of the most accomplished men in the country. Adams had a broad vision of politics. Early in his political career, he had distanced himself from New England maritime commercial interests and supported Jefferson's embargo against England. Madison had rewarded him for this stance with the post of United States minister to Russia, where he had witnessed Napoleon's invasion and retreat (evening host Everett had assisted Adams there). Almost three years had passed since Jackson had won the 1828 election, and the former president had agreed to reenter politics, stand for election to Congress, and counter the backroom deals that characterized Jacksonian party politics. That evening, he appeared keen on practicing his excellent French with a highly intelligent young French aristocrat, and the two soon recognized that despite their differences in age, nationality, and status, they had much in common. Much of their dinner conversation concerned Southern slavery, which Adams severely condemned as "responsible for nearly all our present difficulties and fears about the future."[16] They agreed on the value of work contrary to aristocratic idleness.

Although Adams had risen further politically than anyone Tocqueville had met so far on his travels, a more important connection was formed through a series of conversations with Jared Sparks, a Unitarian minister, former editor of the *North American Review*, and future history professor and president of Harvard College. Sparks was the highly regarded editor of the lives of George Washington, Gouverneur Morris, Benjamin Franklin, and others. A century later, the historian and literary critic Van Wyck Brooks called him the Plutarch of America.[17] It is likely that Tocqueville had met Sparks briefly in Paris in 1828, when Sparks visited Guizot, and renewed the acquaintance with him in Boston.

Over the course of several exchanges, Sparks raised two issues that found a prominent place in *Democracy in America*. The first Tocqueville had already heard about in New York City—the power of the majority. Tocqueville wrote in his notebook that Sparks observed that "the political dogma is that the majority is always right." Although admitting that "sometimes the majority has sought to oppress the minority," Sparks viewed "the governor's veto and above all the power of judges to refuse to enforce unconstitutional laws" as reliable institutional guarantees against "the passions and errors of democracy." Sparks objected later when Tocqueville developed his theory of the tyranny of the majority, but he had unleashed a line of inquiry that Tocqueville could not resist following.

Sparks also revived an age-old principle to explain the history of New England: the importance of the *point of departure.* "Our government and mores are best explained by our origins," Sparks posited. "Upon arriving here, we were already republicans and zealous Christians." But perhaps most importantly, he added, "we were left to ourselves." Such a condition strengthened "the town spirit." Sparks's emphasis on the way early settlers were "forgotten in a little corner of the world" and left to govern themselves made an impression on Tocqueville, who would embark on a systematic reflection on a political system based on self-government in small communities.[18] Sparks told Tocqueville, "Our ancestors founded *towns before there was a state.* Plymouth, Salem, and Charleston [Charlestown] existed before there was any government of Massachusetts to speak of. Only later did they join together, and then by an act of their own will." In all other nations, Sparks insisted, centralization prevailed: "government had concentrated in a particular place and subsequently expanded around that central point."[19]

When writing *Democracy in America,* Tocqueville generalized this New England sequence to the United States at large: "the local community was organized before the county, the county before the state, and the state before the Union."[20] Sparks also insisted that the larger governmental units in America never fully replaced the smaller ones that preceded them. For instance, the state of Massachusetts mandated that each town should maintain elementary schools, but design and implementation remained a matter of local decision making.[21] A puzzled Tocqueville felt the need to compare this situation with France. He wrote to his former prefect father for a refresher on administrative matters: "The word centralization has been dinned into my ears incessantly, but the thing has never been explained."[22] In this questioning, we find the origins of Tocqueville's insistence on a theoretical distinction between *government* and *administration.* He admitted that an efficient government rested on centralized authority but only if administration remained in local hands to avoid undue infringement on local liberties.

Tocqueville continued to mull over the conversation with Sparks during the rest of his journey. While traveling down the Ohio River, Tocqueville carefully read *The Town Officer,* a compendium on town government that Quincy had given him.[23] On studying it, Tocqueville puzzled over the level of detail for duties of various town officers, such as fence viewers or sealers of weights, appointed by the town, and the heavy dose of social control entrusted to them.[24] Selectmen had the authority to post in taverns names of drunks barred from the premises, while constables could prosecute blasphemers.[25] These instructions, Tocqueville felt, did not conform with his understanding of consensual self-government in a town meeting. He wondered whether any of these regulations from the days of the first settlers were still enforced. He sent Sparks an inquiring note.

In his response, Sparks was pedagogical, yet avoided writing a historical account. In terms borrowed from John Locke, he described the first arrivals to Massachusetts Bay as being in a "state of nature," setting forth in their initial covenants a "system of social and political regulations for mutual convenience and security" (defense against Indians, protection from neighbors' encroachment on property, and so on).[26] Sparks did not really address specific regulations but emphasized instead that the most important lesson Tocqueville could draw from the American experience was that the people had acquired the all-important habit of self-government.[27] Democracy rested on local self-rule practiced over a long period of time. Tocqueville was to echo this view in *Democracy in America*, writing that "local institutions are to liberty what elementary schools are to knowledge."[28]

Tocqueville, however, remained confused about the place of religion in local government. His informants had repeatedly pointed out to him that the separation of church and state was a characteristic of American governance. His reading in *The Town Officer* seemed to contradict these statements. He wrote to Sparks, "There is one article in particular in which I confess I am unable to understand anything, the one entitled 'Parish and Parish Officers.' Indeed, it seems to imply that each town is obliged to support a Protestant minister or else pay a fine to the county's court of common pleas. To a certain extent this seems to me to establish a state religion and to mix politics and religion in a way that Americans appear to have taken care to avoid."[29]

Tocqueville was correct to point out this inconsistency. The New England states had been remarkably slow in following the federal model of disestablishing religion. Massachusetts, for that matter, was last, disestablishing the Congregational church only in 1833, or forty-two years after ratification of the First Amendment and two years after Tocqueville returned to France. In responding to Tocqueville's query, Sparks ignored the conflicted process of disestablishment—a succession of court rulings and legislative decisions allowing residents to have their taxes go to their own denomination (and not just the Congregational church), culminating with the formal separation of church and state.[30] Sparks simply advised Tocqueville that disestablishment was about to be fully implemented and that Tocqueville could safely maintain that church and state were separated in America.[31]

The many forms of religious experience in the United States also baffled Tocqueville. Among the class of Bostonians that Tocqueville met, the Unitarian church was in ascendance. It was anchored at Harvard, where its ministers trained, and had spread in and around Boston. While in that city, Tocqueville interviewed William Ellery Channing, the Unitarian minister who spelled out the anti-Trinitarian position of the church and its belief in a benign God, not the harsh and arbitrary God of Calvinism.[32] Thirteen of the sixty churches in Boston were Unitarian.[33] Hence Tocqueville feared, as he told Channing, that "the end of the road will be natural religion." Having himself come to doubt Catholic dogma, Tocqueville worried that people "if deprived of dogmatic faith, believe in absolutely nothing,"[34] a view reinforced, not surprisingly, by the Catholic priests he met in New York.

Tocqueville at the same time wrote to Chabrol, "Protestantism has always seemed to me to stand in the same relation to Christianity as constitutional monarchy to politics. It is a kind of compromise among contrary principles, a half-way point between two opposite states—in short, a system incapable of tolerating its own consequences or fully satisfying the human spirit. As you know, I have always believed that constitutional monarchies would end up as republics, and I am similarly convinced that Protestantism will soon end up in natural religion. Many religious people here feel this strongly."[35]

Tocqueville would have developed a more balanced view if he had paid attention not just to the Unitarians but also to the other reaction to Calvinism, the popular Protestantism that embraced Arminian free will and salvation by character. Evangelical Methodist, Baptist, and Presbyterian churches had taken root mostly in the western parts of the state and promoted an experiential, anti-intellectual, and anti-establishment religious fervor.[36] They were the main proponents of disestablishment in Massachusetts. Earlier in the trip, Tocqueville had failed to appreciate the pietistic renewal in New York and in the Mohawk Valley. Caught in the social network of upper-class New England, he missed it again.

Ever since leaving Auburn for the Great Lakes and Canada, Tocqueville and Beaumont had neglected the prison investigation. They had to resume this pursuit in Boston. The travelers visited the Massachusetts State Penitentiary in Charleston, which had adopted the Auburn system only two years earlier as part of its expensive addition of a new wing. This expansion increased its capacity by 250 inmates whom the state employed quite profitably in stone cutting. Tocqueville and Beaumont visited the prison with the warden, William Austin. They saw that women, juveniles, insane prisoners, and the adult male (and presumably sane) population were kept separate. They met with Louis Dwight, founder and secretary of the Prison Discipline Society in Boston.[37] They observed Chaplain Jared Curtis teach Sunday school. While there, they also encountered Francis Calley Gray, who, in addition to being chief inspector of prisons, was a Massachusetts senator, a Harvard trustee, and an avid art collector. In a broad-ranging conversation, Gray echoed Sparks in stressing the New England tradition of resolving political disputes through debate.[38]

Tocqueville and Beaumont also visited the House of Reformation in South Boston, a house of refuge for twenty-five juvenile delinquents, that Episcopalian minister Eleazer Mather Porter Wells ran.[39] Tocqueville rated it well ahead of a similar institution they had visited in New York and was especially impressed that Reverend Wells used juries of young inmates to judge infractions by their peers. In renewing the prison investigation, then, Tocqueville deepened his understanding of American democracy. He would eventually argue that Americans identified the jury "with the very idea of justice" and considered it the natural "consequence of the dogma of popular sovereignty."[40]

Tocqueville and Beaumont departed Boston enriched by all these conversations on local self-government but left practically no notes about the commercial life of this great New England port. They recorded nothing of Boston seamen and their activities on the wharf. And just as they had ignored industrialization along the Erie Canal, they overlooked the new cotton mills of neighboring Lowell, whose significance Michel Chevalier, the French economist and disciple of Saint-Simon, immediately grasped during his visit in 1834. They noted only that Senator Webster had changed his stance on the tariff, abandoning free trade in support of maritime interests and backing instead protectionism for cotton manufacturers.[41] In addition, they had only a brief conversation on morality and sexual mores. A Mr. Clay, a planter from Georgia, told Tocqueville that any man suspected of having an *affair* "would be excluded from society immediately." Francis Gray shared statistics on prostitution, which was "carefully hidden from view" in Boston, while Reverend Dwight reported on the "shame" a venereal disease could inflict.[42]

On their return to New York, Tocqueville and Beaumont stopped at Hartford, Connecticut, unaware of the city's role in hosting a major Federalist convention in December 1814 designed to preserve New England maritime interests during the war with England. At Hartford, New Englanders had heralded their distinctiveness among Americans and made clear their distaste of both slave South and agrarian West. They stopped only briefly to visit a deaf-mute institute and then traveled to Wethersfield State Prison. Wethersfield impressed them because, although the prison was run on the Auburn system, delinquent prisoners were rarely whipped.[43]

## Philadelphia and Baltimore: A Long Stay

Tocqueville and Beaumont stopped only briefly in New York, dropping off notes and books before traveling to Philadelphia. Oddly, Philadelphia's perfect grid plan of rectangular streets and symmetrical open spaces disoriented Tocqueville. Philadelphia, he told his sister-in-law Alexandrine, is "the only city in the world where people have thought to identify streets by number rather than name."[44] He reported to another correspondent a story he had heard about a man reaching the point of distraction by "running from door to door" in a city where all streets appeared alike, "looking at every nameplate" in a vain hope of retracing his steps to the house of the woman he planned to elope with.[45] He did not find the story laughable, confiding to Chabrol that he thought of Marie "constantly" and feared he might never see her again. He somehow managed to stay "cheerful in society" but became "downcast when alone."[46]

Tocqueville found it more difficult to regain focus in Philadelphia than in Boston. Neither the city's French residents, who were descendants of noble families that had fled the French Revolution, nor its French visitors helped. He resented their pompous disdain for American manners.[47] He thought no better of local French diplomats, whose stupidity was, as Beaumont said, "difficult to overlook."[48] The two friends saw one play in French, and one was enough. They found French theater in Philadelphia "awful," performed by "horrible" actors.[49] While they turned their backs on the French community, they were increasingly concerned about their families in France, which was experiencing an outbreak of cholera. They shipped vials of cajeput oil to France, though without many illusions as to its efficacy.[50]

While in Philadelphia, Tocqueville and Beaumont made an excursion to Baltimore, their first foray into the American South and their first exposure to slavery. This too was disorienting. Tocqueville sensed that the framework he had been developing to understand the United States might not survive this dramatic change of milieu. Entering the border state of Maryland, Tocqueville felt "something feverish, chaotic, revolutionary, and impassioned in the way business is conducted, something that does not leave me with the same impression of strength and permanence."[51]

Fortunately, Beaumont remained on an even keel all this time and kept them going. And the stay in Philadelphia and Baltimore was far from unproductive for Tocqueville. After languishing for a few days, Tocqueville recovered his energy. His experience in Philadelphia added impetus to his view of the role of political and civil associations in American life. Quaker Philadelphia shared this same characteristic with

Puritan Boston, at least as Sparks described it, and this commonality led Tocqueville to begin assembling the component parts of a larger theory of political and civil associations and their impact on political culture. Despite being in Philadelphia, Tocqueville made no reference to Benjamin Franklin's pioneering role in fostering an active civil society. But the anti-tariff convention that was taking place in the city deepened his appreciation of like-minded people associating to achieve common goals.

The two friends had learned about the convention by chance. Before reaching Boston in early September, they had called on the novelist Catherine Sedgwick in Stockbridge. Although the well-known author was away, her family welcomed the visitors. They were proponents of free trade, important to the maritime interests of New England, and were in the process of organizing a national anti-tariff convention in Philadelphia with the goal of orchestrating repeal of the so-called restrictive system of trade.[52]

For Tocqueville, this was a new kind of political manifestation, and he resolved to observe it closely. Tocqueville remarked in his journal that the 200 delegates who attended the meeting from various parts of the country had been in conversation "by the power of the press from Maine to New Orleans." He also noted that sixty-three of them came from the Carolinas, a fact that was not surprising since South Carolina planters were leading the resistance to a federal tariff that favored Northern industrialists.[53]

There was no agreement among attendees about South Carolina's push for so-called nullification—that is, a flexible federal system, where states had license to apply federal law selectively—and the threat it posed to the Union. Tocqueville did not immediately grasp the theory behind nullification. There is no evidence in his Philadelphia notes that he was as yet aware of Vice-President John C. Calhoun's 1828 *Exposition*, which the South Carolina legislature had adopted as its program, and to which he later devoted a significant part of *Democracy in America*. Calhoun's proposal, based on several precedents, aimed at accommodating both majority and minority views in the national community, a view that President Jackson eventually defeated with his Force Bill and preparations for armed intervention in March 1833, when South

Carolina refused to apply the federal tariff—a full seventeen months after Tocqueville and Beaumont attended the convention and twelve months after their return to France.[54]

Protectionists were at the same time holding their own equally large convention in New York City. All the prominent Boston manufacturers were there, and John Quincy Adams, who had told Tocqueville in Boston he feared such conventions might "usurp the rightful place of our representative institutions," made a well-received appearance.[55]

Tocqueville did not heed Adams's premonition that organized private interests might rival the prerogatives of democratically elected legislatures. Instead, he recognized the Philadelphia free trade convention as a real innovation—that is, as a mechanism to bring together similarly inclined people to advance a shared goal. He originally thought of the Philadelphia convention not only as a means to an end but as an end in itself, possibly the nucleus of a new political party. Local informants, however, downplayed this view. Charles Jared Ingersoll, a lawyer and state legislator, himself an active participant in the competing protectionist convention, explained it was important to separate opinion from action.[56] "The purpose of a convention is not to act but to persuade. It represents an opinion, an interest, and does not seek to represent the nation, which is fully represented in Congress."[57]

Tocqueville observed in Philadelphia other forms of association in response to other impulses and needs, among them temperance societies, and decided that their success was "one of the most remarkable things about this country." He was struck by the use of association to achieve moral ends. He immediately generalized, jotting in his notebook, "The power of association has developed to the full in America. People associate for commerce as well as for political, literary, and religious interests. No one ever seeks success by recourse to higher authority; people rely instead on individual resources acting in concert."[58] A few days later, in Baltimore, John Latrobe, son of Benjamin Latrobe, the architect of the US Capitol, concurred with these observations. Latrobe told Tocqueville what the latter had already heard from Sparks, that the most important reason for Americans' ability to "administer" themselves is that they were "*used*" to doing so. "What must be explained is how we acquired that habit."[59] That associations vied to gain influence in the bodies that constituted "higher authority," Tocqueville ignored by focusing his attention on Americans' skills at forming and running associations. Thus began, with only modest empirical observation, Tocqueville's ambitious theory of association, which was destined to become a major contribution to American political theory.

But what, then, of political parties? Tocqueville and Beaumont had left Boston aware that the clashing Federalist and Republican parties of the early Republic had lost their constituencies. Sparks had even explained that Jackson transcended party, and this was correct, for the president was for a strong union, like his National Republican opponents, heirs to the Federalists, but against their program of national economic coordination. In Philadelphia, Tocqueville and Beaumont had a chance to interview Nicholas Biddle on the topic. Biddle was president of the Second Bank of the United States, a joint public-private institution headquartered in Philadelphia.[60] The bank had state branches, and its redeemable bank notes were honored throughout America.

Biddle repeated what Tocqueville had already heard in Boston regarding causes of the original parties' decline. Great debates were things of the past. Now "political passions must inevitably attach themselves to details of administration rather than to principles."[61] John Quincy Adams, who attended that meeting at Biddle's home in Philadelphia, agreed, and Tocqueville repeated this position verbatim in his notes and later in *Democracy in America*.[62] "The parties that I call great are those that dedicate themselves more to principles than to consequences; to generalities and not particulars; to ideas and not men. . . . America has had major parties, but they no longer exist."[63]

The timing of this conversation was unfortunate. If only it had occurred four months later, the conclusion might have been quite different. Thanks to his growing opposition to Jackson, whom he had earlier supported, Biddle was about to become one of the men responsible for the return of great parties in American politics. In January 1832, Biddle (on Clay's advice) sought to renew the bank charter ahead of schedule as a way of insulating it from the politics of the upcoming presidential campaign. This ploy failed: Biddle had not anticipated the depth of Jackson's opposition. The conflict between the bank and the president intensified and dragged on. When Jackson, in his second term, illegally removed the federal deposits from the bank, an action for which he became the only president ever censured in the Senate, opponents of "King Andrew" formed the Whig party to combat his arbitrary rule.[64] With Whigs and Democrats arguing opposite visions of political economy, great parties were indeed returning to the center of political life. Tocqueville recognized in *Democracy in America* how these conflicting visions of political economy, bank and tariff alike, posed a threat to the Union but failed to observe the formation of a new two-party system, which historians have since labeled the second party system.[65]

These great parties were different in important ways from the old ones, reflecting as they did a greater level of participation at the grass-roots. Over the previous two decades, states had progressively erased property requirements for suffrage and instituted popular elections for many offices and for presidential electors. By the time Jackson was in the White House, nearly all white men could vote. Tocqueville collected much evidence of the democratization of politics in both Philadelphia and Baltimore. Upper-class informants decried the poor choices of voters, which they ascribed to the growing presence of the "common" people in national politics.

Some politicians whom Tocqueville met continued to claim politics as a gentleman's preserve, albeit under new populist conditions. For instance, politicking now involved stagecraft. Ebenezer Finley, a prominent Baltimore lawyer, made this point to the French visitors during a dinner hosted in their honor by Governor George Howard of Maryland. The guest list included representatives of several old aristocratic Maryland families. Finley told Tocqueville and Beaumont that his Jacksonian opponent in the race for the state legislature was also his best friend. After addressing the crowd, the two often retreated to a local inn where they shared a good meal and pleasant conversation. Meanwhile, the audience argued their respective points with fistfights and occasional broken bones. To them, their oratorical jousting on the hustings, which their adherents took so seriously, was merely a show.[66]

But most realized that the people were not always easily manipulated. Pierre-Etienne Duponceau, French-born resident of Philadelphia and president of the American Philosophical Society, repeated the common complaint that men of talent were seldom selected.[67] Charles Carroll, at ninety-four the last living signer of the Declaration of Independence, offered a nuanced view of democratic transformation. One of the great landowners of Maryland, Carroll insisted to Tocqueville and Beaumont that "a mere democracy is but a mob" but admitted that "the people are being educated, knowledge is spreading. . . . Society, though less brilliant, is more prosperous."[68] Benjamin W. Richards, Jacksonian Philadelphia mayor (and prison inspector), saw in the greater political participation the political triumph of a middle class "as capable of dealing with public affairs as anyone."[69] And Baltimore's James Carroll (unrelated to Charles) added the most important note to Tocqueville's observations that "whatever the shortcomings of democracy may be, it stimulates activity and energy throughout society."[70]

Tocqueville had overlooked the populist strain in American religion before. Although he had yet another opportunity, he remained blind to changes in Protestant churches in Philadelphia and Baltimore. Baltimore was the center of American Catholicism, and Tocqueville, always attuned to the Catholic voice, was receptive to the message of the local clergy, who effectively restated the position of their colleagues in New York City that "America is destined to become the homeland of Catholicism. It is spreading here freely, without assistance from the civil authorities and without arousing hatred, thanks solely to the power of its doctrine and in total independence from the state." Most vocal in this conviction was Father John Mary Joseph Cranche, vice-president of Saint Mary's School in Baltimore.[71]

Several informants tried in vain to dissuade Tocqueville and point to equally deep and appealing convictions among Protestants. Dr. Stewart, "a distinguished Baltimore physician," insisted, "People [Protestants] are true believers."[72] James Brown, in Philadelphia, a former minister to France, hence somebody who understood Tocqueville's prejudices, insisted that Protestants believed in traditional Christian doctrine and held "a firm belief in the immortality of the soul and in the theory of rewards and punishments."[73] Tocqueville listened politely but remained committed to his view of Protestantism as a denatured form of faith, diagnosing "a vast reservoir of doubt and indifference hidden beneath these external forms" while again pointedly ignoring evangelical, populist alternatives.[74]

Tocqueville's Versailles friend Louis Bouchitté had asked Tocqueville before his departure for a report on Philadelphia's Quakers. Tocqueville only partly complied. He predicted the Quakers would be "one of the first Protestant sects to disappear," for they had lost their popularity by siding with England during the American Revolution and had continued to wane ever since by "squander[ing] their power over souls in minute regulations."[75]

Two Quakers, Roberts Vaux and Samuel Wood, however, were influential in Philadelphia's prison system, which ran on a different plan than the Auburn model. Vaux, who "heads all the charitable institutions, including schools for the poor, institutions for the deaf and mute, hospitals,"[76] conceived of the plan for Eastern State Penitentiary, or Cherry Hill Prison as it was known at the time, and Wood was warden.

Investigating Eastern State Penitentiary occupied a large part of their time in Philadelphia. It provided a contrast to Sing Sing, Auburn, Charlestown, and Wethersfield, which all practiced the Auburn system of collective labor during the day and isolation at night. At Eastern State, Tocqueville and Beaumont confronted an alternative system of imprisonment based on full-time solitary confinement.

Quakers had long insisted on the need for criminals to repent and had implemented reforms at the Walnut Street Jail in the 1790s. They improved the cleanliness of the prison and instituted solitary confinement to give prisoners time to reflect on their crimes. Previous French visitors—notably the duc de La Rochefoucauld-Liancourt when in exile and Girondin Jacques Pierre Brissot—had reported favorably on work at Walnut Street.[77]

The Pennsylvania legislature adopted the Quakers' stance while also considering John Howard's pioneering experiments with solitary confinement in England and Edward Livingston's widely read recommendations for humane treatment in his proposed Louisiana penal code.

The legislature commissioned English architect John Haviland to design a 250-cell prison, meeting the requirement for solitary confinement.[78] Haviland provided a hub-and-spoke, or radial, floor plan inspired by Bentham's panopticon to facilitate "watching, convenience, economy, and ventilation."[79] Cells were large enough to include a workbench and give prisoners the opportunity to ply a trade in isolation; each cell had plumbing and access to a small individual exercise yard. The prison was opened in 1829. It was an experiment Tocqueville and Beaumont were eager to study.

The visit did not disappoint. Although conceding that the costs of building and maintaining large individual cells might outweigh the benefits, Tocqueville unequivocally favored the Pennsylvania model, as his notes to Casimir Perier, the French prime minister and interior minister, attest.[80] In Pennsylvania, prison work—shoemaking, spinning, weaving, dying, dressing yarn, blacksmithing, carpentry, sewing, wheelwright work, washing, last making, brush making, tin working, and a few other tasks—was not intended to reimburse the state for the expense of incarceration, as in the Auburn system, but designed to help prisoners reform. Prisoners were also encouraged to acquire familiarity with the scriptures and engage with the chaplain.

Tocqueville made a point of interviewing as many inmates in their cells as possible and wrote reports of his conversations with forty of them. Minimizing the very real threats to mental balance long-term solitary confinement posed, Tocqueville reported in his journal that inmates found the discipline of the penitentiary "mild and conducive to reform."[81] Inmates, who were isolated in their cells and hooded whenever outside, presumably expressed hope that their anonymity while imprisoned would allow them to reenter society.[82] They recognized the benefit of seclusion. "For a well-bred man," one interviewee said, "it is better to live in absolute solitude than to be mixed indiscriminately with people of the most wretched sort."[83] Tocqueville eventually assessed punishment at Cherry Hill "at once milder and more terrifying than any other punishment yet invented. It aims solely at the prisoner's mind but achieves incredible power over it" as inmates adapt to the trauma of isolation and then settle into a rhythm of work and reflection. Regarding religious sentiments expressed by the inmates, Tocqueville cautioned the minister not to read too much into them, as he felt prisoners had a stake in appearing more religious than they were.[84] He concluded that most simply relished human contact, including the chaplain's, but some seemed to be genuinely exploring their spirituality in their confinement.[85]

Yet the Philadelphia penitentiary did not function as smoothly as Wood suggested to his visitors. Tocqueville and Beaumont wrongly affirmed to Perier that "in the Philadelphia penitentiary, corporal punishment was never used," and this seems the primary reason for their preference (and eventual endorsement of it).[86] In fact, just four years later, a damning report provided the legislature with an alarmingly long list of extrajudicial punishments inflicted on refractory inmates. These ranged from deprivation of food and exercise to the use of a device called the iron gag, a kind of bridle attached to ropes that bound the inmate's hands behind the head, applying dangerous pressure to the jaw and jugular veins. Conversely, total relaxation of the rules also occurred, undermining the system. Corrupt prison personnel had opened cells and made inmates serve as servants at parties in Wood's quarters, among other suspected improprieties.[87] Lieber, whom Tocqueville had befriended in Boston, and who translated Tocqueville and Beaumont's penitentiary report, was drawn into the Pennsylvania investigation and did much work to correct the infractions it identified. But there is no indication that Tocqueville and Beaumont ever learned of these violations at Eastern State.

It was also first in Philadelphia and then in Baltimore that Tocqueville and Beaumont began to think harder about race. Their location afforded them the perfect contrast between free and slave states. Philadelphia had about 15,000 free persons of color in 1831. But as Beaumont noted, though nominally free, free Blacks did not have civil rights. He correctly added, "laws do not change mores."[88]

In Maryland, there was gradual emancipation, but slave owners wielded control over entire families, some free, some manumitted. Tocqueville reported routine episodes of shocking racial oppression. A caning he witnessed at the horse race in Baltimore "occasioned no great surprise in the crowd or, for that matter, in the Negro himself."[89]

Many of those who discussed race with Tocqueville and Beaumont in Philadelphia and Baltimore believed that the country was at risk of a race war. Duponceau told them that Blacks would someday avenge themselves violently for the contempt in which they are held. "The Blacks will arm themselves against their enemy, and they will be exterminated. There is no way out of the situation our ancestors created when they brought slavery here other than massacre."[90]

For Beaumont, these conversations were critical. In Albany, Tocqueville and Beaumont, sensing their different interests, had decided not to publish a book together beyond the penitentiary report (see chapter 2). Beaumont did not want to devote himself to a book on democracy, especially as he was not a proponent. By contrast, he found the fault line of race to be more compelling. He told his brother Achille, regarding slavery, "On this point I made any number of observations, which in my mind do not reflect very favorably on the people to whom they apply. But I will probably publish all of this in the great work that is to *immortalize me*, and it is to that book that I refer you if you wish to know the rest."[91]

Tocqueville, for his part, remained fascinated with the American democratic experiment, but he as yet had no real conception of the book he might write. He told his mother:

> If I ever write a book about America . . . what I have . . . is a jumble of notes, any number of disconnected ideas to which I alone possess the key, and some isolated facts that call to mind a host of others. . . . Will I ever publish anything about this country? I truly do not know. It seems to me that I have some good ideas, but I still don't know how to frame them, and publicity frightens me.[92]

In Philadelphia, Tocqueville and Beaumont received new instructions from the minister of justice to return to France (no reason was given).[93] Even though Tocqueville and Beaumont understood their days in America were numbered, they wanted to see more of it. They briefly considered eliminating New Orleans from their itinerary,[94] but Charles Carroll had described the West as democracy's safety valve— "we can send our upstarts out west"[95]—so they resolved to push ahead.

By heading west and taking a very roundabout route back to France, it is clear they were trying to squeeze in the very last bit from their trip while technically obeying the minister.

## Down the Ohio River to Cincinnati; Crossing Kentucky and Tennessee; Down the Mississippi to New Orleans

From Philadelphia, Tocqueville and Beaumont traveled by coach through the Pennsylvania interior. From a distance, they observed German communities, the Pennsylvania Dutch, who seemed to "have preserved intact the spirit and mores of their homeland."[96] They briefly visited the Western State Penitentiary in Pittsburgh,[97] where, unlike at the Eastern State Penitentiary in Philadelphia, full-time solitary confinement had been abandoned. Almost immediately, they left for Cincinnati, Ohio, with the idea of gathering more information on the workings of local government in the West. But the weather did not cooperate. Not only had winter arrived, but it was the coldest on record. It took only ten miles down the partly frozen Ohio River from Pittsburgh for the steamboat to hit a reef amid "enormous floating chunks of ice."[98] All passengers, including women, showed admirable self-control, noted Beaumont, while a passing steamboat pulled them off the reef, and they reached Cincinnati on December 2.

Tocqueville noted, "This is the place that one must visit above all to have an idea of this social state, which is so different from ours."[99] This city of 25,000, a critical transit point between east and west and north and south, Tocqueville realized, was "in too much of a hurry to grow to bother with establishing any kind of order. . . . No external signs of luxury, but images of industriousness and labor abound at every turn."[100] English novelist Fanny Trollope, who lived there, notoriously complained about a "total and universal want of manners."[101] But Tocqueville felt that Cincinnatians possessed exactly the manners that made a democracy on the move. He marveled at the immense energy he saw deployed around him: "Everyone has come to make money. Nobody was born here, nobody is keen to stay here, no one—absolutely *no one*—is idle, no one is engaged in intellectual speculation, and everyone is occupied with something, to which he dedicates himself with passion. Nobody yet has any notion of an upper class. The jumble is complete. Democracy is unlimited."[102]

Although Tocqueville did not find what he felt was a constituted upper class in Cincinnati, he was able to identify the city's leading personalities to act as informants, like John McLean, a Jackson appointee to the Supreme Court, who spoke favorably of the role of the Second Bank of the United States in fostering local development and expressed fears regarding the durability of the Union. Tocqueville talked to a younger lawyer, Timothy Walker, recently arrived from Massachusetts and soon to be founder of the Cincinnati Law School. Walker recited the familiar complaint that at election time, people's "choices are almost always mediocre or bad."[103] Tocqueville was also introduced to Salmon Chase, Walker's law partner, who was only three years older than he. The future chief justice under President Lincoln made the same point, as did local physician Daniel Drake.[104]

One noticeable feature of Cincinnati that struck Tocqueville—he made a note of it in *Democracy in America*—was the virtual absence of a Black population, yet another manifestation of the deep racial divide of the country. Cincinnati's whiteness was by design. To keep the number of African American residents low, the city had passed a local ordinance requiring Black residents to post a significant bond.[105] Moreover, Tocqueville was seemingly unaware of, or insensitive to, the fact that Irish immigrants had attacked the free Black community during a race riot in 1829. Many African Americans relocated farther north, and some crossed into Canada. Cincinnati had yet to become a center of abolitionism and a route of escape for enslaved people.

The trip down the Ohio vividly displayed the contrast between a free and a slave economy. The disparity was manifestly displayed on opposite banks of the river, with the state of Ohio on one side and the slave state of Kentucky on the other. Tocqueville wrote to his father that the river journey was their "first opportunity to examine the effects of slavery on society." Down the Ohio, he explained in a passage he reproduced in

*Democracy in America,* "On the right bank, activity and industry are everywhere; work is honored; there are no slaves. Cross to the left bank,
and the scene changes so suddenly that you would think you were at the
other end of the world. The spirit of enterprise ends abruptly; work is
not only a hardship, it is shameful, and the man who submits to it de-
grades himself."[106]

On December 3, Tocqueville and Beaumont departed from Cincinnati, still determined to explore more deeply a society shaped by slavery.
The initial portion of this trip was a series of disasters. On the second
day out, their boat was blocked by ice. They took refuge at the mouth
of a little creek, where they waited twenty-four hours for a thaw that did
not come. Forced to disembark, they walked twenty-five miles, with
snow up to their knees, until they reached Louisville, Kentucky. As the
Ohio was still not navigable, they abandoned the river, traveling by
coach for two nights and two days, hoping to reach the Cumberland
River and take it down to Nashville. Discovering the Cumberland River
was also frozen, they hired a coach to continue their trip, but on December 11, the coach broke down. They had reached the Tennessee River by
then, which they crossed on a ferry. Tocqueville, however, fell sick. Shiv-
ering and without appetite, he could not go on.

During his bout of depression in Philadelphia, Tocqueville had jotted
in a travel notebook the three "human miseries" as "1. diseases, 2. death,
and 3. doubt."[107] Beaumont had helped Tocqueville rebuild his confidence. Now he found a refuge for them at Sandy Bridge in the primitive
log cabin of postmaster Zephaniah Harris and his wife, Martha.[108] During the four frigid days it took for Tocqueville to recover enough
strength to move on, he had his only opportunity to experience slavery
up close, albeit slavery as practiced on a small scale rather than the large
cotton or sugar plantations that they did not visit.[109]

Tocqueville realized that even poor whites took full advantage of
owning slaves. "In this impoverished setting . . . our host nevertheless
did the honors of his house easily and courteously. Not that he lifted a
finger himself." Rather, "quietly seated in front of a fire hot enough to
roast an ox to the very marrow," he "soon enveloped himself in a cloud
of smoke, while between puffs he beguiled the time for his guests by

recounting all the great hunting exploits he could remember."[110] Tocqueville concluded, in words that echoed the conversation he had in Boston with John Quincy Adams, "The habit of giving orders without restraint instills a certain haughtiness that makes men impatient of opposition and irritable at the sight of obstacles to their will. Slavery makes work dishonorable. It turns the entire white race into a leisure class, which deprives money of some of its value. . . . The people of these states are southerners, slave masters made half savage by solitude and hardened by life's miseries."[111] They felt free by keeping the other race in bondage.[112]

With Tocqueville feeling better, the two friends resumed their travels toward New Orleans. Their plan was to take a steamer from Memphis to New Orleans, but they found that even the Mississippi was frozen in places, making it impassable. Marooned in Memphis temporarily, they amused themselves by going bird shooting in the "most admirable forest in the world," often with help of local Chickasaw guides.[113] Tocqueville saw the election of Davy Crockett to the House of Representatives as yet another example of the disastrous effects of the social state that existed on the frontier, which left voters incapable of judging the qualities he regarded as necessary for leadership. Tocqueville noted that with universal suffrage, the people of Memphis had entrusted such a responsibility to "a man with no education, who can barely read, who owns no property, and who has no permanent address but lives in the woods and spends his life hunting, selling game in order to live."[114]

Once the river thawed, Tocqueville and Beaumont resumed their trip, encountering Native Americans for the third and last time. The first time, in western New York, they had come across Native Americans who, inebriated and begging, fell far short of the stereotype of the noble savage. Their second encounter was more pleasing to them because it came close to their preconceived notions. They caught glimpses of Indian life as it survived in the Michigan forest and islands of the Great Lakes. Now, as they passed into Arkansas, they witnessed President Jackson's policy of removal firsthand, the forced relocation of the Choctaw Nation, the first stage of the Trail of Tears.

Tocqueville was shocked by the spectacle of the tribe approaching the river.

> Horses had been sent ahead. . . . Then came the men, who . . . carried nothing but their weapons. Then the women, carrying children fastened to their backs or wrapped in blankets. They also bore bundles that contained all their earthly belongings. Finally, the elderly were led aboard. Among them was a woman aged 110. I have never seen a more terrifying figure. She was naked except for a blanket through which one could glimpse the most emaciated body one can imagine. She was escorted by two or three generations of offspring. What a wretched fate, to leave her homeland at that age to seek her fortune in a foreign land![115]

What to make of this bewildering spectacle? As Tocqueville and Beaumont completed the last leg of their journey to New Orleans, they received some answers from a remarkable passenger who arrived at the embarkation point "riding a superb stallion."[116] It was none other than Sam Houston. Raised on the Tennessee frontier, Houston had been a rebellious child who had for several years deserted his family to live among the Cherokees. Largely self-educated, he was an avid reader, known to have read Homer's *Iliad* by himself in the wilderness. He served with distinction under General Jackson in the Creek War, practiced law, and was elected to Congress from Tennessee before becoming its governor.[117]

When Tocqueville met Houston, the latter had just resigned the governorship under mysterious circumstances following separation from his young wife after only a few weeks of marriage. He had returned to the Cherokees where he was known as the Raven, and he was traveling to Washington as a Cherokee citizen to advocate for their causes with Congress, and with his friend the president.

Tocqueville and Beaumont could not have met a person more knowledgeable about Native American traditions and at the same time more aware of the policy of Indian removal. Houston, however, did not condemn the policy. Jackson's friend argued against all evidence that the federal government could protect the integrity of Indian land against land-hungry white settlers. He also believed that Native Americans, if protected, would adopt white mores. Houston defended the position that, if only the United States government would "act wisely for a period of twenty-five years," respect solemn treaties, and encourage Indians, once relocated in Arkansas, to become civilized, they would prosper. Houston described the Indian as "born free," already half-civilized, with "an ever-active mind" and a "subtle and often admirable intelligence."[118] He explained that some Southern tribes like the Cherokees had demonstrated immense progress, living entirely by farming and having developed a written language. Others had also made strides. The Creeks lived by farming as well as hunting, and they formulated a legal code. For once, Tocqueville heard a white man promoting the Native Americans' intelligence rather than justifying the unilateral seizure of their uncultivated lands as right and just. At the same time, he did not question Houston's assumptions or probe the rationale behind moving tribes from their historic lands.

By the time Tocqueville and Beaumont reached New Orleans, they felt the pressure of time. Although anxious to see New Orleans, they knew the visit had to be short if they were to reach Washington, DC, while Congress was still in session. They had already been delayed in Sandy Bridge, Memphis, and farther south when the steamboat had been grounded on a sandbar for two days—and their observations were desultory. They arrived on New Year's Day, and they introduced themselves to the French consul, François Guillemin. They discussed with him their sense of French subjugation in Canada, and Guillemin assured them that the French here, unlike the French in Canada, lived "truly and completely on a footing of equality" with Americans.[119] They were not a conquered people. Also, on New Year's, they pursued their investigations of slavery with Étienne Mazureau, a French lawyer who invoked the climate to justify the practice, a position that John Quincy Adams in Boston had forcefully rejected.[120]

Of race relations in the city, Tocqueville and Beaumont saw little, failing again to record the city's street life or even to mention its slave markets. They did notice race hierarchy during an evening at the theater, where "colored women and white women with some African blood" were seated separately in boxes in the upper circle.[121] They had heard from Louisianan James Brown, US minister to France under John Quincy Adams, whom they had met in Philadelphia, that there was in New Orleans "a class of women dedicated to concubinage. . . . Girls of color destined from birth to become the mistresses of white men."[122] Following the performance, the two friends seem to have made an appearance at a ball designed to match such women of mixed color with wealthy white men, and this prompted Tocqueville to write to Chabrol. "What mores one finds in a southern region where slavery is allowed! You cannot imagine it." Tocqueville also noted, as if to prove Montesquieu right (and John Quincy Adams wrong), that "when you meet people who say that climate has nothing to do with the constitution of nations, tell them they are wrong. We have seen the French in Canada: they are a tranquil, moral, religious people. In Louisiana we found other Frenchmen, anxious, dissolute, and loose in all respects. Fifteen degrees of latitude separate these two groups, and that is the best explanation I can give for the difference."[123]

But there was much more than climate involved, which would have been clear to Tocqueville if he had connected the dots. Mazureau spoke of the "*bedlam* that reigns here" with a legislature "that is constantly making, changing, and unmaking laws."[124] Tocqueville missed his opportunity to think through the implications of Louisiana's grafting of an American legal system based on court precedents onto a French one that followed legal codes. In Philadelphia, Tocqueville had studied American law, intent on finding why American lawyers held such sway. Much of the answer, he had realized, was that lawyers were the repository of special knowledge nobody else could easily access. In Philadelphia, Tocqueville filled up an entire notebook of conversations on the subject with Henry Dilworth Gilpin, US attorney for the Eastern District of Pennsylvania (and later attorney general of the United States under Martin Van Buren),[125] and Philadelphia recorder Joseph McIlvaine.[126]

The two legal traditions collided in Louisiana. Creoles had inherited property and contracts negotiated under French and Spanish codes.

They feared dispossession by American settlers as contracts would no longer be honored in a system where judges' decisions became law. Edward Livingston, already known to Tocqueville for his liberal Louisiana penal code and whom they would soon meet in Washington, DC, had spent much of his political career in New Orleans protecting Creoles from such negative consequences of the fusion of different legal systems.[127] Tocqueville and Beaumont, however, were passing through too quickly to notice this momentous cultural collision.

## From New Orleans to Washington, DC, and New York

In concluding their journey, Tocqueville and Beaumont went straight from New Orleans to Washington, DC. They reached Montgomery, Alabama, on January 6, then spent the next nine days in uninterrupted travel, taking a coach that took them through Georgia and the Carolinas, reaching Norfolk on January 15. They had intended to go to Charleston and from there to Montpelier to visit James Madison (Joseph Coolidge Jr. in Boston had given a letter of introduction). Tocqueville calculated the exact mileage to Charleston and identified all the stops.[128] But they changed plans en route due to impassable roads and collapsed bridges. They were in a rush and realized they could gain at best, as Tocqueville told Édouard, "only a superficial idea of the south of the Union."[129]

Among his sparse notes on this last leg of the trip, Tocqueville recorded that somewhere near Montgomery a local lawyer broached with them the issues of Southern violence, lack of education, and evangelical fervor, arguing that these qualities were naturally entwined. Of violence, Tocqueville recorded his informant as saying that "there is not a person in the state who does not carry a concealed weapon," and of religious feeling that "in the North you have religion; here you have fanaticism," but he did not investigate these claims further.[130]

Reaching Norfolk on January 16, Tocqueville and Beaumont traveled by boat to Washington, DC. They had the good fortune to reconnect on the boat during the five-day trip with an interesting personality they had met in Philadelphia, Joel Roberts Poinsett, who had served as the first

United States minister to the Mexican Republic. A Jacksonian and a Southerner, Poinsett was returning from campaigning against nullification in his home state of South Carolina.

They engaged, for the first time in depth, with the critical fear of disunion.[131] What were the strengths and weaknesses of the Union? Could it be broken? Tocqueville had extensively prepared for this conversation by using much of his time on the steamboat down the Mississippi to read the *Federalist Papers* and to reflect on the US Constitution. He had arrived at the conviction that "only a very enlightened people could have created the federal constitution of the United States, and that only a very enlightened people singularly accustomed to representative forms is capable of operating such a complicated machine and of maintaining within their separates spheres the various powers, which otherwise would not fail to clash violently with one another."[132]

Part of the discussion turned on the risk of rebellion that African Americans and Native Americans posed to the country. Tocqueville was especially keen on getting Poinsett's view of race relations, a topic on which he had made observations of his own. When crossing Alabama, Tocqueville recorded a scene of interracial psychology that struck him so vividly that he reproduced his notes almost verbatim in *Democracy in America*, contrasting Native Americans' natural defiance toward whites with African Americans' habit of submission, even before a child. "Near the home of a planter, a young Indian woman held an adorable white girl (the planter's daughter) in her arms and lavished maternal affection on her. With them was a Negress, who entertained the child. In her every movement the child betrayed the sense of superiority that, as her brief experience of life had already taught her, raised her above her two companions, whose caresses and attentions she received with an almost feudal condescension. Squatting in front of her and watching her every gesture, the Negress seemed clearly divided between devotion to her young mistress and respectful fear, while the Indian's effusive tenderness bore the mark of a certain freedom and even savagery, which made a strange contrast with the submissive posture and humble manners of her companion."[133] Tocqueville was curious whether Poinsett could somehow validate this contrast.

Poinsett believed that there was no danger to the country from a slave revolt, even though Nat Turner's rebellion in Virginia in 1831 had renewed fears. Poinsett argued that "a slave revolt would never succeed," adding that if slaves "ever became intelligent enough to join together and create a powerful force, they would also be intelligent enough to see that, given their situation, ultimate success is impossible," especially as "Mulattoes" felt themselves "much closer to Whites than to Blacks." He believed that only emancipated Blacks threatened the Union and that "Washington set a very bad example by freeing his slaves."

When it came to Indians, Poinsett, who was no Houston, echoed the argument, widespread among white Americans, that Native Americans were "a race that does not wish to become civilized." Therefore, "civilized people have the right to take the Indian land that the Indians themselves are incapable of exploiting and where white men will prosper and grow rapidly in number."[134] Tocqueville, who admired the independence of mind of Native Americans, did not endorse this theory in his heart but grudgingly admitted that it accurately described the inevitable outcome of a fight between unequal combatants.

For Poinsett, if there were a true danger to the Union, it would come neither from a commercial war between North and South nor from a race war between Blacks and whites, but as an unexpected outcome of American prosperity. He pointed out that adventurers, who were ruling western and southwestern states and territories, did not abide by rules conceived for mature societies. They subjected the US Constitution's elaborate balance between branches of government to the harshest of tests. These conversations made a strong impression on Tocqueville, who devoted a part of *Democracy in America* to dangers that the Union might break up. South Carolina's Poinsett joined New York's Spencer, Massachusetts's Sparks, and Pennsylvania's Biddle among Tocqueville's most significant informants.

In Washington, DC, in late January 1832, Tocqueville finally met his fifth major informant in the person of Secretary of State Edward Livingston, who invited them to dinner at his home, with great hospitality (if bad music again). Livingston, married to the daughter of a rich planter from the French Caribbean, was fluent in French. Tocqueville and Beaumont erroneously identified him as born in Louisiana as they knew him only as the author of the proposed penal code for Louisiana. They did not realize at the time that Livingston was from New York, a member of the large family they already knew, indeed the younger brother of the Robert Livingston who had helped negotiate the Louisiana Purchase. Edward Livingston had relocated to Louisiana after facing legal challenges early in his political career. They had with Livingston an excellent conversation on the penitentiary system as the most viable alternative to the death penalty.[135]

Livingston and Poinsett turned out to be extraordinarily solicitous and made it possible for Tocqueville and Beaumont to attend sessions of Congress in both House and Senate and collect government documents. In some ways, Washington demonstrated Tocqueville's and Beaumont's ability to form a social circle. They met again with congressman Edward Everett, whom they had first seen in Boston at his brother Alexander's house and with whom Tocqueville would develop a lasting epistolary friendship. John Quincy Adams invited them to dinner at his Washington home. They attended one ball at the home of Daniel Patterson, a commodore in the American navy, and another at the home of Louis McLane, secretary of the treasury, and they also met with Nicholas Philip Trist, who had married Thomas Jefferson's granddaughter, Virginia Jefferson Randolph, and served as personal secretary to President Jackson.[136]

Thanks to French minister Louis Barbe Charles Sérurier, they also visited the president. This was of course a much-anticipated meeting, as Jacksonian politics had been at the center of so many conversations throughout the trip. But the visit was anticlimactic. They found the White House to be only a modest home, where, Beaumont reported to his mother, "we spoke about rather insignificant things. He [President Jackson] served us a glass of Madeira, and we thanked him and called him 'sir' just as any other visitor would."[137]

They left Washington, DC, on February 2 and reached New York after a brief stop in Philadelphia. In New York, they collected their notes and made a few last-minute inquiries before the return voyage on February 20. Tocqueville left the country admiring the American people's resourcefulness in utilizing the vast possibilities their country offered for the benefit of the greater number in ways not yet conceivable in France. But he was apprehensive about sorting through the vast amount of information they had collected, organizing his ideas, and presenting them to a skeptical French readership. He seriously doubted his ability to succeed, yet cautiously hoped, he wrote to his brother Édouard, that he "might be able to write something passable" about the United States.[138]

# 4

# Writing America in Reverse Order: Prisons First, Then Freedom

TOCQUEVILLE AND BEAUMONT reached France in late March 1832 as the country was in the midst of a major cholera epidemic. Alexis immediately went to Versailles, where he reunited with Mary for a few days.[1] We know that he was in Paris on April 2, reporting on his American travels to his cousin Le Peletier d'Aunay, who had helped make the trip an official government assignment. Alexis then joined his brother Édouard and the rest of the family, who had taken up residence in the country estate of the Ollivier family, Édouard's in-laws, at Saint-Germain-en-Laye, to escape the cholera that had swept through the capital.[2] The epidemic, which Tocqueville and Beaumont had first heard news of while in Philadelphia in October 1831, claimed over 18,000 lives in Paris.[3] The dead were interred in mass graves; the sick feared being mistaken for dead and buried alive; ragpickers rioted against sanitary measures that prevented them from scavenging. There were victims among the wealthy, too. Elizabeth de la Ferté-Meun, Tocqueville's cousin and comte Molé's daughter, a woman he described as "shining with youth and health," died a few hours after being stricken, as did another cousin.[4] Prime Minister Casimir Perier died after visiting the Hôtel-Dieu hospital.[5]

The epidemic consuming Paris left Tocqueville even more disoriented. He was anxious about his future, with no clear sense of what he could do with his trunks full of documentary evidence and personal notes. Indeed, it would take a full eighteen months—until October 1833—for Tocqueville to begin organizing his vast inventory of recorded conversations, letters recovered from family and friends, and preliminary theories about democracy.[6] Meanwhile, from Saint-Germain-en-Laye, Tocqueville communicated with difficulty with Beaumont, who had sought refuge with his parents in the Sarthe. A disabling depression, signs of which had appeared in his last weeks in America, was now worsening, and he feared that his listlessness was becoming a chronic disease. He realized the first task at hand was to deliver the penitentiary report, but he could not muster energy to work on it.[7] "My mind is in a fog," he wrote his travel companion and coinvestigator.[8] He was not even trying. "Eyes half-closed, I await the moment when I can see into the genius of the penitentiary system," he added.[9] With Eugène Stöffels, Tocqueville diagnosed his low spirits as *spleen*—a combination of "boredom, sadness, and moral despondency."[10]

Political instability shook Tocqueville out of his torpor and forced him to decide where he stood and what he wanted to do. The July Monarchy still appeared precarious in spring 1832, with police discovering a series of plots hatched by rivals banding together against the government. In the February rue des Prouvaires conspiracy, Legitimists and Republicans had joined forces in a plot to murder or kidnap the royal family during a ball at the Tuileries Palace. The Legitimists had distributed arms to the Republicans. Chateaubriand, who had been kept abreast of the plot but declined to take part, commented, "The heroes of July, cheated out of the Republic by the *juste milieu*, were happy to work with the Carlists in exacting revenge on a common enemy, if only to slit each other's throats after victory."[11] Just as the two friends returned, two incidents pitting the dethroned Bourbons and their Legitimist supporters against the reigning Orléans, occurring simultaneously in April and May 1832, led Tocqueville to make a critical career change as well as affirm his independence of judgment in political affairs.

## Resignation from the Courthouse

The first pivotal incident was a celebrity prosecutorial investigation. Gossip about the intricate case was on everybody's lips: Charles X was still king in 1829 when the aging duc de Bourbon (who had long ago lost his only child, the duc d'Enghien—Napoleon Bonaparte had had him shot on suspicion of conspiracy) designated as heir to his vast fortune his godson, the duc d'Aumale, son of the now-king Louis Philippe. The choice of heir surprised many. Rumors swirled around the duke's mistress, the baronne de Feuchères, also known as Sophie Dawes, an Englishwoman of great beauty, whom the duke had made the "queen" of his Chantilly estate. She had presumably convinced her lover the duke to designate Louis Philippe's son as heir in exchange for Louis Philippe having her readmitted to Charles X's court, from which she had been banned. She might also have held the duke's hand while he secured a part of the inheritance for her.

Although the duc de Bourbon claimed he accepted the outcome of the July revolution, and the ascendance of the Orléans branch of the royal family to the throne, some suspected he might cut the duc d'Aumale out of his will. If that was ever his intent, he did not have the chance to do so. In August 1830, not even a month after the Revolution, the duke was found dead in his bedroom, suspiciously hanging from a window knob.[12] The official inquest concluded it was a suicide.[13] But the Rohans (the family of the duke's estranged wife), in a bid to invalidate the will and recover the inheritance, argued it was murder, and the baronne de Feuchères became a suspect.

Beaumont had briefly worked on the case for the court prior to his departure for America. He presumably refused to remove from the record evidence that exposed the duke's mistress's loose morals, thus supporting the Rohans' claims.[14] On rejoining the Ministry of Justice in May 1832, Beaumont declined to return to this financial and political intrigue on the pretext that he had not stayed abreast of developments while in America, and his first obligation was to the prison report. If Beaumont was disinclined to defend the Orléans against the Bourbons, he did not say so. But he was instantly fired for insubordination, losing a much-needed source of income. Upon receiving news of Beaumont's "destitution,"[15] Tocqueville immediately resigned his own prosecutorial position, informing the Justice Ministry that he too was leaving "a career in which service guided by conscience is no protection against unmerited disgrace."[16] He had already begun contemplating leaving behind law practice while he was still in the United States, but now he decided to act on it.[17]

## Tocqueville Defends Kergorlay

His timing proved propitious. No longer a civil servant, Tocqueville was released from his half-hearted oath of loyalty to the regime just as the duchesse de Berry, mother of the "legitimate" heir to the throne of France, the twelve-year-old duc de Bordeaux (also known as comte de Chambord), attempted a coup against the July Monarchy.

From exile in Tuscany, the duchess had been counting on strong pockets of Legitimist support in Provence, and then in Vendée, to support her bid to be regent. To boost her popularity in Paris, she had relied on Chateaubriand to distribute money to cholera victims, which he did through a network of Legitimist priests and friendly mayors of Parisian arrondissements. Among the duchess's ardent supporters was Florian de Kergorlay, Louis's father.

Both Tocqueville and Beaumont suspected the Kergorlays might have had a hand in the coup and therefore had probably been arrested and jailed for conspiracy against the regime. This turned out to be true.[18] Father and son had joined the vicomte de Saint-Priest and a few other accomplices in the duchess's coup. From Massa (Tuscany), they boarded the *Carlo Alberto*, a Sardinian steamer, on April 24, 1832 and sailed to a port near Marseille, where the duchess disembarked on the night of April 28 with some of the passengers, including Florian but not his son.[19] This group launched an insurrection on April 30, but only a handful of local nobles rallied to their cause. The duchess traveled incognito to Vendée, where she fomented yet another insurrection, this one fully repressed by June 9. She managed to live in hiding for five months. Finally captured, she was taken to the fortress of Blaye and put under General Bugeaud's surveillance.[20]

Louis de Kergorlay, who had stayed aboard the *Carlo Alberto* with Saint-Priest, two other accomplices, and the duchess's maid, proceeded to flee to Rosas, Catalonia. Forced to refuel at La Ciotat near Toulon on April 29, the steamer was spotted, pursued, and stopped.[21] Once on board, the French police mistook the maid for the duchess and thought for a moment that a Black sailor was the young duc de Bordeaux in disguise (they even rubbed his skin to expose what they believed would be his true color), but the prince had never left his grandfather, who was exiled in Prague. All passengers were taken to Corsica, then to Marseille where they were jailed on May 10. The elder Kergorlay, captured outside Marseille, joined them.[22]

Tocqueville visited his friend in prison. He was allowed to see Kergorlay only after difficult negotiations with the authorities, and he used the visit to assure his friend of his support. Kergorlay wrote a pamphlet in jail to state his case, and Tocqueville distributed it, following Kergorlay's precise instructions. He sent it to influential politicians, the press, and various bookshops, over eighty copies in all. In it, Kergorlay insisted he did not recognize the authority of an illegitimate government—that is, the July Monarchy. At the same time, he made the argument, based on legal precedents, that he had been arrested illegally aboard a defenseless ship of a French ally (Sardinia), and in defiance of international law, this amounted to piracy.

Moreover, Tocqueville and Beaumont inserted in *La Quotidienne*, a Legitimist newspaper, a jointly signed statement calling for the release of the duchess, who was detained as a prisoner of war, outside the reach of the judiciary, with no appearance in court planned.[23] Unlike his brother Hippolyte, who wrote an impassioned defense of the duchess in an act of devotion to the Bourbons (in a "lettre aux Normands"),[24] Tocqueville maintained that he was above the fray. He felt free to defend the duchess, he would later claim to voters in his district, precisely because "I did not share the convictions of her supporters." He built his case on principle. He argued that the government had no right to keep her in prison arbitrarily as a war prisoner without access to a court of law. "I maintained that if the duchesse de Berry was being held as a prisoner of war, she should be released, as the war was now over. If she was being held as a criminal, she should have her day in court. But to detain her without trial was unlawful and offensive to the liberty of all citizens." Challenged on this point during an electoral campaign, Tocqueville invoked his great-grandfather's historic defense of the king: "I remembered that I was the grandson of a man who had defended Louis XVI while he was in irons, a man honored today by all parties."[25]

It turned out that the duchess's worst enemy was herself. She had secretly remarried an Italian nobleman, was pregnant when arrested, and had given birth to a child in captivity (the child died in infancy). The duchess's second marriage caused her to lose her French citizenship and with it any claim to a regency. In his prison cell, the bombastic Florian de Kergorlay refused to believe this was true. No longer posing a threat to the regime, she was eventually released in June 1833 and took refuge in Sicily.

The conspirators were tried in Montbrizon in March 1833, where they had been transported after their incarceration in Marseille and Aix. At the trial, public sentiment was visibly with the defendants. Tocqueville served as a second lawyer for his dear friend. In the only closing statement he ever delivered in a courtroom in defense of a client, he acted perhaps more like a character witness than a defense attorney. He highlighted Kergorlay's patriotism in the Algerian conquest and strongly asserted his right to act according to his conscience. To the charge that Kergorlay was the "Gothic champion of outdated opinions," Tocqueville retorted with the dubious claim that "no one is better fit to understand the spirit of our age." In the end, the jury acquitted.[26]

Tocqueville's pronouncements in defense of his childhood friend have been interpreted as outspoken expressions of support for the Legitimist cause. Tocqueville remained suspected of Legitimism for years. But if Kergorlay was an unrepentant Legitimist, Tocqueville's only commitment was to political liberty. Tocqueville had rushed to the rescue of his friend while at the same time voicing disagreement with his cause. Walking such a tightrope between conflicting principles would become one hallmark of Tocqueville's political career. In their correspondence of the day, Tocqueville and Beaumont referred to themselves as "former royalists." Not only were they not Legitimists, but they were no longer committed to monarchist principles.[27] But they were not democrats either, at least not yet. Tocqueville was leaning toward becoming one, but he needed to ponder his American experience more deeply in light of all that had happened since his return before he could arrive at that position.

## Penitentiaries

During this time, Beaumont and Tocqueville worked on the penitentiary report to fulfill their initial assignment. Their first task was to brush up on French prisons, which they had not studied since the time of their initial proposal. Tocqueville began responding to his friend's repeated requests and encouragements by collecting statistics at the Ministère de la Marine, in May 1832, on French forced labor camps (although technically outside the report's focus on reforming "*prisons centrales*") and then go the *bagne* or labor camp in Toulon for "a long and attentive observation period."[28] Tocqueville cut the Toulon investigation short to visit Kergorlay in jail in nearby Marseille, but he had seen enough of the labor camp to be deeply troubled. In Toulon, he witnessed just about every incarceration practice he opposed. There was no concern whatever for repentance and rehabilitation. In America, enforced silence and solitary confinement, however inhumane, were supposed to lead to reform. In Toulon, inmates were always free to talk among themselves and prone to plotting escape and to recidivism. Instead of separating the more recalcitrant prisoners at night with something resembling a cellular system, the guards chained them together. Inmates could huddle together and plan their next misdeeds. In short, the *bagne* was a huge breeding ground for further crimes, devoid of any official attempts to encourage moral rehabilitation. With not a single priest in sight, Tocqueville fretted that "an inmate can spend his whole life in the work camp without ever being reminded there is a God."[29]

After reconnecting with Kergorlay in Marseille, Tocqueville moved on to Geneva and Lausanne to visit two penitentiaries in Switzerland, where he was hoping finally to meet with Beaumont for the first time since their return from America.[30] On the way, he read a book their Versailles friend Ernest de Blosseville had just written, *De la question des colonies pénales en Australie* (On the question of penal colonies in Australia), and concluded that it was not a good solution to merely export wrongdoers out of France.[31]

Beaumont did not travel to Switzerland after all, leaving Tocqueville to visit its penitentiaries by himself. He liked what he saw, noting that Swiss authorities had introduced a cellular system at night, without American silence during the day but fortunately also without "French anti-Christian philanthropy."[32] He was surprised by, and disapproved of, the comforts Swiss criminals enjoyed, and he concluded that Geneva was "a candy store prison [*prison bonbonnière*]: full-size bed, monthly baths, library, free time on Sunday, constraints on punishments, regular pay. Everything is plush like a mistress's boudoir." The same was true of Lausanne. He noted critically, "The point of genuine philanthropy is to make prisoners better people, not to keep them happy."[33]

Tocqueville returned to Paris in early June just after the government brutally repressed a large riot that Republican societies had orchestrated during General Lamarque's funeral procession. The popular general had fallen victim to cholera; his funeral-turned-riot was an epic event Victor Hugo would recount in *Les Misérables*. Tocqueville severely condemned the governmental repression and wrote to Kergorlay's mother that he saw in it the sure sign of a coming tyranny.[34] This abuse of power strengthened his resolve to defend her son.

In Paris, Tocqueville and Beaumont finally reconnected in person and visited various penal establishments. Beaumont visited La petite Roquette in August, making no analysis of its panoptic design but only expressing his displeasure that wasteful architectural extravagance distracted from any effort to institute a replicable, sober reform program.[35] Tocqueville conducted his own inquiry into a *maison de refuge* in the rue de l'Orne, an establishment not unlike an American almshouse, accommodating beggars and finding work for them.[36] He visited a prison for about 1,000 women, including young prostitutes, and some abandoned children, all crammed into 128 filthy cells in the former convent of

Lazaristes. Paradoxically, they attended services in a luxurious chapel built at great expense. He also visited a *maison de correction* (something like a reformatory) for twenty-five to thirty recalcitrant young men sent there by their families and described the inmates in three words: "dirty, careless, lazy."[37] What a contrast with a house of refuge he visited in Boston, where children were carefully separated at night, given instruction during the day, and given some freedom to judge misdeeds committed by their peers.[38]

Having completed these visits in France and Switzerland, Tocqueville and Beaumont were ready to write a report, complete with useful comparisons and policy recommendations. From Philadelphia, Tocqueville had written Ernest de Chabrol that their prison notes "must be worth something, if only by the pound."[39] Now they proceeded to compose a draft. Tocqueville and Beaumont cosigned the report, but Tocqueville, when supporting Beaumont's candidacy to the Académie des sciences morales et politiques years later, credited him as "the sole author."[40] Tocqueville most likely wrote some of the appendixes and most of the notes, while influencing the general shape of the manuscript. They completed *On the Penitentiary System in the United States and Its Application to France* in September 1832, delivered it in October to the Ministère du Commerce et des Travaux Publics with six volumes of documentary evidence,[41] and it was printed in December with a publication date of 1833.

The authors naturally posed the large question of how applicable American innovation was to France, a problem also at the heart of *Democracy in America*. If there was one overall message, it was that the American penitentiary was not a cure-all for society's ills but a mechanism designed to alter the minds of depraved men.[42] "Perhaps in leaving the prison he is not an honest man; but he has contracted honest habits. He was lazy; now he knows how to work. His ignorance prevented him from doing productive work; now he knows how to read and to write, and the trade that he learned in prison furnishes him with a means of existence that he previously lacked. Without loving the good, he can detest crime, whose cruel consequences he has experienced; and if he is not more virtuous, he is at least more reasonable: his morality is not honor, but interest. Perhaps his religious faith is neither lively nor deep;

but even if religion has not touched his heart, it gave his mind habits of order and his life rules of conduct; without having a great religious conviction, he acquired a taste for the moral principles that religion teaches; finally, if he has not in truth become better, he is at least more obedient to the laws, and that is all that society has the right to ask of him."[43]

In his prison cell in Aix, where some of the conspirators had been transferred, Kergorlay was one of the report's first readers, and he did not like it. He found it too descriptive. He told Tocqueville, "It's all very well that your readers are decent folk, but for three quarters of them, there's something missing: either charlatanism or brilliance."[44] He was tough but correct: the report was largely factual. In it, Tocqueville and Beaumont provided background on the origins of the penitentiary system. They gave significant credit to Philadelphia Quakers for abolishing barbaric sentences such as flogging, the pillory, and public humiliation, replacing them with a system of reflection and atonement through solitary confinement. Throughout, they strongly advocated that French prisons adopt a cellular system. But they followed their mentor Le Peletier d'Aunay's advice not to "become irrevocably bound to ideas that can take you down with them if they fail."[45] They did not state a strong preference for either the Philadelphia model of complete solitary confinement in cells large enough for the inmate to work in or the Auburn variant with solitary confinement only at night but silence enforced during gang labor in the day. Contrary to letters from America in which they showed a distinct admiration for Philadelphia, the report gave a slight edge to Auburn for being easier to establish and generating significant revenue for the state. They concluded that the Auburn system produced more docile citizens, but Philadelphia went further in the transformation of personal character.[46] Much of the report focused on the details of penitentiary administration. It provided information on construction costs, expenses and revenues, and many technical details. The authors put material they could not naturally develop in the narrative into the appendixes.

Although Tocqueville and Beaumont hoped to adapt American reforms to the French context, they were prudent. They identified a host of barriers: The French were generally opposed to corporal punishment, which was the basis of enforcement in the Auburn system. Evoking durable stereotypes, Tocqueville and Beaumont also hypothesized that a law of silence would be more difficult for a Frenchman to bear than for a "taciturn" American.[47] Other practical barriers included the large expense of building prisons with individual cells and the fact that prisoners' work products would likely be less valuable in France than in the United States.[48] Another major obstacle was the absence in France of a religious movement strongly committed to reforming criminals.[49] In America, religious conviction led individuals and denominations to offer financial and moral support for reform. In France, religious involvement in French prisons would appear suspect. There were legal barriers as well. In France, the courts assigned a variety of punishments that necessitated different types of prisons while in the United States only the length of the sentence was specified. But even after conceding all this, Tocqueville and Beaumont stood their ground for a principle that was important to them, which they had explored in depth in the United States—decentralization. They wanted to counter the *"yoke of centralization"* and have local authorities enact prison reform with a large degree of autonomy.[50]

The French Academy gave the two authors its Montyon Prize, an annual award reserved for the book deemed most "useful" for the improvement of mores.[51] "Useful" was the operative word, but there was more to the report than factual reporting. For all its middle-of-the-road prose, one brief segment of the report clearly anticipated one of Tocqueville's major contributions in *Democracy in America*—the mutual reinforcement of liberty and equality. In *Democracy in America*, Tocqueville would explain, "I know of only two ways to achieve the reign of equality—rights must be given either to each citizen or to none."[52] The prison report, which preceded *Democracy in America* by two years, focused on the second way. Through his work on the American penitentiary system, Tocqueville applied the conceptual framework Guizot had first suggested of viewing institutions through the lens of equality. In this case, the focus was on the equality that remains when you take freedom away. The report highlighted that all criminals in the American penitentiary were treated equally regardless of what their rank had been in free society. In prison, they were all reduced to the lowest common denominator. The language could not be clearer: "There is even more equality in the prison than in society. All have the same dress and eat the same bread. All work."[53] The American penitentiary, then, was the creation of an inverted America.[54] For free Americans, equality meant access to opportunity; for imprisoned criminals, equality kept them all at the same low level. Life in American penitentiaries, the report eventually showed, had much to say about democracy. It was a microcosm of an extreme social state of equality for all, with liberty for none, a cautionary tale of what could be called a failed democracy.

Worth noting is that Tocqueville later modified his position on prisoners' equality considerably. In *Democracy in America*, he recognized the fundamental inequality that separates a wealthy American criminal, who could avoid imprisonment by paying bail, and a poor criminal "compelled to await justice in prison" where "enforced idleness will soon reduce him to misery."[55] These conclusions reflected further thought. The prison report itself said nothing of the indicted, only of the convicted.

Tocqueville had long before considered the concept of equality in powerlessness as part of French history. Under French kings, who practiced absolutism for centuries, all had to obey, even nobles. In the report, he and Beaumont even made a subtle analogy between subjected French nobles and American criminals. They stated that American prisons "offer the spectacle of the most complete *despotism*."[56] They did not elaborate. Francis Lieber, when translating the report into English, did not understand what the authors meant. He felt compelled to add a translator's note to correct what he took to be Tocqueville and Beaumont's misconception and point out the "impropriety of calling a system despotic which mainly grew out of the feeling of humanity and continues to be kept by it."[57] Clearly, the time had come for Tocqueville to give the concept of equality a fuller treatment. Tocqueville, however, was not quite ready to write his book on America.

## Five Weeks in England

Tocqueville had for a long time intended to travel to England; early in his student years, in 1824, he had envisioned an excursion up the Thames with Kergorlay, but it had not happened.[58] Tocqueville and Beaumont had hoped to stop in England on the way back to France in 1832, but the press to return home had prevailed.[59] With the penitentiary report completed, Kergorlay out of jail, and Beaumont fond of quoting the famous dictum that John Bull was the father of Jonathan,[60] the time had come for an exploration in person of the British aristocratic sources of American liberty.

Guizot had taught his students to think of France in 1830 as a version of England in 1688—a modern Glorious Revolution. Tocqueville acknowledged the point but went to America with a mind unencumbered by ideas of British constitutionalism.[61] What had been a fortuitous move that enabled him to see America with few preconceptions was now becoming a hindrance. If Tocqueville kept France constantly on his mind when thinking of America,[62] England was the natural *tertium quid* of a comparative assessment.

Tocqueville did not arrive in England with a blank slate. From John Lingard's history of England (see chapter 1), Tocqueville had retained the idea that the British aristocracy had flourished freely over the centuries because English acceptance of aristocracy's local leadership had helped keep royal power at bay. Tocqueville had also learned much English common law from American legal sources during the American trip. Still, a visit seemed urgent because British aristocratic traditions appeared to be coming under siege, as evidenced by the 1832 electoral reform and working-class riots. Tocqueville told his cousin Laurette de Pisieux he wanted to see the British system before it was changed. "One hears that they are positively taking to revolution," he wrote, "and it is necessary to hurry to see things as they are. So, I hasten to England as to the last showing of a fine play."[63]

As if to put himself in the proper aristocratic frame of mind, Tocqueville stopped on the way at the old family manor at Tocqueville, vacant since the French Revolution. He had gone there only once before, in 1828. To Mary, he reported with emotion exactly what he had said to Beaumont five years earlier: that he could see from the top of the tower the coast where his ancestor embarked on the conquest of England. Now, he told Mary, it was up to him to do something worthwhile with his own life.[64]

Tocqueville was not sure what to expect on his arrival. In the penitentiary report, he and Beaumont had blandly blamed the British Poor Laws for swelling the number of the poor and criminals by "giving work and money to all the unfortunate."[65] This was at best a half-truth likely borrowed from Jean-Baptiste Say's *Treatise*.[66] Upon disembarking in Southampton, however, and on his trip to London, Tocqueville did not see poverty; he admired instead a lavish aristocratic lifestyle on display: "parks, country houses, carriages, footmen, horses; luxury top-to-bottom."[67] Once in London, thanks to his cousin Laurette's letters of introduction, Tocqueville entered high society at once. Shocked by so much extravagance, he felt like a social inferior, writing Beaumont, "You have to borrow from what the mathematicians call 'negative numbers' to compute my social rank here."[68] High society had its limits. It was hard to have an interesting conversation with hosts who talked exclusively of balls and elegant parties and moreover approvingly assumed he was a "committed Legitimist."[69] Fortunately, the *Système pénitentiaire*, which Tocqueville thought would be useless as a means of introduction, turned out to be his passport for engaging Whig reformers, including the Archbishop of Dublin, who had read the report with appreciation.[70]

Tocqueville was in good spirits in England. Months earlier, he had confided to Charles Stöffels about his depression. Now he was writing him about how much he enjoyed traveling by himself, reporting "a feeling of freedom and independence, a vivacity and clarity to my impressions."[71] He relished observing a debate on the abolition of slavery in the House of Lords. The Frenchman had expected the Duke of Wellington to give a grand performance but, as someone who struggled with oratory himself, was gratified to see "the hero of Waterloo" not know where to "put his arms or legs nor how to balance his long body."[72] He witnessed a riotous by-election amid "cheers, whistles and shouts," the kind of disorder that, he concluded, "contributed more than anything else in maintaining the aristocracy, by giving the middle classes a horror of purely democratic forms."[73]

Tocqueville visited Oxford, awed by its gothic "lace-work of gleaming stone"[74] but critical that such a huge land endowment maintained comfortably only a small group of fellows.[75] At Oxford, he introduced himself to Nassau Senior, an economist at work on reforming the Poor Laws.[76] Senior was a staunch conservative, and Karl Marx would later lambast him for his argument that manufacturers made a profit only in the thirteenth hour of work and his praise of factory conditions for keeping child laborers warm.[77] For Tocqueville, Senior was a knowledgeable informant, who would become a lifelong friend. From Oxford, it was a short trip to Bath. At the nearby castle of Warwick, Tocqueville found "the wild grandeur of feudal times."[78] Then, traveling by horseback, he arrived at night at Kenilworth, where he let his imagination reenact the lives of Walter Scott's characters.[79]

Tocqueville had gone to England to broaden his understanding of aristocracy. He felt he had achieved his goal when, armed with a letter of recommendation from cousin Eugénie de Grancey, he visited Lord Radnor at Longford Castle, near Salisbury. Radnor was a highly influential "great English Lord of his lands."[80] There could be no better example of the contrast between the three countries Tocqueville wanted to compare. Lord Radnor was a Whig leader and a very religious man who exerted both national and local influence. He embodied the importance of large, landed estates passed from one generation to the next in maintaining aristocracy's grip on English society. In France, by contrast, much aristocratic property had been divided a long time ago.[81] America had ended the practice of entail entirely because, as Jefferson argued, "by the law of nature, one generation is to another as one independent nation to another."[82] But primogeniture still dominated England.

Tocqueville observed Lord Radnor perform his functions of justice of the peace in Wiltshire County.[83] He accompanied him to a court session adjudicating cases of public aid, where he observed for the first time how the poor could at times abuse the Poor Laws, and he recorded this discovery in his notes.[84] The experience confirmed England's place in Tocqueville's mind as the model of a country run by land-owning aristocrats. England was decentralized. This was the important point. It may have a powerful government, but administration remained local and respected local liberties. To this critical distinction between centralized government and decentralized administration fostering local autonomy, Tocqueville attributed "the worthy cause of material progress."[85]

Moreover, aristocracy maintained its ascendency throughout England by remaining open to men who became rich.[86] It was grounded in money as much as in birth. Tocqueville joined here many other contemporary observers who noted that "'gentleman' in England is applied to every well-educated man whatever his birth, while in France *gentilhomme* applies only to a noble by birth," a "grammatical observation more illuminating than many long arguments." Although Tocqueville saw that democracy was "like a rising tide; it only recoils to come back with greater force,"[87] he found in England an aristocratic model for his evolving theoretical construction of democracy resting on local political control and access to the upper classes via wealth acquisition.

It now really was time to write *Democracy in America*, but the allure of new distracting projects was difficult to resist. While still in London, Tocqueville corresponded with Beaumont regarding the possibility of creating a new magazine[88] and making it a political organ for like-minded friends who were lukewarm about the July Monarchy but wanted to mark their distance from hardline Legitimists. In addition, the journal would foster spiritual reform against bourgeois materialism and reconcile democracy and religion.[89] This would become one of Tocqueville's major goals in writing *Democracy in America*, but perhaps founding a magazine was a faster, more efficient way of spreading these views. As Tocqueville explained to Kergorlay, one needed to "rehabilitate the spiritual in politics, and make it popular again by making its utility felt."[90] Beaumont approached Montalembert who, still under the shock of Pope Gregory XVI's condemnation of his newspaper *L'Avenir*, declined to join them in the venture.[91] They thought of their Versailles friends Blosseville and Chabrol as possible funders for their magazine, but Tocqueville decided not to recruit them, finding them too closely associated with Legitimism. The project withered. Tocqueville finally came to the realization that the only way to promote his ideas was to write his book, which he set out to do on his return from England.

## Writing *Democracy in America*

Tocqueville reminisced years later that he had written *Democracy in America* with "faith in a cause and hope."[92] He was convinced after visiting America that democracy was perfectly compatible with religion. By highlighting this essential fact at the outset, he would grab the reader's attention and prepare him to see democracy in an uplifting new light. Kergorlay not only agreed but even suggested to present democracy as "the will of the divinity."[93] In the introduction, Tocqueville momentarily overcame his crisis of faith and declared having written the entire book "in the grip of a kind of religious terror" in the face of "indubitable signs of God's will." Not unlike Blaise Pascal who uncovered some of "God's best kept secrets,"[94] it was Tocqueville's turn in this book to reveal the inevitability of democracy. Tocqueville wanted his readers to know that Providence had brought to the New World, after centuries of slow development in the Old World, a new moral order promising freedom under the conditions of equality. Democracy had all "the essential characteristics" of a "providential fact": it was "universal, durable, and beyond the reach of man's powers."[95]

Even as precise a writer as Tocqueville needed flexibility in his choice of words. Tocqueville often used "equality" and "democracy" interchangeably because he saw a new kind of equality as a prominent quality of democracy. One must recall that Tocqueville's family, friends, and most French aristocrats thought of equality as a malicious force destroying their caste—the result of leveling at the hands of despotic French kings intent on turning nobles into mere subjects. French aristocrats, who experienced equality only in demotion and powerlessness, had no conception of democracy's elevating equality. Tocqueville, however, was no ordinary aristocrat. He sought to figure out a means of escaping leveling that restricted human freedom. With his visit to America, Tocqueville understood that democracy could promote liberty without despotism—whether the latter originated with an individual or "the crowd."[96] The new kind of equality Tocqueville recognized enabled a large part of the American population to achieve their potential freely. As no nobility—a class privileged by birth—existed to monopolize opportunities, Tocqueville designated "equality of condition" as democracy's prerequisite and model. America was therefore, he wrote, "more than America"—it was the future of human societies.[97]

Tocqueville spent fifteen months of uninterrupted writing before crafting this introduction. He began his work in the fall of 1833, upon his return from England, by compiling an elaborate index of his travel notes, then building up a bibliography of books available at the Institut de France's library in Paris. He also returned to the legal works of New York chancellor James Kent, Supreme Court Justice Joseph Story (who later complained that Tocqueville borrowed too much from him), and the debates over the Constitution he had begun reading while traveling on American steamboats. For help summarizing relevant US documents, Tocqueville hired early in 1834 two young Americans at the American Legation: Theodore Sedgwick III, whom he had met briefly in Stockbridge, and Francis Lippitt. Sedgwick became a lifelong friend. Tocqueville also had the benefit of conversations with his American acquaintance Edward Livingston, who was now American minister to France.[98]

Tocqueville settled into a rigorous but pleasant routine: writing during the day, locked up in his parents' attic on the rue de Verneuil in Paris, but spending the evenings relaxing with Mary.[99] "From morning until dinner, I'm in my head, but in the evenings, I go to Mary's. And there I taste the extreme pleasure of very sweet and very tender intimacy, and long chats by the fire in which I am never bored," he told Kergorlay.[100] Now and then, he broke the routine to share his drafts with a select group: his father, his brother Édouard, his friends Kergorlay and Beaumont, all of whom pushed Tocqueville to perfect a style that would reach the widest possible audience.

For Kergorlay especially, style was as important as substance. Kergorlay knew little about America, but he had definite ideas about style. He felt "people are very superficial, and their judgment of what is deep and substantive is in reality a surface-level appreciation of *style*." Kergorlay advised Tocqueville early on to emulate a trio of great masters:

"Read a few sentences of Montesquieu, Rousseau, and Pascal; these ought to be your mentors."[101] Tocqueville took the advice to heart and practiced it daily.[102] Tocqueville meant to express his ideas "in as few words as possible . . . in the simplest and most intuitive order."[103] Beaumont testified that "form was his master," so much so that he occasionally rewrote the same sentence twenty times.[104] Tocqueville read his drafts out loud to family and friends. He once told Beaumont, "I'll end up asking you to comment on how to sign my name."[105] One can see in Tocqueville's manuscripts his many rewrites to achieve perfect form.

As was the case for young aristocrats raised in the Restoration years who were aspiring writers, Chateaubriand was, at least initially, a vital guide. In Tocqueville's case, his influence was further strengthened by their family association. Tocqueville later explained, Chateaubriand knew how to embellish classical French, "adding ornamentation to clarity and concision."[106] Tocqueville emulated Chateaubriand in his youth, and while in the United States, he appreciated Chateaubriand's descriptions of the sights that he too had encountered in America during his voyage of 1791–92. Tocqueville attempted a competing description of Niagara Falls and wrote *Two Weeks in the Wilderness* in a romantic descriptive style reminiscent of Chateaubriand's *Voyage en Amérique* as well as his novels set in America. But for *Democracy in America*, Tocqueville chose a classical style—the means of expression best adapted to a rigorous inquiry and the presentation of a "new political science for a world completely new."[107] He so thoroughly adhered to this standard that Hervé de Tocqueville at times reminded his son not to be too theoretical and to animate his descriptions for the benefit of the reader.[108]

Family and friends were concerned about a potentially hostile readership that was not yet ready for democracy and required convincing. Tocqueville's father and his brother Édouard insisted that he should communicate clearly that he was not proposing simply to import American solutions to France, lest readers dismiss the book outright. Hervé de Tocqueville and Kergorlay especially wanted to make sure that their fellow Legitimists pay attention to what Tocqueville had to say. At the same time, Hervé advised his son to tone down conclusions that might be seen as critical of the Orléans regime, and not to attack King Louis

Philippe in ways that could be damaging to his career.[109] Édouard several times intervened firmly to prevent his brother from too obviously addressing current political fights rather than the larger issues of democracy.

All this fueled Tocqueville's innate penchant for complexity. As Tocqueville explained to Chabrol, "The deeper one goes into any subject, the vaster it becomes, and behind every fact and observation lurks a doubt."[110] His doubts and the advice of others led Tocqueville to make a number of concessions to opponents of democracy. French critic Sainte-Beuve pointed to Tocqueville's overuse of such qualifiers as "*mais*," "*si*," and "*car*" (but, if, because) that distracted the reader from the main message.[111] That Sainte-Beuve and Tocqueville never warmed up to each other may partly account for the criticism, but Sainte-Beuve was correct that Tocqueville rarely made a point without giving ample space to the opposing view. Tocqueville highlighted opposing viewpoints as a rhetorical strategy designed to bring readers around to the one the author advocated. Tocqueville always expressed his conviction. But as he gave contradictory opinions almost equal time, readers often found ammunition for positions contrary to the one Tocqueville favored. An unexpected outcome is that Tocqueville has inspired readers of opposite political persuasions who have always felt free to choose their preferred formulation to claim him. Only readers who have engaged the text fully have come to recognize the author's deep convictions, as he revealed them in small installments, by virtue of subtle repetitions, throughout the volume. All along, Tocqueville strove to reach stylistic purity while presenting controversial ideas. The peculiar result was a book at once pleasurable to read and hard to grasp fully.

Despite the complexity, Tocqueville forcefully advanced a positive view of democracy, and he did so using a rigorous, logical progression. After the bold introduction positing democracy as God's work, Tocqueville presented North America as an "empty cradle awaiting the birth of a great nation."[112] Although he acknowledged the ancient presence of Amerindians, he postponed to the last chapter any consideration of white Anglo-American conquest and domination. Turning to Montesquieu as guide, again in frequent conversation with Kergorlay (who had read Montesquieu's *Spirit of the Laws*, pencil in hand in his jail cell), Tocqueville sought to identify an American "national character" as a unique combination of "prejudices, habits, and passions" that would foster democracy.[113] He recognized that the Anglo-American family had divided into two branches, North and South, with different "social states" generating different "laws, customs, and ideas,"[114] but focused his attention on the "civilization" of early New England and said little about those he called the "gold seekers" of Virginia.[115] He affirmed only that the two families had joined in their revolution against England and the creation of a Union.

In emphasizing the early role of New England, Tocqueville followed the counsel Jared Sparks had given in Boston, but he was also indebted to Rousseau. In a passage Tocqueville struck from his final manuscript, he drew a parallel between the Puritan covenant he was describing and "the social contract in proper form that Rousseau dreamed of in the following century."[116] Although Tocqueville acknowledged his debt to Montesquieu, he avoided crediting Rousseau, whom much of his audience held responsible for inspiring the Jacobin Terror. For opposite reasons, Tocqueville never recognized his debt to Guizot, who had by this point turned his back on the liberal views he espoused as a young professor.

Tocqueville stressed that the New England Pilgrims had fought for the triumph of an idea. They endowed America in its infancy with a powerful understanding of liberty that was critical in developing democracy because they did not conceive of liberty as a license to do what one pleases but instead as a call to moral and material self-improvement. Tocqueville borrowed this demanding vision of liberty from John Winthrop as quoted in the writings of the Puritan divine Cotton Mather. Citizens were truly free when they could engage "what is just and good without fear." Liberty was therefore a positive act of will. Liberty was not an "enemy of all authority" but "a civil and moral" quality that made it possible for individuals, singly or in groups, to realize their potential.[117] Tocqueville, who believed in the possibilities of human achievement,[118] embraced the idea of liberty as capable of fostering equality. With liberty empowering individuals, equality could spread.

There began the great challenge of modern history, that of balancing liberty and equality. Tocqueville kept arguing in successive formulations that the two concepts of liberty and equality, so easily at odds, actually touch and join.[119] For one cannot be free without being equal to others; and one cannot be equal to others, in a positive sense, without being free. For Tocqueville, the combination of equality and liberty was the best possible human condition, while equality without liberty was among the worst, as he had argued in the prison report.

Although Tocqueville asserted that equality and liberty ideally should be mutually reinforcing in democratic life, he recognized that men loved equality passionately but often resented the kind of demanding liberty that democracy required. It was simply too much work to set positive liberty in motion and sustain it. Indeed, Tocqueville underscored that "nothing is harder than the apprenticeship of liberty."[120] As a result, Tocqueville charged, too many accept "equality in servitude" (the result of leveling) and prefer it over the more demanding condition of "inequality in freedom."[121] Only by acquiring the habit of liberty, Tocqueville argued throughout the book, could a democratic society make creative use of equality. He concluded that the mutual reinforcement of equality and liberty was the precondition for the dogma of popular sovereignty to "emerge from the towns," "take possession of the government," and become "the law of laws."[122]

The American people, Tocqueville explained, had found at the local level a special strength and a free spirit that they forged into a Union.[123] Because the larger units of government never replaced the smaller ones, multiple centers of authority coexisted, and this protected against centralized tyranny. But, again, Tocqueville insisted, only a long habit of liberty and constant vigilance could maintain an otherwise precarious mutual strengthening of liberty and equality.

## An Analytical Description of the US Constitution

In March 1834, Tocqueville wrote Nassau Senior, the British economist he had recently met in Oxford, that he was writing a book on "American institutions."[124] Tocqueville had reached a point in his writing where he needed to convince French readers that in America, one could be both Republican and moderate, have a central government but respect local autonomy. The Constitution would be his proof. For although the history of New England provided key ingredients, the framing of the Constitution marked the real founding of a durable Union that nevertheless preserved states' power.[125] In elaborating a federal constitution, the founding fathers gave the central government great authority while simultaneously protecting the parts from the whole. In dividing sovereignty, Tocqueville insisted, they sustained and fostered liberty.

Tocqueville described the relevant institutional mechanisms rigorously. French readers, many of whom were legislators, therefore turned to *Democracy in America* as a text where they could gain knowledge of American institutions. But for Tocqueville, a mini course on the US Constitution was only a means to demonstrate that powerful national institutions need not eradicate local liberty as kings and emperor had done in France. He pointed to the key distinction he had recognized while traveling in America between government and administration. A central government must be strong but at the same time respect local autonomy. In the United States, most administrative functions remained not only decentralized but also independent of the federal government.

Tocqueville therefore credited the framers of the federal union for going further than merely dividing the work of legislation among several bodies, which had become an "axiom of political science."[126] Remarkably, he saw the founding fathers as having combined two "theoretically irreconcilable" systems of national and local governance.[127] The American federal government was powerful because unlike the previous federations of states, it derived its authority by governing individuals *directly* without the intermediary of state or provincial governments. This was a real innovation. The American federal government's strength, Tocqueville explained, was "not borrowed [from the states] but drawn from within. It has its own administrators, its own courts, its own law enforcement officers, and its own army."[128] State governments had their own institutions and functions. This was a tough sell to a French political audience committed to administrative centralization inherited from kings, imitated by revolutionaries, and codified under Napoleonic rule. As former prefect, Hervé de Tocqueville defended administrative centralization; Édouard judged the attack on French centralization far too political.[129] But Tocqueville kept pressing the point that both central and local power needed to coexist. He condemned excessive centralization and excessive decentralization with equal vehemence. Regarding the latter, he added as an appendix to the twelfth edition (1848), a disquisition on federalism in Switzerland, where the diet had no direct authority over the citizens of the autonomous cantons, a situation that crippled government.

Only the Americans had gotten the balance right with citizens accountable to both state and federal authority. Tocqueville, then, saw the framers had succeeded in creating a country "glorious and strong" like a large nation and "free and happy" like a small one.[130] James Madison had correctly speculated (*Federalist* 10 and 14) that a system could be created "to combine the various advantages of largeness with those of smallness." The happy outcome, in Tocqueville's mind, was that the United States enjoyed the political liberty that Montesquieu had thought achievable only in small nations.[131]

To protect their innovation, the framers built into the Constitution safeguards against abuses of power. Tocqueville praised them for instituting checks and balances that limited the authority each body could claim. He admired leaders who dared "to limit [liberty] because they were sure they had no wish to destroy it."[132] He was impressed by the power of judicial review in America, living in a time when no French court could dream of invalidating a law by deeming it unconstitutional. As for American officials who abused their position, they were subject to scrutiny and could be removed by impeachment.

A few criticisms aside, Tocqueville drew a highly favorable portrait of American constitutional principles. His father, brothers, and other readers told him he was too pro-American and advised him to moderate his praise, but he made only stylistic, not substantive, revisions. Tocqueville enlivened his analysis of Constitution, otherwise a somewhat dry and detailed exercise, with vivid descriptions of presidential elections that still resonate today. Modern-day readers familiar with American presidents seeking second terms feel they are reading a text written for our own times. Tocqueville did not name any president but entertained his readers with the portrait of a president "consumed by the need to defend his record" who "no longer governs in the interest of the state but rather in the interest of his reelection." Indeed, "he prostrates himself before the majority, and often, rather than resist its passions as his duty requires, he courts favor by catering to its whims."[133]

## Popular Sovereignty: Citizens Control Political Institutions

After seeing democratic principles embedded in a constitution, Tocqueville turned to tools of popular sovereignty emanating directly from the American people, which he praised equally. Especially important was Tocqueville's understanding of associations in democratic life. In the *Federalist*, Madison and Hamilton had recognized not associations but factions as a reality of American politics, and they feared them. Madison defined a faction as a "majority or a minority of the whole, who are united and actuated by some common impulse of passion, or of interest, adverse to the rights of other citizens, or to the permanent and aggregate interests of the community."[134] The only way Madison saw to counter factions' negative effects was to multiply them so that they would cancel each other out. In his farewell address (1796), Washington blamed factions for obstructing the work of government. John Quincy Adams still echoed some of that feeling in his conversations with Tocqueville in 1831.

Tocqueville rejected this analysis, conceiving of political associations in a new and positive light. This was the strangest of theoretical leaps, considering that when he was in America, Tocqueville missed much of the emerging benevolent empire of Bible, tract, and missionary societies, Sunday schools, educational associations, and local charities of the Jacksonian era. Americans had not yet fully absorbed their consequences and talked little about them. But in retrospect, and on the basis of sparse observations on political parties and political associations whose messages were broadcast by a partisan but free press, Tocqueville built a powerful new theory. Throughout *Democracy in America*, Tocqueville hewed closely to conversations he had with informants such as Jared Sparks on the New England town, John Quincy Adams on the South and slavery, John Spencer on the Constitution, or Sam Houston on Native Americans. But he had not engaged his informants on the topic of associations beyond the free trade convention in Philadelphia and brief conversations on the temperance movement. He nonetheless connected the dots, arguing that "there is nothing the human will cannot achieve through the free action of the collective power of the individual."[135] He felt that "the freedom most natural to man, after the freedom to act alone, is the freedom to combine his efforts with those of his fellow man and to act in common" and concluded that the right of association was "by its very nature almost as inalienable as the freedom of the individual."[136]

In praising a nation of joiners, Tocqueville became, unexpectedly, wildly influential. With a series of brief chapters on political parties, the press, and political associations, Tocqueville made a large and original contribution to American political theory. In analyzing the Constitution, he had rendered his American sources faithfully. Now he went beyond them and taught Americans how to understand themselves anew, quite a daring thing to do for a young man who had not even spent a full year in the country. He taught Americans how to view a social practice he himself knew only dimly in a new and positive light, and Americans believed him.

Tocqueville explained that Americans knew how to employ voluntary associations to initiate change. He described the process so concretely that one would believe he had observed it in detail, though of course he had not. Tocqueville constructed the associative impulse in his own mind and rendered it remarkably accurately: "Suppose a person conceives of an idea for a project that has a direct bearing on the welfare of society. It would never occur to him to call upon the authorities for assistance. Instead, he will publicize his plan, offer to carry it out, enlist other individuals to pool their forces with his own, and struggle with all his might to overcome every obstacle. No doubt his efforts will often prove less successful than if the state had acted in his stead. In the long run, however, the overall result of all these individual enterprises will far outstrip anything the government could do."[137] The free circulation of ideas in the press only further facilitated the process. Americans recognized themselves in this imagined but largely correct portrait, and this made all the difference.

Had he realized it when in America, Tocqueville might have added that Protestant sectarianism only reinforced the associational impulse. Religious disestablishment that encouraged the creation of new churches was proceeding under his eyes, and Sparks tried to alert him to it. Old denominations fractured and new ones emerged. Tocqueville, however, was concerned primarily with problems of dogma in his discussion of American Protestantism. He did not focus his discussion of religion on the voluntaristic sources of Protestant denominationalism. Still, he rightly insisted that American churches had been a pillar of liberty, in contrast to a French Catholic Church that had sided with monarchs.

Remarkably, it was partly the French political situation that influenced Tocqueville to develop a theory of association that turned out to be so significant in American political theory. In praising American democracy in these terms, Tocqueville was fighting political repression at home, where all associations were experiencing a renewed level of political scrutiny from a repressive government. The problem was old, and Tocqueville had been aware of it since childhood. Much of his father's job as a royal prefect had been to keep presumably politically dangerous associations under control. As Tocqueville was writing these lines, the French law of associations had just been tightened after a workers' insurrection in Lyon in April 1834. All associations of more than twenty members had to be granted prior authorization (the previous threshold had been thirty).[138] "What can public opinion accomplish when there are not *twenty* people united by a common bond?" Tocqueville inserted in his text to be sure the French reader recognized his target.[139] Moreover, when "associations are free, secret societies are unknown" and joiners "do not become conspirators."[140] Édouard of course objected to the critique of contemporary French politics implicit in this section.

Tocqueville was not done with dispensing praise for Americans. Americans could take pride in a healthy pragmatism that mitigated majority opinion and its potential for abuse. They respected politically independent elites—mostly lawyers who, by reasoning in terms of common law precedents, thus advancing tradition over innovation, were the closest American equivalent to an aristocracy moderating political power. They trusted the jury as a "free school" "shaping the people's judgment."[141] Overall, a widespread religious practice elevated the mind. All these qualities added up to "mores," or "habits of the heart," that were the most "robust and durable power" capable of sustaining democracy.[142] Moreover, even the American's desire for wealth could be a constructive force. Americans enjoyed exceptional access to abundant resources, "rivers that never run dry, verdant, well-watered solitudes, and boundless fields yet to be tilled by any plow,"[143] that they could peacefully exploit with no threat from a foreign nation's invasion (Tocqueville conveniently dismissed the War of 1812). "Happy is the New World," Tocqueville concluded, "where man's vices are almost as useful to society as his virtues."[144]

Thus emerged a picture of American democracy with multiple centers of power and enduring habits of liberty and self-government. Tocqueville conceded there was a price to pay for democracy. "Democracy does not give the people the most skillful government," he pointed out, "but what it does even the most skillful government is powerless to achieve: it spreads throughout society a restless activity, a superabundant strength, an energy that never exists without it, and which, if circumstances are even slightly favorable, can accomplish miracles. These are its true advantages."[145] This was the very positive image of American democracy that Tocqueville meant to convey.

## The Tyranny of the Majority

Having showered praise on American democracy, Tocqueville could also be critical, if only to be credible. To be free to criticize America without causing his American informants "embarrassment and chagrin" was Tocqueville's excuse for not mentioning any of them by name in his book.[146] He did not want to implicate them, or so he claimed, when exposing the danger of excessive popular sovereignty. American minister to France Edward Livingston, still in Paris when the book came out, was the only exception; he was given credit for providing documentary evidence on the workings of the federal government.[147]

Tocqueville charged that Americans lived under the constant threat of a tyranny of the majority—an alternative despotism—that muzzled dissent and killed freedom of opinion in America. He claimed, "I know of no country where there is in general less independence of mind and true freedom of discussion than in America."[148] What Tocqueville feared most from equality was a deadening uniformity of thought, which he believed he detected in America. He depicted Americans as victims of a crippling conformity of opinion, justified only in part by the great instability of conditions inherent in a new country, yet aggravated by an extreme case of national pride that made self-criticism unlikely. He complained that one could not even criticize the weather in America.[149]

Again, Tocqueville's attack on the tyranny of the majority was not just the result of his observations in America. It was also a reaction to the tactics of the French left, and it was meant in part as a rebuttal to them. Tocqueville was criticizing uniformity of thought in France and America simultaneously. In denouncing the tyranny of the majority, Tocqueville pursued his debate with the more radical republicans who, heirs to the Jacobins, defended unicameralism and rejected the idea of checks and balances, and with Rousseau who had formulated the political dogma of a "general will." Tocqueville unmistakably targeted Rousseau when he wrote, "There are those who have made so bold as to insist that a people, insofar as it deals with matters of interest to itself alone, cannot overstep the bounds of justice and reason entirely, hence that there is no reason to be afraid of bestowing all power on the majority that represents that people. But to speak thus is to speak the language of a slave."[150] Tocqueville praised associations because of their ability to counter abuses of the general will.

# Could Democracy, This Providential Act, Fail?

Tocqueville reserved his most direct challenge to American democracy for the last and longest portion of the book, the chapter on the "three races," in which he unequivocally condemned the forced displacement of American Indians and the harsh realities of life for Blacks—slave or free. He was wise in devoting a separate chapter to race and stating bluntly that the topic required a distinct treatment, for there was no way he could think of the lives of nonwhites on American soil as democratic. Treating race relations independently was thus a way of highlighting for Americans the deficits of their democratic experiment. Tocqueville was a universalist who, although recognizing the "civilizing mission" of advanced societies, never accepted the inherent superiority of one race over another and remained a committed abolitionist. Tocqueville had not seen enough of the American South to anchor his thinking in a sustained observation of race relations. He therefore attempted in this chapter only to evaluate the threat that racial conflict posed to democracy.

Tocqueville was not immediately sympathetic to the plight of the Indians. He had a difficult time overcoming a prejudice derived from his first sight of intoxicated Native Americans begging in upstate New York, a repudiation of his romantic and Rousseauian vision of proud and independent savages. But he threw off his preconceptions to the extent of severely condemning Jackson's policy of removal and the subsequent Trail of Tears, an early manifestation of which he witnessed while traveling down the Mississippi. He denounced it as legal form of extermination.[151] He condemned the hypocrisy of whites in dictating Indian treaties to the tribes only to immediately violate them. He denounced moral and physical violence. He praised aristocratic traits of bravery and honor in Native American culture. But he was seemingly resigned to the outcome. In asking the question as to whether Native Americans could stop white settlers from encroaching on their land and destroying their ancient civilization, the answer, based on the evidence, was no. For all the sorrow he expressed, he distanced himself from the Native Americans, concluding simply that the "Indian race" was "doomed."[152]

When he turned to African Americans, Tocqueville sensed a potentially far more volatile situation and resultant threat not only to the South but also to the Union. As an abolitionist, yet one who favored some compensatory compromise with slave owners, Tocqueville reasoned that slavery was as poisonous a system for the masters as for the slaves. This conviction led him to introduce at the end of his book a discussion of the concept of "self-interest" that would occupy so much of his later thinking. He argued that it was in the "self-interest of the master"[153] to abolish slavery and realize as soon as possible the advantages of free labor, even though he realized this was unlikely to happen.

Tocqueville predicted that keeping democracy *white* was not viable in the long run. Tocqueville saw that whites had only two options: "either free the Negroes and fuse with them; or remain isolated from them and keep them in slavery as long as possible." He speculated that "any intermediate measure will lead imminently to the most horrible of all civil wars and perhaps to the destruction of one of the two races."[154] Tocqueville published this in 1835. He predicted a race war within the South, not one between the states, but his forecast of a dire outcome was correct.

In finishing his book, Tocqueville pursued his analysis further. He feared that race and sectional economic conflicts might combine and compromise the very survival of the Union. During his visit, the cultural and economic divide between the free-labor industrializing North and the agrarian slave South erupted in the public sphere as bitter tariff wars between Northern industrialists and Southern planters. As a result, the Constitution was under attack. The emerging nullification crisis threatened to tear the country apart as John Calhoun argued that states could apply federal law selectively. Tocqueville's narrative of the nullification crisis in finishing his volume was strangely inaccurate. Tocqueville failed to give President Jackson his due in ending the crisis, even though he was in regular communication in Paris with Edward Livingston, who had edited Jackson's nullification proclamation in 1832.[155] Tocqueville did not listen to Sparks either, who advised him in the summer of 1833 that the crisis was over.[156] He wanted to underscore the underlying fragility of the Union. He therefore concluded with anxiety, "It is difficult to imagine a durable union between two peoples, one poor and weak, the other rich and strong, even if the strength and wealth of the one are known not to be the cause of the weakness and poverty of the other."[157] The complex institutional edifice of the Union might collapse should race conflicts and sectional divisions combine, and democracy would vanish in the same movement.[158]

At the end of this long analysis of democracy, after recognizing and outlining serious threats of American disunion and collapse, Tocqueville was anxious to return to his main message of a resilient democracy. He credited his ultimately optimistic outlook on shared mores. He restated that "society exists only when men see many things in the same way and have the same opinions about many subjects and, finally, when the same facts give rise to the same impressions and the same thoughts."[159] Tocqueville repeated his conviction that "laws and above all mores could allow a democratic people to remain free."[160] Tocqueville placed mores over laws and again pushed the idea, already promoted in the introduction, that a democratic society that favors the welfare of the many is far better than an aristocratic society that values the brilliance of the few.[161] Tocqueville recapitulated all the reasons for unity: a "*consensus universalis*" on the republican *principle*, shared values regarding the mutual reinforcement of equality and liberty, "the habit of thinking for oneself and governing oneself," a shared commercial spirit, and a number of institutional innovations that maintained "powerful intellectual bonds."[162] Tocqueville asserted that the world faced a choice between liberty and servitude. Contemporaries could readily see that Russia had sided with servitude. America was instead the hope that "God had held in reserve."[163] Tocqueville knew which side he was on. With his book, he had expounded his own vision of democracy.

# 5

# Testing American Equality against British Inequality

TOCQUEVILLE EXPERIENCED a familiar bout of anxiety shortly before *Democracy in America*'s publication in January 1835, with a modest printing of 500 copies. After having locked himself up in his parents' attic to write, he was reentering society. Fearing being misunderstood, he told his cousin Camille d'Orglandes, "The best thing that can happen to me is if no one read my book, and I have not yet lost hope that this happiness will be mine."[1] His enthusiastic readers did not cooperate. Tocqueville became a celebrated intellectual overnight. His work was discussed in literary and political circles alike, and his opinion valued. A bemused Tocqueville found himself wondering "whether they are really talking about me."[2]

Political circumstances were propitious for a book on America. The relationship between France and the United States reached a crisis in 1835, as the long-simmering dispute over reparations for French seizure of American ships during the Napoleonic blockade of the continent boiled over. The French had paid scant attention to it for years, but when Andrew Jackson became president in 1829, he made it a point of national honor to have the French pay. He sent William Cabell Rives as minister to France to resolve the matter. Rives signed a treaty in 1831 that obligated the French government to make good on its obligations. When the French Chamber repeatedly refused to appropriate the necessary funds, Jackson appointed his secretary of state, Edward Livingston (whom Tocqueville had first met in Washington), as minister to France in September 1833 and charged him with settling the affair. This effort proved equally unsuccessful. Frustrated, and hoping to divert attention from the censure he had received from the Senate for removing federal deposits from the Bank of the United States, Jackson resorted in December 1834 to threats of economic "reprisals," including seizure of French property in the United States. These actions alarmed French political and business circles.

By the time *Democracy in America* came out, Franco-American relations had reached a complete impasse. The French demanded that Jackson apologize for his intemperate remarks while the Americans insisted on their payment. Although nobody wanted war, there was talk of it. Formal diplomatic relations were suspended: Minister Sérurier left Washington in January 1835 while Livingston left Paris in April.[3] Tocqueville's celebrity as an expert on American government had reached the point that the Chamber asked him for an opinion on the extent of the diplomatic powers of the American president.[4] As it turned out, confrontation was avoided. Jackson toned down his rhetoric in late 1835 and the French Chamber consented to allocate the monies Louis Philippe had promised long ago.[5]

This drawn-out affair, however, served to enlarge the readership for *Democracy in America*, although few readers grappled seriously with Tocqueville's message on democracy. Among them, two elder figures of national stature—Chateaubriand and Royer-Collard—hailed Tocqueville's new political science. The great romantic novelist was first to express enthusiasm for the new book, promote it, and introduce the author to all the right people. Certainly, Chateaubriand was promoting a family member, but he and Tocqueville had much in common beyond family ties. They shared the conviction that democracy was inevitable. In sending a presentation copy to his famous relative, Tocqueville invoked the memory of how M. de Malesherbes (Tocqueville's great-grandfather) "had been pleading with the king for the cause of liberty while at the same time fighting for equality of rights, even though he himself was among the privileged." Chateaubriand answered that there was indeed no turning back: "The democratic idea is ubiquitous: it tunnels under thrones, brings all aristocracies to ruin."[6]

The two also shared in the conviction that Catholicism was not only compatible with liberty but that religion and democracy were indispensable to each other. As Chateaubriand put it, "Liberty may have saved the world but will flounder without the aid of religion."[7] Tocqueville felt the same even though he had lost the faith of his childhood and settled for an instrumental view of religion—one that never brought him solace. From Philadelphia, Tocqueville had confided into Charles Stöffels the pain of living without absolute truth.[8] Tocqueville revealed as much to readers of *Democracy in America* when alluding to men "who abandon the faith they love in order to follow doubt that leads to hopelessness."[9] In 1835, upset at the sudden death of a cousin who was a young mother, he despaired that he had become a heathen.[10] But no matter his personal tragedy of faith, Tocqueville felt it imperative to help foster a harmony between the kingdom of God and democracy. With that determination, Tocqueville dispatched one advance copy of *Democracy in America* to the Abbé de Lamennais as a sincere "tribute" to the priest who had founded *L'Avenir* and who was finally banished for attempting to reconcile religion and democracy.[11]

The other great figure who emerged as an advocate for Tocqueville and his book was Royer-Collard, forty-two years his senior.[12] The aging statesman found in *Democracy in America* "an inexhaustible source of instruction and pleasure" and widely praised it. He put Tocqueville on par with Aristotle and Montesquieu, and repeatedly said so publicly.[13] Tocqueville, in turn, referred to Royer-Collard as having been the "master of the country" during the Restoration.[14] When president of the Chamber before the 1830 Revolution, Royer-Collard had addressed the Crown to reassert the principles of parliamentary government and affirmed the liberal interpretation of the charter.[15] Moreover, as the former *maître à penser* of the Doctrinaire school (intent on combining parliamentary government with hereditary monarchy), Royer-Collard had combined intellectual and political work in a way that Tocqueville wanted to emulate. The two were committed to freeing liberalism from revolutionary violence. Essentially, they wanted to implement the promise of 1789 without descending into the chaos of 1793. Tocqueville admired Royer-Collard's consistency of thought and action. His feelings redoubled after Royer-Collard condemned the September laws restricting freedom of the press and implementing other reactionary measures, which the government passed in 1835 in the wake of Fieschi's attempted assassination of King Louis Philippe.[16] An admiring Tocqueville told Royer-Collard, "You are the spokesperson not for *Magna Moralia* but for morality applied to great ends, and that is quite different."[17] Could Tocqueville ever reach this harmony of goal and action?[18]

Various literary salons opened their doors to the newly discovered writer of genius, introducing him to several important cultural and political figures who would become his friends for life. The heyday of salons had passed with the Restoration because so many participants in that aristocratic culture of conversation were Legitimists now in political exile. But salons were still important gathering places, where social elites mingled with politicians, writers, artists, and diplomats and advanced political, social, and philosophical agendas. Hostesses played an important role by bringing together guests capable of finding common ground on important political or literary matters. Mary Clarke, a young English friend of Madame Récamier, saw Parisian salons as "the most complete exercise of the social faculty."[19] Charles de Rémusat spoke of the conversation salon hostesses stimulated as art, and literary critic Sainte-Beuve put it on a par with literature.[20]

Chateaubriand took the new author to l'Abbaye aux Bois, Madame Récamier's salon, where admirers regularly heard the great man read excerpts from his in-progress *Mémoires d'outre-tombe*.[21] There, Tocqueville met Jean-Jacques Ampère, son of the famous scientist, a literary scholar who became a lifelong friend, and Sainte-Beuve, who was Ampère's friend. He also encountered philosopher Pierre-Simon Ballanche, a disciple of Chateaubriand and Joseph de Maistre. Ballanche credited Christianity as a force in periodic regenerations of society, or "palingenesis."[22] At Mary Clarke's salon, which Ampère also attended, he mixed with Christian moralist Charles de Montalembert, historian François Mignet, and philosopher Victor Cousin; he would interact with all three for years to come.[23]

Royer-Collard actively advanced Tocqueville's career. He used his considerable influence with members of the Académie française to

award *Democracy in America* the Montyon Prize.[24] He introduced Tocqueville to the duchesse de Dino in March 1836. The duchess, a niece by
marriage of Charles Maurice de Talleyrand, had accompanied the diplomat, thirty years her senior, to the Congress of Vienna and become
his mistress. She ran a salon in the heart of aristocratic Faubourg Saint-
Germain, from where she influenced the voting politics of the Académie des sciences morales et politiques and Académie française, and she
took a genuine interest in Tocqueville's chances to someday be elected
to these bodies.[25]

Tocqueville also benefited from the influence of his cousin Prime
Minister Louis-Mathieu comte Molé. Molé was a remarkably adroit politician who managed to serve Napoleon, the restored Bourbons, and now
an Orléans king.[26] He opened the door to the salon of his well-mannered
mistress, Madame de Castellane, and to that of Madame d'Aguessau, his
aunt.[27] Among the more literary salons Tocqueville attended was Virginie Ancelot's.[28] Madame Ancelot was married to a successful play-
wright, Jacques-Francois Ancelot. At her salon, Tocqueville again saw
Ballanche and Sainte-Beuve as well as Prosper Mérimée and Stendhal
among the regulars.[29] Tocqueville also frequented the salon of émigré
Milanese princess Cristina Belgiojoso, admired for her beauty, literary
talent, and leadership from abroad in the cause of Italian unification.[30]

These hostesses sought Tocqueville because he spoke brilliantly and
not just on America. George Ticknor, whom Tocqueville had befriended in Boston and who was quite familiar with salon circles from
his European visits, remembered Tocqueville's ease of conversation, in
contrast with his poor abilities as an orator.[31] At Madame Ancelot's urging, Tocqueville pressured his friends for reviews in the press, but he
had reasons to be apprehensive.[32] Having raised ambiguity to the level
of a literary technique, he recognized that he appealed "to many people
whose ideals are contrary to my own, not because they understand me
but because they lift out of context arguments that align themselves
with their fleeting passions."[33]

A handful of reviewers embraced Tocqueville's program for a new
liberalism and endorsed his call for "citizens to be involved in public
life."[34] One such reviewer was Léon Faucher, a young journalist, who

shared with Tocqueville and Beaumont a commitment to prison reform (but opposed solitary confinement[35]) and who traveled in the same literary circles. Faucher published an advance review in December 1834 in the paper he directed, *Le courrier français*, an organ of the "dynastic left" (comprising the more liberal Orléanists). Faucher predicted that *Democracy in America* would "strike readers as a revelation," for they would discover a "foreign society comprising neither lords nor commoners, neither rich nor poor, drawing only from the twin sources of power: enlightenment and hard work."[36] More reserved in his review for *Le Temps*, Sainte-Beuve nevertheless endorsed Tocqueville's claim of establishing a new political science. As this was an important part of Tocqueville's agenda, Tocqueville dashed off a quick note of appreciation.[37]

The most supportive reader, Francisque de Corcelle, had been marquis de Lafayette's aide de camp in the National Guard and had married one of Lafayette's granddaughters.[38] His reading of *Democracy in America* in the *Revue des deux mondes* captured not only Tocqueville's intent but also the urgency of his message.[39] Corcelle was uniquely equipped to appreciate the book. During the Restoration, Corcelle had joined the ranks of the Charbonnerie, a secret society that orchestrated opposition to the Bourbons.[40] With the July Monarchy in place, Corcelle expressed his dismay at the modesty of reforms, calling them mere "amendments to the principle of the divine rule of kings." He denounced the government's blindness to the popular sovereignty to which it owed its existence and advocated a program of social regeneration (borrowing from Ballanche's vocabulary). Corcelle rejected Cousin's eclecticism and Hegel's synthesis as not proposing strong enough moral principles.[41] With Lamennais, he advocated the separation of church and state. He demanded, like Rousseau, that political rights be on par with natural rights. At the same time, Corcelle remained a realist. He refused to be lured into utopian thinking, whether it be Saint Simonian pseudo-religion, Owen's "convents," Fourier's phalansteries, or calls rewarding "each according to his work."[42] To no one's surprise, he found much to like in *Democracy in America*.

Corcelle read *Democracy in America* as a "revelation," just as Faucher had predicted. He endorsed the idea of an inexorable march toward equality and recognized the need for a new political science that France's intelligentsia had heretofore failed to provide. Corcelle rightly interpreted Tocqueville's book as recommending that France "regularize its democratic movement" and "educate its society" as to the inevitability of equality of conditions so that democracy be sustainable.[43] Tocqueville and Corcelle began a friendship, at times troubled by clashes of personality but enduring.

Unexpected support also came for some of the early socialists. Young Louis Blanc wrote an equally penetrating review of *Democracy in America*. He diagnosed properly why the book would endure because, as he put it, society changes individuals. "More than ever, society modifies the individual." We therefore need "books that encourage men to seek out greater happiness and virtue by actively modifying the laws that dominate them." Blanc did not agree with everything Tocqueville had written, far from it. But he understood Tocqueville to be joining in the fight against despotism. Blanc especially approved of the difference Tocqueville posited between legitimate "government" and invasive "administration," which he saw as an "enlightening distinction" between "power" and "despotism."[44]

Blanc could have repaired a significant blind spot in Tocqueville's observations on democracy. Industrial organization, fundamental to early socialist thinking, was notoriously absent from Tocqueville's gaze. Tocqueville had based his observations on largely rural Jacksonian America while the early socialists were focused on the growing industrial towns of England and France. In late November 1831, while the twenty-six-year-old Tocqueville was still journeying down the Ohio River observing log cabins and isolated woodlots, silk weavers of Lyon (the "Canuts") had erupted in a massive labor riot. Nineteen-year-old Louis Blanc, an impoverished student shedding his own conservative background, was then busy teaching groups of workers in Arras, a town in northern France's most industrial region.

Tocqueville did not see fit to initiate a dialogue with Louis Blanc as he had with Corcelle. Not that Tocqueville was indifferent to the events that moved Blanc. When political economist Pellegrino Rossi in his first lecture at the Collège de France suggested that society would be better off if Lyon's Canuts did not have children, he and Kergorlay became alarmed that the professor might be helping the government cast "overlapping nets" of repression.[45]

Tocqueville's reasons for ignoring Blanc were both ideological and personal. Blanc believed that the Terror, which had decimated much of Tocqueville's family, was justified. On that point, there could be no reconciliation, for Blanc did not recognize the Terror as despotism. He felt the convention had been "forced to strike its external enemies by the sword and its internal enemies by the axe"; that both "victory and scaffold" were imperative to "save France and the future" was something Tocqueville could not concede.[46] With aristocratic aloofness, Tocqueville refused to engage in dialogue with people he considered enemies of freedom, especially those far from his social circle. For most of their careers, Tocqueville and Blanc talked past each other until they finally faced off in the Revolution of 1848.

Louis Blanc was not the only early socialist to recognize the value of *Democracy in America*, but he was the only one to do so in print. Proudhon left behind passionate reading notes of *Democracy in America*, part of his search for a broader definition of democracy that went beyond simple access to suffrage.[47]

These reviews were proof that Tocqueville's message resonated with dedicated reformers. Other reviewers in the literary establishment dispensed praise but did not go beyond a superficial reading. Narcisse de Salvandy, historian, novelist, deputy in the Chamber, and about to be inducted into the Académie française, called Tocqueville the Blackstone of America in the ministerial *Journal des débats*. Tocqueville appreciated being compared to the author of *Commentaries on the Laws of England* but thought it the article's only merit. Otherwise, he judged "you could not find a more ignorant analysis of the subject, nor one so superficially recounted."[48] Abel-François Villemain, secretary of the French Academy, and grand mandarin of French literature (Balzac was his student) did better when recycling as a review the citation he had written for the Montyon Prize. The lesson for Europe from Tocqueville's work, he explained, was that laws and ideas must "gradually increase equality among men in a way that promotes self-governance" and enables "stability" of the kind once achieved under monarchy.[49] Villemain praised Tocqueville for defending justice against the will of the majority.

At the same time, opponents vocally resented Tocqueville's use of the United States as a model for France. If the indemnity controversy had fueled interest in Tocqueville's work, it had also rekindled anti-American sentiments. In some quarters, America could never be a model. The Legitimist marquis de Custine rejected the idea of American democracy "emerging from God's design for human societies" but saw it instead as "the dangerous consequence of eighteenth-century philosophy's encroachment on the religion of our fathers" while the Legitimist *Gazette de France* lashed out at American racism.[50] At the same time Philippe Buchez's newly created periodical, *L'Européen—Journal des sciences morales et économiques,* displayed the liberal Catholic's prejudice against Protestants by painting a picture of American democracy as "selfishness in social form."[51]

The most significant and enduring pushback came from the victors of 1830. As the July Monarchy's political leaders, they were promoting an altogether different political vision. Tocqueville resented some of them. Adolphe Thiers, a historian with immense energy, Tocqueville despised instinctively: "What I love, he finds ridiculous and loathsome; what he loves, I fear and despise."[52] Tocqueville no longer admired François Guizot, who had turned conservative. Guizot and his followers drew a sharp contrast between American democracy and French constitutional monarchy. American democracy was serving the numerical majority. France's government, they argued, should instead represent the growing French middle class, or bourgeoisie. The Doctrinaires claimed that the bourgeoisie (which formed their political base) was the social class best equipped for democracy, since its ranks were significantly more open than those of the old aristocracy.

Tocqueville agreed with limits on voting, did not endorse American "universal" suffrage for white males, and even mounted a sustained attack on what he called the tyranny of the majority. But his pro-American book disturbed Guizot and his followers, and they made it known, although it took until 1837 for their argument to appear in the press. Louis de Carné expressed the Guizot position most fully in a long essay published in *Revue des deux mondes* perfectly titled "American Democracy and French Bourgeoisie." Carné was a contemporary of Tocqueville's, the founder of the newspaper *Le Correspondant* in 1829, *conseiller général* for Finistère (eventually becoming *député*, like Tocqueville), and one of the founders of the Société d'économie charitable that Tocqueville had joined. In his essay, he posited the "manifest incompatibility between our ideas and those of America." Economic conditions in the two countries were vastly different, he explained, for France did not have a Mississippi Valley where it could send pioneers with axes in hand. More importantly, the coming of a government of the bourgeoisie, an outcome of the July Revolution, carried with it a real chance for a more inclusive alliance with the church that France needed, and that Tocqueville wished to see. With that alliance, the bourgeoisie would fulfill its true and great "providential mission": "the moral improvement of the lower classes." For Carné, the bourgeoisie had a historical destiny, and it could not possibly be confused with the "numerical majority" that you find in America.[53] Carné felt the property qualifications for voting in France, if tampered with, should be raised instead of lowered. In reality, limited extensions of the franchise allowed just enough mobility to maintain the illusion of growing inclusiveness. The dominant view Carné conveyed distinguished voting from other civil rights (such as association and freedom of the press). Voters had to possess significant financial resources before expressing political judgment at the polls; but in voting, they merely served a function rather than exercising a right open to all.[54]

Carné aligned perfectly with Guizot, who doubled down in a review of two mediocre books—one defending the status quo, the other advocating a republic—for the *Revue française*.[55] Guizot seized that opportunity to attack Tocqueville in print, albeit without mentioning him by name. The mentor turned against the student in heralding the historical mission of the bourgeoisie. He stressed not the inevitability of democracy but the urgency of limiting its reach. "There are those who tell us that when it comes to contemporary democracy, we can wring our hands all we like, speechify as much as we please; that all our words, all our thoughts shall be in vain; that what we have before us is final, a foregone conclusion, before which we are powerless to act. What is done is done, no doubt. But shall we stand by and let things run their course? And if there are things we can do or say, are we so infatuated with ourselves that it would be in vain to speak out?"[56] Tocqueville remained friendly with Carné, but he did not forgive Guizot, even though his own qualms about numerical majority made his personal position ambiguous in the larger and fraught debate on political participation.

## New Directions: Poverty and Pauperism

Tocqueville's recognition as a political philosopher strengthened his resolve to try politics itself. Under the Restoration, the minimum age for election to public office was forty. The 1830 Charter had changed that to thirty, and for Tocqueville, born in July 1805, that was only six months away after the publication of *Democracy in America*. As he told Kergorlay, he had no "blind enthusiasm for the intellectual life" alone; the time was near when he could perhaps fuse letters and politics.[57] When sending a presentation copy of *Democracy in America* to cousin Le Peletier d'Aunay, several times vice-president of the Chamber, Tocqueville apologized that his prose reflected a real lack of firsthand political experience. "Forgive me," he wrote, "if I have been forced to retreat into theory but I am only twenty-nine years old."[58] In the dedication to Lamartine, Tocqueville recognized not only "the first poet of our time" but also a "statesman."[59] The opportunity to try entering the Chamber did not arise immediately. Tocqueville would have to wait several years before running his first electoral campaign.

He needed a new project; after a few months of social engagements in Paris literary circles, Tocqueville confided to his father and his brother Édouard that he could not tolerate more evenings out.[60] He was pushing his fragile constitution to the limit and experiencing recurrent episodes of painful gastritis, which crippled him for days at a time. He summed up his condition later to Mary Mottley: "My body is a machine that craves rest, but rest is lethal to the spirit operating the machine."[61] Tocqueville and Beaumont, who participated in many of the same events, agreed they should worry less about salons and more about their new books: for Tocqueville, the already announced second volume of

*Democracy* and for Beaumont, *L'Irlande*. Beaumont rightly counted on salon attendees "who forget you easily" to "suddenly recover a prodigious memory so long as you return with a successful book."[62] Enough wasting time in Parisian salons.

As critics were debating *Democracy in America*, Tocqueville sought new directions of inquiry. He turned to the issues of poverty and pauperism he had neglected both in his travels and his writings. It is not entirely clear why Tocqueville, responding to a suggestion from a local scholarly society in Cherbourg, made pauperism the subject of his first work after *Democracy in America* was published, but he read a paper on the topic to the society in April 1835.[63]

Tocqueville's firsthand knowledge of poverty was minimal. In childhood, he had seen his father practice charity when delivering bread to the poor at Verneuil. When a young magistrate, Tocqueville had read and annotated Jean-Baptiste Say's *Cours complet d'économie politique* (1828–29).[64] He read it again during the voyage to America, took notes on early parts but not on the relevant section on "*secours publics*" in the second volume, where Say traces the word *pauperism* to the pauperization British Poor Laws presumably generated by making alms broadly available.

When in the United States, Tocqueville and Beaumont recorded only a few observations of the poor. New York politician John Spencer explained to them that Americans had realized that the English system of public charity at the parish level was too costly, and they had begun to demand work in exchange for alms. Thus, an almshouse in New York State employed inmates to raise crops to cover the cost of their housing.[65] Altogether, Tocqueville and Beaumont blithely reported few destitute in America and devoted only a brief appendix of the prison report to the application of poor laws in Maryland and New York.[66] Their account was purely descriptive, not offering any criticism or suggestions for reform. Moreover, they showed little interest in the prison report in investigating the relationship between poverty and crime.

Tocqueville's first substantive interaction with welfare policy came in 1833, during his travels to England. In the company of Lord Radnor, one of the leaders of the Whig Party, he attended a court session adjudicating cases of public aid. He emerged highly critical of British public charity after observing alms seekers receiving help they did not absolutely need and justices of the peace allowing them to get away with it.[67] At the same time, Tocqueville was not blind to the causes of poverty. He noted, also in his 1833 travel diary, that the "extreme disparity in land ownership" in England added to the ranks of the landless poor.[68]

Tocqueville did not include any considerations of poverty based on his brief encounters with it in America and England in the 1835 volume of *Democracy in America*, except when addressing it indirectly in the last chapter devoted to race. In a rare instance of anachronism reminiscent of the author's aristocratic roots, Tocqueville used the word *poor* to describe not the real poor but most of the American population who had to work to live comfortably.[69] He understood partible inheritance laws (abolition of entail), and the great availability of western land to have saved Americans from facing real poverty and its social consequences.

Because his own experience with poverty was limited, Tocqueville turned to the experience of others when preparing for his address to the Société savante in Cherbourg. Tocqueville read Alban de Villeneuve-Bargemont's *Économie politique chrétienne* (1834) closely. This was an influential work by a social conservative Catholic, Legitimist, and agrarian reformer who had held the post of prefect in the rapidly industrializing département du Nord. Tocqueville borrowed from Villeneuve-Bargemont the main paradox of modern poverty: the largest number of poor live in prosperous countries. England is the "Eden of modern civilization," but "one sixth of the inhabitants of this flourishing kingdom live at the expense of public charity." But the "ignorant and coarse" population of Portugal contains only "one pauper for every twenty-five inhabitants."[70] In his book, Villeneuve-Bargemont indicted Say, Adam Smith, and Malthus for giving good advice but no work or bread to the poor, and he condemned British industrialists as well as large landowners as a "greedy and arrogant class exploiting the human race."[71] Tocqueville was more impressed than Villeneuve-Bargemont with the theorists, especially Malthus,[72] but he agreed with him that political economy ought to be a moral discipline and not be reduced to an exercise in economics. As Tocqueville wrote to Kergorlay, "While all the efforts of political economy in our day seem to me to be about material issues, I would like . . .

to highlight the more immaterial side of this science . . . to include in it the ideas, the feelings of morality as elements of prosperity and happiness . . . to rehabilitate spirituality in politics."[73]

Villeneuve-Bargemont, who published his book in 1834, said nothing of the Poor Law reform under way in England and approved that same year. As it turned out, it was Tocqueville's acquaintance, Nassau Senior, in collaboration with Jeremy Bentham's former secretary, Edwin Chadwick, who had written the report that led to the 1834 reform. In preparation for his essay, Tocqueville asked Senior for his report, a copy of the legislation, and some related documents.[74] Senior and Chadwick had not challenged the basic Elizabethan principle of poor relief but had persuaded Parliament to bring a degree of centralized control to parishes and to provide "relief" in "community" spaces rather than at "home." They paid scant attention to the spiritual life of the poor. Their reform implemented a system of local workhouses where treatment of the poor, who had to earn their relief, was harsh.[75]

In the *Memoir on Pauperism*, Tocqueville painted in broad strokes a "gradual and irresistible movement," accelerating since the Middle Ages, which brought into the world "an immense number of new commodities" and generated modern inequality. Rousseau had condemned this development.[76] Tocqueville instead approved of it but exposed the corollary that a huge expansion of perceived needs necessarily followed that of available goods, hence dramatically increasing the danger of falling into poverty.

Reading the legislation and Senior's papers, Tocqueville correctly concluded that the 1834 English reform was designed to make welfare as unappealing as possible. "The goal of the law's amendment, not merely on the surface but at its core, was to make receiving public welfare so unpleasant to the indigent that they were deterred from seeking it out."[77] It obliged recipients to work on the dreaded treadmill for grinding corn, a workhouse feature Charles Dickens famously exposed in *A Christmas Carol*. But no matter the law's effects, Tocqueville still adopted Say's indictment, as he had in the penitentiary report. He blamed the availability of alms through public charity for the perpetuation of poverty and called the mechanism *pauperism*. By perpetuating dependencies, public charity, Tocqueville charged, delivered "a dowry of infamy," without creating a "moral tie" between giver and recipient capable of fostering community and fellowship.[78]

Tocqueville eventually disavowed the position he took in his memoir but only after visiting England and Ireland, talking to Senior again, and seeing real poverty for himself. When politician Prosper Duvergier de Hauranne wrote to Tocqueville in 1837 to request a copy, Tocqueville reluctantly sent it with the injunction to "accept it for what it is, and then promptly forget it," so upset he was for having treated superficially "one of the greatest, if not *the* greatest, question of modern times."[79]

## Visiting England: Another Route to Reform

Tocqueville returned to England in 1835, this time with Beaumont, to "complete" his political education.[80] This trip proved critical for Tocqueville's evolving understanding of democracy. After visiting England and Ireland, Tocqueville reconceived the second volume of *Democracy in America*. He had announced to readers a volume on American mores to follow the one he wrote on institutions, but now he chose to give democracy a general theoretical grounding, irrespective of place, and with it, his own political program as a "liberal of a new kind."[81] In America, Tocqueville had observed poverty only incidentally. But observation of the naked poverty of English industrial towns and the Irish countryside brought a whole new measure of the reality of inequality in modern society.

It was the perfect time for a visit. England was enacting major reforms that laid the foundation of the modern state. Already in 1832, prior to Tocqueville's first visit, the Great Reform Act of 1832 had transformed the electoral system.[82] Thereupon followed the Factory Act of 1833, which initiated the regulation of children's hours, and the Poor Law Amendment Act of 1834, which brought a degree of centralization to welfare. When Tocqueville and Beaumont arrived on April 23, 1835, Sir Robert Peel and his Tory cabinet had just resigned. Whigs had returned in a second Melbourne cabinet. The Prison Act and the Municipal Reform Act of 1835 created a national prison inspectorate and borough councils elected by taxpayers, respectively. For historian G. M. Trevelyan, this latter act was "the high-water mark of Benthamite Radicalism acting through the Whig machine."[83] Tocqueville, who was in London during the parliamentary debate on municipal reform, reported on it in detail to his cousin Le Peletier d'Aunay and explained to him why Robert Peel and the Tories could not seriously oppose it.[84] All this legislative activity amounted to significant democratic reform, prompting Tocqueville to observe, "The Whigs used democracy like an instrument, until the instrument overpowered the hand that had been guiding it."[85]

To meet people in power, there was no better passport than a note from the French prime minister. Comte Molé had already done much to bring his young cousin into the most august political and social circles in Paris. Molé now agreed to introduce him (and, at Tocqueville's request, Beaumont whom he did not know) to his British counterparts. Molé wrote notes to two of England's most influential Whigs, Lord Lansdowne and Lord Holland. Lansdowne, who had been close to Bentham, was a friend of Senior. As lord president of the Council, he had helped pass the Great Reform Act and had just returned to the new government, as had Lord Holland. Molé also sent a note of introduction to General Sebastiani, French ambassador to the Court of Saint James.[86]

Tocqueville was also making connections on his own, having reached out to Senior to promote *Democracy in America* in England. Senior immediately dampened expectations by advising Tocqueville that in his country, "there is great difficulty in getting a review of any book requiring much thought,"[87] but he suggested Tocqueville send copies prior to his visit to Lords Brougham and Lansdowne. A former Lord Chancellor in the first Melbourne cabinet, Brougham was one of the more iconoclastic of the aristocratic Whig elite, especially active in the abolitionist movement. Senior suggested several journals as well, including the *Athenaeum* and John Stuart Mill's *London Review*.[88]

London appeared gloomy at first. In late April, streets still looked like "mine tunnels lit by torches" at high noon, and the air was "thick and humid."[89] But thanks to their connections, the two travelers quickly enjoyed hospitality in the highest political and social circles. They delivered Molé's letter to Lansdowne House on April 28. Lord Lansdowne paid them a personal visit the next day and invited them to dinner.[90] They had dinner with Lord Holland on May 4.[91] At Holland House, "a delightful gothic chateau," they dined and chatted with Lord Granville and Lord Melbourne, the prime minister.[92] Lord Brougham also attempted to find the much-talked-about young author and his friend at their residence, but he missed them.[93] They dined at his house three days later.[94] Tocqueville reconnected with the devout Lord Radnor,[95] who had them for lunch at his residence. They were surprised to see all the servants in the household fall on their knees in unison around their master as he recited a prayer before they served the meal.[96]

Tocqueville and Beaumont dutifully reported their visits not only to their families but also to their salon hostesses in Paris. Tocqueville explained to Madame Ancelot how servants in these great aristocratic homes were suspicious of them, as they arrived on foot, not by carriage, but their attitude changed completely after the host welcomed them. By the time they left, servants had become obsequious. It was "the same way each time: greeted with marked insolence at the door, extremely well looked after in the drawing room, and treated with the utmost reverence upon my return to the vestibule." Tocqueville also described his encounter with Lord Byron's daughter, the twenty-year-old Lady Ada: "I sought to discern the great poet's gaze in her eyes, his smile on her lips, his gestures in the subtleties of her movements, so vivacious was Lady Ada in the prime of her youth."[97]

At other times, they attended political events, with toasts reminiscent of similar gatherings in America but now in aristocratic England. Tocqueville told again Madame Ancelot, a little caustically, "I attended a grand political dinner presided over by Lord Brougham; we were two hundred close friends, seated in a room as big as a church. . . . Eating was a mere excuse; the real goal of the meeting was to talk of the House of Lords, the House of Commons, to discuss magistrates, the army, the press, public education."[98] At times Tocqueville and Beaumont retreated to the Athenaeum, a "grand club, a magnificent palace with beautiful libraries stocked with the finest collections and the best restaurant you could ever imagine."[99] They also spent time with Tories as guests of John Murray, founder and guiding spirit of the *Tory Quarterly Review*.

Even middle-class Britons had an air of aristocracy about them, Tocqueville observed. When Tocqueville and Beaumont dined with a manufacturer, they felt like they were at the table of a New York City or Philadelphia alderman, except that their host imitated the aristocracy and made fun of Americans, who he maintained, had no notion of manners in good company.

All this busy social activity was temporarily interrupted when, as was bound to happen, too many social events got the better of Tocqueville's fragile constitution. Indisposed after a lavish dinner hosted by Lord Lansdowne, Tocqueville sought refuge on May 10 at the home of Henry Reeve, in Hampstead, a suburb northwest of London.[100] The two had met a few months earlier in Paris. Twenty-one-year-old Reeve, raised partly in Switzerland and fluent in French, with good family connections into Parisian literary society, had joined a dinner with Tocqueville, Sainte-Beuve, Ampère, and Ballanche by chance.[101]

Reeve had conservative leanings and was not inclined to pay attention to a work on democracy. However, after meeting the brilliant author at dinner, hearing him telling irresistible stories of Native American tribes, and then reading his book, he changed his mind. He decided he would be the one to translate it into English and welcome Tocqueville in London. A lifelong collaboration was born. Tocqueville stayed with Reeve and his mother until May 22. He insisted Beaumont remain in London and not visit more than every other day. The family doctor and Reeve's mother took care of the patient while Reeve used the opportunity to revise his translation and clarify ambiguities while Tocqueville was on hand.[102]

Conversations with congenial British intellectuals had a lasting influence on Tocqueville's thought. The encounter with John Stuart Mill, one year Tocqueville's junior, led to a historic collaboration between two of the greatest minds of their generation.[103] Although still broadly utilitarian, Mill had distanced himself from Bentham, whom he had begun to see as reductionist. Mill recalled in his autobiography that *Democracy in America* "fell into my hands" by chance. In reality, Senior had sent him a copy. Having read it, he was anxious to meet Tocqueville. Indeed, Mill had just commissioned Joseph Blanco White to write a review of Reeve's translation of *Democracy in America* in his revived *London Review*, which would be merged with the *Westminster Review* the following year. When White did not come through, Mill took on the assignment himself.[104] His essay, which appeared in the October 1835 issue, was a magisterial introduction to *Democracy in America* for the British public. Mill reproduced many key excerpts and rejoiced to see the book in "an English dress."[105] Mill was naturally anxious to recruit Tocqueville for his journal, who agreed to write a substantial essay on France's transformation since the old regime and to contribute shorter pieces as well. Although their relationship would be tested by diplomatic rifts between England and France, the two remained mutual admirers.

Tocqueville and Beaumont also had an opportunity to spend time with other prominent Radicals and Utilitarians of the day, as well as the more reformist Whigs. Tocqueville renewed earlier contacts with the novelist Edward Bulwer-Lytton and with John Bowring, Member of Parliament and first editor of Bentham's *Westminster Review*. He conversed with outspoken reformers in Parliament—Joseph Hume, John Roebuck, and especially George Grote, a historian of ancient Greece. Grote's wife, Harriet, became one of Tocqueville's most supportive friends.[106]

Tocqueville admired this small group of so-called Radicals, which had no counterpart in France. Unlike the French, these English Radicals respected the principles of democratic rule, they were not trying to impose utopian systems on an unwilling society; they respected the right to property as the basis for civilized society, they saw the political necessity of religion, and they were well educated. Tocqueville felt at ease with them, perhaps because, like him, they combined elitist manners with reformist ambitions.[107] He recognized in them the type of politician he wanted to become.

Tocqueville discussed the pressing issues of the times with his new British friends. Especially with Senior, Reeve, and Mill, Tocqueville shared his fears of centralization and its negative effects on both administration and justice. He sought to understand the extent to which the English were willing to centralize their institutions and how they divided responsibilities between national and local authorities. Tocqueville eventually recognized how a mix of centralized and local courts operated together in ways he had not understood from his study of British common law during his American trip.[108] There was much more to Poor Law reform than he had perceived in his *Memoir on Pauperism*. By implementing a degree of centralization, the new law limited the abusive control of the local gentry over the poor.[109]

Mill sought to reassure Tocqueville that there was little reason to worry about excessive centralization in England because "centralization rests on general ideas," and the English, Mill added, "have difficulty grasping large and abstract ideas." This helped explain Tocqueville's observation, which had puzzled him, that the English gave a great deal of care to legal details while keeping large principles loose.[110] Tocqueville did not have a chance to pursue the theory of centralization further while in England but noted this was an "important question to be dug into."[111]

Tocqueville impressed this group of reformers so much that they arranged for him to serve as a witness in the House of Commons regarding the French practice of the secret ballot. Grote was trying to gather support for the secret ballot as a way to limit the immense influence great property owners exerted on their constituents. Prior to the testimony, constitutional historian Henry Hallam gave Tocqueville a full view of electoral bribery. Tocqueville then proceeded to explain in detail in front of a parliamentary commission the technical conduct of elections in France.[112] The open ballot, however, remained the law for years to come.

Tocqueville tried to synthesize his observations of England, but he found it "a more complicated case than America."[113] In America, he told comte Molé, "all laws issue, so to speak, from a single idea. All of society, as it were, is founded on a single fact; everything flows from one principle. One could compare America to a great forest with a myriad of straight roads built through it, all of them leading to the same point. One need only find the crossroads, and everything will become visible in a single glance."[114] But in England, Tocqueville argued, legal reform had outpaced social change, making it difficult to pinpoint a crossroads. He wrote to Molé from London that "democratic ideas were rapidly impacting political life but at a standstill when it came to civil society." In this respect, England stood opposite to France. A good example was the Great Reform Act of 1832, which considerably extended the franchise. "The reform bill gave political power to the Commons. Peers can still direct the course of business, but they are no longer its sole arbiter."[115] Nonetheless, "money and privilege still power English society. . . . It costs a great deal to run for office, to be a lawyer, to be a JP or occupy some other unpaid office . . . to attend Oxford or Cambridge."[116] Beyond justices of the peace, there was no tribunal for the poor. As a nation, England was more preoccupied with legal equality than equality of conditions. Tocqueville restated the same argument to his cousin Le Peletier d'Aunay: "Though the movement of democracy is at a standstill in the mores and ideas of the rich, it continues to work through the legal system."[117] Altogether, "the respect people attach to wealth in England is cause for despair."[118]

Tocqueville also shared his views on the disjunction between legal and social reform with people he met. Twenty-five-year-old Camillo Cavour, the future leader of Italian unification, came to England as part of a European tour during Tocqueville's stay. The young traveler had made Senior's acquaintance, and he arrived at the Oxford professor's home to find him in conversation with Tocqueville. Cavour had read *Democracy in America* just before arriving in England and found it "the most remarkable work of modern times."[119] He subsequently dined with Tocqueville, Reeve, and Mérimée in London. With them was also Sutton Sharpe, whom Tocqueville referred to as "a very smart lawyer," a Francophile, friend of writers Vigny, Mérimée, and Stendhal, whom he met when in Paris at Madame Ancelot's salon.[120] In England, Sutton was close to the radical Whigs.[121] At that dinner, Cavour had a chance to hear Tocqueville elaborate on his theory of England torn between access to political rights for the many and concentration of wealth in the hands of a few. He noted in his diary that "this anomaly cannot last long without grave danger to the State."[122]

That democracy did not penetrate society was most noticeable in land ownership. Tocqueville observed again, as in 1833, that in England, the peasant was never inclined to purchase land because he never saw small holdings available.[123] In making again this important observation, Tocqueville was arguably developing at the same time a more positive view of the French Revolution's focus on land acquisition. "France always had a sizeable population of yeoman farmers, and the desire for land is widespread amongst the people. This only became more general with the Revolution," he noted. But in England, men were leaving the fields for the factories where all the desirable objects were manufactured, "not only for British consumption, but for that of the whole world."[124]

## Poverty and Inequality in Industrial England and Rural Ireland

Armed with the idea that legal change was not translating into social change, and with the fine dining in London's aristocratic homes behind them, Tocqueville and Beaumont went on a whirlwind tour of industrial England. They left London on June 24, arrived at Coventry on June 25, at Birmingham, the city of iron, copper, and steel, on June 26, and at Manchester, "that great manufacturing city of fabrics and cottons and threads," on June 30.[125] In all these cities, they could see poverty everywhere, not as the outcome of poor laws, as Tocqueville had once imagined, but of industrial exploitation.

Tocqueville interviewed some of the manufacturers who had stood firmly behind the reform bill, determined to march to London, armed, if necessary, to force Tories' assent.[126] He took copious notes regarding local tax rates, population growth, and other demographic and economic indicators, but he did not attempt to see any labor leaders.[127]

Tocqueville and Beaumont observed the great industrial city of Manchester with special acuity. A local physician, Dr. James Phillips Kay, author of *The Moral and Physical Condition of the Working Classes in Manchester* (1832) guided them.[128] Dr. Kay took them to a charitable organization where they collected various documentation, then to town hall. He took them to Little Ireland, where they saw "a cluster of hovels in which 50,000 Irish were packed in cages. . . . Dante himself could not invent for the nasty rich a more awful torment than to live in these hideous dwellings," before an evening of conversation at a local scientific society.[129]

Unlike Engels, who knew every alley, Tocqueville surveyed the town rather rapidly, but his description of abject poverty in the workshop of the world is just as powerful. It was from this "foul drain" that "the greatest stream of human industry flows out to fertilize the whole world. From this filthy sewer pure gold flows. Here humanity attains its most complete development and its most brutish; here civilization works its miracles, and civilized man is turned back almost into a savage."[130]

By July 4 they were at Liverpool, a city "destined to become the center of trade."[131] Misery was not immediately apparent there, but Tocqueville estimated again that about 50,000 poor lived in cellars, most of them from Ireland, which was the pair's next destination.

Inspired by Montalembert and Duvergier de Hauranne, Tocqueville and Beaumont had desired to explore Catholic Ireland for some time. Montalembert had praised Irish Catholicism as exemplary in *L'Avenir* in 1830, and he had promoted the cause of Ireland in Mary Clarke's and Virginie Ancelot's salons in Paris.[132] Tocqueville and Beaumont were in Dublin from July 6 through 17, where they visited George Ticknor, their friend from Boston.[133] They then proceeded south. If Tocqueville had initially found it hard to penetrate the paradox of English law and society, he had no difficulty in capturing the predicament the Irish found themselves in: "If you wish to know what the spirit of conquest, religious hatred, combined with all the abuses of aristocracy without any of its advantages, can produce, come to Ireland."[134] The contrasting extremes of poverty and wealth were beyond what Tocqueville and Beaumont had imagined. After visiting the poor house in Dublin, Tocqueville reported in his diary on "*The sight inside.* The most hideous and disgusting aspect of destitution. A very long room full of women and children whose infirmities or age prevent them from working. On the floor, paupers are lying down pell-mell like pigs in the mud of their sty. One has difficulty not to step on a half-naked body." Following this visit, they were taken to the university where they could admire "an immense and magnificent garden kept up like that of a nobleman. A palace of granite, a superb church, a wonderful library. Lackeys in livery, fourteen fellows, seventy [scholars]. Enormous revenues. Men of all religions are educated there. But only members of the Church of England can administer the establishment and receive its revenues."[135]

In conversation with Tocqueville, the Bishop of Kilkenny compared the Irish to the Greeks under Turkish rule.[136] Ireland was very much a colonized nation. The Irish sent their harvest and meat to England and ate only potatoes.[137] "Go to Mayo," the bishop said, and "you will encounter thousands of men literally nearly dead of hunger. The Marquis of Sligo has, in the same province, seventy thousand acres of land, the revenue of which he consumes in England. Should not the law force this man to give his fellows some part of his surplus? Why are so many people dying of hunger in Mayo? Because the landlords find it in their interest to increase their grasslands, and if they can make a little more money, they laugh at us besides. At the present time, gentlemen, it is the interest of the landlords of Ireland to render the people as wretched as possible, for the more the cultivator is threatened by starvation, the readier he will be to submit to every condition they wish to impose on him. Let us give the landlords an interest in making the poor comfortable." Tocqueville noted that this long democratic tirade was listened to with enthusiasm and interrupted several times by cries of "Hear!" from the bishop's other guests.[138]

M. W. Murphy, a lawyer friend of political leader Daniel O'Connell, added in conversation with Tocqueville that absentee owners held on to even uncultivated land.[139] Tocqueville realized again that poverty was rooted not in immorality, as he had naively argued in the *Memoir on Pauperism*, but in political history. The extreme concentration of landownership in the hands of a people of a different religion and national origin than the Irish masses created a system of oppression akin to slavery. John Revans, the secretary of a commission investigating the possibility of establishing a poor law in Ireland (which would become reality in 1837), joined with the Bishop of Kilkenny in hoping that such a law might make landowners see their tenants' economic self-sufficiency as aligned with their own interests. That was wishful thinking, Tocqueville concluded. In Ireland, there was "no moral tie between the poor and the rich."[140] Only the poor helped the poor, leading to more general impoverishment.

In traveling the country, it was common for Tocqueville and Beaumont to seek shelter from the rain. Tocqueville told his cousin Eugénie that if they saw only humans in a house, they would bypass it in favor of finding a home with a pig inside, for a pig was a sign they could count on relative comfort."[141] He added facetiously, "I have infinite respect for pigs, but I doubt it was the intention of providence to make them the everyday companions of men." Tocqueville concluded that Ireland displayed "all of the evils of an aristocracy without any of its advantages,"[142] generating extreme poverty and taking no blame for it.

By contrast, Tocqueville found Ireland's other major institution, the Catholic Church, a force for good, just as Montalembert and Duvergier de Hauranne had reported in Parisian salons. The church was on the side of the poor, not concerned that education might lessen faith and intent on maintaining its independence from government. The Bishop of Kilkenny told him, "I would despair if the State wished to pay me. . . . It would break the union that now exists between the clergy and the people."[143] Tocqueville heard Irish Catholic priests even come out in favor of freedom of the press as "the only weapon the oppressed can resort to against the oppressor."[144] The Irish church seemed to him to embody a democratic ideal he approved of: instruction, the separation of church and state, freedom of the press, and faith in the future.

Tocqueville and Beaumont returned to Dublin on August 9 to attend sessions on social statistics at a meeting of the British Association for the Advancement of Science.[145] They left Ireland on August 13, Beaumont traveling to Scotland while Tocqueville returned to France, where he arrived on August 16.

Impatient to explore new territory, Tocqueville had used his fame as an entrée to explore a new topic in a new place: inequality in Great Britain. In a few months, he gained a perspective on poverty that was lacking in *Democracy in America* as well as deeper knowledge of British institutions, its legal system, and the workings of British society, all of which were to become critical foundations of the second volume of *Democracy*. He found enduring role models in the group of reformers he befriended, and he corresponded with them for the rest of his life. With encounters and observations in England and Ireland, Tocqueville strengthened dramatically his comparative thinking and expanded his study of democracy.

Tocqueville kept detailed notebooks during his travels in which he recorded his observations, conversations with informants, and personal impressions, parts of which are brilliant pieces of description. Whereas he had relied on his American notebooks extensively in piecing together the first volume of *Democracy in America*, he would not extract passages from his English or Irish notebooks in the second; although this volume would address the broader phenomenon of the democratic revolution, it was still advertised as a book on America. There was another reason why Tocqueville would refrain from referring to specific places in England and Ireland. Tocqueville and Beaumont agreed while in London that they would not compete with each other. One would write on the United States and the other on Great Britain.[146] A similar understanding had earlier led Tocqueville not to publish his romantic description of their exploration of the Michigan forest ("Two Weeks in the Wilderness") as an appendix to volume one of *Democracy in America*. Beaumont claimed this same landscape for the final scenes of *Marie*, his novel narrating the tragic story of a French immigrant's forbidden love with an American woman marked by a visually imperceptible but nonetheless terrible stigma of Black ancestry.

What England inspired, Tocqueville would in time subsume under his more general discussion of democracy. Tocqueville had bypassed industry in America only to watch it closely in England. This had been a serious omission. In the second volume of *Democracy*, Tocqueville would be able to correct that by theorizing about the grave danger an emerging industrial aristocracy posed to democracy.[147] He would base his reasoning entirely on his notes on industrial England without ever mentioning England. The English trip, then, broadened Tocqueville's gaze and helped him turn his rich anthropological observations into political theory.

Mill also played a role in this move toward comparative political theory by extracting from Tocqueville a promise to write a theoretical essay on France. The eventual outcome would be Tocqueville's first attempt to think through the French Ancien Régime, well in advance of the famous book Tocqueville would write on that topic in the 1850s.[148]

During all this time, Tocqueville heard little from America. Perhaps Tocqueville had counted on Edward Livingston to promote his book on his return to the United States. Unfortunately, the minister showed no intention of playing in America the role that Chateaubriand and Royer-Collard were performing so effectively in France. Only two brief reviews of *Democracy in America* appeared in the United States in 1835 and only three in 1836. One was significant. The one that appeared in the *North American Review* was written by Edward Everett, an ex-Harvard professor, congressman from Massachusetts, and leading figure in the increasingly important Whig Party. He had talked to Tocqueville first in Boston and then in Washington. He praised Tocqueville for recognizing "the necessity of commencing his inquiries" from the "municipal corporations," in particular the New England towns, and the "separate States" rather than from the federal government, and for showing the power of local civil society in preventing the "curse of centralization." Tocqueville, who still feared he might have made some significant error, dashed off a note to Reeve. "I read this [review] with extreme pleasure. I spent so little time in the United States that I had no opportunity for depth. I so often had to reason by analogy, like Cuvier with his animal fossils, that I truly feared having committed one of those blunders that lose those readers who know better right away. Thank God this is not the case."[149]

The necessary precondition for a larger critical following for *Democracy in America* was an American edition, but no publisher seemed interested. On June 6, 1837, Jared Sparks wrote to Tocqueville, "I am vexed and mortified that an edition of your 'Démocratie' has not yet been published in America." He reminded his friend that the work had come out in France just at the time of the unfortunate "Indemnity Controversy." Sparks noted a second reason for the lack of enthusiasm for an American edition. Several British reviewers dwelled on the negative aspects of American democracy. "Our newspapers," Sparks wrote, "have been filled with extracts from the English reviews, containing the parts of your work most objectionable to American readers; that is, your remarks on the defects of democratic institutions." Sparks tried to promote an American edition, but his discussions with a Boston publisher (while Tocqueville was clearing the way for a French edition of Sparks's volume on Gouverneur Morris) were unfruitful.[150]

Tocqueville was aware that the English reviews might dampen his American readership. He had realized while in London that Tories had been appropriating his book (and Beaumont's *Marie*) to highlight the flaws of American democracy and complained that one ultra-Tory review, *Black Magazine*, had published cleverly selected excerpts that made him look like an "enraged Tory."[151] The near-fatal blow to an American edition of *Democracy in America* came during former prime minister Sir Robert Peel's famous oration in Glasgow in 1837 on his inauguration into the office of lord rector of the university. He heralded Tocqueville's book as the definitive evidence of the absolute tyranny of the majority in American politics and the oppression under which the minority suffers. Peel used Tocqueville to buttress his claims that English institutions were superior to their American counterparts. Peel's oration led to multiple American rebukes, including one that Edward Everett sent directly to the former prime minister turned opposition leader. Everett had praised *Democracy in America*, but he told Peel that on the topic of the tyranny of the majority, Tocqueville had merely dwelt on "generalities" and given "no facts by way of illustrating the character of this tyranny."[152]

Help in the United States finally came from John C. Spencer, arguably the second most important informant for *Democracy*, whom Tocqueville had met in upstate New York. Spencer convinced a New York publishing house to hijack the British translation. Americans did not respect international copyright laws until the 1890s and rarely paid royalties to foreign authors—and indeed Tocqueville never earned money from the American editions of his book.[153] Spencer wrote a preface and some explanatory notes. Volume 1 came out in 1838, almost four years after the French and British editions. Spencer, in his notes to the American edition of *Democracy in America*, put the best face he could on the chapter on the tyranny of the majority by explaining that Tocqueville was criticizing not Americans in general but only the Jacksonians and the "tyranny of party."[154] The Jacksonians, for their part, flatly rejected Tocqueville's views and joined the Whigs in a rare display of unity. Thomas Hart Benton, senator from Missouri, took care to distinguish Tocqueville from "the riffraff of European writers who come here to pick up the gossip of the highways, to sell it in Europe for American history, and to requite with defamation the hospitalities of our houses." But "Old Bullion Benton," renowned for his advocacy of Jacksonian hard money positions, spoke for all in rejecting Tocqueville's claim of a "tyranny of the majority" in the United States.[155] Benton pointed instead to the "intelligence of the masses" in guiding the country. Was such a misunderstanding not enough to incite Tocqueville to publish his second volume of *Democracy in America* and clarify his position?

# 6

# When Political Theory
# Becomes Politics

AS HE WAS ABOUT TO EMBARK on his first electoral campaign for the French Chamber in March 1837, Tocqueville explained to Reeve that because aristocracy was already dead when his life began and democracy did not yet exist, he had none of the "aristocratic or democratic prejudices" people attributed to him. He was instead "perfectly balanced between past and future" and not "instinctively drawn toward either."[1] He felt he was in a good position to enter politics as an independent who could apply impartially a much-needed comprehensive theory of the great transformation from aristocratic to democratic society.[2] Whether politician or writer, he would be his own guide, free from pressures of government officials of the *"juste milieu"* or their Legitimist or liberal opponents. But political independence quickly proved a liability in electoral politics even as it remained an asset in formulating political theory.

## A New Phase of Life: Marrying for Love
## and Settling in in Normandy

Tocqueville's Legitimist family was first to reckon with Alexis's commitment to independence, which he asserted in marrying Mary Mottley (hereafter Marie), the middle-class English woman he loved but whom they were reluctant to welcome. Tocqueville confided to Mrs. Austin,

Reeve's aunt, that his family barely tolerated his "audacity" in choosing a wife for himself, yet he had great hopes for a marriage he thought could help him combine "two things not easily found united in this world—a busy intellectual, and a tranquil, calm, home-life."[3]

The family should not have been surprised by Alexis's choice. He had virtually announced it in volume 1 of *Democracy in America*, which they had read closely in manuscript, when declaring his admiration for the ways Americans respected "the marriage bond" and "subscribe[d] to the loftiest and most just ideal of conjugal happiness," in contrast to Europeans, who were "scornful of natural ties and permissible pleasures."[4] Tocqueville never changed his mind. When advising his nephew Hubert on the prospect of marrying, he did not hesitate to say, "There is nothing more solid and genuinely sweet in this world than domestic happiness and the company of a woman who understands you. I've experienced that too much not to be convinced of it."[5] Tocqueville acted on his conviction that Marie was the one to support him for life when he interrupted his stay in England in mid-June 1835 to meet her for three days in Boulogne. There, priests of the local diocese advised English visitors wishing to become Catholic and officially registered their renunciation of Protestantism. In pursuing this path, Marie hoped to enhance her chances that the Tocqueville family would accept her.[6] Tocqueville decided at the last minute to join her. He rescheduled a meeting he had with John Stuart Mill in London to support her conversion so that Marie could see "with her own eyes, with what ardor I loved her."[7]

Was it love? Tocqueville said so to Marie, unequivocally and repeatedly. With his friends, he was more ambiguous. To Louis de Kergorlay, who had called their potential union a disastrous misalliance, he insisted that it was love.[8] To others, Tocqueville admitted to feelings of "deep attraction rather than love" but said he had made up his mind all the same because Marie had an "elevated soul and character" capable of giving him the "peace of mind and happiness" he needed after the "adventurous and chaotic life" (presumably emotionally and sexually) that he had heretofore led. He realized that Marie had no money and that she was merely "attractive rather than beautiful," unlike his cousin Camille d'Orglandes's "gorgeous and wealthy wife." But he had simple tastes and did not care for a life of social pretension. When returning from adventures of discovery in distant lands, he felt most comfortable at home by the fire. Combining their modest means, he and Marie could be independent and comfortable, and that was really all he had ever hoped for.[9]

Hervé de Tocqueville overcame his misgivings and supported his youngest son. After Édouard and Alexandrine expressed anxiety about how such a union might loosen their family bonds, Alexis, writing from Ireland, reassured them that Marie's simplicity should instead help tighten these bonds even more.[10] Hippolyte and Émilie were less forthcoming. Émilie promised her support when, back from England and Ireland, Alexis recovered at his brother and sister-in-law's home at Nacqueville from a traumatic sea crossing that had left him quite sick, but she never followed through on her promise.[11] The marriage was celebrated on October 26, 1835 at the church of Saint-Thomas d'Aquin in Paris with only the immediate family and a few friends present. Louise-Madeleine, Tocqueville's mother, already ailing, had been warming up to Marie. She was in attendance a few days earlier at the law office where a marriage contract was drawn up but not at church on the wedding day. Kergorlay and Gustave de Beaumont served as witnesses for the marriage contract and both the civil and religious ceremonies.[12]

Louise-Madeleine died three months later. A grieving Tocqueville mused on the fate of the Rosanbos, his mother's family, whose downfall paralleled the great political transformation he wanted to explain. Uncle Louis was now the only survivor of this "tribe broken by providence." Tocqueville recapitulated his uncle's singular destiny. Louis de Rosanbo had witnessed his "grandfather" (the great Malesherbes), his parents, and one sister and brother-in-law (Chateaubriand's brother) go to the scaffold, seen another sister die prematurely, and now watched his other sister, Louise-Madeleine, who had never recovered from the same events, finally "succumb after twenty years of misery."[13]

The family partly redistributed its assets again after Louise-Madeleine's passing, and these included several pieces of landed property in Normandy. Among these, Tocqueville had already received the long-abandoned château of Tourlaville, near Cherbourg, and its dependencies. But he had a marked preference for the nearby Tocqueville château (also uninhabited and in an equal state of disrepair) that was now going to Édouard. Tocqueville had visited the place briefly in 1828 and then again in 1833, before his first trip to England. He liked this "old house flanked by two heavy towers where nothing is comfortable and even less is pleasing to the eye: dark rooms, vast chimneys that provide more cold than heat. . . . The walls lining the drafty hallways dripping with condensation." Outside, "a long meadow going out to the ocean."[14] Édouard agreed to trade real estate with his younger brother. He and Alexandrine were already comfortably settled at Baugy, a property near Compiègne that had come to them from the Ollivier family, and where Tocqueville would continue to spend much time until he and Marie could make substantial improvements in Normandy. Hippolyte also had his say. With his two older brothers' consent, Tocqueville would in time inherit their father's title of comte associated with the land (a title Louis XVIII had confirmed early in the Restoration), but he always refused to use it.[15]

The newlyweds experienced greater-than-expected difficulty in personality adjustments. Marital bliss was not so easily achieved. Although "we will one day get ashore," Alexis told Édouard, they were battling the storm.[16] Alexis was controlling, critical of his wife's every move. He loved her so much, he explained, that he wanted her to be perfect in everything, and this caused sorrow and resentment. When in Normandy, Hippolyte and Émilie in nearby Nacqueville made things worse. "Hip," an unfaithful husband, attempted to repair his relationship with his wife by supporting her every whim, and this resulted in Émilie's constantly displaying an air of superiority that reinforced Marie's feelings of inadequacy.

But Alexis was also considerate. The couple had not been married a year before they traveled to Switzerland for Marie's health. Marie suffered from severe menstrual pain. Her husband set aside his work on the promised second volume of *Democracy in America* to take her to a cure at the sulfurous springs in Baden, Switzerland, for two and a half months in the summer of 1836. He had begun working on the general influence of democracy on ideas in late 1835 and first half of 1836, but departing for Switzerland broke the momentum.[17]

The couple reached Baden in late July for Marie to begin the cure. However frustrating the interruption seemed to Tocqueville at the time, it ultimately proved beneficial. Tocqueville made important comparative observations in Switzerland. He sharpened his understanding of federalism by observing the Swiss diet in Bern. He reported to Francisque de Corcelle that he had "in [his] capacity as an American conceived an exceptional disdain for the federal constitution of Switzerland" that "has divided the population into twenty-two different nations."[18] Switzerland stood in striking contrast to the United States he had described in volume 1 of *Democracy in America*, where the federal government could directly govern its citizens without relying on the states as intermediaries. Meeting with the French ambassador, duc de Montebello, in Bern, Tocqueville became dismayed at the ardor with which the French government was tracking down political refugees in Switzerland, which only reinforced his commitment to fight political repression at home.[19]

With Marie at the spa, Tocqueville, away from his study, fumed that he could not pursue his writing, but he immersed himself in reading classic books he had long neglected, by Plato, Aristotle, Plutarch, Thomas Aquinas, Machiavelli, Montaigne, Bacon, Descartes, Pascal, Montesquieu, and Rousseau.[20] Bossuet's providential reading of history in *Histoire des variations des églises protestantes*, a book duchesse de Dino admired, was also on the list. Many titles, he was ashamed to admit, he was reading for the first time. He ruefully compared himself to "marshal Soult learning geography when minister of foreign affairs."[21] He exchanged ideas on Plato with Royer-Collard, who had the advantage of being able to read the text in the original Greek.[22] Machiavelli's *The Prince*, a treatise on what Tocqueville saw as the "art of crime in politics," however, inspired his distaste and the interesting thought that Machiavelli must have been "Mr. Thiers' grandfather—that says it all." The journalist François-Adolphe Chambolle, in his *Mémoires*, wondered why Tocqueville disliked Thiers so much. The animosity began when Tocqueville first read Thiers's multivolume history of the Revolution, which justified uncritically each and every one of its steps. That book, Tocqueville reflected, "provoked a singular horror in me and a violent antipathy towards its author. I saw Mr. Thiers as the most perverse and dangerous of men."[23] In reflecting on materialism with Kergorlay, Tocqueville settled for an honest moral middle ground, somewhere between the moral laxism of Roman emperor Heliogabalus and the exacting rigor of Saint Jerome.[24] Kergorlay expressed only contempt for such a compromised position.

The travel, rest, and long periods of time spent together did much for marital harmony. Tocqueville told Kergorlay of "the inexpressible charm I found in being alongside [Marie] for such a prolonged length of time."[25] But it was also during this time together that the couple realized they might remain childless. Tocqueville shared the news with his closest friends but eventually reconciled with it, telling Édouard, "I did passionately want children, as I understand them, but I share no ardent desire to try my luck at the lottery of fatherhood."[26]

On their return to Tocqueville, Marie proved to be a superior mistress of the domain she was rebuilding. By August 1837, she had made their château livable enough that the Corcelles could spend two weeks there, and the Beaumonts followed them. Workers were still tearing up floors and ceilings in the spring of 1838. Two years later, Tocqueville could proudly offer to his now–close friend Jean-Jacques Ampère a quiet room bearing his name at the top of one of the towers.[27] Tocqueville loved the peaceful surroundings and tranquil life, but he insisted on friends' frequent visits. He had no intention, he told Corcelle, of becoming a "modern anchorite in a new Thebaid."[28] Marie restored not only the building but also the tradition of noblesse oblige. She had bread made and distributed locally to the poor, as in the Verneuil days of Tocqueville's childhood, when Mayor Hervé de Tocqueville made bread every week for the poor and visited the sick.[29]

## Entering Politics

Tocqueville was determined to enter politics and run for the Chamber at the first opportunity. From the moment he settled at Tocqueville, he looked into the possibility of joining the Conseil général, the elected body governing the *département*, which he judged to be the institution most truly representing the needs of the people. He did not mean to abandon political theory for politics but wanted a career contributing to their mutual enrichment. He told Édouard that holding office would give him, "he who was lost in theory," a chance to "handle the most precious interests of the population."[30] This was especially true in local elections where property qualifications to vote were significantly lower than in national elections.[31]

One can only be struck by how timid Tocqueville was in his early political overtures. Tocqueville drafted a modest program in an electoral circular in early October 1836, while in Normandy between stays in Switzerland and Baugy, and he sent it out in December to electors of two cantons (Beaumont and Pieux) to let them know he was available for the Conseil général. He claimed as his main credentials his book on America. He also promoted public education to "open the mind to all useful innovations," and good roads.[32] Tocqueville's chances of success, however, were limited. The château was still unoccupied, and the available seat on the Conseil represented two cantons that did not include Tocqueville. Their residents were naturally suspicious of the heir to an ancient aristocratic family, as they considered him to be just another Legitimist. Realizing this, Tocqueville did not campaign.[33] After Nicolas-Jacques Noël-Agnès, a leading merchant, mayor of Cherbourg, and local notable, was elected, Tocqueville developed a good rapport with him. For instance, he took it upon himself to write to Académie française member Abel-François Villemain, endorsing the mayor's nomination of a local woman for the Académie's annual *prix de vertu*, awarded to an ordinary person of exemplary character. Although he did not know Villemain personally, Tocqueville thought he might be receptive to his recommendation, as Villemain had awarded the Académie's Montyon Prize to *Democracy in America*.[34]

Political instability in 1837 gave Tocqueville the opening he needed for his first electoral run. Thiers had fallen as prime minister in August 1836 after failing to convince the king and the Chamber that France should invade Spain in support of the queen regent in her fight against her liberal opposition. A subsequent power-sharing arrangement between Molé and Guizot was filled with friction and misunderstanding and did not last. Guizot left the cabinet in April 1837 and turned against Molé. Adding to the feeling of chaos, Louis-Napoléon attempted a coup in Strasbourg on October 30, and before the year was over there was yet another assassination attempt against the king.

The charged political climate led to a major argument on May 5 and 6, 1837 in the Chamber between Odilon Barrot, leader of the dynastic left, and Guizot over the future of the country. Tocqueville followed the exchange closely as the protagonists focused on the very issues he raised in his work on democracy. Barrot, whom Karl Marx later characterized as the "chief of the liberal wing of the parliamentary bourgeoisie," pushed for reforms while Guizot was unwilling to go beyond the 1830 status quo.[35]

Barrot began with a remarkable speech in which he questioned how the Doctrinaires could claim to want a more inclusive society while insisting on a narrow political order.[36] Barrot called for a large extension of the suffrage. He could not possibly endorse the notion that just 150,000 to 160,000 electors represented the entirety of the middle class, not to mention France as a whole. He gave voice to the widespread sentiment that the concept of *capacité* (a person without wealth possessing sufficient status and/or knowledge to be entrusted with the vote) was too restrictive and eloquently reminded the Chamber that on the battlefield, all classes had paid with their blood for France's standing in the world.[37]

In his response, Guizot coined the phrase *"pays légal"* to designate the select group he believed should exercise the right to vote. Guizot argued that the 1830 charter already granted equal access to public jobs, freedom of the press, and individual freedom to all citizens, whether they voted or not, but he launched a sustained attack on what he considered the revolutionary theory of universal suffrage and the universality of political rights. He denounced that kind of equality as "absurd." He posited that only an enlightened portion of the nation could exercise full political rights. These were citizens free from manual labor, independent of salary, and endowed with the freedom and leisure time to devote to affairs of state. He insisted, however, that one should not confuse them with the nobility of old because their ranks were so much larger and continuously growing.[38]

Tocqueville felt, rightly, that he could add a valuable perspective to the debate if only he could join it. He sent detailed letters about the goings-on to Beaumont, who was fighting a cold in a vermin-infested apartment in London. Tocqueville told his friend that Guizot had based much of his argument in the Chamber on the contrast Louis de Carné had drawn, when discussing Tocqueville's work a few months before, between the French "bourgeoisie" and the American "numerical majority." Thiers, Tocqueville recounted, had participated in the debate and managed to ease tension by suggesting all that was needed to restore confidence in the government was to loosen the September laws restricting civil liberties.[39]

Molé, who had remained silent during the exchange, decided he needed to consolidate his majority, hence there was talk of Chamber dissolution. Tocqueville was waiting for new elections to enter politics, but he felt alienated from all the main players in the debate. Tocqueville could not envision being embroiled in the governmental electoral corruption his cousin Molé was so good at orchestrating. Temperamentally, he had no sympathy for Thiers. Guizot was not personally corrupt, merely complicit; Victor Hugo once suggested thinking of Guizot as an "honest woman running a brothel."[40] For Tocqueville, the issue was more concrete; Guizot had given up on the liberal agenda that had once inspired him. Tocqueville, who had not yet been elected to the Académie des sciences morales et politiques, was unwilling even to give Guizot credit for creating an institutional space for the political philosophy that had become his métier. Tocqueville could possibly see a rapprochement with Barrot, but he had serious misgivings about extending the franchise, a reform at the top of Barrot's agenda. He was too much of an elitist to give up his fear of the tyranny of the majority.

King Louis Philippe delayed authorizing Molé to dissolve the Chamber until October 3, and the election was scheduled for November 4, 1837. Tocqueville revealed his political aspirations to Royer-Collard, indicating that, while in Normandy, he had been cautiously talking to "lots of people belonging to the *pays légal*, as M. Guizot would say." He had been careful not to broach the topic of elections directly but, when asked, had signaled that he would gratefully accept a mandate if offered. Royer-Collard was not impressed. He confirmed the likelihood of an impending dissolution but advised Tocqueville that he thought of him as a man of high principles whose real calling was writing and that he should devote his undivided time to making the second volume of *Democracy in America* as important as the first. Moreover, he pointed out that Tocqueville's poor oratory ability, made worse by a voice that did not carry, would make it frustratingly difficult for him to perform in the Chamber.[41] Tocqueville resisted the advice, not because he was stubborn, although he was. He had a genuine desire to contribute to the historic change he was helping diagnose, believing he could do so without having to compromise with leaders he did not trust, but he had not figured out how to turn his ideas about democracy into a political program.

Prime Minister Molé tried hard to attract his young cousin, whom he admired, to the government coalition, which he was committed to enlarging with a campaign of public relations. The duc d'Orléans's marriage to the duchess Hélène de Mecklenburg-Schwerin (on May 30, 1837), the outcome of elaborate negotiations with several European courts, served Molé's purpose, becoming the occasion for liberal measures of reconciliation and national celebration in advance of an electoral campaign. These ranged from amnesty for political crimes to festivities surrounding the grand opening of King Louis Philippe's Musée de Versailles, which was dedicated to displaying "all the glories of France." Molé took these measures preceding Chamber dissolution with the hope that new elections would give the government a reliable majority.[42]

Favors followed. First, Tocqueville and Beaumont received from Minister of Public Instruction Narcisse de Salvandy, by order of the king, the splendid inventory of Egyptian monuments compiled during Napoleon's 1798 expedition (published in twenty-two volumes between 1802 and 1830). The official reason for the gift was to recognize that the two had conducted the American penitentiary work on behalf of the French government at their own expense.[43] Then came the Légion d'Honneur at Salvandy's behest. The government had included Tocqueville and Beaumont among personalities recognized with this honor on the occasion of the duc d'Orléans's marriage. The two friends seriously considered declining "this piece of ribbon whose price is servility," lest their political independence be jeopardized. Tocqueville was not about to "pin this rag on a buttonhole."[44] But in the end, they followed Royer-Collard's and Le Peletier d'Aunay's counsel and accepted the honor. Only hardline Legitimist Kergorlay argued for turning it down. Salvandy eventually presented the *croix* during a private visit to his office.[45]

Tocqueville simply refused to be "a pawn that you move surreptitiously."[46] After accepting the Egyptian book and then the Légion d'Honneur, he turned down the official invitation to attend Louis Philippe's new Versailles museum opening ceremony and banquet following. Tocqueville's failure to attend generated controversy. A political opponent in Normandy later accused Tocqueville of having played a double game, suggesting that Tocqueville had fabricated a medical excuse to justify his absence from the museum ceremonies in order not to offend officials while using his nonappearance as a sign of freedom from government. An infuriated Tocqueville responded to the slander by demanding an immediate retraction and even alluding to the possibility of a duel, as if a long-forgotten impulse from the aristocratic past had just resurfaced. The man recanted.[47]

With the decision to run for office, Tocqueville knew he had to position himself both politically and geographically. He explored electoral possibilities in Cherbourg, Paris, Versailles, and finally settled on Valognes, not far from the château. It is revealing to see how Tocqueville approached the electorate and what issues he was prepared to address in the various districts where he might be a candidate. Being independent was not enough; he also needed to navigate dirty electoral politics and make his own, concrete proposals—two areas in which the young Tocqueville lacked experience.

When meeting Eugène Stöffels in Metz on his way to Switzerland a year earlier, Tocqueville had defined his political position as that of a "liberal of a new kind," neither with "the friends of order" nor with the "dirty democrats of our age." Stöffels could not figure out what Tocqueville meant and was troubled to think his friend might be adopting American republican principles. Abstractly, Tocqueville wanted to see "the taste for liberty developed in all the political institutions" of the country, together with a "refined taste for justice, honest love of order, and a profound and reasonable attachment to morals and religious belief."[48] Tocqueville had explained this system in *Democracy in America*, but a complex book was not an easy program to circulate. Regular liberals had no patience for the elaborate reasoning of a "liberal of a new kind." Tocqueville realized this, telling Beaumont there were too few potential recruits "in the middle ground between enlightened men and the friends of order who have read my book and understood it."[49]

Tocqueville attempted therefore to adjust his political rhetoric to the different places where he might run. Cherbourg was a natural choice. Close to his château, it was a large port town with an important navy arsenal, commanding a strategic position on the English Channel. Tocqueville had set his sights on Cherbourg for a while. As early as the fall of 1836, Tocqueville had thought that the Cherbourg seat might become available. The local representative, the Bonapartist comte de Bricqueville, who, as it happened, was Hippolyte's brother-in-law, was in poor health and had indicated that he might be retiring. Tocqueville began identifying influential people and figuring out how to cultivate them. But replacing Bricqueville in Cherbourg was a long shot, even as a designated successor. Hippolyte Quenault, a well-entrenched competitor, had been trying to unseat Bricqueville since 1834, and he was using his position in the Justice Ministry to exchange government jobs for votes. This was a formidable advantage, as Tocqueville well knew, for "in Normandy as everywhere else in France, people are famished for patronage jobs, even the humblest ones. In the district of Cherbourg, all the jobs available to rural people—justices of the peace, tax collectors and the like—are granted through the spoils system."[50] Tocqueville considered Quenault an arrogant prig. Moreover, Quenault, born of a union between a local priest and a local nun, could count on a significant anticlerical vote in town, yet an additional reason for Tocqueville to try to defeat him![51] But Bricqueville did not step down in 1836 after all.

With the 1837 dissolution, Tocqueville turned his gaze on Cherbourg again as he hoped that Bricqueville would let him run in his place this time. He took the opportunity to explore in depth the life of workers at the navy arsenal whose interests he might represent. In England, Tocqueville had developed a new sensibility toward working-class life, and his curiosity about the associations they formed was a logical outcome of his work on associations in *Democracy in America*. Unlike the navy arsenal in Toulon, where socialist Flora Tristan would be actively proselytizing, there was no sign of radicalization in the Cherbourg arsenal. But workers' associations were spreading. No fewer than ten societies of mutual aid were founded at Cherbourg between 1836 and 1845.[52]

Tocqueville asked Beaumont, who was in England in May, to collect information on savings banks in Scotland and consult with statistician Charles Babbage in London on matters related to working-class life.[53] Tocqueville collected at the time many brochures on savings banks, friendly societies and loan societies in England and Scotland, and histories of savings banks as they were created, first in Switzerland in the late eighteenth century and in England and Scotland early in the nineteenth century. Benjamin Delessert opened the first one in France in 1818. Tocqueville annotated these brochures. He studied mathematician Charles Dupin's legislative testimony of 1834 and his lectures at the Conservatoire royal des arts et manufacture in 1837, which provided detailed information on workers' deposits in the savings banks of different departments. Tocqueville also studied closely the work of Félix de Viville in Metz, published in 1834, which proposed a system that would provide workers with low-interest loans and attractive returns on savings, an alternative to the exploitative practices of unregulated pawnshops. At Metz, Viville was in the unique position of heading both a pawnshop and the city's savings bank. A reformer, he stressed the philanthropic origins of the pawnshop, which he wanted to restore. He proposed utilizing workers' savings in one institution to make loans in the other, guaranteed by the security the borrower gave to the pawnshop, thus making the poor both lenders and borrowers. Tocqueville meant to promote this innovative idea with a second memoir on pauperism he was preparing for the Société académique de Cherbourg, where he had presented the first, but he never finished, read, or published it.[54]

All this preparation was for naught because electoral prospects at Cherbourg evaporated as Bricqueville, once again, declined to step down. Meanwhile, Quenault, promoted conseiller d'état, had expanded his patronage network, enabling him to defeat Bricqueville on election day.[55] In due course, however, Tocqueville would continue to investigate social issues in Normandy in ways that reflected a genuine commitment to social betterment.

Friends explored electoral possibilities in the tenth arrondissement of Paris (which included the Faubourg Saint-Germain), but these did not materialize either.[56] Prospects were brighter in Versailles, where his father had been prefect and where he had begun a career as apprentice magistrate in the courthouse. Tocqueville had kept his local friends and connections. From his Versailles days, he remained closest to Louis Bouchitté, a philosopher who taught at the local Collège Royal. Bouchitté had even read *Democracy in America* four successive times prior to publication.[57] Bouchitté's brother-in-law, Baudry de Balzac, owned a local newspaper, *La presse de Seine et Oise*, and Tocqueville had purchased a share to gain a platform for his views.

Tocqueville did not address local political issues concerning Versailles residents. He instead seized the opportunity to express his views on the colonization of Algeria, arguably the biggest national project of the day. He wrote two "letters" on Algeria, which appeared in *La presse de Seine et Oise* in June and August 1837. There was nothing startling about his position: he joined a near-complete national consensus, from Guizot to Louis Blanc, in heralding colonization as national glory.[58] As he put it, "with time, perseverance, ability, and justice, I have no doubt that we shall be able to raise a great monument to our country's glory on the African coast."[59] The letters are the first public declaration of Tocqueville as an ardent colonialist.

Tocqueville had a long-standing interest in the conquest of Algeria dating back to his friend Kergorlay's participation in the military invasion. Already in 1833, with the conquest still incomplete but with the prospect of colonization in the not-too-distant future, Tocqueville and Kergorlay had thought of investing in Algeria by acquiring fertile land on the presumably safe hillside of Algiers and attracting settlers. They had not pursued the project, but Tocqueville had been sufficiently intrigued to seek out noted orientalist Silvestre de Sacy and ask him how difficult it would be to learn common Arabic and for advice on what to read.⁶⁰

Tocqueville conceived of his letters as a response to pamphlets by representative Amédée Desjobert (Seine maritime) that had espoused a minority view that colonialism was incompatible with representative institutions.⁶¹ Tocqueville saw Algeria as a great outlet for French settlers fleeing the life of mediocrity imposed by the July Monarchy. In Algeria they would find the opportunities denied them at home. He penned the letters in the months between General Bugeaud's Tafna peace treaty with Abd-el-Kader and the French army's successful assault on Constantine and expressed optimism for a successful colonization. Without drawing the obvious parallel with the settlement of the American West one might have expected from him, Tocqueville nevertheless adopted a line of reasoning he had first heard from white American pioneers. He remarked there was plenty of land available in Algeria, for "the Arab population is quite sparse; it occupies much more terrain than it can possibly cultivate every year. The consequence is that the Arabs sell land readily and cheaply, and that a foreign population can easily establish itself next to them without causing them to suffer."

Tocqueville had not visited Algeria any more than Desjobert. He conveniently ignored the multiple civil, religious, and political conflicts on the ground between French military and civilian authorities and between French and local populations. This allowed him to foster an unrealistic hope for a peaceful blending of French with local Berber and Arabic populations, which he believed would take place as long as some basic rules were followed. Tocqueville criticized how Ottoman janissaries had remained aloof from the population, just collecting taxes, despite a mixed population of kouloughlis (the offspring of intermarriage between janissaries and Arab women). He imagined that in French Algeria, the different populations would eventually "melt into a larger whole" despite their initial cultural differences, but he went no further in explaining how this would happen. He was content to declare, "If only the political leadership is common to both races but everything else is different for a long time, fusion will come at last, of its own accord." He would in time have to drastically revise this poorly informed and utopian prediction.

Verneuil château, near Paris, where Alexis de Tocqueville spent part of his childhood.
(Archives départementales des Yvelines)

Louise Madeleine de Tocqueville.
(Archives départementales, Maison de l'histoire
de la Manche; photo Alexandre Poirier)

Alexis de Tocqueville as a child.
(Archives départementales, Maison de l'histoire
de la Manche; photo Alexandre Poirier)

A family scene:
Hervé de Tocqueville tutoring his
son Alexis; Louise-Madeleine with
Édouard, Alexis's older brother.
(Archives départementales, Maison
de l'histoire de la Manche; photo
Alexandre Poirier)

The prefecture at Metz, where Alexis lived with his father, prefect of the Moselle département.
(Archives Moselle)

Alexis de Tocqueville is awarded
first prize in Latin composition
while in high school in Metz.
(Archives départementales, Maison
de l'histoire de la Manche)

INSTRUCTION PUBLIQUE.

ACADÉMIE DE METZ.

COLLÉGE ROYAL DE METZ.

CLASSE *de rhétorique.*

M. *Mougin* — Professeur.

LE Proviseur certifie que l'Elève
*charles alexis de Tocqueville*
a obtenu le *1er* prix de *discours*
*latin ( prix d'honneur )*
à la distribution générale et solennelle
de l'année classique 1821 – 1822.

*Le Proviseur du Collége royal,*

Hervé de Tocqueville.
(Archives départementales, Maison de l'histoire
de la Manche; photo Alexandre Poirier)

Louis de Kergorlay, Alexis's cousin and childhood
friend. (Bibliothèque nationale de France)

Alexis de Tocqueville.
(Yale Tocqueville manuscripts, 1802–1860,
Beinecke Rare Book and Manuscript Library)

Mary Mottley, Alexis's future wife.
(Bibliothèque nationale de France)

Gustave de Beaumont's rendering of himself and Alexis de Tocqueville at Lake Oneida in the Mohawk valley, New York. (Yale Tocqueville manuscripts, 1802–1860, Beinecke Rare Book and Manuscript Library)

Gustave de Beaumont's drawing of the church in Stockbridge, Massachusetts. (Yale Tocqueville manuscripts, 1802–1860, Beinecke Rare Book and Manuscript Library)

Gustave de Beaumont's drawing of Eastern State Penitentiary, Philadelphia.
(Yale Tocqueville manuscripts, 1802–1860, Beinecke Rare Book and Manuscript Library)

Gustave de Beaumont's drawing of Choctaws crossing of the Mississippi, which the two
travelers witnessed. (Yale Tocqueville manuscripts, 1802–1860, Beinecke Rare Book and
Manuscript Library)

Jared Sparks by Rembrandt Peale, c. 1819.
(Harvard University Portrait Collection,
Bequest of Lizzie Sparks Pickering)

Virginie Ancelot.
(Bibliothèque nationale de France)

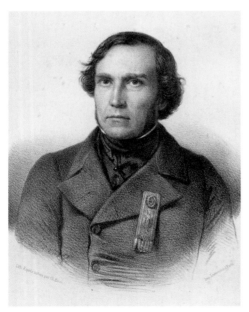

Gustave de Beaumont.
(Archives départementales, Maison de l'histoire de
la Manche; photo Alexandre Poirier)

Francisque de Corcelle.
(Alamy)

Jean-Jacques Ampère.
(Bibliothèque nationale de France)

John Stuart Mill.
(Bibliothèque nationale de France)

Nassau Senior by Henry Wyndham Phillips, 1855.
(National Portrait Gallery, London;
Art Resource, New York)

Sofia Swetchine
(Bibliothèque nationale de France)

Tocqueville château.
(Archives départementales, Maison de l'histoire de la Manche)

Alexis de Tocqueville's study at Tocqueville.
(Archives départementales, Maison de l'histoire de la Manche; photo Alexandre Poirier)

Théodore Chasseriau's Moorish women. (Bibliothèque nationale de France)

Théodore Chasseriau's Arab horsemen.
(Bibliothèque nationale de France)

Léon Juchault de Lamoricière,
the only general Tocqueville trusted.
(Bibliothèque nationale de France)

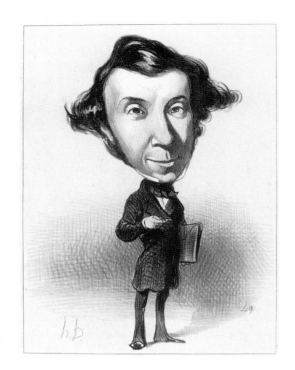

Alexis de Tocqueville by Honoré Daumier, 1849. (National Gallery of Art, Washington, DC)

Pierre-Joseph Proudhon by Honoré Daumier, 1849. (National Gallery of Art, Washington, DC)

Adolphe Thiers by Honoré Daumier, 1849. (National Gallery of Art, Washington, DC)

Odilon Barrot by Honoré Daumier, 1849. (National Gallery of Art, Washington, DC)

Tocqueville's briefcase.
(Archives départementales, Maison de l'histoire de la Manche; photo Alexandre Poirier)

The newspaper *Le Commerce*, the first issue under Tocqueville's leadership.
The text reads, "The newspaper *Le Commerce* is now under a new management."
(Archives départementales, Maison de l'histoire de la Manche; photo Alexandre Poirier)

*[Handwritten table of contents, in French]*

1° Moniteurs du 21, 22 et 23 février 1837 qui contiennent une discussion très importante sur les caisses d'épargnes — celle où le danger de l'accumulation des capitaux des caisses dans les mains de l'état est traité.

2° La caisse d'épargne et les ouvriers (1837) Charles Dupin.

3° Divers Documents sur la caisse d'épargne de Metz.

4° Des banques d'épargne pour Niville (1834)

5° recherches sur l'origine de l'institution des caisses d'épargne par de candolle. (1834)

6° Les caisses d'épargne de la Suisse par le même.

7° Divers Documents sur la caisse d'épargne de Genève.

8° Tableau général de la situation des caisses d'épargnes en angleterre, et irelande en 1831.

9° Divers Documents sur les caisses d'épargne d'angleterre.

10° La loi anglaise des caisses d'épargne.

Tocqueville's handwritten table of contents of a volume of brochures on workers' savings banks. (Archives départementales, Maison de l'histoire de la Manche; photo Alexandre Poirier)

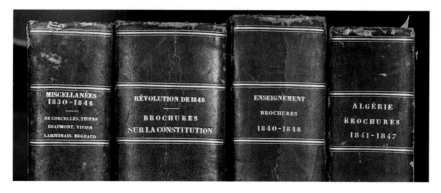

Four bound volumes of brochures Tocqueville kept in his library.
(Archives départementales, Maison de l'histoire de la Manche; photo Alexandre Poirier)

Théodore Chassériau's official portrait of Alexis de Tocqueville, 1850.
(RMN/Grand Palais; Art Resource, New York)

Tocqueville warned accurately, however, that simply imposing French social and political norms on native Algerians was bound to fail. "Above all, in Algeria," he wrote, "we must take care to give up this taste for uniformity that torments us, and to realize that it would be as dangerous as it is absurd to apply the same laws to different beings." Tocqueville advised the government that "tribal organization" was "the most tenacious of all human institutions" and cannot "be taken from them . . . without overturning all their sentiments and ideas." He added, "The Arabs name their own leaders; we must preserve this privilege. They have a military and religious aristocracy; we must by no means seek to destroy this."[62]

In the end, Tocqueville ran in neither Cherbourg nor Versailles but Valognes, another electoral district about fifteen miles away from the château, where local electors actively recruited him to the race.[63] Once drafted, Tocqueville became committed to Valognes. The political sociology of that rural district rather than colonization came now to dictate his political strategy. This was familiar ground for Tocqueville, away from either workers or colonists. The arrondissement of Valognes included the cantons of Valognes, Barneville, Bricquebec, Montebourg, Quettehou, Sainte-Mère-Église, and Saint-Saveur-le-Vicomte. There were only 457 votes cast in 1837, which meant that one out of about thirty adult males voted. Three-quarters of voters were *agriculteurs* (rich farmers, landowners, and livestock ranchers). Among the remainder, 7 percent were bureaucrats, 10 percent belonged to liberal professions, another 8 percent were merchants running local businesses, and all of these were wealthy owners of real estate. Half of the constituency paid a *cens* between 200 and 300 francs, but 11 percent paid more than 1,000 francs.[64] Tocqueville reminded his correspondents that the electors belonged to a "small number of enlightened and independent men"[65] while also telling them that "the gradual development of democratic institutions is the great event of our times."[66] The reality was that a legislature constrained by such a limited electoral system was highly unlikely to deliver a democratic revolution.

Not being in residence, Tocqueville reached out to select voters who had positions of importance in Valognes and relied on them for greater contact with the electorate. Paul Clamorgan, a liberal lawyer, became his most important electoral agent. Tocqueville also interacted with Auguste-Irénée Moulin, mayor and conseiller général of Bricquebec; Honoré Langlois, who also sat on the Conseil général and became his personal lawyer; as well as Zacharie Gallemand, Jacques-François Hervieu, and Jacques Louis Auguste Marie-Deslongchamps, who all sat on the Conseil d'arrondissement. "It's for the likes of you that I work," he told Moulin. The reverse was also true. Tocqueville's contacts did considerable electoral work on his behalf with the "wood merchants and butchers" who would decide the election.[67]

On October 14, 1837, Tocqueville distributed an electoral circular in which he outlined a modest program.[68] Again, he was prudent and conservative. He informed electors that he had now settled at nearby Tocqueville and suggested, as he had done earlier for the Conseil général, that they read his book on America to know his program. They would find him to be an advocate of gradual change, an enemy of revolution, and a defender of freedom of the press and of association, both freedoms being necessary for citizens to express themselves and to act in concert. Tocqueville did not believe in or propose an extension of the suffrage despite his published commitment to democracy, but he advocated fighting electoral corruption. He also came out against the lavish subsidies that the government had granted to King Louis Philippe's family.

Tocqueville's opponent, Jules Polydor Le Marois, already occupied the seat. He was a wealthy local figure, whose father had been Napoleon's aide de camp and enriched himself from the spoils of war. Le Marois spared no expense wining and dining electors in local taverns, exciting their anti-Legitimist feelings and rallying them under the banner "no nobles."[69]

Molé, who did not give up easily, ordered the prefect to ask civil servants to vote for Tocqueville. Learning of this step, an indignant Tocqueville, who had waged war on government corruption, immediately notified Molé that he intended to gain the seat on his own merit, without government support, and insisted Molé give instructions accordingly.[70] Molé had no option but to allow Minister of the Interior Camille de Montalivet to support Le Marois, who professed to be supporting the government while pledging his loyalty to Barrot's dynastic left. *Le Siècle* exposed Le Marois's persistent duplicity, but Tocqueville remained stubbornly independent.[71] An exasperated Molé warned him that "isolation is not independence."[72]

As the election neared, an elector pointed out the vagueness of Tocqueville's program, which was designed to alienate neither Republicans nor Legitimists, the latter voting for him because of his name and family history. It was an astute criticism, for in fact, Tocqueville needed their combined support to challenge Le Marois. Unfortunately, Tocqueville's response would attract neither party. He declared that he wanted to improve constitutional monarchy, which neither Republicans nor Legitimists had an interest in.[73] A second attack prompted Tocqueville to write a response, but the local postmaster, a supporter of Le Marois, failed to send out Tocqueville's rebuttal. Tocqueville eventually had the postmaster reprimanded, but it was too late. He lost the election, with 210 votes to Le Marois's 247. It was a respectable score, Tocqueville assured Royer-Collard. He was now well known in Valognes, to which he would regularly return to keep his prospects alive.[74]

Tocqueville finally won his seat in the Chamber in March 1839 after another Chamber dissolution offered a second chance to run for office. No major issue had been resolved since 1837. By then, Thiers, Barrot, and Guizot had formed a temporary but powerful coalition dedicated to ending Molé's government and creating a Chamber more independent of the crown. For a while, the Chamber narrowly continued to support Molé, but eventually gridlock set in. Lamartine captured the depressing political climate in an address to the king from the Chamber in January 1839, famously claiming, "France is bored. You have let the country sink into lethargy."[75]

Only a month before the 1839 dissolution, Chateaubriand had knocked at Tocqueville's door unannounced to hear Tocqueville read excerpts from his manuscript in progress.[76] The old man was satisfied, but Tocqueville struggled to keep writing with his mind on the election. After five or six hours, he told Beaumont, "the machine will not run."[77] With new elections announced, Tocqueville advised Beaumont also to put aside his book on Ireland and get back to Paris to meet with politicians he needed if he were to launch a campaign of his own. "This is our big chance. . . . It would be a terrible shame to lose it."[78]

Tocqueville ran again in Valognes, where he was now a known quantity. He also learned some lessons from his first campaign.[79] He claimed loudly and clearly that he was not a Legitimist and that he favored the separation of church and state, as in America.[80] His Legitimist family publicly confirmed that Tocqueville was speaking the truth.[81] His message regarding his personal loyalties was unambiguous: "They tell you that because I belong to an old family I want to bring the country back to the old prejudices, to the old privileges, and the old ways: these are not only odious but ridiculous calumnies." We must "without exiting monarchy, arrive slowly but surely at a government of the country by the country."[82] Tocqueville ran again without party support. He challenged the government as an independent, not as a member of the Thiers-Barrot-Guizot coalition that had overcome Molé's government.

Le Marois was to pay for his earlier duplicity. Although Thiers continued to support him, Barrot did not trust him any longer, and no amount of pleading by Le Marois gained him Barrot's support.[83] In addition, Tocqueville had adopted a few tricks from Le Marois's playbook. Not only had he bought real estate in Valognes, but he had also established residence at the central Hôtel du Louvre during the campaign. He visited with electors and asked Marie to meet their wives.[84] He even financed a few rounds of electoral gastronomy, as he called it.[85] On March 2, Tocqueville, who had this time conducted a respectable get-out-the-vote campaign (though he had still never defined a strong political program), soundly defeated Le Marois, 318 to 240, in the first round of voting. He then pledged to serve all the residents of Valognes, whether they were voters or not.[86] Exhausted, he moved to Tocqueville to rest only to be besieged by visitors and buried under a huge pile of letters. Rest would wait. At the prospect of entering the Chamber, Tocqueville wrote to Beaumont, "Over the next six months, I am going to play the game of my life."[87] To Uncle Rosanbo, upset at his nephew for having betrayed the Legitimist cause, Tocqueville wrote that he was following his conscience by working for "the greater political good of his

compatriots."[88] At the same time, he worried that his political responsibilities would interfere with completing volume 2: "I must at all costs
finish this book. It and I have a duel to the death—I must kill it, or it
must kill me."[89]

## Tocqueville as Writer

Ever since the publication of *Democracy in America*, Tocqueville had
contemplated an ambitious sequel in which he would articulate an overarching theory of democracy, as bold as his political campaign was
timid. But first he honorably set about satisfying other writing commitments he had made. In 1836, before going to Switzerland, Tocqueville
made good on his promise to Mill to contribute to his journal. Mill had
welcomed the translation of *Democracy in America*, and Tocqueville was
eager to show his gratitude. He sent his *État social et politique de la France
avant et après 1789* via diplomatic mail in February 1836. Although
Tocqueville had to put off work on the second volume, this essay shows
that he was working on its themes. The essay was in part a continued
reflection on the opposing fortunes of the British and French aristocracy. Tocqueville conceded the superiority of the British aristocracy for
"making the democratic classes believe for so long that the common
enemy was the prince." This is how the British aristocracy, he explained,
was spared the fate of its French counterpart, which was destroyed by a
powerful alliance between French kings and the people against the local
nobility. Building on his personal observations during his time in
England, Tocqueville criticized the way that legal equality in England
too often coexisted with social inequality. He presented the French as
having followed the opposite route. The French crown had formally
maintained legal inequality by keeping the privileges of the nobility intact but, unlike in England, social equality had progressed in France. It
would not be long for the hated privileges to be challenged. With the
French Revolution dramatically accelerating access to landownership,
mores inevitably became more democratic because "there is nothing
more favorable to the reign of democracy than the division of the land
into small independent properties." This is how France became, early

on, "the most really democratic nation of Europe," a point Tocqueville would assert again, much later, in his book on the Ancien Régime.

In the essay, Tocqueville drew a sharp distinction between "aristocratic" and "modern" liberty. Unlike aristocratic liberty, modern liberty was not an egoist claim of privilege but the outcome of a right more broadly shared as society became more equal and distinction of ranks faded. "Every man [is] presumed to have received from nature the intelligence necessary for his own general guidance, is inherently entitled to be uncontrolled by his fellows in all that only concerns himself, and to regulate at his own will his own destiny." Tocqueville asserted, it is "the modern, the democratic, and, we venture to say, the only just notion of liberty." He would emphasize that point repeatedly in the second volume of *Democracy in America*. Mill and John Bowring translated the essay and published it in the April 1, 1836 issue of the *London and Westminster Review*.[90] Mill asked for additional contributions from Tocqueville, and he managed to extract a few book reviews, but Tocqueville made it clear to his British friend that he now had to devote his energy to his second volume.

Yet there was another task pending. With renewed talk of prison building and reform in governmental circles, Tocqueville and Beaumont felt they had a chance to influence policy with a new edition of the penitentiary report. Tocqueville had a conversation in late 1835 with Thiers, who was then minister of the interior, on a French government's plan for a 200-cell jail in Limoges and a military prison in the Saint-Germain-en-Laye château.[91] As a trusted expert, he accompanied Thiers's successor, comte de Montalivet, to the prison de la Roquette and showed him American prison floor plans William Crawford had reproduced in his book.[92] He recommended prisoners be kept in individual cells and that architects refrain from excessively adorning monumental structures.[93]

Tocqueville had left Beaumont to write most of the original report, but this time he was concerned about how it would be received and personally composed much of the new preface they appended to the second edition. They noted that modern judicial systems were increasingly reluctant to use the death penalty; it was carried out only in remote places where "the executioner hides like a wanted man."[94] They came out strongly against penal colonies, declaring that England should no longer send convicts to barbaric Australian camps from which they could sometimes escape. With imprisonment the only future of punishment, they advanced the idea that it should be a route to rehabilitation.

Tocqueville and Beaumont were still not ready to recommend the Philadelphia system of twenty-four-hour isolation, but they came close. For economic reasons, they advocated for a version of the Auburn system instituted at Wethersfield, which prescribed isolation only at night and removed the whip. Reformers in other countries were advocating a similar path. William Crawford, following in Tocqueville and Beaumont's footsteps in England, had also investigated American prisons and endorsed the cellular system of solitary imprisonment, and the British parliament had adopted it. Support for this idea also came also from Nikolaus Julius in Germany.

It is only in 1838 that Tocqueville and Beaumont finally decided to advocate the Philadelphia system of complete isolation in full. By then, another French reformer, Frédéric-Auguste Demetz, had gone to Philadelphia and reported not only that solitary confinement did no harm to the sanity or health of the prisoners but that officials at Wethersfield had restored use of the whip, without which they could not ensure silence and order in gang work. Even though Demetz "hated America" and "condemned everything in three months," said Tocqueville, his report on prisons was valuable and the combined weight of Crawford, Julius, and Demetz pushed him for good into the Philadelphia camp.[95]

In anticipation of implementing reform in French prisons, Interior Minister Montalivet circulated a questionnaire regarding the treatment of prisoners to the Conseil général of each department, thus reviving the debate between proponents of the Auburn and Philadelphia systems of incarceration.[96] Upon receiving it, Honoré Langlois, a member of the Conseil général for La Manche and Tocqueville's personal lawyer, sought Tocqueville's opinion and then took it on himself, without notifying Tocqueville, to publish in the local press the full endorsement of the Philadelphia system Tocqueville privately sent. The national press immediately reprinted it, and it became public knowledge.[97]

Tocqueville apologized to Beaumont for not having consulted him before distributing these views, but Beaumont agreed with Tocqueville's assessment.[98] Not everybody did, however. Léon Faucher, author of the first published review of *Democracy in America* and a respected prison expert, maintained that solitary confinement would affect the mental and physical health of prisoners. Well-known prison expert Charles Lucas also took a definite position against the Philadelphia system. Prison reform would remain the object of tense policy debates that intensified in the 1840s.[99]

All this time, Tocqueville's reputation as an author and reformer only grew. In 1838, the "jolly fat man," as Tocqueville called Gosselin, his publisher, was already sending to press the tenth printing of *Democracy in America*.[100] The Académie des sciences morales et politiques became interested in attracting the rising star among its members. The founding of this organization, in 1832, had been Guizot's dream since the Restoration. His idea was to revive a section of the Institut de France that First Consul Bonaparte—whom Tocqueville deemed "one of the greatest adversaries of human freedom the world had ever known"—had abolished because he deemed its members ideologues and dreamers.[101] Loosely allied with the state, Guizot's new Académie was to be a bastion of free, though nonrevolutionary, thought. Its purpose was to undertake research for the government, promoting the study of history and economics to inspire more principled political action. The Académie did not play a pivotal role in the political or intellectual debates of the nation, but it recognized and publicized important studies, such as Villermé's statistical works on hygiene and Villeneuve-Bargemont's on poverty that influenced Tocqueville's first memoir on pauperism.

At the invitation of the Académie des sciences morales et politiques, Tocqueville made a presentation to its members in 1836 entitled *Mémoire sur l'influence du point de départ sur les sociétés*. Using the opportunity to draw attention to ideas expressed in *Democracy in America*, he based the lecture on its first chapter.[102] The members were impressed. Philosopher Victor Cousin even advanced Tocqueville's name for election, unbeknownst to Tocqueville, although the proposal did not garner enough support. Historian François Mignet, however, pursued the idea.

When Pierre Laromiguière, one of the members of the older generation, died in 1837, there was a vacancy in the philosophy section. To attract Tocqueville, the Académie transferred Théodore Jouffroy to the philosophy section to free up a seat in the morality section that would be appropriate for Tocqueville. Tocqueville read of the effort to recruit him in a newspaper and wrote to Mignet that he did not wish to offend the members but did not want to appear to be seeking the seat. Ambitious as he was, young Tocqueville had already set his sights on the Académie française. He did not want his election to a lower branch of the Institut de France to diminish his chances of joining the group of "immortals" later, and he said so openly. In Parisian salons, it was quickly rumored that the great-grandson of Malesherbes did not want to be associated with a less prestigious institution.[103]

The Académie des sciences morales et politiques elected Tocqueville in early January 1838 by a vote of twenty to two, "against my will" (as Tocqueville protested, perhaps too much, to Royer-Collard).[104] He was nonetheless gratified that a vote for him was one against fellow prison reformer Charles Lucas, who had systematically attacked Tocqueville and Beaumont's penitentiary report. Mignet, full of good intentions, was naturally taken aback when Tocqueville subsequently informed him that he was too busy to attend sessions at the Académie. "I have withdrawn to the country for a few months in order to finish in peace the second and final portion of my work on democracy in America," Tocqueville wrote him. "It will be several more months before I will get the chance to return to Paris." Tocqueville attended only six of fifty meetings in 1838 and gave no public readings or lectures, despite the urging of Mignet.[105] Ultimately, though, Tocqueville would realize the benefit of membership and would play a significant role in the Académie's development, justifying Mignet's gamble.

## The Grand Theory

All along, Tocqueville expected to make great strides in writing the second volume of Democracy in America and offering the world his grand theory of democracy as a guide. With this book, he wanted "to bring forth liberty from the midst of the democratic society in which God has decreed we must live."[106] The goal was uplifting but the work slow and twice interrupted by political campaigns. To escape distractions in Paris and the discomfort of home renovation at Tocqueville, Tocqueville took frequent refuge in the comfort of Baugy, Édouard and Alexandrine's estate near Compiègne, where he could write. "I enclose myself in a kind of *donjon*," he reported to Royer-Collard. "In fact, a more modest pigeon coop of sorts that I have fashioned under the roof of the château. There I am suspended between heaven and earth, and the stirrings of the house do not reach up to me."[107] Away from distractions, Tocqueville attempted to build a theory of democracy no longer specifically rooted in America but in a broader, more generalizable process of political and social change. Would he succeed in explaining the basis of a new social state? It remained to be seen, he told Royer-Collard, whether readers will prefer "America to me."[108]

It is difficult to trace the writing of successive parts of the second volume of *Democracy in America* with accuracy. Only rarely did Tocqueville note the date on his drafts. Most of the time, he wrote on loose leaves of paper that he kept reshuffling as he reworked his ideas. As he explained to Mill, "My mind is full of things of which I can discern no clear order and I struggle to draw out my ideas one by one; I want to run but I can barely drag myself along. You know that I do not write mechanically or with a mad drive towards predetermined objectives. I follow the natural flow of my ideas, allowing me to be guided in good faith by the logic of the arguments. The result is that so long as the volume is not finished, I know not where I am going, nor if I will ever get there. This sense of doubt ends up being unbearable."[109]

After Switzerland, Tocqueville applied himself "like the devil" to make up for lost time. "I have never written with so much ardor in my life; I think about my project day and night," he wrote to Reeve from Baugy.[110] When called to Paris for jury duty, he fumed at the interruption and wondered how he could ever have praised the jury system as a school of democracy.[111] Appointed to a Comité des travaux historiques (committee on historical publications) by Education Minister Salvandy, he never showed up for meetings.[112] Tocqueville found a productive routine at

Baugy. He was at his desk at six in the morning and worked for four hours. He then took a three-to-four-hour break with exercise and returned to work for another three-to-four-hour writing stint before dinner. He told Beaumont, with an unusually optimistic outlook, "I am moving very slowly but I am doing reasonably good work. But I am missing companionship and conversation. I wish you or Louis were here."[113]

Tocqueville continued during the next two years of writing to carve out periods of intensive reading. At one point, he told Beaumont, "It's been years since I have read this much and thought so much about what I am reading."[114] He enlisted his close friends to talk about books and ideas. When missing conversation with Kergorlay, who had advised him to read closely Pascal, Montesquieu, and Rousseau, Tocqueville expressed his appreciation by telling his friend he was "missing a fourth, which is you."[115]

In volume 2 of *Democracy in America*, Tocqueville was no longer analyzing the United States of the 1830s but comparing the two distinct "social states" of aristocracy and democracy. He had purported at first to be impartial, but he progressively became ambivalent toward both social states. In a note to himself during a revealing moment of introspection, he admitted to being an aristocrat at heart who had become a democrat by reason. "I am aristocratic by instinct," he wrote, but "I have an intellectual preference for democratic institutions."[116] Tocqueville spelled out his inner conflict as an exemplar of the crucial social conflict of his day.

Ever critical, Tocqueville came down hard on both worlds. He exposed aristocrats as living in soundproof chambers away from the noise of everyday people. As a result, they showed no empathy for people not of their class. Madame de Sévigné, for example, who looked on public hangings as a spectator sport, "had no clear notion of what it meant to suffer when one was not a nobleman."[117] This was the kind of callousness that justified revolutions. Conversely, Tocqueville saw democratic men and women ignoring people in need around them while declaring empathy for humanity, an impulse perhaps generous in spirit but devoid of specific commitments. In democratic times, Tocqueville saw an "excessive weakening of the parts of society against the whole." "This is one of my central opinions," he wrote to Reeve, when the young lawyer from London was putting the final touches on the English translation of volume 2.[118]

Tocqueville rearranged the organization of the second volume several times. In 1835, he had announced a book entirely on "habits, ideas, and mores."[119] He was true to his words in only two of the book's four parts: part 1 on the "influence of democracy on the evolution of the American intellect" and part 3 on the "influence of democracy on mores properly so-called." In part 2 on the "influence of democracy on the sentiments of the Americans," Tocqueville provided the most focused exposition of his theory of democracy, while he reserved part 4 "on the influence that democratic ideas and sentiments exert on political society" for a general assessment of the value of democracy.

In exposing his core theory of democracy, in part 2, Tocqueville largely reiterated the relationship between equality and liberty already proposed in 1835. Tocqueville was concerned about repeating himself, but he could not avoid it; it was the "necessary result of such a large work done in two stages."[120] He explained in abstract but carefully reasoned terms: "One can imagine an extreme point at which liberty and equality touch and become one. Suppose that all citizens take part in government and that each has an equal right to do so. Since no man will then be different from his fellow men, no one will be able to exercise a tyrannical power. Men will be perfectly free, because they will all be entirely equal, and they will all be perfectly equal because they will be entirely free. This is the ideal toward which democratic peoples tend."[121] But in the real world, Tocqueville insisted, people desired equality so much that they were willing to sacrifice their political liberty for it. They would rather limit opportunity for all than see some people getting ahead at the expense of others. To combat this degrading form of submissiveness, one had to work constantly at keeping political liberty alive. Tocqueville expressed again his sense that liberty was fragile and all too easily sacrificed to the drive for equality. This was the axiom on which he built his new political science.

In these central chapters, Tocqueville formulated his tightest and most abstract theoretical statements contrasting aristocracy and democracy. Gone were the specific examples that peppered volume 1. In carefully crafted propositions, Tocqueville explained how individualism broke asunder the aristocratic chain of solidarity among men. Tocqueville was among the first authors to use the word *individualism*. We can date his first use of it in a manuscript note on philosophical method on April 24, 1837.[122] To him, America was the perfect field for individualism. Where else had the fixed positions of traditional societies so completely disappeared? The American was an individualist, whose obsession with wealth was beginning to be heralded as a national trait. Tocqueville suggested his busyness may not have been based in greed but rather was a means of avoiding the moral misery Pascal ascribed to restlessness.[123]

Yet the same American saved himself from the danger of imprisoning himself "in the loneliness of his own heart" by his long practice of political liberty.[124] Associations, in Tocqueville's great theoretical scheme, were engines of liberty. In volume 2, Tocqueville extended his discussion to civil associations in addition to political ones and labeled the art of association "the fundamental science."[125] Associations functioned as the source of education and base for action. By coming together, like-minded citizens exercised their freedom of action. By regrouping "into a multitude of small private societies,"[126] they mustered means not available to any individual. In small groups, they better achieved their personal as well as collective goals. Thanks to their associational habits, democratic citizens might avoid the dangers of homogenization.

Tocqueville went significantly beyond what he had said in 1835 in other ways. For the first time, he established a strong positive connection between "self-interest" and collective betterment. He labeled the mechanism "self-interest properly understood."[127] In his travels, he saw Americans fending only for themselves. But he later posited instead an "enlightened love" of oneself that could lead people to "sacrifice a portion of their time and wealth" to the common good.[128] Using language from Montesquieu, Tocqueville speculated that in America (read democracy), "interest" had replaced "virtue" as the motivation for working for the community, and that was the wave of the future. Turning self-interest into a benefit for all, Tocqueville argued, was a positive development for civilization because, as an impulse, it was in much greater supply than virtue. One could not be more tolerant of human weakness.

As part of his effort to define a new political science, Tocqueville meant to expand the Franco-American comparison that informed volume 1 by introducing a tertium quid—England. Tocqueville asked Beaumont to provide him with a summary of Michel Chevalier's study of the Lowell textile mills, which he combined with his own extensive observations of industrial England to write in May 1847 a chapter on the threat a new industrial aristocracy posed to democracy.[129]

Tocqueville preceded this theoretical part 2 with a discussion of democracy's impact on the life of the intellect. In part 1, Tocqueville argued that Americans (individualists and Democrats) believed only in their own reason—they were products of a de facto Cartesianism. You could detect it easily in reading their books or listening to their speeches. Nowadays, poets turned primarily to personal introspection to represent mankind. They claimed, "I have only to consider myself."[130]

Tocqueville extrapolated from this observation that authors in a democratic society reason only about general causes, while in an aristocratic society, they focus on superior individuals. He borrowed from marquis de Lafayette the idea that historians in democratic centuries outlined only general causes of change. Following this trend, democratic orators abandoned precise words for generic words.[131] In these chapters, Tocqueville was at times guilty of the reification he exposed—that is, of turning "equality into a living being." He admitted attributing to "social state and political constitution" more than they were likely to be responsible for. He recognized having "personified equality in several places," saying "that equality did certain things or refrained from doing certain others."[132]

In his chapters on mores in the book's third part, Tocqueville was especially interested in gender roles. He saw that the same great "social movement that is bringing son and father, servant and master, and in general, inferior and superior closer to the same level is raising woman and will make her more and more the equal of man," albeit fulfilling clearly distinct roles.[133] During his summer 1837 visit, Corcelle suggested that Tocqueville make his thoughts on the influence of equality on morals clearer.[134] Tocqueville rewrote the chapter on the equality of men and women in democracy shortly after Corcelle's departure and read the new version, in August 1837, to the Beaumonts, who seemed very satisfied with it.[135] The more conservative American feminists who had faith in separate spheres as a means of equality between men and women were pleased, too. In *A Treatise on Domestic Economy for the Use of Young Ladies at Home, and at School*, published in 1842, Catherine Beecher approved effusively of Tocqueville's specific understanding of the division of labor between sexes. It helped that Tocqueville had concluded that the "superiority" of American women was "primarily responsible for the singular prosperity and growing power of this people."[136]

Tocqueville moved on to a chapter on manners, "a difficult subject for me," he told Corcelle, "as I am never comfortable in the little details of private life. So, I will be short. I hope to have finished in eight days or so and to then be able to get into the big chapters which end the book."[137] But when Tocqueville returned to the manuscript at Baugy in early 1838, after his electoral defeat, he stumbled. He had difficulty theorizing the impact of democracy on ambition. Kergorlay came to spend four days with him and helped him out. At that time, Tocqueville reminisced with Beaumont, "I was ensnared in a tangled web of ideas from which I could not free myself. It was a real intellectual dead-end, and he helped me out of it in a matter of hours."[138] Overall, progress remained slow. Tocqueville's spirits lagged even as he was drafting, in March 1838, an ultimately famous chapter on why revolutions become rare when comfort comes to be the purpose of life.[139] It was a powerful argument that Tocqueville released as a separate essay "Des révolutions dans les sociétés nouvelles" in *Revue des deux mondes* in mid-April 1840, just as the book was coming out. The prediction may have appeared fantastical amid a backdrop of successive riots threatening the regime, but Tocqueville presented it quite logically. What Tocqueville meant was that equal conditions bred identical ideas and interests and therefore narrowed the possibilities of revolution. One should therefore not fear the extension of civil liberties—freedom of speech and freedom of association—if there were no threat of revolution. We could regard liberty with serenity and not indulge in repression.

Tocqueville was still complaining to Corcelle in June 1838 that he worked slowly and tediously, besieged by house renovations. "Finishing my book is crushing me and will assuredly give me jaundice if I don't find the momentum to finish it."[140] Tocqueville finally did but only after the deliberate interruption of the 1839 electoral campaign. In his fourth and concluding part, he allowed himself to pass judgment on democracy. He had envisioned expressing his main thoughts in a substantial prologue but decided not to encumber volume 2 with an introduction competing with the powerful one he had written in volume 1 but instead summarize his ideas in a brief epilogue.[141] This is the clearest indication we have that Tocqueville intended for the two volumes to be read as a single work.

In this long concluding part, Tocqueville drew together the lessons of American history for France. Insisting again, as in volume 1, that the habit of self-government, acquired early on, at the point of departure, determined the course of American history, Tocqueville explained to the French that they had to work doubly hard to make democracy work, for they had instead started out on the wrong foot. Equal only in their lack of liberty, the French "had to overthrow or coerce the old powers. This led them to make revolutions and inspired in many of them the unbridled taste for disorder."[142] The opposite was true of America where "liberty was old and equality comparatively new."[143] Tocqueville insisted on these opposite historical sequences as a means of warning his countrymen that they had to reverse course. Only if the French changed their ways could equality lead to "liberty" rather than "servitude."[144]

To drive the point home, Tocqueville stressed the need for individual initiatives in democracy. Tocqueville had shown in his central theoretical part that democracy had severed the aristocratic chain and, with it, social hierarchies. But in concluding, he saw a multitude of atomized individuals lacking in energy and initiative. He blamed widespread popular indolence on the supervisory grip of the state on citizens' lives that amounted to soft despotism. Democratic men submitted to the authority of "an immense tutelary power, which assumes sole responsibility for securing their pleasure and watching over their fate. It is absolute, meticulous, regular, provident, and mild. It would resemble paternal authority if only its purpose were the same, namely, to prepare men for manhood. But on the contrary, it seeks only to keep them in childhood irrevocably."[145]

Moreover, Tocqueville decried the lesser theoretical value of arts and sciences in a utilitarian democracy. In a rare instance of giving specific examples, he reminded his readers of great individual intellectual accomplishments across the ages. Archimedes, as portrayed by Plutarch, was a model to emulate. Archimedes was "so high-minded" that his work was purely theoretical; "he never deigned to write any treatise on the construction of war machines."[146] By contrast, Americans committed themselves only to practical work. They did not risk scientific abstractions. They were too busy making money. American society could never have produced a genius like Pascal. "Had Pascal only some great profit in mind," Tocqueville insisted, "I cannot believe that he would have been able to concentrate the powers of his mind as he did to uncover the Creator's best-kept secrets."[147]

The finish line for the book was delayed not only by interruptions but because Tocqueville was constantly rewriting sections. In November 1838, while revising early chapters on the influence of equality of conditions on the philosophical method of Americans he had written before going to Switzerland, Tocqueville disliked what he had written so much that he simply threw these chapters in the fire and rewrote them from scratch, retaining only the "idée mère."[148] Even as he was about to send the manuscript to the printer in late 1839, Tocqueville was still integrating new evidence. For a fragment on how democracy affected the master-servant relationship, he requested from Ampère at the last minute some literary examples he could use to enliven his theoretical treatment.[149]

But as he closed his volume, Tocqueville finally stopped equivocating between his two worlds. Completing the book achieved what two electoral runs had not. Having conceded much, Tocqueville came down firmly, at last, on the side of democracy in a way he had not before. In a democracy, he concluded, people found true greatness not in crowning achievements that benefited only a few but in progress for most. Tocqueville had hinted at this throughout the volume but now stated his conviction with force: "Equality is less lofty, perhaps, but more just, and its justice is the source of its grandeur and beauty."[150]

# 7

# A Synthesis of Thought and Action

WITH TOCQUEVILLE's great theoretical work now published and his seat in the Chamber secured, Lamartine challenged the author to apply his ideas. "Now you will act; you have articulated your thought. You must now embody it."[1] Tocqueville recognized he had to set theory aside to master, as he told Édouard, "the entirely different sphere of practical politics through the study of an infinite multitude of small details."[2] But he was reluctant to choose between the two. He could perhaps have attempted parallel lives, one in political philosophy and one in politics, but he sought instead to strengthen one with the other. He believed he had it in him to achieve an original synthesis of thought and action and turn his principles into concrete policies.

## Marking Independence in the Chamber and at the Polls

If he were to accomplish this, he decided, his course must be to remain independent. But in practical terms, this meant holding himself apart. Consistent with his electoral promise, Tocqueville entered the Chamber, when the session began on March 25, 1839, determined to be his own man. He could not imagine submitting to either of the Chamber's two dominant figures, Thiers or Guizot. Tocqueville was telling his friends, "Both are, at bottom, antithetical to my manner of thinking and feeling.

I despise them." He was more favorably inclined toward Barrot but still harbored a distrust, finding "all the existing parties repugnant." He told Royer-Collard, "The *liberal*, rather than *revolutionary*, party—the only possible fit for me—does not exist, and it is not up to me to create it."[3]

To make clear that he would not answer to any parliamentary authority, Tocqueville was particular about where he would sit in the Chamber. "Where you put your behind is a matter of first importance,"[4] he wrote. His preferences notwithstanding, few seats were available. Tocqueville understood the power of public perception. There was an empty seat with the center left, which was in principle acceptable, but because it was adjacent to the seat of Interior Minister Montalivet's brother-in-law, Tocqueville feared this would signal he was a cabinet yes-man. Another seat near Lamartine was available, but sitting next to him might bring Tocqueville too close to the Legitimists, with whom he would have nothing to do. Tocqueville ended up in seat no. 319, located between Thiers's center-left party and Barrot's dynastic left but at a safe distance from both.[5] Proud isolation perhaps felt better than meddling in petty coalitions, but it was no way to begin a political career.

## Lost in the Complexity of Electoral Politics with a Moral Argument Nobody Wanted to Hear

Tocqueville clearly failed his first test of influence when he was appointed in July 1839 to a committee on electoral reform.[6] In response to mounting grassroots pressure, the left wanted to broaden the electorate by lowering the property requirements of the franchise (the *cens*) and by expanding the ranks of the so-called *capacités* whose numbers had been dramatically restricted in the 1831 electoral law. Officers of the National Guard led the movement for this change.[7] They were offended at not being electors even though they were regularly called on to protect the country. They had influential Republican allies in the Chamber (Arago and Garnier-Pagès). Barrot and the dynastic left were equally receptive, even though Guizot accused them of posturing and grandstanding. Tocqueville had followed previous iterations of the debate from outside the Chamber. Now he was able to have his say.

Guizot and the conservative Doctrinaires opposed expanding the electorate. As Charles de Rémusat, close to Thiers, explained, they insisted on voters owning (primarily landed) "wealth as the guarantee of enlightenment and independence."[8] And Félix Le Peletier d'Aunay, Tocqueville's older cousin and protector, asserted, the Chamber could always consult with *capacités* (lawyers, professors, intellectuals, local notables), but only economically independent men were impartial in casting votes.[9] Representative Duvergier de Hauranne best delivered the obvious rebuttal: if representation was to remain this selective, "the chosen sample must be good enough to gauge the wants and needs of the country" and fire up common energies.[10] Yet the law, as Louis Blanc put it, "condemned intelligence to cede to wealth."[11]

Surprisingly, Tocqueville too resisted broadening the electorate. He jotted in a diary note, "As for electoral reform, my feeling is this: I absolutely reject any lowering of the property qualification or equivalent additions," and he held to that position throughout the 1840s.[12] This seems like an inexplicable contradiction from a candidate who, during his electoral campaign in Normandy, had envisioned progressively broader political participation leading to "the government of the country by the country."[13]

Tocqueville's first public declaration that he was opposed to lowering the franchise qualifications came in opposition to a manifesto for global electoral reform that a group of deputies on the left issued following exploratory meetings at Barrot's home.[14] When Tocqueville, who had attended only one meeting, found his name among the signatories, he rushed a letter of dissent to *Le Siècle*,[15] while privately worrying that public dissociation might endanger his fragile working relationship with the left.[16] Tocqueville insisted that he was not against all the suggested reforms. He fully supported the abolition of small districts where politicians could more easily intimidate voters, but he refused to consider lowering the franchise as long as there was widespread electoral corruption. He sought "an election law that is not more radical but more moral, and an electoral system that would render corruption through government appointments more difficult."[17] He vowed to end pork-barrel legislation of the type Guizot himself supported. (Guizot once said at a banquet speech that "those who lend their firm and sincere support to policies that benefit the general interest will reap the fruits of their own local interests.")[18]

To his credit, Tocqueville's focus on the workings of government rather than electoral participation was consistent with his position in *Democracy in America*. He had never endorsed universal male suffrage in the United States. Tocqueville feared that his French compatriots, unlike Americans, lacked the habit of political liberty. Without such a habit, enlarging the electorate would lead to a French version of the tyranny of the majority not mitigated, as in the United States, by a system of checks and balances, and further aggravated by corruption. Ending corruption was therefore the first step toward learning to live in a lawful system of representation.

Tocqueville was especially scandalized that so many of his Chamber colleagues were civil servants who owed much of their livelihood to the government, not independent and disinterested people like himself. About 45 percent of the deputies occupied posts such as magistrates, armed services officers, and high-level officials in various ministries, and most owned just enough property to qualify for the franchise.[19] Because they were themselves the recipients of government favors as well as their distributors, they voted systematically with the government. With so many Chamber members reporting to the ministers, the perceptive Duvergier de Hauranne talked about "a chamber that represents the ministers rather than the country."[20]

Tocqueville did not mince his words in denouncing the French "unlimited taste for spoils" and deputies who enter public life not to work in politics but to advance their careers.[21] In February 1840, the Chamber agreed to take up a proposal Charles Gauguier, deputy from the Vosges, had repeatedly introduced, to exclude civil servants from the Chamber. Tocqueville seized the occasion to make the case for freezing the civil service career of deputies during their time in the Chamber. A sound idea, perhaps, but the newly minted representative could not refrain from haranguing the assembled deputies who joined the Chamber "only to become civil servants or gain a promotion" as a bunch of mercenaries.[22] If Tocqueville had wanted to isolate himself in the Chamber, without allies among either conservatives or reformers, he could not have adopted a better stance.

What Tocqueville learned in the process, however, was that reform, however modest, was nearly impossible to implement. Thiers, returning to power in May 1840, tabled the issue of electoral reform for fear that any change in the law would automatically lead to a call for new elections. Lamartine pointedly concluded that if the genius of a political leader in charge of a government was to turn down every reform, one might as well replace the statesman with "a roadside mile-stone."[23]

A disappointed Tocqueville wondered whether the effort it took to be elected to the Chamber was worth it. He confided to Kergorlay that the political life of a representative was not as uplifting as he had expected. "I fear that the time of great men and great events is gone forever. And that the destiny of our generation is to exert ourselves endlessly and without glory in this confining ant hill. . . . I cannot tell you how painful it is to live a political life amidst these half-hearted pieties, fickle ideas, and mediocre men with whom you must deal every day, despite the contempt they inspire in you. I have made great strides to get here and now that I am here, I regret having given up the position of observant philosopher, and I despair of having been condemned to live in such a society, among such wretches for colleagues."[24] Of the Chamber, he told Eugène Stöffels, "Nothing is really generous about it: nothing in it that pumps the lifeblood of the heart. In a word, there is no youth in it, even amongst the young."[25]

The feeling of disaffection was, not surprisingly, mutual. Most Chamber colleagues found Tocqueville aloof and unfriendly, did not see him as a potential leader, and made little effort to introduce themselves to him. Indeed, he knew only a few by name.[26] He appeared frail and mannered in his pince-nez. His unimpressive oratorical skills, compounded by his stage fright, produced speeches better read than listened to.[27]

## Reception in Letters, Politics, and the Press: Praise, Criticism, and Indifference

Dissatisfaction was not limited to the Chamber. Tocqueville had begun his term with the second volume of *Democracy in America* almost finished. He could only hope that publishing it would boost his visibility and increase his moral authority and influence. It became apparent quickly after its publication that most critics would not give the second volume of *Democracy in America* the endorsement they accorded to the first. Tocqueville had developed a comprehensive theory of democracy. Today, it is widely acknowledged as a pioneering work of modern social science, but at the time, it was much too new and too abstract. Only a handful of admirers fully grasped it.

Two intellectual figures close to the author recognized the second volume of *Democracy in America* as a truly innovative work offering a theory of modern democracy. British friend John Stuart Mill celebrated the breakthrough. Tocqueville had told Mill that he wanted to show "the influence of equality on the ideas and feelings of men."[28] Mill recognized Tocqueville as having done so much more: it was "the first analytical inquiry into the influence of democracy"; a study of democracy's "influence upon society in the widest sense; upon the relations of private life, upon intellect, morals, and the habits and modes of feeling which constitute national character." Moreover, Mill credited Tocqueville for seeing that democracy, in the modern world, was inevitable as "man cannot turn back rivers to their source" and that democracy was, "on the whole, desirable; but desirable only under certain conditions, and those conditions capable, by human care and foresight, of being realized, but capable also of being missed." Mill did not agree with all the points Tocqueville made, but that hardly mattered. The value of Tocqueville's work, he felt, was "less in the conclusions than in the mode of arriving at them."[29] In providing a comprehensive view of democracy, Tocqueville had opened a new way of thinking about society. In the final analysis, how Tocqueville thought of society was more important than what exactly he argued.

In France, Royer-Collard, the older political leader whom Tocqueville considered a mentor, hailed his protégé for creating a new topic of reflection and study. Royer-Collard praised Tocqueville for imposing on himself "the task of invention" and fulfilling it by fitting all of democracy's components into a coherent whole. If volume 1 of *Democracy in America* was "description," volume 2 was now "invention." Although "invention," Royer-Collard noted critically, is "within certain limits, arbitrary," Tocqueville had credibly envisioned a democratic society in a masterpiece of political imagination.[30]

Another close friend, Jean-Jacques Ampère, expressed his admiration in verse:

Pour conjurer ces maux nés de l'égalité
Aimez, nous dites-vous, aimez la liberté![31]

The liberty Tocqueville loved was neither the aristocratic liberty of privilege nor the negative liberty of rights but a demanding personal exertion to achieve great things—the positive liberty of effort from which everything else flows. Liberty so conceived, Tocqueville believed, was a "sacred thing" because it was "the *free* choice of what is good."[32]

Tocqueville, however, lost those intelligent readers who had used volume 1 of *Democracy in America* to understand America but were not ready to follow the second volume's theoretical acrobatics. Thus Pellegrino Rossi, professor of political economy at the Collège de France, expressed a common reserve about Tocqueville's penchant for abstraction in the *Revue des deux mondes*.[33] A frustrated Tocqueville acknowledged the defect. "When I was speaking only about the democratic society of the United States," he said to Mill, "that was readily understandable. If I had spoken of our democratic society in France, as it exists today, I would also have been understood. But starting from ideas about American and French society, I meant to depict the general features of democratic societies, for which there is not yet a complete model. This is where I lose the ordinary reader. Only men very accustomed to looking for general and speculative truths like to follow me in this direction. I think the comparatively lesser impact of my book comes from this original sin of the subject matter much more than from the ways in which I have dealt with this or that part of the topic."[34]

Some critics pointed out factual inconsistencies as a means of casting doubt on the model. Even good friends did that. Thus, Nassau Senior wrote to Tocqueville after a close reading: "You appear to consider France as eminently democratic—England as eminently aristocratic. And yet many of the qualities which you describe as marking democratic societies appear to belong to us much more than to you"—that is, "the desire for 'wellbeing,'" "individualism," and "pacifism."[35]

Even though the second volume of *Democracy in America* was more about democracy in the abstract than about American democracy, readers questioned its relevance for France. Journalist and literary critic Samuel Silvestre de Sacy, the great orientalist's son, was one of them. In a review Gustave de Beaumont had urged him to undertake and publish in the *Journal des débats*,[36] Sacy responded to the new book with visceral anti-Americanism. Sacy misread Tocqueville's project as an attempt to transplant American-style democracy directly onto French soil. And he understood America only through the lens of his prejudices. Even though Tocqueville had dropped the phrase *tyranny of the majority*, Sacy attacked him for using as his model a country "where everything, including feelings and beliefs, is ruled by the majority. I call such arithmetic liberty a harsh form of slavery—the harshest of all: moral slavery." Sacy asked whether one could be "free" in a country where, for example, "the rich hide to enjoy their wealth"; or where "men of intelligence pretend to be stupid lest their superiority cost them a few votes."[37] To this angry critique of both *Democracy in America* and the United States, Tocqueville responded that he had a higher purpose in mind: "To show our contemporaries that in order to prevent this equality, which we rightly hold dear, from becoming the leprosy of the human race, one must work tirelessly to sustain the flight of ideas, to lift souls and to show that in the democratic age that is just beginning, political liberty is not only beautiful but also necessary for nations to become great and even to remain civilized."[38]

As for the defenders of equality on the left who had genuinely praised the first volume of *Democracy in America*, they seemed indifferent this time around. Men like Louis Blanc, Proudhon, and the radicalized Lamennais who, unlike Tocqueville, trusted centralized power to deliver more equality and protect basic rights, did not comment on Tocqueville's new speculations. For them, Tocqueville's American moment had passed. Blanc, so supportive initially, had moved on to issues of labor organization and remained silent on the second volume. Neither did Proudhon leave any notes as he had five years earlier. Lamennais, who had wanted to learn about America in 1835, had lost interest by 1840. They did not perceive that Tocqueville was, like them, preoccupied with the general welfare.[39]

Tocqueville's first year in the Chamber and the publication of his new book did not secure for him the foothold in public affairs he craved. He had few listeners and readers in the Chamber and few readers in the public. But he still retained a clear-eyed perspective on his situation. Tocqueville realized that he had not replicated with his 1840 volume his 1835 success and that he could not count on it to endear him among colleagues in the Chamber, who showed no interest in his exercise in political philosophy. Nonetheless, he had faith in his work and found satisfaction in the thought that enough people in high literary circles saluted it, he told Eugène Stöffels, "as a great effort of the human spirit."[40]

So sure was Tocqueville of his book's significance that he sought, on the strength of this conviction, to realize his ambition to be elected to the Académie française, "this academic society that is all that remains of France's old culture of urbanity."[41] Tocqueville carefully prepared his campaign for the Académie française. He sent a copy of volume 2 of *Democracy in America* to Madame Récamier. He understood that her support and Chateaubriand's were indispensable, but he knew that the older Ballanche, also their friend, had precedence. In London, Henry Reeve presented a copy to Ambassador (and academician) Guizot, who answered he was disappointed not to see a more fully elaborated section on the role of religion in democracy. Royer-Collard had his hands tied, for, as he told the duchesse de Dino, he had already pledged his vote to Jacques-François Ancelot.[42]

Historian Michaud's passing in September 1839 freed a seat, but academicians agreed that Victor Hugo, who had been knocking at the door for some time, had priority.[43] There were other ailing members. Beaumont told Tocqueville that he was following "with interest the health reports of the Archbishop of Paris."[44] Tocqueville, for his part, was hoping he would succeed Louis de Bonald, whose career he would enjoy invoking, as tradition required, in his acceptance speech.

Friends were helping. François Mignet, who had engineered Tocqueville's election to the Académie des sciences morales et politiques in

1838, arranged for Tocqueville to visit with members and even secured Thiers's vote for Tocqueville. Abel-François Villemain was on board.[45] Tocqueville, for his part, called on Victor Cousin to pressure poet Casimir Delavigne for his vote. He also asked Charles Stöffels to lobby "Lacretelle, that old Anacreon," a poet who happened to live, like Stöffels, in Metz.[46] This electoral chess game lasted a year and a half, but Tocqueville finally attained his goal in December 1841, gaining election to a seat that had been occupied by the comte de Cessac, who had been in charge of the dreaded conscription of the French army under Napoleon. Instead of praising Bonald, Tocqueville would have to confront this Napoleonic legacy when inducted into the academy.[47]

## Reelection to a Second Term: Breaking Political Isolation at Last

Joining the Académie française did advance Tocqueville's political interests, at least locally in Normandy. The government dissolved the Chamber in June 1842 with a view to strengthening its majority. This meant that Tocqueville had to campaign anew in Valognes to keep his seat. Both Guizot and Barrot, whom Tocqueville had challenged, naturally backed his opponent, Le Marois, who was trying to recover his former position. "I was facing an unchecked administration and a millionaire opponent," Tocqueville noted. He had to fight the renewed accusation of being a Legitimist, "a Carlist in disguise" who "under cover of liberalism . . . wanted to bring back Henri V."[48] Le Globe even printed speculations that Tocqueville wanted to overthrow the government.[49] Le Marois treated electors to lavish meals, while Tocqueville, whose health was too fragile to match these dietary excesses, hoped "that God can inspire the denizens of Lower Normandy not to linger too long at the dinner table."[50] Tocqueville reflected, "There are days when I am ready to trade in the Academies, the Chamber, and all the trappings of literary vainglory for a good stomach."[51] But Tocqueville benefited from his literary recognition and from Marie's visits with wives of electors in Valognes, as well as her help distributing electoral material.[52] He insisted that he was free from the bonds of any party, telling electors that his "opinion had always been moderate and dynastic" against "the two extremes: the partisans of 1793 and the regime of absolutism."[53] He was neither Republican nor Legitimist, but instead a "liberal and nothing more."[54] Tocqueville swept the polls on July 9, 1842, with 465 votes against 177.[55] Following this success, Tocqueville also won his seat on the Conseil général of the *département*, in November, a post he had long sought because it allowed personal investment in the community. Jaded by his experience in national politics, Tocqueville relished the chance to get involved locally, where "one discovers here and there some good sides of the human spirit."[56]

Tocqueville had more luck in his parliamentary maneuvering during his second term. By chance, he broke isolation and entered a coalition. The unexpected sequence of events came only a few days after he was reelected, in July 1842, with the fatal carriage accident of the popular duc d'Orléans at age thirty-two. The duke's father, the king, was already sixty-nine; the duke's son, the comte de Paris, suddenly heir to the throne, was only five. The future of the Orléans dynasty became uncertain. There ensued a vigorous parliamentary debate over a likely regency. Guizot and the king wanted to settle the issue by guaranteeing the regency would go to the duc de Nemours, the king's second son, and not to the duke's wife, the duchesse d'Orléans. She was the daughter of the duke of Mecklenburg-Schwerin and still very much considered a German. Thiers sided with the king and Guizot in favor of Nemours, and he convinced Barrot as well. Taking the opposing view, Lamartine chastised them and defended the duchess.

Tocqueville had a different view altogether, advocating that they postpone the debate until a regent was needed, allowing the Chamber to assess the situation in due course, and only then voting on who the regent should be. Tocqueville rose to the tribune to propose to postpone their decision. He felt he had spoken unconvincingly. He told Marie, "It was nearly six o'clock. The Chamber was in a hurry [to adjourn]. That flustered me. Once again, I learned by experience last night that I have no talent for improvisation, which in this government means everything."[57]

Tocqueville was more effective than he thought. He broke the political alliance between Thiers and Barrot. Although the Chamber approved

the government's approach to the regency, Tocqueville was able to convince Barrot to join him in supporting the delayed option. So long as
Thiers controlled Barrot in opposing the Guizot government, Tocqueville wanted to "stay all alone in my corner rather than be absorbed in the
bosom of the left."[58] But Tocqueville had managed unexpectedly to sever
their pact, at least temporarily. Thiers felt betrayed. This gave Tocqueville
the opportunity to propose a partnership to Barrot. Tocqueville immediately told Francisque de Corcelle he thought of acting "in concert"
with Barrot, and with François-Adolphe Chambolle, who represented
Vendée and edited the pro-Barrot newspaper *Le Siècle*, on the condition
that Barrot would distance himself from Thiers.[59] Tocqueville told Barrot
bluntly, "Do you know anyone in the Chamber as fundamentally illiberal
as Monsieur Thiers? More antagonistic to individual rights? More of
a centralizer, more determined to march towards his ends by any
means necessary?"[60]

Tocqueville could bring to Barrot what Rémusat understood to be a
very small but "distinguished and difficult coterie" of followers.[61] Among
them were Tocqueville's close friends, also elected in 1839: Corcelle, who
was Rémusat's brother-in-law, and Beaumont, who had become his
cousin; all three had married Lafayette's granddaughters. Tocqueville
initially kept his distance from Rémusat, considering him to be too close
to Thiers, but he developed other friendships in the Chamber. A few
members especially appreciated him, notably lawyer and economist Victor Lanjuinais, who represented the Loire inférieure; Jean-Charles Rivet,
a former prefect elected in the Corrèze; and Mathieu Combarel de
Leyval from Puy-de-Dôme. Tocqueville also broke the ice with lawyers
Jules Armand Dufaure and Alexandre-François Vivien, two cabinet
members in the Soult government that Louis Philippe had formed after
the May insurrection.[62] Marking this new alliance with Barrot, Chambolle opened the pages of *Le Siècle* to Tocqueville. In a series of six articles in January 1843, Tocqueville explained he wanted to implement the
liberal principles of 1789 without the revolutionary spirit of 1793; in other
words, he wanted to deradicalize the left by separating "the principles of
the revolution from revolutionary habits."[63] If Barrot would lead this
movement, Tocqueville would support him.

What was necessary, Tocqueville enjoined Barrot, was to abandon revolutionary rhetoric and adopt a genuinely liberal program of "loving liberty for its own sake; sincerely respecting the independence and the rights of the neighbor even when such exercise is unpleasant; reining in governmental power and limiting its action, even when that power is acting on our own desires; gradually and reasonably decentralizing administration."[64] Barrot seemed to agree. He committed to revisiting the September laws, enforcing the charter, guaranteeing independence for juries, fighting against parliamentary corruption, and promoting morals in politics.[65]

Seeing in this new alliance hope for his political future, Tocqueville called for a robust defense of liberal institutions and separation of powers. For too long, Tocqueville wrote, the threat of revolution had served as an excuse to suppress civil liberties. But in fact, as he had explained in volume 2 of *Democracy in America*, there was no revolution to fear, no realistic possibility of a renewed alliance between the people and the bourgeoisie as in 1789 and 1830. The Revolution had produced a complacent nation of bourgeois seeking to enrich themselves in such a way that made future revolutions unlikely. Playing down Republican agitation in larger cities, Tocqueville saw a France prone to vocal opposition but conservative in its behavior. "A population composed of small landowners shows itself to be freely defiant and oppositional, but we could not imagine one less inclined to violate its laws and overturn the government." With the pursuit of well-being leading to political quietism, Tocqueville observed, "the revolution, by its outcome, has killed the revolution."[66]

The real problem, Tocqueville went on to say, was not revolution but bad governance resulting from a huge administrative machinery that included 100,000 civil servants, 400,000 soldiers and sailors, and kept Paris under the surveillance of 60,000 bayonets.[67] The regime had clamped down on civil liberties in a betrayal of the spirit of 1789 and 1830. Because of its virtually exclusive focus on the electoral franchise, Tocqueville argued, the opposition had lost ground just about everywhere else, and had given up on guarantees granted in the charter's tutelary laws. Recovering these rights and guarantees was the one means the nation had to acquire the habit of liberty, without which there could be no democracy.

Regrettably, the rapprochement with Barrot against Thiers did not last. Thiers recovered his dominance over the left and therefore came to control more of the press, including not only *Le Constitutionnel* but also *Le Siècle*, where Tocqueville had publicized his ideas. Having had a platform for his views, Tocqueville did not welcome the idea of being shut out. He resolved to keep a public voice and strengthen his status by pursuing a combination of intellectual and political work. Tocqueville did not immediately break with *Le Siècle* but seized the opportunity in March 1844 to buy an ailing newspaper, *Le Commerce*, a progressive voice on industrial, agricultural, and commercial affairs. He joined forces with a large landowner, five other deputies (Corcelle, Viard, Combarel de Leyval, Dezeimeris, and Lanjuinais but not Beaumont who stayed with *Le Siècle*), and two lawyers to raise the required funds. They renamed the newspaper *Le Commerce: Journal politique et littéraire* and launched it anew.

Tocqueville was the leading force behind the acquisition. He wrote to Reeve that he planned to have a "habitual influence" on the newspaper to use it as a forum for his own political ideas.[68] His close friend Corcelle became copublisher. Together, they hired as editor in chief Arnold Scheffer, brother of the well-known painter Ary Scheffer, a friend of Corcelle from Carbonari days and one-time secretary to Lafayette. An attentive reader of early socialist theories, Scheffer was attuned to the worsening condition of the working classes as an economic recession loomed. Tocqueville wrote the manifesto that was published in July 1844 to accompany the relaunch. It stated that the newspaper would be political but not partisan. "Its mission shall never be to serve special interests but to make ideas triumph."[69] *Le Commerce* would be the "only authentic representation of liberal ideas."[70] To codirector Corcelle, Tocqueville made clear he wanted to "create an opposition paper independent of Monsieur Thiers that can fight him on the great domestic and foreign questions."[71]

In embracing journalism, Tocqueville demonstrated his belief in the role of a free press, even though, as it turned out, he had little taste for the work itself. He told Corcelle that he had "the style and mentality least fitting to newspapers that one can imagine."[72] He soon realized that the public subscribed to a newspaper not necessarily to follow the movement of ideas but to find entertainment in serial novels. For instance, *Le Constitutionnel* achieved wide circulation by printing the vaguely socialist *feuilletons* of Eugène Sue. Tocqueville entered into ultimately fruitless negotiations for material with Honoré de Balzac, who deeply resented Tocqueville's election to the Académie française while he was left out. The resentment became mutual; Tocqueville referred to the writer as "Balzac, that swine of letters."[73] He had no more success in attracting Alexandre Dumas.[74] But having chosen middlebrow culture, Tocqueville was determined to promote his cause with articles "intended to produce, by constant repetition, a temporary effect . . . on hurried and rather ignorant" newspaper readers, with "simple arguments easily understood on the fly."[75]

After breaking political isolation, successfully challenging the Chamber leadership, and acquiring a newspaper to influence public opinion directly, Tocqueville's next enterprise was to take on the large question of the role of religion in democracy. What Tocqueville most wanted to accomplish in his political life, he told his friend Corcelle and his brother Édouard on several occasions, was to "reconcile the liberal spirit with that of religion, the new society and the church."[76]

## Prison Reform

This meant pursuing his work in the Chamber on prison reform. He was by now a well-known voice in the field; his study of American penitentiaries, coauthored with Beaumont, had gone through several editions and translations. Tocqueville prepared in 1840 an initial report for a Chamber ad hoc commission on prison reform in which he promoted the Pennsylvania isolation system under supervision of a chaplain as the most promising route to reform criminals. The idea was not to isolate the prisoners in a cruel way but to create the conditions of individual repentance with the help of regular visits from chaplain, doctor, and teacher while daily work kept body and soul together. Among commissioners, Beaumont, Lanjuinais, and Duvergier de Hauranne added their voice to the rapporteur's while moderate Republican Hippolyte Carnot dissented.[77] But the report, scheduled for deliberation in June 1840, was tabled, causing Tocqueville significant frustration.

Although deputies passed on the opportunity to debate Tocqueville's report, Interior Minister Agenor de Gasparin, who knew Tocqueville from the Abolitionist Society, listened to him independently and instituted the isolation system on an experimental basis at the juvenile jail of La petite Roquette.[78] There, juvenile inmates could no longer see one another and develop partnerships in crime. They were given religious instruction in their individual cells. When it proved impractical for chaplain Abbé Crozes to administer Holy Communion to each boy alone, he assembled them in the chapel where they received the sacrament with their eyes veiled.[79]

Based on these experiments and others, Tocqueville championed the benefits of isolation in a fuller commission report in 1843. Tocqueville again insisted that the isolation system was aimed at reform.[80] He explained that cellular isolation "provokes an energetic and salutary influence on the soul" by "the fear that it inspires," especially in the first few months of solitude.[81] In addition, Tocqueville endorsed new prison regulations forbidding the use of money and the consumption of wine and tobacco. He called for more priests, both to counsel inmates and to perform religious ceremonies. "To bring about these grand, good, and sacred things, do you think it is possible without the clergy?" he asked.[82] He believed that through religious means, the French had an opportunity to foster the democratic goal of reinsertion into society.

Tocqueville's new influence is perhaps best seen in the strength of the opposition his views generated. Beaumont, not a member of the 1843 Chamber commission, hoped to prevent criticism of Tocqueville's report by praising it in Le Siècle.[83] But it faced pushback from prison experts and Chamber colleagues alike. In an about-face, Chambolle opened the pages of Le Siècle to Léon Faucher, who renewed his attack on a cellular isolation system that he believed induced madness.

Faucher pointed to political prisoners in isolation at Mont-Saint-Michel, among them popular republican figures Armand Barbès and Louis-Auguste Blanqui, who had been driven to despair. Tocqueville went to Mont-Saint-Michel, not far from his Normandy home, "to observe with my own eyes what I know already, that the regime so fatal to the political inmates currently held there, which Faucher speaks of with such bad faith and flawed logic, has nothing to do with the one I intend to bring about in France."[84] Beaumont and Tocqueville wrote a rebuttal to Faucher, but Chambolle did not bother to publish it.[85] At the same time, Charles Lucas launched another line of attack, claiming that isolation worked only for austere Pennsylvania Quakers.[86]

Tocqueville's report provoked a Chamber debate for several weeks in the spring of 1844. With a newfound eloquence on behalf of rehabilitation, Tocqueville injected his views of the Catholic religion into arguments about costs, prison size, and time of isolated incarceration. "All French Catholics," Tocqueville argued, should support the cellular system because "it's the only one that gives the larger share to religious ideas, and Catholic ideas (consolation, education, prayer)." Without isolation, the prisoner mixed in with fellow criminals is "locked up in a legal hell from which one does not emerge once admitted." The cellular system not only defeats "this forthright paganism" but is a means of "secularizing Christianity," the achievement of which would redound, Tocqueville insisted, "to the greater glory of the French Revolution." With the cellular system, the legislator, who "transfers the maxims of Christianity from the sphere of religion to the practical sphere of law" conforms to the wishes of the revolutionaries themselves. Had not Mirabeau's "first consequence of the French Revolution" been "precisely the introduction of this idea of improvement and rehabilitation at the heart of the penal code?"[87] Even though critics, Republican Arago most vocally, retorted that there was no way that prison personnel and chaplains could give prisoners enough individual time to make Tocqueville's blueprint work, the Chamber approved much of the report and voted for the law. The Chamber of Peers never acted on the lower Chamber's vote and therefore the law never went into effect, but Tocqueville had his voice heard and his ideas reckoned with.

## Education: Joining Religion and Democracy

Bringing religion to prison was only the first step. Tocqueville's much bigger ambition was to reconcile democracy with religion. In the Chamber, Tocqueville asked, "What is democracy, good democracy, if it isn't society's constant and powerful effort to ameliorate, elevate, and raise to a higher moral standard the lot of each of its members. . . . What is that, if not Christianity translated into politics?"[88] America had convinced Tocqueville that the coexistence of religion and democracy was necessary to liberty and public morality. In volume 1 of *Democracy in America*, he declared the American example of religious toleration the indispensable example of how "religion showed the way to enlightenment."[89] Tocqueville was especially in awe of American Catholics' embrace of religious pluralism. In volume 2, he generalized beyond America to say that the "nature of the human soul" led men to develop a "conception of God."[90] The time had come finally to reconcile religion and democracy in France. Otherwise, France would need "soldiers and prisons if we abolish belief."[91]

Tocqueville had the opportunity to pursue and deepen his thoughts on religion and democracy at the Académie des sciences morales et politiques, where he now spent more time as a welcome retreat from the Chamber. In 1841, at the government's behest, the Académie undertook a general survey (never completed) of moral and political sciences from 1789 to 1830. The Académie appointed four of its members to lead the inquiry, Cousin (philosophy), Tocqueville (moral philosophy), Rossi (political economy), and Mignet (history), providing each with funds to hire a research assistant. With this assignment, Tocqueville undertook research on moral doctrines and their application in policy and administration. He hired as his assistant Henri Charles Savoye, a young lawyer who had studied in Germany, but the two did not work well together.[92] In 1843, Tocqueville replaced him with Arthur de Gobineau. This young, impecunious writer (future author of the *Essay on the Inequality of the Human Races*), was trying to make a name for himself in Parisian society. Through tenacious maneuvering, Gobineau had slipped into aristocratic salons, met with Ballanche, and published some essays. These evidently came to the attention of Tocqueville, and he hired him.[93]

The two men were consumed with the question of the changing role of spiritual matters in an increasingly materialist world, but they disagreed on the answer. Tocqueville doubted his faith yet was convinced that to prosper, society needed religion. He credited the idea of equal rights and the obligation of the better off to come to the aid of the poor to Christian beliefs. He praised Christianity for making soft virtues such as humility and pity more important than courage and honor. He saw the modern challenge as enforcing moral laws in this life rather than relegating punishment or reward to the afterlife.

Gobineau, whom Tocqueville entrusted with compiling documentary evidence, instead understood modern morality as an outgrowth of the eighteenth century and downplayed its Christian roots. He pointed to major differences between contemporary and Christian morality: modern society aimed to eliminate suffering while Christianity considered suffering sacred. In modern life, everyone had the right to work and should desire to do so; Christianity instead held that man was condemned to labor and that only God could do worthy work.[94]

Tocqueville repeatedly criticized Gobineau for his "absolutely contrary" opinions and for presenting old ideas as new ones.[95] Tocqueville urged Gobineau to think more deeply, work more quickly. He always maintained a tone of superiority—accusing Gobineau of laziness and referring to his generation as falling prey to the "epidemics of the times."[96] But in the process of debating contrary opinions, Gobineau helped Tocqueville dig in deeper.[97]

One thing Tocqueville and Gobineau agreed on was the need for more relaxed mores in modern life. Tocqueville had expressed that idea clearly in volume 2 of *Democracy in America*, arguing "a certain well-being of the body is necessary for the development of the soul. . . . It was necessary to tie this world to the other or one of the two escapes us."[98] He repeated the same to Gobineau: "Our society has moved away much more from theology than from Christian philosophy. Since our religious beliefs have become less firm and the view of the other world more obscure, morality must show itself more indulgent for material needs and pleasures. It is an idea that the Saint-Simonians expressed, I believe, by saying that *it was necessary to rehabilitate the flesh.*"[99] Well-being was a natural desire.

This academic conversation on Christianity turned out to be a rehearsal for a much larger political debate on liberty of teaching in France, a public controversy developing over whether Catholic schools and a state-run lay system of education could peacefully coexist. Tocqueville was deeply invested in the political debate. He wanted to see religious and lay educators respect one another in a rejuvenated democratic alliance.[100]

The two distinct systems of secondary education, lay and ecclesiastical, overlapping in the July Monarchy, were of roughly equal size. *Collèges royaux* (secondary schools under university control) educated about 18,700 students, not significantly more than the approximately 18,500 students enrolled in *petits séminaires* (secondary schools under church control). Moreover, another 58,000, or most students, received some secondary education in a wide array of municipal and private institutions. Beginning at age fourteen, *petits séminaires* students were required to wear an ecclesiastical frock and were expected to graduate to *grands séminaires* to become priests. Many neither wore frocks nor continued to the priesthood. They could not, however, take the state-administered baccalauréat exam unless they completed two years of schooling in a *collège royal* or in a state-accredited private school, of which there were only about one hundred. In numerous cases, this meant graduates of Catholic schools had to repeat two years, an unattractive proposition.[101]

Early in the July regime, it seemed that the state and church systems would live in relative agreement. Tocqueville was pleased to see a fragile reconciliation between church and state alongside renewed religious practice in the population. This renewal was especially visible among the young. "Many believe, all would like to believe," Tocqueville wrote to his English friend Lord Radnor in 1835. Tocqueville reported huge attendance at the Sunday sermons that "a young priest gifted with rare eloquence," by the name of Henri Lacordaire, was delivering weekly at Notre Dame.[102] Cabinet members may not have been churchgoers themselves, but the government reaffirmed the existence of a number of religious orders as "recognized orders."[103] Dominicans and Jesuits, if not formally recognized, were tolerated, as Lacordaire's and the influential Father Ravignan's fame attested.

The government's tolerance extended to education. Guizot's 1833 law on primary education endorsed Catholic primary schools as equal to state schools, conforming to the spirit of the 1830 charter that had promised freedom of education.[104] Some priests had remained among the administrators of the state system, like Abbé Daniel, rector of the Academy of Caen, near Tocqueville's estate.[105] Most Royal Colleges had in-house chaplains. Although the Restoration years, when throne and altar were allies, were gone forever, there was still some interpenetration of the two systems as well as competition for students between royal and Catholic schools, which sometimes required arbitration. In 1840, Tocqueville himself intervened in Normandy to prevent the Bishop of Coutances from creating a *petit séminaire* at Montebourg because of the real threat to the established Collège Royal.[106]

This entente cordiale did not last, however. The spirit of the French Revolution resurfaced. The university authorities, in charge since the Napoleonic reforms of regulating secondary education, asserted that Catholic schools indoctrinated their students against the state. They feared that Catholic educators were claiming the freedom granted to them by the charter to impose their antidemocratic views on impressionable children. This assertion is behind Rémusat's insistence on drawing a fundamental difference between freedom of the press and freedom of teaching. There should be no restriction on the press, he argued, because "readers are men, masters of their own thoughts and actions, who are not constrained in what they read and can correct one newspaper's bias with that of another." Teaching could not be allowed the same freedom because students were still "children, quartered within disciplines and forced to listen exclusively to the lessons they receive." A government therefore cannot tolerate that students be indoctrinated "in hatred towards its institutions and leaders."[107]

In response, Catholics accused the university heads of the state system of advancing their institutional interests ahead of the legitimate right of parents to elect the schools they wanted for their children. They did not believe university authorities were speaking for the nation. They pointed out that with freedom of teaching written into the 1830 charter, the university had no legal basis for authority over Catholic schools. Charles de Montalembert and Abbé Dupanloup repeatedly made this point.

Unsurprisingly, Tocqueville attempted to distance himself from both camps, promoting diversity and competition in education. Once again, however, he could not prevent himself from being drawn into the fray. As Kergorlay noted, Tocqueville could not tolerate Thiers's idea of "submitting all the nation's children to a single mode of teaching, in order to create a uniform public mind," but he also resented the clergy's strategic use of education to gain political influence and erase much of the heritage of the French Revolution.[108] Conflict between the two camps erupted when Education Minister Villemain attempted to implement state supervision of the *petits séminaires* in 1841. Villemain demanded that *petits séminaires* teachers, heretofore exclusively under the authority of bishops, obtain from the local mayor a certificate of morality and a certificate of teaching competency.[109] Villemain's bill, once it reached the Chamber, was never reported out of committee (of which Tocqueville was a member[110]), and most bishops preached to their own clergy to be moderate in their response. Nevertheless, battle lines were drawn in the press and exchanges became sharp. Montalembert tried in vain to restrain the militant Louis Veuillot, editor of the conservative Catholic daily *L'Univers*, in his attacks against the university authorities. Angry pamphlets circulated, including a 700-page tract issued by Chanoine Desgarets in Lyon condemning the government for daring to question the teaching qualifications of the very people God had chosen to "*make disciples of all nations.*"[111]

The university camp was equally adamant. Two prominent historians at the Collège de France, Jules Michelet and Edgar Quinet, launched a polemic against the Jesuits, by whom they meant all priests, or all who resisted university control of teaching. In his lectures, Michelet called on educators to turn each student into "a free being, able to act and create according to his own will." He enumerated the ways Catholic schools taught instead "a police mentality" mixed with "God talk."[112] Quinet, in turn, asserted that the mission of nineteenth-century Jesuitism was to replace the heritage of the French Revolution with a theocracy.[113] Church authorities won a round of the fight when Guizot agreed to suspend Quinet's lectures in 1843 and 1844. This hit close to home for Tocqueville. He was on excellent terms with Michelet at the Académie des sciences morales et politiques; in 1841, when Michelet proposed to have Quinet join the Collège de France faculty, Tocqueville had pressured Villemain to appoint him. In one instance during Quinet's lectures, Tocqueville sent him a note of appreciation for challenging "the lethargy of the mind."[114]

As Tocqueville sought a route to the high ground, his friend Louis Bouchitté from Versailles days, a Catholic philosopher who taught at the local Collège Royal, provided him with an approach that seemed promising. In 1840, Bouchitté had published *Histoire des preuves de l'existence de Dieu, considérées dans leurs principes les plus généraux, depuis les temps les plus reculés jusqu'au Monologium d'Anselme de Cantorbéry*, where he advanced the complementarity of religion and reason.[115] Tocqueville, who had never showed a penchant for metaphysical speculation but was keen on promoting his friend's work, arranged for Bouchitté to give lectures at the Académie des sciences morales et politiques and lobbied for his appointment as corresponding member of the Académie. Tocqueville redoubled his efforts on behalf of Bouchitté in 1842, when Bouchitté translated and edited Anselm's *Monologium* (1076), written at the Abbey du Bec before the Norman Benedictine monk became Archbishop of Canterbury. The publication was timely. In this landmark essay, Anselm had introduced "Christian rationalism," as Bouchitté called it, endorsing the use of reason in discovering God— provided that faith came first. Seen from the proper perspective, Anselm argued, reason helped confirm the existence of God. When faith precedes intelligence, intelligence affirms faith, a proposition that Immanuel Kant rejected but that Hegel, whose work Cousin introduced in France, embraced. Anselm's was a text for the day.

Tocqueville hoped that an endorsement from the rationalist Cousin for the Catholic Bouchitté would suggest that the two sides could overcome their antagonism and even approach education from the same philosophical position. Tocqueville could not directly nominate his friend's book for the Montyon Prize because, although already elected to the Académie française, he had not yet been inducted. So he convinced Cousin to do so. He also lobbied Royer-Collard, who assented to help only if he did not have to read Bouchitté's book![116] Bouchitté did not win the prize, but Cousin's support was promising. Regardless of Cousin's own commitment to reason over revelation, the philosophy taught in public secondary schools, under his leadership, remained squarely, Rémusat explained, "between faith and unbelief." Cousin pursued generalized Christian truths while stopping short of doctrinal Christianity.[117]

At the same time as Tocqueville was helping to promote his friend's interpretation of Anselm's theological view, Catholic leaders, first among them Montalembert, recruited Anselm to support the Catholic political agenda. Rallying Catholics to protect Catholic schools from university control, Montalembert issued a pamphlet titled *Devoir des catholiques* (November 1843). On the cover was a quotation from Anselm: "God loves nothing in this world more than the freedom of his church."[118] This came not from the saint's theological work from his days as monk but from his time as Archbishop of Canterbury when he courageously resisted the encroachments of King William Rufus on the English church. In other words, Montalembert cited Anselm as an example of fighting undue control from the state.

Montalembert's pamphlet was a sure sign that the situation had badly deteriorated and that Tocqueville's attempt to bridge the divide between church and state had failed. Tocqueville said to Édouard in December 1843 that he blamed the church for wanting not just independence from the state but the whole "direction of education."[119] Tocqueville addressed the Chamber a month later announcing that the new war had become "philosophical and religious."[120] After reprimanding the church, Tocqueville also condemned the university. Borrowing from Benjamin Constant, he worried that if the state was solely in charge of public education, "opinions will be dictated by privilege."[121]

All the newspapers commented on Tocqueville's speech. *Le Siècle*, trying to make up for the damage done by Faucher's article on prisons, praised Tocqueville's Chamber speech for its "gravitas" and "elevated character." *Le Constitutionnel*, more reserved, defended Villemain but appreciated Tocqueville's condemnation of the clergy's "wild declamations." Not every critic thought that Tocqueville's contributions were valuable, though. Predictably, the governmental *Journal des débats* judged the speech empty and pretentious while the legitimist *L'Univers* found it a singular mishmash of contradictions.[122]

Tocqueville, however, was quite clear that, as he told Bouchitté, "secular education guarantees freedom of thought. The University must remain the principal home of education, and the state must conserve its supervision of even those schools that it does not control." But Tocqueville also wanted "serious competition that could thrive alongside the University." "Education, as with all things, must perfect itself, enliven itself, and regenerate itself according to the stimulus of competition. This is what I want—no more, no less."[123] After promoting Bouchitté's translation of Anselm in 1842, Tocqueville turned to promoting his Chamber colleague Hyacinthe Corne's essay *De l'éducation publique dans ses rapports avec la famille et l'état* for the Montyon Prize. His *député* friend argued that public secondary schools should attract students "by liberty not monopoly, by the institution's demonstration of moral and scientific excellence, not constraints on heads of households."[124] The Académie judged the book too political for entry into the competition.

The controversy reached new heights as Villemain doubled down. Villemain submitted to the Chamber of Peers a new reform project in February 1844, which the peers adopted in May. This version demanded that *petits séminaires* teachers meet state qualifications. But regardless of their credentials, only university professors were trusted to administer the baccalauréat, and the state retained the right to visit and inspect private schools at any time. Countering Villemain, Abbé Dupanloup wrote public letters to the duc de Broglie, who oversaw passage of the law in the Chamber of Peers. The abbé argued that the complete independence of the *petits séminaires* was integral to the Church mission and its ability to attract young people to the priesthood. To tamper with it was to jeopardize the Church's ability to foster a calling and to place in further peril the already badly shaken Christian values of the nation.[125]

Pamphlets calling parishioners to action multiplied, some quite violent. The court sent Abbé Combalot to jail in March 1844 for three months for incendiary preaching that amounted to "inciting hatred between social classes" and defamation of a public administration of the government. Veuillot, whom Tocqueville blamed as "the principal author" of this evil, also went to jail for one month.[126] In April, Montalembert declared in the Chamber of Peers, "We are the sons of crusaders. We will not back down before the sons of Voltaire,"[127] and he created the Parti catholique to rally laymen (including many fathers who wanted to send their children to independent Catholic schools) in regional committees to advance the cause of the Church. Thiers, in charge of reviewing the bill the peers had passed, wanted instead to multiply restrictions on the clergy; he proposed reverting the *petits séminaires* to their original status as schools only for aspiring priests and demanded the renewal of prerequisites that had been relaxed in 1841.[128]

Tocqueville took his own views to the pages of *Le Commerce*. His thoughts on this topic became his most significant contribution to the newspaper. He reaffirmed that "the state has the right to enforce standards from teachers."[129] But he criticized Villemain for his reductionism, for "drawing around the human spirit a fixed circle and preventing it from leaving"; "we force everyone to learn the same things in the same way"; "we confine the human mind to a cramped circle."[130] Privately, Tocqueville admitted to Corcelle that "the most recent declarations of the bishops have really been intolerable," especially "the violence of their insults towards certain people, the exaggerations of their attacks on the University . . . their secret thoughts about dominating the whole education system."[131] But more nefarious was the parliamentary opposition—that is, the Thiers-Barrot coalition. The freedom of education controversy, Tocqueville maintained, was merely a smokescreen. It had become the left's excuse for avoiding the real issues that undermined society. By heralding it continuously, Thiers could hope to take over the government without committing to any substantive reform. Elections remained corrupt, September laws still held, popular classes were suffering, the press was not free. The diversion was an old trick. It was a modern version of the tale Plutarch told of Alcibiades docking his dog's tail: "the old Greek story in modern guise: while the Athenian people busy themselves with Alcibiades' dog, they forget his master's ways."[132]

This public controversy caused a deeply painful break in Tocqueville's friendship with Beaumont. Tocqueville courted Beaumont throughout 1844 for *Le Commerce*—including printing a glowing review of Beaumont's *L'Irlande* in October 1844—but Beaumont remained loyal throughout the year to *Le Siècle*. He even momentarily replaced Chambolle at the helm when the latter broke his collarbone in a carriage accident.[133] Tocqueville's resonant article, however, was too much for Chambolle to take. *Le Siècle* was silent at first, perhaps so as not to embarrass Beaumont, but the answer was coming. *Le Siècle* charged that Tocqueville had joined Montalembert's call to close ranks with "the sons of crusaders," and "the vestrymen of l'Univers and the Legitimist Party" to abandon liberty for despotism and priestcraft.[134] As if to prove *Le Siècle* right, *L'Univers* rushed to reproduce Tocqueville's "remarkable" article.[135] For *Le Siècle*, the entire staff at *Le Commerce* were now Jesuits and Carlists in disguise.[136]

After *Le Siècle*'s ad hominem attack on Tocqueville, exposing him as a Legitimist, a troubled Beaumont refused to write for the newspaper, but he stopped short of resigning from its board. He did not want to appear to be in league with Tocqueville.[137] However, in Tocqueville's mind, Beaumont's failure to explicitly defend him against *Le Siècle*'s accusation of Legitimism was an unforgivable act of betrayal. An aggrieved and somewhat spiteful Tocqueville broke off with his closest friend and confidant. To the travel companion who had singlehandedly come to Tocqueville's rescue during major bouts of sickness in Tennessee in 1831 and then in Algeria in 1842 (see next chapter), Tocqueville wrote, "I would rather you had abandoned me in the virgin forest or in the Eddis campsite." He reminded him, "I have but one weak point. My birth and the opinions of my family lead others to believe I am attached to Legitimists and the clergy." He added snidely, "Unlike you, I did not marry a granddaughter of General Lafayette."[138]

The vocal and contentious legislative debates and violent arguments in the press on the respective teaching missions of church and government in the end produced no tangible change in national policy. The battle that had mobilized such energy soon appeared futile. The Chamber session ended without a vote on the Villemain proposal, and Villemain himself was in deep trouble. When blackmailers threatened to reveal his homosexuality to the public, the minister attempted suicide. In an episode of madness on the place de la Concorde, he mistook a pile of stones for plotting Jesuits, cursing at them and flailing about until he was arrested and committed to an asylum. As for Tocqueville, the blowup over education had come to an end without resolution and with a dear friendship seriously imperiled.

## Tocqueville's Social Conscience: Reform and Social Work

A large part of Tocqueville's reflection on Christianity and democracy was on the obligation to lend a hand to the disadvantaged. Ever since he attempted to produce a second memoir on pauperism when he envisioned electoral prospects at Cherbourg, Tocqueville had been concerned about pauperism and welfare. While he had Gobineau on hand at the Académie des sciences morales et politiques, he put him to work on the issue. He told Gobineau in September 1843 that although Christianity had introduced the idea of charity, the concept was evolving in response to the complexity of the industrial age. Modern society therefore necessarily relied on the government to redress inequality and assist the weak. Accordingly, Tocqueville asked Gobineau to research charity not only in France but also throughout Europe and especially in Germany.[139] Gobineau sourced a number of references related to the transformation of charitable work since the late eighteenth century—sources that added to those Tocqueville had collected for several years on institutions of public assistance.[140] He documented a great rise in the number of private charitable groups beginning in 1816. In 1828, the first attempts to organize and publicize the efforts of these resulted in the Société des établissements charitables, and a move toward scientific theories of charity commenced. Gobineau provided documents on work done in Hamburg, Germany and in Bern, Switzerland. He also retraced duc de la Rochefoucauld-Liancourt's recommendations to the Constituent

Assembly for a centralized system of public assistance, which was never adopted, and other blueprints.[141]

Tocqueville took the occasion of France's ongoing economic contraction to advocate for relief for the poor in the pages of Le Commerce. He and his colleagues were equipped to assist in the effort. Corcelle was knowledgeable about government finance, having written about ways of making taxation more equitable.[142] Tocqueville, for his part, had introduced legislation for revising the census to create a fairer tax assessment.[143] Editor in chief Arnold Scheffer was the person most invested in issues of economics and social work. Drawing on these strengths, Le Commerce regularly addressed inequality. A few articles quoted Ledru-Rollin approvingly; one publicized effort for improving urban health; another endorsed Lamartine's program of public works and welfare; yet another called for state aid to workers' associations; some mentioned favorably Fourier's and Saint-Simon's emphasis on the benefits of community.[144] Unfortunately, these articles would be among the last for Le Commerce. Its readership was declining. Efforts to attract new investors and two attempts to restart the newspaper under a new name failed, and Tocqueville lost his investment as the paper folded.[145]

Nonetheless, these expressions of a commitment to social improvements would inform a larger political program that Tocqueville was developing. Tocqueville pursued the effort in Normandy at the Conseil général of his department, where he had become the most influential member. The days when he resisted the idea of public charity were long gone. Now he felt that in the absence of a national welfare program like the British poor laws, it was up to the department budget to fill the void and for local authorities to rescue those in need. Tocqueville invested himself heavily in four extremely well-researched reports meant to encourage the department to support abandoned children and help unwed mothers and their offspring. He thought no other question was "more governmental in nature" than child abandonment.[146]

In composing the reports, complete with statistics on infant mortality, Tocqueville was much influenced by the work of baron de Gérando, who had recently died. Gérando was an authority on administrative law and had promoted philanthropic institutions and authored De la bienfaisance publique. He and Tocqueville had mutual friends in Ballanche,

Ampère, and Madame Récamier.[147] Gérando advised suppressing the "towers" where children could be abandoned anonymously and replacing them with admission centers where mothers would be listened to. Tocqueville embraced this recommendation. He developed an apprentice system for orphaned children with monthly certificates of attendance. He wondered whether the local government should be responsible for providing clothing to abandoned children each year, given the expense and especially since the clothing thus provided was often better than the adoptive mother could give her own children. Tocqueville also addressed whether "unwed mothers" should be given small welfare payments, on what conditions of moral rectitude, and for what duration. All of Tocqueville's recommendations were adopted and appear to have been carried out. By 1847, two-thirds of *enfants trouvés* in the department were attending school.[148]

Having made his influence felt in Normandy, Tocqueville decided to champion similar programs in the Chamber, whose political makeup had changed after the elections of 1846. Tocqueville easily secured his seat in an election that otherwise returned a solid majority to the government and put Montalembert's Parti catholique on the political map. These gains were made at the expense of Barrot's dynastic left, which lost thirty seats.[149] Ensuing political realignments gave Tocqueville an occasion to pursue a coalition of his own making, relying once again on a few friends in the Chamber to launch a small parliamentary group with a distinct voice.

Tocqueville approached Dufaure in 1846, a former minister of public works whom Tocqueville befriended upon first joining the Chamber. Tocqueville proposed that Dufaure create "an association of a few men of talent and heart to stay out of political intrigue and crude electioneering and focus on the general and long-term interests of the country." If successful, he believed, the group had the potential to blossom into a "party that would take upon itself the principal mission to actively and practically work for the moral and material wellbeing of the lower classes, without stroking their prejudices nor inflaming their passions, in order to play an entirely new and important role in public life." Such reforms had so far been left to the "unintelligent and egotistical contempt of the conservative majority" on the one hand and to the "dreams and passions of the utopians" on the other.[150] To be clear, Tocqueville insisted that there should be no compromising collaboration with members of the current government. Also off limits was the Legitimist party. Tocqueville then asked his good friend and Chamber colleague Corcelle to "consider our intimate union with Dufaure . . . as the only way to create if not a party then at least a gathering of men that can stand fast between both Guizot and Thiers, and, with even more difficulty, between *Le Siècle* and *Le Journal des Débats*."[151] Tocqueville was also keen to maintain his connection with Rivet, from Corrèze, even though Rivet had lost his seat in 1846. Beaumont, however, remained firmly in Barrot's camp. Despite the mediation of common friends, affectionate words of reconciliation from both Tocqueville and Beaumont, and a renewed correspondence, the wound was still open.[152]

Tocqueville worked with this tiny group of Chamber colleagues to prepare a political platform of economic and social reform as a base for a possible Young Left party. In his working notes for such a party platform, Tocqueville for the first and only time gave serious and favorable consideration to early socialist theories. He read and reflected on "the different systems of Owen, Saint-Simon, Fourier, the ideas now called socialist in the work of Louis Blanc, in various novels, and even in the passing pages of serials." He noted the "cries of the people or at least those attributed to the people" and the innovation of "proposed remedies: communism, labor organization, phalansteries. . . . All these remedies point to the making of a new social order that is without precedent in the world." The Young Left hoped to bring about concerted action in the Chamber to "guarantee that the poor benefit from full legal equality."[153]

Tocqueville had only a few conversations, however, with prominent personalities on the left. Among Fourierists, he crossed paths with Victor Considerant at Madame Ancelot's salon, but the encounter was superficial. He knew the Saint-Simonian Gustave d'Eichthal, a student of Auguste Comte; he had had him contribute articles on Greece to *Le Commerce*. It is likely that the Urbain who worked briefly at *Le Commerce* was in fact Saint-Simon's disciple Ismaÿl Urbain.[154] As Tocqueville's newfound interest became known, Père Enfantin, Saint-Simon's most prominent disciple and the leader of the sect, sent Tocqueville his *Correspondance philosophique et religieuse*. Tocqueville responded that he shared Enfantin's "powerful sense of what miseries the poor endure" and the goal of "developing greater equality on earth with a fairer distribution of wealth."[155] The same socialists who had ignored volume 2 of *Democracy in America* now regularly reported on Tocqueville's Chamber speeches in their newspapers.

Although Tocqueville's relationship with the socialists never went further than mutual curiosity, his developing social conscience led him to join a group of Catholics promoting social reform under Armand de Melun's leadership. He subscribed to Melun's *Annales de la charité* in 1845. Besides advocating good works, the journal focused on the science and art of charity. Both Tocqueville and his brother Édouard became charter members of Melun's Société d'économie charitable at its first meeting in January 1847, together with Corcelle, Louis Cormenin, Louis-René Villermé, and Abbé Landmann (whom Tocqueville had met in Algeria).[156]

In his admittedly preliminary draft program for the Young Left, Tocqueville proposed a two-pronged approach. He envisioned "expanding political rights to those beyond the middle class" so that "the lower classes become more consistently and peaceably interested in public affairs." And then "making the intellectual and material lot of these classes the principal object of the care and concern of the legislator."[157] Meanwhile, he pursued his older goals of holding civil servants accountable by introducing the right to sue them, working on reforming the Conseil d'état into an independent judiciary, ending voting fraud, and keeping Conseils généraux as administrative, not political bodies.[158]

As a legislator and public intellectual, then, Tocqueville traveled a long road from inexperience to becoming a respected voice. He strove to marry thought and action as he attempted to reconcile democracy with religion. Although his commitment to social change left few concrete traces, he reflected enough on inequality to write with conviction: "There is no doubt that one day the political battle will pit the haves against the have nots; that the battlefield shall be property, and that the great political questions will relate to property law and its modification."[159]

# 8

# Abolitionist, Nationalist, and Colonialist

TOCQUEVILLE'S POLITICAL CAREER put into stark relief the conflicting elements of his own identity, between the political theorist and the French imperialist, between the advocate of democracy and the advocate of conquest. Tocqueville wanted to see France recover its role as a power broker in world affairs and regain its place as a major colonial presence as it had been in the lost days of New France. This meant working both within and without the Chamber toward the long-term economic viability of the French Caribbean islands; countering England's domination of the seas; ensuring that France had its say in international treaties concerning the Middle East; and most importantly, promoting the French colonization of Algeria. Tocqueville devoted immense time and energy throughout the 1840s to restoring French grandeur. He sought to be at once a patriot, a colonialist, and a democrat, even though these identities failed to cohere. He tried again and again to merge his view of national interest and democratic values, only to find this melding unsustainable.

## Slavery in the French Caribbean Islands

Tocqueville was most easily able to reconcile his desire for French grandeur with his democratic ideals in promoting the abolition of slavery in the French colonies. His first Chamber assignment was to a committee on the abolition of slavery in the French Caribbean islands. The sweeping British emancipation legislation of 1833, which freed over 800,000 slaves throughout the British colonies, rejuvenated French abolitionism. Tocqueville and Beaumont were members of the elite Societé pour l'abolition de l'esclavage (a re-creation, in part, of the Société des amis des noirs of the Revolutionary years), which welcomed the two authors known for their condemnation of slavery in the United States. There, Tocqueville and Beaumont met the politicians who were the voices of abolition in the Chamber, most prominent among them the duc de Broglie, Victor Destutt de Tracy, Hippolyte Passy, Xavier de Sade, and Alphonse de Lamartine. Victor Schœlcher, who would lead the French abolitionist movement to success in 1848, joined the society late and radicalized slowly.[1] Society meetings were perfunctory, typically limited to the exchange of documents.[2]

Members regularly petitioned the Chamber for partial emancipation, but these efforts yielded little. The Chamber normally referred these petitions to the minister of colonies and/or the minister of the navy or debated them as part of its consideration of the colonial budget. It appointed an occasional ad hoc commission to make recommendations. Although commissioners were often sympathetic to the petitioners' views, Caribbean planters and their mercantile creditors in Bordeaux, Nantes, and Saint-Malo maintained solid allies in the Chamber (François Mauguin, baron Dupin) who made sure petitions circulated only from commission to commission without a recommendation ever going to the floor for a vote.

In 1838, a year before Tocqueville's election, Passy, who had since become finance minister, submitted to the Chamber a motion to free all children born in the colonies, to allow enslaved people to purchase their own freedom with a *pécule* (peculium), and to recognize slave marriages, all measures aimed at progressive emancipation. After a heated exchange in the Chamber, Guizot presided over a commission to study the proposal, with Rémusat as rapporteur. In its April 1838 recommendations, never brought back to the full Chamber for a vote, the commission advocated that the French state assume responsibility for implementing the abolition of slavery. The commission also suggested the state wait until

1840, the year scheduled for emancipation in British colonies, to formulate policy.[3] Because the Chamber never heard the recommendation, Tracy reintroduced the Passy motion in July 1839, and the Chamber created yet another commission, this time with Sade as president and Tocqueville as rapporteur.[4] Tocqueville was thus tasked with assembling evidence and suggesting means of emancipating slaves in Martinique and Guadeloupe, the Caribbean remnants of the French empire, as well as in French Guiana and La Réunion.

Tocqueville expressed on multiple occasions his loathing for the notion that an "innate and permanent inequality within the great human family" could exist.[5] In an improvised speech at the Académie des sciences morales et politiques in 1839, Tocqueville characterized slavery as "unjust, immoral, violating the most sacred rights of humanity . . . a horrible abuse of power, a disdain for all laws, both human and divine."[6] He took special pride in the fact that the French had freed their slaves during the Revolution several decades before the nonconformist evangelical movement led England to do so. The French had been the first, Tocqueville argued, to "spread the notion throughout the universe that all men were equal before the law, just as Christianity had created the equality of all men before God; we are the legitimate authors of the abolitionist cause."[7] Tocqueville recognized, however, that Napoleon's 1802 decree restoring slavery in the colonies, a brief eight years after the French Revolutionary Convention decreed its abolition, muzzled the French abolitionist movement for a generation.

As the commission's rapporteur, Tocqueville seized the opportunity "to treat a great problem with a pen in hand."[8] Tocqueville pressed for abolition on the grounds that "the status quo will lose the colonies."[9] In Tocqueville's judgment, the obsolete sugar cane industry in the French Caribbean could not survive competition from both a growing beet sugar enterprise at home and free labor in British colonies. As it turned out, the British government had accelerated emancipation by shortening the period of apprenticeship to which slaves had to submit. British slaves were freed in August 1838, two years ahead of schedule. Martinique and Guadeloupe had therefore become islands of slavery in a sea of British freedom.

This development was foremost on Tocqueville's mind as he argued for abolition and the responsibility of the French state to arbitrate conflicts between planters and freemen. Tocqueville feared that British-dominated islands would attract runaway slaves—and that a small arm of the Caribbean Sea, like the Ohio River between free and slave states in the United States, would prove to be no obstacle. Moreover, how could the planters not see that a slave revolt could at any moment destroy their livelihood and ruin them, not realize that "the races are merging; classes are drawn ever closer together"? Tocqueville thought it was imperative to turn the "Mediterranean of the new world" into a sea of liberty and equality.[10]

Assuming abolition a foreordained conclusion, regardless of planters' deep-rooted convictions to the contrary, Tocqueville championed the immediate and simultaneous emancipation of all slaves in French colonies. Tracy and Passy had proposed a plan that would allow some slaves to purchase their freedom, but Tocqueville noted that such a measure would only have introduced a new division between the few slaves able to afford emancipation and all those still trapped in bondage. Neither did Tocqueville support the idea of freeing children first, which similarly would divide slaves by disturbing or even severing the natural bond between mothers and children.

In his report, he adopted a dispassionate tone in hopes of minimizing colonial opposition.[11] He also looked for ways to ease the transition for planters. From conversations with Nassau Senior, Tocqueville realized that the British had implemented their system of apprenticeship for freed slaves not as an intermediate step between slavery and freedom but as a means of compensating British planters.[12] Aware of the limited resources of the French state, which could not match the generous compensation the British government had provided, Tocqueville suggested, without specifying how, that the government pay freemen yet withhold some amount to provide an indemnity to former slaveholders—details for this plan to be determined during the 1841 legislative session.

French planters were not persuaded. At least one of them invoked none other than Tocqueville, whom he called "the Montesquieu of our days," in arguing *against* abolition. The vice-president of the Conseil colonial, comte de Mauny, a sugar planter in Martinique, put *Democracy in America* to good use in a pamphlet that circulated in the Chamber. He quoted Tocqueville as saying that "for all the uncertainty of the future," the one "sure" and "imminent" reality was that "the Anglo-Americans alone will blanket the vast region comprised between the polar ice cap and the tropics and stretching from the Atlantic to the South Seas." Maintaining slavery, Mauny concluded, was the only possible way of competing with the British and, he added, preserving "the gentleness of the French regime" against "the cruelty of the English system."[13] Perhaps as a reminder of the power of the colonial lobby, Tocqueville kept Mauny's tract at hand in his library.

Slavery interests in the Chamber predictably managed to bury Tocqueville's proposal. It was never discussed by the full body and therefore had little political impact. The Société pour l'abolition de l'esclavage printed it as a brochure, which circulated modestly in England and in the United States. Tocqueville was at the time corresponding with his American friend Jared Sparks about the danger of expanding slavery in the US territories.[14] Mary Sparks translated Tocqueville's text and had it published in Boston in 1840. The one place where Tocqueville's proposal seems to have resonated was in Louisiana, which had a large contingent of former French planters from Saint-Domingue. An alarmed French consul to New Orleans sent a special communiqué to the government in Paris reporting on the fear sparked by a "mere reading of a proposal" there. If ever enacted, it "would cause a veritable revolution in the colonies and would not be without effect on the future of the United States."[15]

In keeping with the practice of replacing one commission on abolition by another, Thiers, prime minister in April 1840, asked the duc de Broglie (former president of the Société pour l'abolition de l'esclavage and former prime minister) to head a new effort. Tocqueville was one of the more active participants of the Broglie commission, which submitted its conclusions in 1843. He deemed the report a "masterpiece . . . breathing a sincere love for the human race."[16]

The Broglie commission conducted an extensive inquiry that amply justified Tocqueville's estimation of its work but took the view that immediate emancipation was not politically acceptable. Broglie and his team not only documented the existing situation on the French islands but also contemplated realistic institutional reforms needed to turn the colonies into a free society. They studied possible reforms of the courts, adjustments in law enforcement and prison management, expansion of the school system, and encouragements to church attendance to Christianize freed slaves.

For his part, Tocqueville continued to argue for complete emancipation, with the French state responsible for organizing work, paying the newly freed slaves, authorizing the creation of civil associations, fostering religious practice, and encouraging marriage among former slaves. Abolition seemed to him within reach considering the comparatively small number of slaves in the French Caribbean (a quarter of a million versus three to four times that number already emancipated in the British colonies) and the fact that there was only a single industry to regulate.

In the end, Tocqueville compromised. Broglie could not convince his commission members to make a unified recommendation. The majority (including Tocqueville) recommended the colonies be given ten years to prepare for emancipation. A minority opted for progressive emancipation over twenty years beginning with freeing children and then allowing slaves to purchase their freedom with their savings. In either case, France would pay a significant indemnity to slave owners and guarantee a remunerative price for colonial sugar after emancipation. The French government, however, was not ready to act on any of the commission's proposals, concerned about the cost of compensation to slave owners, a problem further aggravated by a major earthquake that shook Guadeloupe in February 1843.[17]

As the Broglie report was not debated in the Chamber any more than the preceding ones, Tocqueville publicized its findings and recommendations in several articles in Le Siècle in late 1843. To help secure planters' cooperation, Tocqueville further compromised his initial position by proposing an additional concession to them not in the Broglie report. The planters were concerned about competition from former slaves becoming successful planters themselves. This had happened in British Jamaica where freemen had been able after 1838 to acquire cheap land.

To protect French plantations from similar rivalry, Tocqueville suggested that freemen be temporarily forbidden from acquiring land.[18]

Tocqueville's concessions were inadequate to alter the colonies' adamant resistance to even the idea of change. Colonists persisted in painting slavery as a social arrangement working for the "perpetual and absolute benefaction" of all.[19] Navy Minister Admiral Mackau, the most timorous and conservative member of the Broglie commission, provoked a tempest by proposing that the French state at least guarantee the right for slaves to purchase their freedom with their own money. It was a modest proposal for a small reform that promised to have no effect, as it did not set a maximum price the owner might demand and required the "freed" slave remain in the service of the former owner for another five years. Even this timid suggestion provoked a flurry of complaints from the colonies and outrage in the Chamber of Peers when Mackau introduced the measure. When the Chamber of Deputies finally approved the Mackau law in 1845, Tocqueville, who for years had been calling for so much more, spoke in favor of passage only because the law was a small wedge in the planters' resistance. Its real innovation was that it made it possible for the French state to regulate a transaction between master and slave for the first time. Such a modest move, he thought, was at least a step in the right direction of involving the government in the endlessly postponed task of emancipation.

But when it came to allowing the British Navy to interfere with the French slave trade, Tocqueville drew a line. However desirous Tocqueville was to see the end of slavery, his commitment to national sovereignty took precedence over his abolitionism.[20] British patrol boats diligently policing the slave trade at sea did not hesitate to arrest French captains and their crews who carried African slaves to the Caribbean.[21] Yet Tocqueville abhorred the idea of ceding to England any authority over ships carrying the French flag. No British patrol boat should have unrestricted authority to board French ships and decide whether to arrest their crew. Tocqueville admired the British emancipation project, but that was no reason for letting the British police infringe on French rights. He was determined to put an end to British unilateral domination of the seas, even if that meant relaxing the hunt for the illicit human trafficking.

Tocqueville argued in an address to the Chamber in May 1842 that the right to search (*droit de visite*) was an ineffective way to end slavery and that it provoked further acts of savagery. He pointed to instances where slave traders had evaded British surveillance ships by dangerously increasing speed after packing as many bodies as possible in their cargo. Fearing being caught, some had thrown hundreds of slaves into the sea. One must find another way to abolish the trade. This one leads only to "atrocities." He suggested it would be more effective to close the slave markets in Cuba and Brazil.[22]

Tocqueville redoubled his efforts in January 1843 in attacking in the Chamber a (still unratified) treaty renewal on reciprocal rights to inspect boats at sea that Guizot had entered, in France's name, with England, Prussia, Austria, and Russia.[23] Tocqueville denounced Guizot for conceding too much authority to England over French captains who should answer only to French courts. The assault he delivered on that day on Guizot, he rehearsed carefully.[24] Tocqueville failed to provoke a cabinet crisis, but Guizot eventually renegotiated the treaty so that the two countries would be collaborating in policing the seas.

Tocqueville objected to Britain's excessive might. How should "the armed forces of a nation have the extraordinary right to arrest the criminals of another nation: and where is this to be done exactly? On the high seas, where anything can happen, and where anything can be expected."[25] And given America's history with Great Britain, Tocqueville looked to his American friends for common ground. When John Spencer was appointed secretary of war in the Tyler administration in 1841, Tocqueville wrote him to convey his concerns: "In our day, Great Britain is to seafaring peoples what Louis XIV was to the Europe of the 17th century. She destroys many of them and threatens the others with the same fate."[26]

Tocqueville's attacks led Lord Brougham (who had been among Tocqueville's hosts in England in 1835) to chastise Tocqueville publicly in the House of Lords by pointing out that England respected the terms of an 1823 agreement with the United States on policing the slave trade, and by ridiculing Tocqueville's "marvelous ignorance" of precedents. Tocqueville struck back in the press that ignorance was on Lord Brougham's

side. He asked his British translator, Henry Reeve, to translate his response and Mill to publicize it, which they did. The conflict was wide
open. Tocqueville proved unwilling to cede even a small fraction of national sovereignty in defense of the universal human freedom he claimed
to support.[27]

## Promoting France's Interests in the Orient Crisis

The argument over the slave trade and the right to search was part of a
larger struggle between France and England for international supremacy.
In spring 1839, that contest centered on the future of the Ottoman Empire and influence in the Middle East. The dispute very nearly brought
England and France to war. Tocqueville became a strident advocate of
the French position, much to the dismay of his British friends. Mill felt
that Tocqueville's reflexive reactions to his perceived attacks on French
honor were unbecoming of a theorist of democracy, who should have
higher values. As in the right to search controversy, Tocqueville felt he
had to defend France's international standing.

The facts are intricate but worth following in some detail. Ottoman
sultan Mahmud II had already lost Greece to independence and Al-
geria to France when, in the spring of 1839, he attempted to recover
Syria, which his former subject, the Egyptian pasha Mehemet Ali, had
invaded and occupied in 1832. In the span of a few days at the end of
June and beginning of July, however, Egypt routed the Ottoman army.
The defeated Ottomans surrendered their fleet to the Egyptians in
Alexandria.[28]

As this dramatic Ottoman capitulation was still unfolding, Tocqueville gave his first speech in the Chamber on July 2, 1839. He underscored European influence in Asia as the "undertaking of the century,"
and he argued that France could not let the Russians and British dictate
the future of the Ottoman Empire and that it was a matter of "national
honor" that France has a say in any negotiated settlement between the
sultan and the pasha.[29]

In analyzing the conflict in the Chamber, Tocqueville saw that Russia
and England had different objectives in taking the side of the Ottomans.

Czar Nicolas I had heretofore protected the Sublime Porte but only to extend his reach over its territory. His expansionist policy was not to the liking of British foreign secretary Lord Palmerston, who sought instead to maintain the integrity of the Porte to protect British trade routes to India and other commercial and strategic interests. The French also had an interest in the outcome, but they sided with Egypt. Tocqueville pointed out that the French had maintained a real presence in Egypt long after Napoleon's retreat; there were numerous French officers in the Egyptian army and there were influential French religious ministries building schools in Egypt. He supported an alliance with Mehemet Ali necessary to consolidate French presence in the Mediterranean and dominate Algeria, while preventing England from having access to India through Suez and the Dardanelles. War with England was rapidly becoming a distinct possibility. Tocqueville seriously entertained the idea, leaving his English friends aghast.

The young sultan's inexperience encouraged Palmerston to orchestrate a collective resolution later that month, on July 27, 1839, whereby Austria, Prussia, Russia, France, and Great Britain reserved the right to be party to any settlement between Constantinople and Alexandria. At the same time, England jockeyed with France for influence over Egypt. Palmerston demanded Mehemet Ali return Syria in exchange for recognition of his hereditary sovereignty over Egypt. In France, Marshal Soult (prime minister and minister of foreign affairs) countered England directly by affirming instead France's full support for Mehemet Ali's hereditary position not only in Egypt but also in conquered Syria.

France and England were on a collision course. Soult requested military funds from the Chamber should fighting the British become necessary. Soult resigned in February 1840 because of an unrelated budgetary crisis, and King Louis Philippe called Thiers, who was initially conciliatory toward England, to replace him. Tocqueville had consulted with Thiers on the crisis and had found him placing more importance on securing English assistance in reclaiming the Rhine as France's eastern border—"a glorious dream"—than on defending Egypt and possibly intervening militarily. Thiers was willing, or so he told Tocqueville, to let British influence over Egypt grow if he could secure their help on eastern expansion—a project that briefly provoked a renewed anti-French nationalist surge in Germany.[30]

Back in power, however, Thiers changed his mind, and he too gave priority to French interests in the Mediterranean and came to Mehemet Ali's defense. Assuming a belligerent attitude toward England became part of a larger effort by Thiers and his interior minister Rémusat to revive the Napoleonic legend. They arranged for the return of the emperor's ashes from Saint Helena to France and buried them with great pomp in a newly designed imperial tomb under the dome of the Hôtel des Invalides. Preparing for war, they launched anew the defensive project (dating from the Restoration) of encircling Paris with a military wall to protect the capital from foreign invasion. The Chamber allocated funds for the wall fortifications of Paris in April.[31]

Palmerston set up a European commission to negotiate a solution to the conflict, but Thiers secretly encouraged direct negotiations between the sultan and the pasha. He reasoned that direct talks were more likely to produce an outcome favorable to the Egyptian pasha than a European commission controlled by Palmerston. This arrangement did not stay secret long. An angry Palmerston struck back. Keeping Guizot, then French ambassador to the Court of Saint James, in the dark, Palmerston convinced a reluctant British cabinet to exclude France from the European concert of nations. As a result, with France not invited, England, Russia, Austria, and Prussia signed the Treaty of London (July 15, 1840), pledging to destroy Mehemet Ali unless he removed himself from Syria. If Mehemet Ali complied, the four great powers would agree to respect his hereditary claim to Egypt. The French were outraged at having been excluded. They looked to the new European alliance as an unwelcome and dramatic reminder of the Sainte-Alliance against Napoleon.[32]

Tocqueville disliked Thiers, and he also disliked Napoleon. The second volume of *Democracy in America*, published in April 1840, just as Thiers was returning to power, was in good part an attack on Napoleonic despotism. Tocqueville, however, put national honor first. He took a firm position and held on to it. He wrote to Thiers in July 1840 in support of the prime minister's bellicose stand toward England, telling him,

"There remains only one way to prevent war, and that is to seem very determined to wage it." He opined that "to make a proud and costly demonstration of this seem[ed] wise."[33] Meanwhile, Thiers's Napoleonic rhetoric worked almost too well in public opinion. It generated much popular support for war. By summer's end, a banquet for electoral reform outside Paris ended with shouts of "Mort aux Anglais."[34]

In London, Ambassador Guizot was alarmed by the turn of events. He feared that the revived nationalist fervor of the masses not only favored war with England but also posed a revolutionary threat to the French government. War would awaken domestic revolutionary passions and likely destroy the regime. Although Palmerston had blindsided him, Guizot sought appeasement, an approach that elicited Tocqueville's contempt.

A war broke out in the Middle East as the British delivered on their threat to Egypt. They issued an ultimatum to Mehemet Ali to return to the sultan the territorial conquest as well as the confiscated fleet. When Mehemet Ali did not even answer, the British fleet sailed for Beirut. British troops invaded Syria on September 9. They captured Beirut and Acre in no time. By early November, Ibrahim, Mehemet Ali's son, had evacuated all of Syria.

In Paris, Thiers threatened to prepare France for war unless Mehemet Ali was immediately guaranteed his hereditary sovereignty in Egypt. "If certain lines are crossed, it's war," he declared.[35] The Chamber approved military funding. Thiers, however, was gradually losing the support of the king as well as that of influential cabinet members. Reeve, who visited Paris at the time, noted there was no war consensus among top political personnel. He reported to Lord Lansdowne that Victor Cousin (his former professor at the Sorbonne, now Thiers's minister of public instruction) was in favor of a strong alliance with England against Russia, as were Broglie and Guizot. The conflict between the king and cabinet on the one hand, and Thiers and the belligerent crowd on the other hand, reached a fever pitch when a Parisian worker denouncing royal tyranny attempted to assassinate Louis Philippe in his carriage on October 15. Reeve reported phlegmatically, "Just before dinner, the King has been shot at." The king, for his part, understood that his inclination to look for a peaceful way out had made him that much more unpopular with the masses. "By killing me they sought to kill the peace,"[36] he reckoned. But he stayed the course; he fired his *petit ministre* and replaced him with Guizot and Soult in hopes of restoring "a cordial good understanding" between France and England, in accord with Guizot's position that "Europe's foremost interest is peace everywhere and always."[37]

Although conflicted between belligerent and conciliatory feelings toward England, Tocqueville came out in defense of French national honor. He wrote a detailed letter to Reeve early in November 1840 pleading that the British stop humiliating France lest the situation deteriorate. Reeve, who had gotten to know Guizot well in London (he had translated Guizot's book on George Washington into English), believed in Guizot's policy of appeasement but also took Tocqueville's anxieties seriously. He shared Tocqueville's letter with Lord Lansdowne, who paid attention and advised Prime Minister Melbourne and Foreign Secretary Palmerston accordingly.[38] How much Tocqueville's intervention mattered in lowering the tension is hard to say, but the British cabinet thereafter proved more conciliatory with respect to Mehemet Ali's sovereign position over Egypt. On November 27, 1840, Mehemet Ali agreed to the British conditions of returning Syria to the sultan, and the sultan in turn yielded to British pressure to let the pasha keep Egypt. Reeve concluded the episode by noting that Palmerston had either "superior knowledge" that there would be no war with France or "superior luck."[39] With the diplomatic crisis subsiding, France signed in London in July 1841, in a pacified Europe, a five-power straits convention to keep the Bosporus and Dardanelles closed to foreign warships in time of peace. A humbled France was readmitted to the concert of nations.

Even as the crisis abated, Tocqueville maintained a bellicose stand in public. He told the Chamber on November 30, 1840 that it was unforgiveable that France should have been excluded from participating in transforming the Orient. "Do you think a great nation can bear witness to such a great spectacle without taking part?" He chastised Guizot for temporizing, and he denounced the government's fear of domestic radicalism (which he otherwise shared) as an excuse for not mobilizing the army. "A government that cannot make war is a detestable government."[40]

Tocqueville's British friends were dismayed, and Reeve was the first one to let him know. Tocqueville restated his position. Conceding to the British, Tocqueville explained, amounted to assenting publicly that a timorous French middle class, which dominated the Chamber, was right to value its material interests above those of France. This, he could not possibly do. In response, Reeve felt that Tocqueville had fallen into the "old Girondin error of joining a wrong party to set it right."[41] But Tocqueville persisted in his belief that for once, the crowd was right. Therefore, the best way he could see to contain a revolutionary outcome was to side with it. For, as he put it most pithily, "you can only master the vices of a people by partaking in its virtues."[42]

Mill was not so easily convinced that there was any justification for Tocqueville to embrace the French crowd's belligerent attitude. Mill had lavished praise on the second volume of *Democracy in America* without receiving any sign of appreciation from Tocqueville. Tocqueville finally wrote Mill at length but also complained of British attitudes toward the crisis. An irritated Mill fired back that the whole crisis had been a political game among a few politicians but that the British people, contrary to the French, had never been involved. Let us hang Palmerston and Thiers together, but the "people were not to blame." Senior concurred, telling Tocqueville "whether Mehemet Ali reigned in Constantinople & Alexandria, or Mahmoud in both these countries, not two persons out of London, & not ten persons in London care one sixpence."[43]

Mill openly denounced Tocqueville's bellicose rhetoric and the French "rabid eagerness for war," "explosion of Napoleonism," and "hatred of England." Fortunately, they faced an "English character" "not to be bullied" (presumably by Thiers's double game).[44] Tocqueville, in turn, held his ground that if the "chance of war" had been mitigated, so had the "chance of a new and sincere alliance" between the two nations. Although Tocqueville indicated that he "could not approve the revolutionary and propagandistic language" from the "partisans of the war," he remained far more distrustful of "those who were loudly asking for peace" simply because they preferred their own comfort. War, Tocqueville insisted, remained the solution to the "gradual softening of mores" that plagued the French people. One does not foster grandeur by building railroads. A nation that had "fallen from the level on which its ancestors had put it" required a "proud attitude" if it intended to stay alive, not the "weakness and egoism" of the middle class. Tocqueville wrote all this in March 1841.[45] Mill did not bother to respond.

Tocqueville ended up denying Mill's charge of Napoleonism indirectly in his acceptance speech to the Académie française in 1842, a ritual that marked his ascendance to the pinnacle of France's literary order. Tradition comes with unexpected challenges. Academic electoral politics required that Tocqueville praise his predecessor, none other than the comte Lacuée de Cessac, a writer on military art and a close aide to Napoleon, whose responsibility it was to oversee the conscription, with the consequence that 80,000 young men a year were slaughtered on the battlefield, "cut down systematically like trees in a forest," as Chateaubriand had said.[46] In a draft, Tocqueville called Cessac a man who "did not conceive he could argue with the emperor," but in the speech, he settled for the faint praise of a "servant of absolutism."[47]

Tocqueville was walking a fine line in simultaneously praising French conquests and love of liberty. Although he had to commend Cessac, he also made clear that Napoleon had gone too far. Tocqueville valued liberty more than military glory. He wondered whether the "servant" had finally realized that the "master" had unfortunately "substituted a passion for conquest to a passion for liberty" and "ended in despotism an immense revolution begun for liberty."[48]

There ensued two rebukes. The first came from comte Molé, Tocqueville's older cousin and former prime minister, who had once rallied to the emperor. Molé used his privilege of giving the rejoinder to lecture the new academician, saying that had Tocqueville lived through the dramatic events himself, he would have known that Napoleon had saved France from the chaos of the revolutionary National Convention.[49] A very different rebuke came a bit later by mail. Mill, to whom Tocqueville had sent his induction speech, would have none of it. He resented Tocqueville's persistent underlying bellicosity in the name of "France & civilization." Mill implored, men of influence like Tocqueville, and above all the great theorist of democracy, had a duty to remember that "national glory" depended not on belligerence but on "industry, instruction, morality & good government." Only in prioritizing these factors did a country gain respect and standing in the face of the wider world. Without them, the "English" understood France as operating on nothing less than "simple puerility." International standing and a healthy "civilization" required more." "The real importance of a country . . . does not depend upon the loud & boisterous *assertion* of importance," and Tocqueville should not stoop to the bullying rhetoric of "a nation of sulky schoolboys."[50]

Tocqueville did not hear his friend. He stayed the course in opposing English might around the world in the name of the French grandeur he longed for.[51] He devoted several position papers in *Le Commerce* in summer 1844 to the need to limit England's grip on so many theaters. He defended the French colonization of Polynesian islands to counter British presence in the Pacific. He supported, against Guizot, the expulsion from Tahiti of British representative Pritchard, who had fomented anti-French feelings.[52] Although worried about the extension of slavery in the American west, he sided in the Chamber early in 1846 with the Americans in their boundary dispute with England in Oregon, knowing that their success would challenge the British maritime domination of the Pacific.[53] Then in 1847, Tocqueville's Young Left group threatened the entente cordiale in a French-English rivalry of influence in the Mediterranean. They proposed an amendment to the parliamentary address to the Crown, instructing Guizot not to appease England, when France and England became embroiled in a game of influence with the minutely negotiated marriage of the duc d'Aumale, Louis Philippe's son, with the infanta, the Spanish queen's sister.[54]

## Waging War in Algeria

The largest test of French grandeur, as Mill challenged Tocqueville to understand the term, came in Algeria. Tocqueville was deeply involved in the French implantation in North Africa, and this is where his nationalist instincts most visibly clashed with his democratic ones. It is also where he most clearly failed to find a satisfying compromise. In seeking colonization, Tocqueville was not inspired, like his British friends, by a civilizing mission. If for Mill, despotism was "a legitimate mode of government in dealing with barbarians, provided the end be their improvement," for Tocqueville, colonization worked to the benefit not of "barbarians" but of French settlers. Tocqueville justified the conquest by seeing the colony as a place where French people could rise out of sedentary mediocrity at home, seek a better life for themselves in a new place, and exercise their freedom at last.[55] They could realize in Algeria the democratic promise they could not fulfill at home.

Tocqueville was committed to a successful Algerian conquest from day one. His childhood friend Kergorlay had been among the first soldiers to ship off to Algeria. His brother Hippolyte had wanted to go. Kergorlay and Tocqueville agreed that the conquest offered both geopolitical and economic prospects. France would strengthen its position in the Mediterranean and effectively challenge Britain. Algeria, moreover, appeared to be a golden economic opportunity. Even though France was neither overpopulated nor land hungry, Algeria's abundance of arable land was enticing. Berber country had been Rome's granary in antiquity; now it would be France's. The Tell, or north Algeria, had enough rainfall for settled agriculture.[56]

A broad colonial consensus materialized in France. It extended from the royal family on the right (the king sent his sons to battle in Algeria) to the members of the Chamber furthest to the left. Tocqueville, like most of his colleagues in the French abolition society, had no reservations regarding the conquest. Those few society members who opposed it, like Passy, did so on economic, not moral, grounds. In France, not only liberal circles but also communitarians and socialists embraced imperialism. "We have the Mediterranean to turn French and Algeria to keep," wrote socialist Louis Blanc.[57]

Tocqueville rapidly abandoned the utopian view he had embraced in his first electoral campaign of 1837 that the two populations—French and Arabic—would "blend together." The invaders must unequivocally dominate the country, he now believed. Tocqueville told Léon Juchault de Lamoricière, Kergorlay's classmate at the École Polytechnique, who, as captain of the newly formed Zouave Battalion, had established military intelligence units in Algeria, "one people conquering another is hardly a new thing in this world." Degrees of civilization usually determine the relationships between conqueror and conquered. "We have sometimes seen a highly civilized people fuse with a barbarian people but only in cases where the civilized are weak and the barbarians strong. In cases where one of the two is both stronger and more civilized, it does not allow itself to be subsumed into the other, it either fights it off, or kills it off. I fervently wish it were not so in Africa, but I have little hope it will turn out otherwise."

Tocqueville came to see Algeria as a French version of the American frontier.[58] His experience of democracy in America justified French colonization of North Africa. The conquest should stimulate intelligent people to embark on a pioneering venture, like Americans whom he had observed populating the west. "What great examples to follow! This people that advances five or six leagues a year in a desert of more than four hundred. It is these American property owners, these small-scale capitalists, who with resources large and small seek out their fortunes on the frontier. It is that type of people that we must attract to Algeria."[59] The French had a chance to acquire in Algeria the colonizing skills that had heretofore escaped them. Very early in the conquest, Kergorlay envisioned that "colonists granted large plots of arable land would produce gaggles of children to till the soil."[60]

Tocqueville read the Koran in 1838, one year after his first electoral campaign, when he had speculated it was possible to fuse the two societies into one ("*se confondre*"). Now he found they were in fact "two discrete bodies, utterly distinct."[61] Arabs would neither convert to Christianity nor adopt a secular state. The Koran, by blending divine and civil law into one set of precepts, prevented the creation of a shared western-style civil society. Tocqueville told Arthur de Gobineau, "There have been few religions in the world as deadly to men as that of Mohammed."[62] Among Arabs, justice is served only in God's name, with no possible appeal. Elites receive common training in a single text whether they end up serving as imams, muftis, or qadis. Believers, for their part, are limited to a cult of praying and listening to sermons.[63] All have an obligation of jihad, as evidenced by the war of resistance the sanctified marabout Abd El Kader was waging against the French. "To fuse these two populations together would be a fool's errand."[64]

Tocqueville did not want the French in North Africa to replicate with Arabs anything like the extermination of Native Americans that white settlers had committed on the American frontier. Although "the Europeans of North America ended up pushing out Indians from their territory," he wrote, "we must take care not to do the same *chez nous*."[65] But at the same time, Tocqueville was clear-headed in recognizing that the French faced immense resistance. He had learned early in the conquest that the Arabs dictated the kind of war being fought. Kergorlay had explained how useless the French heavy cannon was against a mobile and rapidly dispersing force. Bedouins were fine horseback riders and accurate shooters. Foot soldiers, too, were good with rifles. The French had better learn how to fight a skilled nomadic population that knew how to recover from defeat quickly by simply regrouping elsewhere. They had to learn speed and mobility. Naively, Kergorlay had suggested early in the conquest that "we have to impose our style of war on them and refuse theirs on us," but this was obviously not to be.[66] To fight the Arabs effectively, Kergorlay soon realized, the French army had to resort to its lightest kind of mountain mobile cannon as prelude to its traditional infantry bayonet assault. In these circumstances, Tocqueville believed that a military response would not be enough. It would be necessary, he felt, to at times resort to violence against civilians and crop destruction to force submission. Even before visiting Algeria and seeing for himself, Tocqueville wrote to Lamoricière, "I am among those who understand and approve the kind of war you are waging at the moment."[67]

Tocqueville certainly considered alternatives to this kind of war in Algeria. But the models of domination Tocqueville reflected on were not designed for settling a population of invaders. Under Ottoman rule, janissaries and other kouloughlis had for two centuries kept North African native populations apart from one another throughout the Maghreb and collected tributes from the separate tribes. The Ottomans never attempted to settle the country.

Tocqueville also considered the British colonization of India as a possible model for France. He became quite absorbed in the case. He read James Mill on the history of India. He took detailed notes from

Abbé Dubois on the caste system.[68] The strict hierarchical structure of a caste society made it possible for the British to ensure their domination of the country by interacting only with a few princes. Tocqueville admired the way the British cultivated rivalry with local rulers and managed to keep all in check. He meant to write a long essay on the topic for the *Revue des deux mondes*, but he never got beyond his detailed notes.

These Ottoman and British models of domination did not include territorial settlement. Tocqueville, however, foresaw a dense French population occupying Algeria. War to defeat the jihad was the first step. Then, at some point, the civilian populations would face one another. "The moment the laborer appears behind the soldier," Tocqueville predicted, Arabs would recognize the French had come "not only to conquer but to dispossess them." In dispossession, "the quarrel was no longer between governments, but between races."[69]

Tocqueville finally went ahead with a long-planned trip to Africa to take the measure of the issue he deemed "foremost among France's interests in the world."[70] In the thick of the Orient crisis, he told Lamoricière, that a "great war" with England would put the Algerian conquest under way on hold. The French risked losing "the first fruits of the immense sacrifices we have made in Africa and that we make every day." But as the *grande guerre* with England did not materialize, Tocqueville departed for Algeria with his brother Hippolyte and Beaumont to apprise himself of the military and administrative situation. He asked Lamoricière to make sure they would see "the people best suited to show us the pros and cons of the matter, putting both sides into perspective."[71]

They disembarked in Algiers on May 7, 1841, where Corcelle joined the group. In Algiers, Tocqueville recorded "a prodigious mix of races and costumes, Arabs, *Kabyles*, Moors, Negroes, *Mahonnais*, French" and even recognized a familiar sound from America of "a feverish busyness . . . all you hear is the noise of hammers . . . Cincinnati transported onto African soil."[72] Tocqueville was impressed by the beauty of the landscape and clarity of the air. He wrote to his Chamber friend Victor Lanjuinais, "During this time of year, Africa is at first blush a marvel to behold. The climate is superb; the land around Algiers is fertile. Everywhere there are pretty houses nested in orange groves and other fruit trees of the south, and we have traced grand beautiful roads through the interior that seem to link together the provinces of a vast empire."[73] To his father, Tocqueville reported he felt as though he had been transported to an episode of the Arabian Nights.[74] He kept Marie, who needed reassurances after mistrust in the marriage, apprised of his every movement. Tocqueville was keen on promising his wife that he was being faithful. Despite the "burning climate exciting the senses," he was "very well behaved, you have my word." "I have not committed any infidelities, nor have I succumbed in any other way. . . . You will see just how much by the delight with which I will take you into my arms."[75] Tocqueville finally admitted to occasional infidelities in a long letter a year later, and Kergorlay had to intervene once more in the private life of his good friend by convincing Marie she was the only woman her husband loved and the only one he trusted.[76]

Initial enthusiasm for Algeria's climate, beauty, and activity quickly gave way to a more somber assessment. Algeria perhaps had great potential, but it was unsafe. Tocqueville told Lanjuinais, "Go three leagues in any direction on these delightful paths and two or three men come bursting out of the bushes to promptly slit your throat. As you can imagine, it takes away one's taste for strolling or at least limits it to very confined areas. As for me, I took care not to stray too far and contented myself with observing the bluffs of the Sahel and the plains of the Metidja from a distance," plains that the Hadjoute tribe was still ravaging in accordance with Abd El Kader's orders.[77] Tocqueville wrote to his journalist friend Léon Faucher, "Do not expect a prompt, explosive, and honorable end to the war; that is an illusion that eight days in Africa will cure you of."[78]

The group met with General Bugeaud, who, just back in Algiers after pacifying the Medea, was preparing a military expedition from Mostaganem to Tagdempt, the headquarters Abd El Kader had established at the edge of the desert. They went with Bugeaud to Mostaganem, where Lamoricière was waiting for them. Once there, Tocqueville, always at the mercy of his fragile health, felt too weak to continue with the army all the way to Tagdempt. Hippolyte and Corcelle moved on, but Beaumont returned to Algiers with Tocqueville by way of Oran and Mersel-Kebir. On May 28, they boarded a ship along the coast to Philippeville intending to move on to Constantine and visit the eastern part of the country. Peace prevailed in this region where the French army recruited light cavalry regiments of spahis among the natives.[79] Tocqueville succumbed to a serious episode of dysentery, however, and returned to France on June 10, a month ahead of schedule.

In contrast to the notes he took in America, England, and Ireland, only a few of Tocqueville's jottings on his first Algerian trip have survived. We therefore get only a glimpse of his observations as he met with civil servants, clergy, soldiers, and sailors. Tocqueville recorded that Mgr. Antoine-Adolphe Dupuch, Algiers's bishop, had been able to negotiate a successful exchange of prisoners with Abd El Kader in what sounded like a dramatic replay from the "era of the crusades."[80] He logged visiting with Louis-Adrien Berbrugger, a French linguist and archaeologist favorably inclined toward Fourierist communal theories, married to an Algerian, and founder of a library and museum. Among some commentaries on local mores, Tocqueville noted that legal polygamy allocated too many women to some men and therefore reduced bachelors to practicing the "vice against nature."[81]

Only after reaching Toulon in June did Tocqueville give his wife an accurate account of how seriously sick he had been. Except for two or three days in Algiers after his arrival, the whole trip had been a lengthy malaise with violent bouts of high fever. Now that he was back safely, he hoped to be fully recovered by the time they would be together again at Tocqueville.[82]

At home convalescing, Tocqueville reflected on his trip. He produced a long memorandum entitled *Travail sur l'Algérie* for the benefit only of his friend Beaumont, who wanted a record of Tocqueville's impressions for a book on Algeria he intended to write. He also left other personal notes that help us to follow his reasoning. His priority was to win the war, even if that meant assuming the army's scorched earth policy. But he did not want to prosecute the war throughout the entire Algerian territory. Unlike his friend Corcelle, however, he did not advocate only a slim coastal settlement.[83] Tocqueville would have preferred that France be selective in conquest. There was no reason to penetrate the parts of the Oran province not under French control—no need to settle west of Mostaganem, a fertile enough region, but five walking days from Oran, with war everywhere. Bône in the east should be avoided for the opposite reason: the population there was friendly to the French and it would be a blunder to provoke them.

But these were geographic nuances. The bottom line was that Tocqueville wanted the French to successfully colonize Algeria, and there was no going back. Much like his complaint about France in the English conflict, he was convinced that "any people that surrenders what it has taken to retreat comfortably behind its former borders proclaims that its former greatness is now gone. It enters willingly into its period of decline."[84] Tocqueville thus supported the brutal conquest Bugeaud was conducting, including the army's tactics of razzias and cave burning.[85]

Tocqueville did not like Bugeaud personally and objected to his absenteeism as well as his character, which exhibited "the vulgarity and violence common to military power."[86] He had resolved to resist being indoctrinated into Bugeaud's military strategy of total conquest, but he should not have been so confident. He supported Bugeaud as he realized Abd El Kader was a formidable adversary, a "most remarkable man," a "Muslim Cromwell" capable of enlisting enormous loyalty. Against Abd El Kader, the army believed, "only terror will work."[87] Tocqueville indicated to Beaumont in his notes that he had personally no desire to "re-create" a "Turkish"-style violence "that deserved the world's abhorrence." But when it came to burning down harvests or destroying silos or capturing "unarmed men, women, and children," Tocqueville indicated that such inhumane tactics were "unfortunate necessities, but ones to which any people that wants to wage war on the Arabs is obliged to submit."[88] Early in the conquest, Kergorlay had reported how Arabs routinely cut the French prisoners' throats and then sold the heads to the Turkish dey; they did not comprehend why French soldiers were not similarly beheading their Arab prisoners. Tocqueville invoked such local mores to justify "violent" campaign against "tribes that have been at war with us." "The mores of the country" suggested that such methods were not "unjust."[89] The French had no alternative to winning. Publicly, Tocqueville remained quiet regarding army violence, neither endorsing nor condemning it. But his silence gave tacit endorsement to the scorched earth policy.

Following victory and pacification, the next step would be for the French to settle in Algeria—that is, for enterprising agricultural settlers to occupy the land, make Algeria home, and create a civil society.[90] This is where Tocqueville vocally distanced himself from the army. With settlement, he believed the army should end its domination of the colony and stop cruel episodes of army violence. He suggested that the French concentrate efforts on Algiers and its hinterland, the first region to reorganize as an extension of France.

Tocqueville, in his memorandum to Beaumont, indicted military rule for its failure to create the conditions for civil society among French settlers. The American government had assisted pioneers' move to the west with land policy. In Michigan, Tocqueville had observed how the federal land office was helping American pioneers acquire and develop land. In Algeria, determining who owned what land was a headache. Lamoricière testified that the Mitidja had been oversold. Land, with a qadi adjudicating, added up to twice the available surface area of the plain. To validate the real owners was an insoluble problem.[91]

Moreover, there were no reliable political institutions in Algeria. The electoral system, freedom of the press, and trial by jury, perhaps not necessary in the "infancy of societies," had become indispensable to ensure "the liberty to make use of one's own person and property" and guarantee prosperity.[92] Military rule, however, took all rights away from French settlers. "You take away his property without compensation, impose all types of barbaric jurisprudence on him, arrest prisoners without warrants, incarcerate without legal recourse. . . . You forbid the colonist a free press, give them no choice in where he might educate his children, and you take away all his agency in local government. He chooses none of his leaders, pays no taxes, and can be banished at any moment."[93] Algeria was thus a part of France where citizens had no French rights. "Municipal government, even in principle, is gone."[94] It was all as if Saint-Simon's parable had come to pass in Algeria.[95]

To Faucher, Tocqueville wrote, "What amazes me is not that anyone comes to Algeria but that anyone chooses to stay." "At the present hour, you would have to be crazy to stay in Africa."[96] Algerian governance was in the hands of generals and administrators who, "in the name of France," put "over-civilized but corrupt lawyers" to the service of their "gruesome ends."[97] "God help us if France is ever governed by the officers of the armies of Africa."[98] Everywhere Tocqueville turned, he saw administrative chaos under army governance.

"I am convinced that so long as the general order of business is determined by military leaders, the work of colonization we are concerned with here will never happen or will be done poorly."[99] Military domination is a means, not an end; the end must be civil. All the army needs to do is to make sure settlers "can farm without a gun."[100] Africa needed colonists free to come and go as they pleased with a real stake in the outcome. Unfortunately, when it came to social organization, "theoretical men," like Abbé Landmann in Constantine, preached only Fourierism and Saint-Simonianism—that is, "destroying individual life." Finally, Tocqueville denounced an "absurd" level of centralization in Paris. A colonial society required "reasonable independence from the Paris bureaus." Instead, nothing was done locally. "The director of finances has written 9,000 letters a year to the minister."[101] It became impossible to attract to Algeria under such circumstances anyone other than speculators and men already heavily indebted and of ill repute.

How was it possible to create a civil colony, Tocqueville added, when power was in the hands of "the rough, violent, tyrannical, arbitrary, and vulgar government" of a "soldier making up civil institutions as he goes along?"[102] Beaumont never wrote his intended book on Algeria but gave a sanitized version of Tocqueville's text in several *Le Siècle* articles he published in 1842 as a response to Bugeaud's request for raising the number of French troops to 80,000 and King Louis Philippe's goal of making Algeria part of France forever. Beaumont recalled Tocqueville's main points. After congratulating Bugeaud on his military achievements, Beaumont denounced his ambition of total occupation. It would be better to focus French military might where Arabs might regroup and become powerful. Beaumont also attacked

Bugeaud's failed attempt at military colonization. You needed soldiers to protect settlers, not turn soldiers into settlers. The goal should be 60,000 French farmers in Africa, not 300 soldier-settlers who submitted to ridiculous drum marriages. It was imperative to implement in Algeria the rule of law to replace the arbitrary powers of the governor-general, to devise a realistic fiscal system, not taxes on Arabs that could not be collected and on properties without owners. It was unacceptable to present the Chamber with a sixty-page fantasy budget. Most critically, if France must lose 12,000–15,000 lives a year and put an additional 25,000 sick soldiers in hospitals, it had to be for a great enterprise from which the French people could benefit. Algeria should be a French-populated extension of France.[103]

In April 1845, Marshal Soult finally created a civilian administration for the three provinces of Alger, Oran, and Constantine. Tocqueville planned to visit Algeria again in 1846 to assess whether the country had progressed. Prior to the second trip, during a very animated June 1846 Chamber debate on the Algerian budget, Tocqueville expressed his frustration with Bugeaud's military administration and his displeasure with the marshal's personal absence from Africa.[104] With Young Left partner Jules Armand Dufaure rapporteur of the commission on Algeria, Tocqueville was in a good position to help frame the Chamber debate. In addressing his colleagues, Tocqueville affirmed that from what he had read and heard just about everywhere, nothing was being done to facilitate civilian colonization. Ordinary French men and women, so visibly frustrated at home with diminishing prospects, could freely exercise their entrepreneurial spirit in Algeria only if the French army facilitated their work instead of hampering it. "Preparatory measures as simple as surveying the land and dividing it up into property allotments were not afoot with any degree of regularity or urgency." Even in Algiers, "one lives by-the-by, as if each day were the morning after the conquest." "Everywhere, and without exception, I encountered this idea that the Maréchal is hostile toward civil society, something he neither understands nor wants."[105] The few colonists in Algeria, Tocqueville reported, live in the most horrifying conditions. "The agricultural population . . . simply doesn't exist." In villages the army created, "half the inhabitants are dead and the other half lives in misery." Overall, "the government is in the hand of second-rate subordinates who could not populate the Plaine St Denis [on the outskirts of Paris] even if they wanted to!"[106]

Tocqueville argued that one should expect from a government only a general framework for colonization: "Create security, clean up the country, build roads that link up with one another as well as to the various markets, protect private property as peaceably as possible." That would be enough. But instead, the army brings settlers and creates villages and then pretends they are prosperous in the face of much evidence to the contrary. "To take a poor man from France and bring him to Algeria, to assign him residence there and build him a house, then to clear the land for him and find some other poor devil to put next to him—in a word, what we did in the Algerian Sahel—that seems to me patently ridiculous and absurd. . . . We must give up on this system of lining up men one by one and planting them in the ground like asparagus. It reminds me of those cardboard villages Potemkin would prop up to impress Catherine the Great as she rode through the countryside."[107]

Tocqueville announced to Bugeaud that he would make another visit,[108] and he prepared for his second trip by corresponding again with Lamoricière, the only officer in Algeria he trusted. Tocqueville was back in Algiers on October 31, 1846. This time, Marie accompanied him, but she remained in Algiers while Tocqueville traveled with Bugeaud, overland, to Orléansville, where Saint-Arnaud was in command; then he traveled across Dhara to Tenes, with Lieutenant Colonel Canrobert as escort, and moved on to Oran to see Lamoricière. This tour lasted a month. Tocqueville returned to Algiers on November 30. Tocqueville left Marie again in the first two weeks of December to visit surrounding settlements. He was no longer escorted by military personnel but by a French journalist named Auguste Bussière (who kept a chronicle of the journey). With Bussière, Tocqueville visited the villages of Sahel and Mitidja. When back in Algiers on December 10, he and Marie sailed to Philippeville and Constantine. The weather turned bad in Bône, but they were in Constantine on Christmas Eve as guests of General Bedeau. They returned to France on December 29.[109]

It was with Bussière that Tocqueville focused on the state of colonization and settlers' conditions in their villages. Unlike his artist friend
Théodore Chassériau, who was at that time painting scenes of Arabic
life,[110] Tocqueville was concerned mostly with the fate of French farmers. Everywhere he went, he inquired into the draining of swamps, the
building of roads, and the maintenance of forests. He took note of the
size of herds and studied the demographic makeup of the population,
the survival rate, and the methods of communication and administration practiced in local settings.

Neither Bugeaud nor any other official had ever visited the villages
Tocqueville went to. In one instance, the entire population of a village
came from Hyères in Provence. The government had built them a forti-
fication but no church or school. In another instance, the government
had been responsible for initiating the settlement of thirty-six original
lots, but ten had been abandoned, and the remaining settlers had no
capital and could not secure credit. In a third, fifty families lived in a village the army created in 1843. It had no school and an unreliable water
supply. Of the thirty children born in the village, only three survived. As
Tocqueville told Lamoricière, "This is not how nations are formed."[111]

The issue of cohabitation with the Arabs loomed large. Tocqueville
returned from his 1846 trip with a clear sense of the conflicts between
the two populations and the intention to present to the Chamber plans
for reorganizing the colony. He became rapporteur on two pieces of
legislation regarding Algeria introduced in the Chamber on February 27, 1847, including one allocating new funding that Bugeaud requested for additional military colonization. As if to revive a painful
dispute, Beaumont, who had been independently traveling to Algeria,
wanted to be rapporteur of the same bills. Tocqueville complainingly
asked Corcelle how Beaumont "had the idea to cross me and prevent
me from carrying out work that I have labored so carefully to understand at such great personal cost?"[112]

In his May 1847 report, Tocqueville took note of near-completed
pacification. He was satisfied that the French army had fulfilled its mandate. France dominated the country; France's grandeur was on display.

Even "independent Kabyles," "surrounded on all sides by our settlements . . . are beginning to submit to our influence and are said to be
ready to recognize our power."[113] Abd El Kader was about to surrender
seven months later to none other than Lamoricière. Tocqueville called
for the creation of a civilian, not military, ministry to administer the
territory. He proposed that would-be Algerian administrators undergo
an education that would prepare them in understanding the "language,
the customs, the history of the country they go to govern"—much as
the "English have done in India" even though they did not intend to
settle the country.[114]

Tocqueville justified the undemocratic conquest of the Arabs as a
necessary show of French military might. But now he felt the French
had a unique chance to create their own version of the American frontier and repeat America's democratic experiment in a new place. He
repeated that Philippeville and Algiers were growing "like Cincinnati."
Adapting the language of many an American pioneer, Tocqueville argued French settlers could develop large parts of the country without
disturbing the natives considering the great availability of land. It was
therefore imperative to turn struggling emigrants into free citizens with
guarantees of property ownership, fair justice system, end of arbitrary
measures of expropriation, a free press, and a functional, locally based
administrative system.

At the same time, now that the French had pacified the country, they
needed to maintain peaceful coexistence with the Arabs and not repeat
"in the middle of the nineteenth century the history of the conquest of
America over again." In short, Tocqueville was willing to use any means
necessary to subdue the Arabs, but once subdued, he wanted to treat
them in an enlightened way. Rather than revert to the "bloody examples that the opinion of the human race has stigmatized," Tocqueville
asked that the French operate in Algeria with respect for "the enlightenment the French Revolution spread throughout the world." Doing
anything else was perilous. "If we surround and embrace their populations not to raise them up to a better life and greater enlightenment,
but to stifle and strangle them with these things, the two races will be
at each other's throats."

For the grand design to work, Tocqueville envisioned at least a partial conversion of Arabs to French mores while maintaining a clear hierarchy of relations between the two societies. Tocqueville proposed to create a native Arab landowning gentry. In a strange phrase that only Tocqueville could coin, he wrote, "Humanitarian and budgetary concerns overlap and blend together."[115] Practically, this meant giving indemnity to Arabs for land seized but also, more radically, persuading the Arabs to abandon communal property for private property, something the Americans failed to persuade Native Americans to do. Tocqueville saw a grand economic and social revolution consolidating the gains of political revolution and imagined new landowners indebted to the revolution that gave them land.

Regarding central political power, Tocqueville insisted it be unquestionably "in the hands of the French." Only when it came to the "secondary powers of the government," Tocqueville advised that such powers "be exercised by the inhabitants of the country."[116] Empower local leaders but do not lead them to believe they are our equals.

On education, consistent with his belief in diversity, Tocqueville recommended, "Let us not force the indigenous peoples to come to our schools, but help them rebuild theirs, multiply the number of teachers, and create men of law and men of religion, which Muslim civilization cannot do without, any more than [the French] can." The aim in terms of reform is not to make the Arab or Muslim a spitting image of the Frenchman in his "mores," "ideas," or "customs" but instead to allow the building of institutions that best suit the Arab and Muslim populations.[117]

Finally, Tocqueville authored a second report, designed to lead the Chamber toward denying Bugeaud a credit of three million francs for new agricultural camps for military men serving or having served in Algeria. The Chamber's denial of these monies led to Bugeaud's resignation the following year, clearly a victory for Tocqueville's vision but also his last pronouncement on the question.[118]

Approximately 110,000 Europeans lived in Algeria by the end of the July Monarchy.[119] History has not been kind to Tocqueville's endorsement of colonial expansion, tolerance of military abuses, and exclusion of natives from government. How could a great theorist of democracy, we ask today, also be an advocate of brutal colonialism? The question is not as anachronistic as it sounds. Tocqueville condemned the extermination of Native Americans by American settlers who claimed all men were brothers while appropriating the continent. Equally blinded by nationalistic pride, he sided with French colonists while harboring the hope that the French settlement of Algeria, if ever successfully completed, would tap into a large reservoir of energy in the French people and expand democratic possibilities of individual self-realization for them.

# 9

# Crushed at the Helm

FROM THE POPULAR INSURRECTION of February 1848 to Louis Napoléon Bonaparte's coup of December 1851, Tocqueville lived through
the sequence of revolution, reform, and despotism he had described in
*Democracy in America* as the curse of French history. Once again, blood-
shed led not to the hoped-for democracy but instead to a new authoritarian regime. Tocqueville concluded that France's political illness was
chronic. "In 1789, in 1815, and even in 1830 it was possible to believe that
French society had been afflicted with one of those violent maladies after
which the social body is restored to a more vigorous and durable state of
health. Today it is clear that the illness is chronic; that its cause is more
profound; that an intermittent form of the disease will persist longer
than anyone imagined; that it is not only a specific government that is
impossible but any durable form of government whatsoever; and that we
are destined for a long time to waver between despotism and liberty
without being able to tolerate one or the other permanently."[1]

Tocqueville would record his own version of the revolutionary events
and the coming of the French Second Republic, still fresh in memory, in
his remarkable *Recollections*. He told his own story of how he managed
the affairs of France while briefly at the helm. He assessed his contribution to the framing of a new constitution for France as an influential
member of the Constitutional Committee, and to the restoration of the
pope's temporal powers during his tenure as foreign minister. Intended
for private reflection (published only posthumously), Tocqueville's narrative, written under the duress of failing health, surprises with its

scathing analysis and unforgettable portraits of men Tocqueville judged harshly but with what he felt was a "clear view."[2] There are none of the self-doubts and misgivings that Tocqueville shared with his readers in other writings, nor does he show any reticence in making personal judgments of others. In *Recollections,* everybody, regardless of political persuasion, is undressed at every turn. Autobiography, however, is not biography. Tocqueville presented himself throughout his memoir as someone deeply frustrated by fickle and untrustworthy political colleagues. He reflected only occasionally on his own blind spots and equivocation, or on his compromises with coalitions of antidemocratic conservatives made up of Legitimists and Orléanists.

Tocqueville began his *Recollections* with the observation that his position in the Chamber had never been a happy one. A decade of busy (and at times important) work on prison reform, on pauperism, and on the abolition of slavery, his efforts as a publicist for these causes, and his advocacy of a settlers' colony in Algeria had not advanced his "life's passion" for political liberty nearly as much as he had hoped.[3] His frustration began with the king himself. In an acid portrait of Louis Philippe, Tocqueville argued that the king's "limited" mind and lack of "elevation and breadth"[4] paralleled the flaws of his era and set the tone for the ensuing events. Tocqueville found no greater good in the incessant, meaningless power plays orchestrated by François Guizot, Adolphe Thiers, his own cousin Louis-Mathieu Molé, and other leaders. He viewed Thiers, whom he considered the most manipulative of the three, as a coward for fleeing the Chamber when armed insurgents invaded it on February 24, 1848. He disparaged his colleagues' endless battles over small things, their lack of respect for civil liberties, and their passion for the personal gains to be obtained from office—one "man's daughter's dowry" or another's "entire fortune."[5]

In recording his side of the story, Tocqueville made it sound as though he had seen the revolution coming before all the others. There may be some truth to this. Three weeks before the revolution erupted, Tocqueville notably told his colleagues in the Chamber, "My deepest conviction, gentlemen, is this: I believe we are presently sleeping on a volcano." He then proceeded to indict them: "When I study other times, other eras, and other nations in search of the true cause of the governing class's downfall, I take note of this or that event, this or that man, this or that accidental or superficial cause, but believe me when I say that the real cause, the effective cause that deprives men of power, is this: that they have become unworthy of wielding it."[6]

Equally true is that Tocqueville himself had stayed on the sidelines of political change when the campaign for enlarging the electoral franchise gained momentum in 1847. Although he feared that moderates would lose control of the movement, all he acknowledged in *Recollections* is that he did not want to get involved in the "agitation" around the banquets (unofficial private political meetings not requiring prior authorization from the government) that moderates Barrot, Duvergier de Hauranne, and other figures of the dynastic left, including Beaumont, had launched to promote modest electoral reform.[7] In Tocqueville's view, their attempt to align themselves with Republicans, who could be satisfied only with universal suffrage, was misguided. As he predicted, the radical agenda prevailed, and most moderates withdrew. Fearing the radicals, the government led by Guizot forbade a banquet to be held on February 22, 1848. But Lamartine led Republican demonstrators in defiance of Guizot's order to the place de la Concorde from where they made their way along the rue de la Paix toward the Ministry of Foreign Affairs on the boulevard des Capucines. Amid confusion, troops fired on them. Widespread rebellion spread with news of the massacre. The 1848 revolution had begun.

To pacify the Republicans, King Louis Philippe promptly dismissed Guizot and appointed Thiers as prime minister, who, in turn, called in Barrot to form a coalition cabinet. The emergency reshuffling of the cabinet worked no better than Marshal Bugeaud's army in restoring order as the crowd erected barricades in the center and eastern districts of Paris and invaded city hall. King Louis Philippe abdicated, and by the end of February 24, a provisional government had abolished the monarchy and proclaimed the republic.

Although Tocqueville had heretofore been a fierce critic of the July Monarchy, when faced with its demise, he was unwilling to see it go. Tocqueville endorsed the Protestant duchesse d'Orléans, widow of the popular duc d'Orléans, for regency until her nine-year-old son could take the fleeing king's place. The duchess made her proposal to the

Chamber as street battles raged outside. Tocqueville called on Lamartine, the man who had defied the order forbidding the last banquet, to speak in favor of the duchess, but the charismatic poet-politician knew better. Tocqueville hoped to save the constitutional monarchy. Instead, a crowd of insurgents invaded the Chamber and the royal party escaped (the duchess eventually took refuge with her two sons in her native Germany). Lamartine and others hastened to nominate a provisional government before leaving the Chamber (Palais Bourbon) for the Hôtel de Ville. This government of the republic, during a brief euphoria, passed the great measures associated in memory with 1848—the national workshops for the unemployed, the Luxembourg Commission (to study work), limits to the workday, universal male suffrage, abolition of slavery in the colonies, abolition of the death penalty for political reasons, and freedom of the press and of assembly.

When Tocqueville retreated to his home on the evening of February 24, the genial Jean-Jacques Ampère shared with him his feelings of empathy toward the winning insurrectionaries. Ampère attributed to them "selflessness and even generosity, as well as courage" only to hear Tocqueville predict in anger not "the triumph of liberty" but instead "its ultimate defeat. . . . I am telling you that these people, whom you so naively admire, have just proven that they are incapable and unworthy of living as free men." Tocqueville anticipated that victorious insurgents would pursue a program of social leveling, which in his view would impose a deadening conformity. After some shouting, the two friends agreed to let the future judge. Tocqueville noted that although the future may be "an enlightened and upright arbiter, alas, it always arrives too late."[8] But in this instance, Tocqueville did not wait for the future to judge before changing his course of action.

## Joining the Republic: America as Model

Once the initial shock wore off, Tocqueville reconsidered and decided to become a participant in a historic republican experiment. It was a pragmatic decision, as when he had pledged his allegiance to the July Monarchy after the July revolution. He recognized the potential of the revolutionary events to bring about the kind of political freedom he had always advocated, and he made up his mind to join the Republic because he believed that it gave him an opportunity to put his ideas to work. The socialists and precocious republicans (*républicains de la veille*), who "ignite genuine passions, embitter jealousies, and stir up class warfare," had nevertheless created an opportunity for him to steer the state in the right direction. Tocqueville soon became a sincere convert to the Republic (*républicain du lendemain*). As he told Eugène Stöffels, "The mind can now rest; there are no longer two roads to follow."[9] He hoped the revolution carried with it the possibility of constructing a real democracy in France and that he, as the scholar of democracy long ago turned politician, had a special role to play in it. But there remained the big question of the kind of republic Tocqueville would agree to promote. It would have to be a political system "giving each individual the greatest possible share of liberty," enlightenment, and power.[10] And the only system that fit this bill, Tocqueville believed, was an American-style democracy.

A month after the February revolution, Tocqueville issued the twelfth edition of *Democracy in America*. In a new preface, he highlighted that democracy was inevitable and that aristocracy was a dead end:

> Reread this book: on every page you will find a solemn warning to all men that the form of society and the condition of humanity are changing and that new destinies are at hand. At the beginning these words were inscribed: *The gradual development of equality is therefore a providential fact. It has the essential characteristics of one: it is universal, durable, and daily proves itself to be beyond the reach of man's powers. Not a single event, not a single individual, fails to contribute to its development. Is it wise to believe that a social movement that originated so far in the past can be halted by the efforts of a single generation? Does anyone think that democracy, having destroyed feudalism and vanquished kings, will be daunted by the bourgeois and the rich? Will it stop now that it has become so strong and its adversaries so weak?*[11]

Tocqueville struck the same note at a popular banquet in Cherbourg on March 19. "Many among us are still frightened by the word *republic* because their minds are filled exclusively with glorious but sad memories of our own history, and they do not consider what has happened and is still happening elsewhere in the world. Let them cast their eyes across to the opposite shores of the Atlantic Ocean, and they will discover a great people occupying a territory much larger than France who for sixty years have enjoyed democratic and republican institutions." He then turned to a description of America for electoral purposes only—a strictly idealized vision, detached from any critical perspective or recognition of the deep sectional and racial conflicts he had highlighted in *Democracy in America*. "No other country in the world can provide us with such useful examples or inspire such legitimate hopes. In America, the republic is not a dictatorship exercised in the name of liberty; it is liberty itself, the authentic, true liberty of all citizens. It is the sincere government of the country by the country, the uncontested empire of the majority, the rule of law. In the shadow of America's laws, property is safe, order firmly maintained, industry free, the burden of public spending light, and the tyranny of one or a few unknown, and so it has been now for the past sixty years. During those sixty years, while Europe has been torn by so much discord, war, and revolution, republican and democratic America has not experienced so much as a riot. I am therefore justified in telling you that you must turn your gaze on America if you are looking for great examples to follow and great hopes to conceive." Tocqueville was similarly animated by his ambition for French grandeur, with uncontested standing in the world. Keeping in mind that, in Cherbourg, he was addressing the denizens of a major seaport who resented British naval superiority, Tocqueville cleverly added, "We must ask still more of America: we must join with her in demanding freedom of the seas."[12]

Tocqueville proved eager to run for election to the Constituent Assembly in April 1848, which was the first test of universal male suffrage in France. He won. In his American travel notes, he had lamented that American men could elect as poor a specimen as Davy Crockett to public office (this was four years before Crockett became the hero of the Alamo). But now, and to his own astonishment, universal male suffrage energized him to run a strong campaign. On the stand in Normandy, he characterized representing his ancestral home not as his birthright but as a contract by which local people would entrust him to defend their interests in the infant Republic. A vastly rejuvenated Tocqueville expressed enthusiasm for the coming of a new era in the letters he wrote to Marie, who had stayed in Paris. The challenge of persuading voters even brought out his latent eloquence—whether in announcing his program of "liberty and human dignity"[13] or in battling radical republicans, whom he labeled zealots. Tocqueville put up with "all the petty vexations and calumnies" and what he called "wars of chamber pots,"[14] firmly rejecting accusations that that he was a closet Legitimist on account of his ancestry and loyalty to family and friends. He overcame temporary economic difficulties as well. Fearing a shortage of ready cash during the campaign, Tocqueville advised his wife "right now to set aside all the money we can to get through this difficult time, because we cannot hope to collect much of our income," to keep that money only in "hard cash" as bank notes might quickly depreciate, and to do so "without saying anything" to anyone.[15]

There was no turning away from the Republic. As he put it pithily in the electoral circular he distributed in late March, "Did we not destroy the old monarchy . . . the monarchy of ten centuries, in three years? The monarchy of the elder branch in three days? The monarchy of the younger branch in three hours? Who could hope to restore with yet another revolution a principle with so little life left in it? Who would wish to make the effort necessary to plant in French soil, and perhaps in blood, a tree that experience has shown to have no roots?"[16] Furthermore, Tocqueville had come to believe not only in the future of the Republic but also in his capacity to play a role in its development. He wrote to Beaumont that "there may come a moment when an opportunity for glorious action may arise."[17]

Under the electoral system of *scrutin de liste* (in which electors vote for slates of candidates and the winners are determined by the percentage cast for each slate), various organizations circulated lists of candidates whom they endorsed. Tocqueville managed to be put on all the important lists—even, he told Marie, "that of the commissioners (of the Republic), who did not dare exclude me altogether. . . . The clergy put me on their list, as did all the former conservatives. The only signs of reluctance and hostility come from my former colleagues in the moderate opposition, who should want me most. But as you have seen, they had no choice in the end but to follow the current."[18]

Tocqueville's own description of election day on Easter Sunday, April 23, 1848, has often been quoted as a moving rendering of the voters' first experience with universal male suffrage and, in this instance, belief in the sincerity of this scion of an ancient family's commitment to the Republic. "The local people had always been kind to me, but this time I found them affectionate as well. Never was I treated with more respect than after posters bluntly proclaiming equality appeared on every wall. We were supposed to vote as a body in the town of Saint-Pierre, one league from our village. On the morning of the election, all the voters— the entire male population above the age of twenty—assembled in front of the church. The men lined up double file in alphabetical order. I took the place that corresponded to my name, because I knew that in democratic times and countries one cannot place oneself at the head of the people but must be placed there by others. Pack horses and carts followed this long procession, bearing the crippled and sick who wished to accompany us. Only the women and children remained behind. When we reached the top of the hill that overlooks Tocqueville, we stopped for a moment. I knew that people were expecting me to speak, so I stood on a mound next to a ditch and, with everyone gathered around in a circle, said a few words inspired by the circumstances. I reminded those good people of the gravity and importance of what they were about to do. I advised them not to allow themselves to be accosted or diverted by people in town who might try to lead them astray. Instead, we should remain together as a body, each man in his place, until everyone had voted. 'No one should go indoors to eat or dry off (for it was raining that day) before doing his duty.' They loudly proclaimed that they would do as I asked, and they did. Everyone voted together, and I have reason to believe that nearly all voted for the same candidate."[19]

Most satisfying to Tocqueville, "there was no corruption or intimidation of any kind."[20] When attempted, it failed. Tocqueville felt he had gained significant popular support, and the vote count proved it. Immediately after submitting his ballot, Tocqueville set out for Paris, where he learned he had been elected in third place in his circumscription, after Léonor Havin and Narcisse Vieillard, who were the candidates with government support.[21] Overall, elections amounted to victory for the conservatives and disappointment for the Republicans. Radical republicans occupied less than 10 percent of the seats.[22] The Constituent Assembly elected a five-member executive committee (Arago, Garnier-Pagès, Marie, Lamartine, Ledru-Rollin) to run a moderate liberal government that, in accordance with the electoral outcome, no longer included socialist theorist Louis Blanc or the worker Albert.

Tocqueville's burst of enthusiasm was soon dampened by a familiar anxiety. The conservative turn of the Assembly renewed street protests for which radical organizers found eager participants among the semi-idle workers of the national workshops, created only a few months before with the lofty ideal of ending unemployment. The program had resulted in groups of workers scattered around the city, without work, "drinking, womanizing or playing cards," with no alternative in sight.[23] As a result, the government came to see the workshops as a threat to order and developed competing plans for reforming and eventually closing them.

In this climate, Tocqueville stood firmly on the side of order. It became unclear whether an April 16 workers' march from the Champ de Mars to city hall was a celebration of, or a challenge to, the nascent Republic. The government was sufficiently concerned to order the National Guard, whom Tocqueville joined again, as he had done in 1830, to surround the demonstrators. Richard Rush, the American minister in Paris, remembers Tocqueville visiting him in his residence on that day, abruptly stopping short a conversation when hearing the "*rappel* beating in the streets. Rising from his chair, he left me, hardly pausing a moment to join his regiment in the national guards. Author; man of genius; independent in his circumstances; addicted to study; not robust in frame; yet off he goes for his musket at the first summons of the drum, to take his stand as a private in the ranks."[24] Tocqueville wrote the next day to Nassau Senior, "All day yesterday (April 16th), I bore arms not quill. 30 or 40,000 workers on the Champ de Mars against 100,000 of the National Guard defending the provisional government against the 'communists.'"[25]

Protests became more frequent. Tocqueville recalled days "filled with anxiety at what was coming. The army and the National Guard responded daily to new alerts. Craftsmen and bourgeois ceased to live at home and moved, armed, into the public squares. Everyone hoped against hope to avoid a conflict, yet all shared a vague sense that conflict was increasingly inevitable. The National Assembly was so obsessed with the idea that it was as if the words *civil war* had been written on the four walls of the Chamber."[26] In *Recollections*, Tocqueville narrates the radicals' May 15, 1848 invasion of the Assembly under the pretext of a demonstration for Polish independence, in which "the ludicrous vied with the terrifying." The threat of class warfare was apparent on that day. Amid the cries of "organize labor" and "tax the rich," several people hoisted Louis Blanc onto their shoulders. The small man, who had created the Luxembourg Commission and promoted what he called the right to work, but was no longer a government official, appeared frightened by what he had created, his supporters "holding him by his tiny legs."[27]

Only a few days later, on May 21, the Republican regime celebrated itself with a review of the troops while staging a spectacle on the Champ de Mars, complete with a giant "car drawn by sixteen plow horses . . . transporting an oak, a laurel, and an olive, symbols of strength, honor, and abundance . . . a plow surrounded by stalks of wheat and flowers. Peasants and maidens clad in white sang patriotic songs." Tocqueville and several of his colleagues were in attendance, concealing the weapons they carried because they feared for their lives. During the review, Tocqueville could see "civil war" coming. He imagined "the day when all those bayonets gleaming in the sun (some 200,000 bayonets) would be raised against one another."[28]

A chance encounter with George Sand gave Tocqueville, who fell immediately under the novelist's charm, further insight into the depth of the coming class war. The occasion was a dinner Tocqueville's British friend Richard Monckton Milnes, Member of Parliament and patron of literature, had organized during a visit to Paris. Milnes had invited both Sand and writer Prosper Mérimée, unaware that the two had had a short but disastrous affair that elicited a round of malicious gossip in the circuit of literary salons. The unexpected reunion was embarrassing, but Tocqueville engaged Madame Sand in conversation, sat next to her at dinner, and commanded her full attention. The novelist warned Tocqueville that "if fighting breaks out, believe me, you will all die." She herself had been fearing the worst since the May 15 invasion of the Assembly. "We spoke for a full hour about public affairs; in those days one could speak of nothing else. In any case, Madame Sand was in a way a political man at that point. What she said about politics made a great impression on me; it was the first time I had spoken directly and familiarly with someone who was willing and able to tell me some of what was going on in our adversaries' camp. Parties never know one another: they come together, they feel one another out, they come to grips, but neither sees the other." Tocqueville appreciated Madame Sand's "singularly vivid and detailed portrait of the state of the Paris workers, their organization, their number, their arms, their preparations, their thoughts, their passions, and their terrifying determination. I thought it was a caricature, but it was not, as ensuing events made clear. She herself seemed afraid of the people's triumph and in rather solemn terms expressed pity concerning the fate that awaited us. 'Try, Monsieur, to persuade your friends not to drive the people into the street by provoking or offending them, just as I hope to persuade my allies that patience is a virtue.'"[29]

George Sand's prediction came to pass. The infant republic faced a giant explosion of anger from the very workers it had vouched to serve. Workers erected barricades again on June 23 to protest the controversial closing of the four-month-old national workshops. Tocqueville sided with the violent restoration of order that Defense Minister General Cavaignac, his friend General Lamoricière, and a few others orchestrated during the so-called June days.[30] General Cavaignac assumed dictatorial powers to end what Tocqueville described as "the greatest and strangest uprising in French history and perhaps in all history. Greatest because for four days more than one hundred thousand men were involved in the fighting, and five generals died. Strangest because the insurgents fought without battle cries, without leaders, without flags, yet with marvelous coordination and a military expertise that surprised even the most experienced officers."[31]

After making sure his father and his nephews were safe, Tocqueville wrote Paul Clamorgan, his electoral agent in Normandy, "My dear friend, I write to the sound of cannon and rifle fire after the most terrible day and the cruelest night you can imagine. This is not a riot. It is the most terrible of all civil wars, a war of class against class, of the have-nots against the haves. I hope we will prevail. National guardsmen from the surrounding area are arriving en masse, along with line regiments. Yet God only knows what the outcome of this great battle will be. If we are defeated, and I do not think we will be, the reddest of republics will control Paris. If that happens, the Assembly will leave Paris en masse and call France to arms. I hope France will heed that call, for what is at stake is not the shape of a political regime but property, family, and civilization—in short, everything that makes life worth living."[32] Cavaignac led a merciless crackdown, which Proudhon saw as the equivalent of the infamous Saint Bartholomew's Day massacre of Protestants three centuries earlier. It was over by June 26.

How best to interpret the class war has been the topic of profound debate. Nobody expressed Tocqueville's dilemma in mid-1848 better than Karl Marx when contrasting February and June. "February 25, 1848," Marx wrote in his *Class Struggles in France*, "had granted the republic to France; June 25 thrust the revolution on her. And revolution, after June, meant overthrow of bourgeois society, whereas, before February, it had meant overthrow of the form of state."[33] Tocqueville supported February but strongly rejected June. Marx, of course, wanted June writ large. Neither got his wish.

Marx, who was following all the revolutionary events from Cologne, made the case that Cavaignac had defeated the real workers behind the barricades only by recruiting an army of the poorest of the poor—the "lumpenproletariat"—"thieves and criminals of all kinds, living on the crumbs of society," most of them "young men from 15 to 20 years" and arranging them in "24 battalions of Mobile Guards, each of a thousand men" and leading them to victory.[34]

Inverting Marx's diagnosis, the bourgeoisie saw the rabble fighting on the other side, claiming the workers fought exclusively out of greed. As Tocqueville attested in a letter to his friend Eugène Stöffels, "It's often said—you hear it every day—that the insurgents of June were the scum of humanity; just worthless looters motivated by love of plunder." But Tocqueville did not accept that view. "That was certainly true of some, but not all of them. By God, I wish it had been! Such men are always in the minority; they never prevail. Prison and the scaffold weed them out." Tocqueville testified that honest workers fought well in both camps.[35] Tocqueville also noted correctly that Generals Cavaignac and Lamoricière (the latter of whom had his horse shot from under him during the battle)[36] might not have been able to dismantle the barricades had not so many revolutionary leaders previously been jailed or escaped into exile after the May 15 invasion of the National Assembly.

Tocqueville looked for the reasons for the class war. He did not find them in the workers' miseries, which he had recognized for some time in his welfare work, but in the socialist rhetoric of their leaders. Instead of blaming a lumpenproletariat for betraying either the workers or the bourgeoisie, Tocqueville focused his analysis on the ideological convictions socialists successfully promoted. He felt that behind the barricades, "many of the men who fought to overturn our sacred rights were guided by a distorted notion of a higher law. They sincerely believed that society had been founded on injustice, and they wanted to give it a new foundation. It is this kind of revolutionary religion that cannot be destroyed by cannons and bayonets. New dangers await us, and our problems are nowhere near over."[37]

Against the urban insurrectionists, peasants arriving in droves from the countryside joined Cavaignac. Tocqueville observed that Paris appeared as a "society divided by revolutionary struggle between two enemy classes. He judged that so long as poor farmers were not taken in by "what has been planted in the heads of urban workers, the social order and civilization can save itself."[38]

Writing to Senior on April 10, Tocqueville insisted that irresponsible socialists had planted unrealistic expectations in the populace. "It was not needs but ideas that caused the great upheaval—fantastic ideas concerning the relative condition of the worker and capital, exaggerated theories concerning the role that social power could play in relations between the worker and his master, and ultra-centralizing doctrines that ultimately persuaded multitudes of men that it was within the power of the state not only to save them from misery but also to make them comfortable and prosperous."[39] Even though he had given socialists a hearing in the months preceding the revolution, he now castigated them for having "filled the heads of workers with chimerical expectations."[40]

He concluded there was no imaginable connection between socialism and his understanding of democracy. Whatever value he had momentarily seen in the utopian treatises he read in the late 1840s, he now rejected indiscriminately. To socialists threatening to "overturn not only laws, ministries, and governments but society itself, by undermining the base on which it now rests," he said, "Take any name you like—*any name at all*, except *democrats*. I forbid you to take that one. You do not deserve it."[41]

At the tribune in the National Assembly, Tocqueville denounced socialism as fundamentally antidemocratic and crassly materialistic. He had worked tirelessly to bring out a fusion of democratic and spiritual values in society, only to witness in socialism "a persistent, strenuous, and immoderate appeal to man's material passions." Some (Tocqueville was referring to Saint-Simon) said that "it was a matter of rehabilitating the flesh." Others (Fourier) said that "work, even the hardest work, must be not only useful but also pleasant." Still others (Cabet, reformulated by Saint-Simon, Louis Blanc, and Marx) said that "men must be paid in proportion not to their merits but to their needs." For yet another (Proudhon), "the purpose of the socialist system and, in his view, of the February revolution was to obtain for everyone a right to *unlimited consumption.*" In sum, all the schools of socialism stirred material passions.

"There is also a second characteristic: an attack, sometimes direct, sometimes indirect, but always unrelenting, on the very principle of individual property. From the first socialist [Tocqueville was quoting Babeuf], who said fifty years ago that *property is the root of all evil in this world*, to the socialist we heard at this podium [Proudhon] declaring that *property is theft*, all socialists—I daresay *all*—directly or indirectly attack individual property."

Tocqueville believed that socialism, by imposing a uniform equality, erased individual autonomy. "Here is the third and final characteristic, which in my eyes applies to socialists of all colors and all schools: a profound distrust of liberty, of human reason, a profound contempt for the individual in himself, for the human state. What characterizes all socialists is a persistent, varied, relentless effort to mutilate, truncate, and impede human liberty in every way possible. It is the idea that the state must be not only the director of society but also the master of each individual. Nay! Not his master but his tutor, his teacher . . . the confiscation of human freedom . . . a new form of servitude."[42]

Tocqueville's contrasting vision of democracy was directly inspired by his personal American experience, which he reformulated for the occasion. America was the country where there was no confusion between democracy and socialism but instead where the spirit of democracy and the spirit of religion joined. In a parting shot at a group of Cabet's disciples, so-called Icarian socialists, who were leaving France for America in hopes of creating a community in Texas, Tocqueville told them (conveniently ignoring a variety of communal experiments that flowered in the 1840s in the United States) not to expect their ideas to take root where democracy thrived, for real democracy and socialism were simply incompatible.[43]

## American Formulae for a French Republican Constitution

Before the June days, Tocqueville had been appointed to the Constituent Assembly's key committee of eighteen representatives in charge of framing a republican constitution, largely in recognition of his deep understanding of the American constitution. Tocqueville had signaled his commitment to constitutional reform in the new edition of *Democracy in America* that he published in March 1848. He added to the volume an essay he had read at the Académie des sciences morales et politiques a few months earlier on the work of Swiss legal scholar Antoine-Elysée Cherbuliez. In this essay, Tocqueville contrasted the efficiency of the huge US federation of states to the paralysis experienced by tiny Switzerland. He restated what he had already explained in *Democracy in America*: that American federal institutions had power because they intervened directly and *autonomously* in the lives of citizens, without mediation from the states. The US federal government had its own court system, army, and so forth. By contrast, the Swiss confederation was "reduced to issuing orders solely to local governments" but never directly to citizens. Tocqueville concluded the Swiss confederation "resembled a creature endowed with life but deprived of organs."[44]

The Cherbuliez essay was relevant because Tocqueville also advocated for a US-style separation of powers. He drew a sharp contrast between the total lack of "separation or even relative independence of legislative, administrative, and judicial powers" in Switzerland to the arrangement that prevailed in a state like New York, roughly the size of Switzerland, with its bicameral legislature and balance of power. Tocqueville was signaling to his colleagues that in the aftermath of the February revolution, they had an opportunity to write American democratic principles into a new republican constitution. They should avoid the Swiss pitfall and follow instead the American example, where "no bill can become law until it has been examined by two assemblies," where "the division of powers exists not only in appearance but also in reality," and where all citizens enjoy the same rights, and where "nothing resembles a class or a privilege."[45] These checks and balances ensured liberty for all by preventing any party or group from claiming a dominant share. Tocqueville valued the US Constitution for dividing power among the various branches of government while granting significant executive autonomy at various levels of authority.

Tocqueville renewed dialogue with American friends, first among them John Spencer, the New York State legislator, who had introduced Tocqueville to the Constitution when they first met in Canandaigua in 1832. Spencer, who had since served as President Tyler's secretary of war and secretary of the treasury, was a strong advocate for bicameral legislatures and reinforced Tocqueville's views. He wrote to Tocqueville, "It is the firm belief of our wisest men, that under Providence we owe the continuance of our free institutions, more than to any other one cause—to the institution of two legislative Chambers." He also reminded Tocqueville that Benjamin Franklin had disavowed the unicameral legislature that he had first proposed for Pennsylvania. It was "abrogated in a short time and two chambers created."[46] Other American correspondents concurred, among them Robert Walsh, Richard Rush, George Bancroft, and Edward Everett.[47] The distinguished jurist William Alexander Duer sent Tocqueville a copy of his lectures on the constitutional jurisprudence of the United States while also advising "a division of the legislature into two coordinate branches, in order to insure the caution and deliberation requisite to the enactments of wise and wholesome laws."[48]

In *Democracy in America*, Tocqueville had praised the American founding fathers for daring "to propose limiting [liberty] because they were sure they had no wish to destroy it."[49] Tocqueville, however, did not expect his fellow members on the Republic's constitutional committee to live up to their example. They "bore little resemblance to the men who, with Washington in the chair, drafted the American constitution sixty years ago— men sure of their goal and thoroughly familiar with the means for achieving it." Aside from his close friend Beaumont, and his Chamber associates Dufaure, Barrot, and to some extent Vivien, he had little respect for their acumen. Most were moderate Republicans. Corbon, initially a printshop worker turned journalist, sat with the moderates in the assembly. There were only three representatives from the left, Victor Considerant, Félicité de Lamennais, and Armand Marrast. Tocqueville dubbed them "chimerical dreamers." Whatever respect Tocqueville had for Lamennais when he first published *Democracy in America* was long gone. He now described him as a "defrocked priest" lacking determination. Lamennais advocated for the local institutions Tocqueville believed in, but he would rapidly resign from the constitutional commission rather than fight for his ideas—or so Tocqueville concluded. Considerant, the other Montagnard, "had he been sincere, would have deserved to be placed in an asylum." Marrast, more moderate, was a "garden-variety French revolutionary of the sort for whom freedom of the people has always meant despotism exercised in the people's name."[50]

Tocqueville delivered a forceful attack on socialism as part of the Assembly debate on whether to insert the "right to work" clause that Louis Blanc had promoted since the early days of the Second Republic in the constitution. Prior to the June insurrection, Tocqueville had not objected to the possibility of such a clause in the constitution's preamble, but after the disastrous ways in which the workshop experiment ended, he vigorously denounced the idea and offered instead an expectation of public charity, which was adopted in the final version ratified in November 1848.

Tocqueville devoted much time and effort to the constitutional project, missing few meetings save for some special circumstances that affected him personally, such as attending Chateaubriand's funeral on July 8, 1848.[51] Nevertheless, Tocqueville failed to convince his fellow committee members to adopt American bicameralism. None wanted to go against a time-tested centralized regime that reconciled monarchical tradition with Jacobin and Napoleonic rule, or swim against the current of public opinion. Even Beaumont and Dufaure, the latter Tocqueville's closest ally among the Young Left, voted for a unicameral legislative; only Barrot and Vivien shared Tocqueville's conviction and supported a second chamber as the best hope for preventing the Republic from "ending in ruin."[52] In France, all political traditions converged to oppose such a separation of power.

Not all was lost, however. To Tocqueville's satisfaction, the principle of the separation of executive and legislative power prevailed when it came to presidential powers, with the president elected by universal male suffrage rather than by the Assembly. The president therefore derived his legitimacy from his election by the people at large.[53] Only if no candidate had an absolute majority would the selection revert to the Assembly (article 47).

The president, however, would not be allowed to serve consecutive four-year terms, to prevent him from devoting time in office to his reelection (article 45). This was the only criticism of the American system Tocqueville admitted—that a sitting president could "enlist the power of government" "with its immense resources," to secure his reelection.[54] Tocqueville would soon regret this clause, which Beaumont had initially proposed, for a strong president might be tempted to "violate the constitution."[55] That is exactly what happened; the Republic ended when Louis Napoléon staged a coup in December 1851 in the face of a constitution that forbade him from serving a second term.

The constitution now voted into law, presidential elections were scheduled for December 10. Tocqueville was a lukewarm supporter of Cavaignac, who had run the transitional parliamentary regime up to the elections. He saw him, he explained later, as "the only person who, possibly, when the day came, could be a bridge between republicans and monarchists."[56] Tocqueville praised Cavaignac in an editorial in *Le Siècle* for keeping order within and peace without. But he did not risk his reputation for a cause he believed "lost in advance."[57] For the only realistic path to the presidency for Cavaignac was the application of article 47 of the constitution. This was a plausible scenario only if Cavaignac faced off with Lamartine, Ledru-Rollin, and François-Vincent Raspail, but not the increasingly popular Louis Napoléon, who had reappeared on the political scene, winning two consecutive by-elections to the National Assembly in September, after years of exile and imprisonment. In addition to gaining popular support, Louis Napoléon became the favored candidate of the Burgraves (the influential politicians of the Party of Order, as they were called following Victor Hugo's play), who believed they could manipulate him. Thiers, the leader of the Burgraves, confided to Tocqueville that "the man is entirely in our hands. He sees exclusively with our eyes. He is a sort of cretin, whom we will push aside the moment he is no longer useful to us. With him we can turn the Napoleonic page of the revolution of 1848, and then we will get rid of him and get on with the rest of history."[58] This turned out to be a delusion. Elected in a landslide, Louis Napoléon soon asserted his authority.

Tocqueville fell ill in early 1849, severely enough to request successive days of leave from the Assembly.[59] During his bed rest in Normandy, he continued to influence the work of his colleagues. From afar, he pushed for the passage of the so-called proposition Rateau, as amended by his friend Lanjuinais, to move up legislative elections, a move Republicans resisted for fear of losing more seats. Tocqueville also prepared his own reelection campaign in Normandy. He now considered male universal suffrage "the only way to govern from a position of strength," he told Eugène Stöffels.[60] With the vote scheduled for May 13, 1849, Tocqueville issued an electoral circular in which he reasserted his commitment to the Republic but vowed to continue to fight socialism. As doctors advised not only rest but a change of venue, Tocqueville, feeling secure enough about his reelection, went to Germany to visit Bonn and Cologne and finally Frankfurt, where he observed the diet contend with Germany's own revolutions. Not knowing the German language proved a real obstacle, but he followed enough of the debates to correctly predict that the princes, who still controlled the armies, would win if only because of the "violence, impatience, indiscipline" and "hatred of liberty" of the revolutionary parties.[61]

## Tocqueville, Minister of Foreign Affairs

Beaumont advised Tocqueville to return to France in time for the gathering of the new, and more conservative, legislative assembly to be available for a possible reshuffling of the cabinet.[62] With Louis Napoléon relying on Barrot for a second but revised ministry, Tocqueville, although still feeling physically fragile, angled again for the job of education minister he had unsuccessfully sought under Cavaignac's provisional regime, but Louis Napoléon gave that post to Catholic Alfred de Falloux. After much haggling, Tocqueville landed the more prestigious post of minister of foreign affairs while securing the post of minister of agriculture for his friend Lanjuinais, to make sure he would not be isolated in the cabinet. Tocqueville's tenure in foreign affairs lasted a short five months, from June 3 to October 29, 1849.

The first days in that post brought an unpleasant surprise. Who would have thought that as soon as "Mr. America" became foreign minister, he would find himself caught in a remarkable diplomatic imbroglio with the United States? Secretary of State John Clayton had asked the French government to recall Guillaume Tell Poussin, the French minister to Washington, for having used offensive language in demanding the censure of an American navy commander who had rescued a French boat in the Gulf of Mexico but detained it for a few days in the vain hope that he would be rewarded for salvaging it.[63] Tocqueville disliked Poussin, whose 1841 *Considérations sur le principe démocratique qui régit l'union américaine et de la possibilité de son application à d'autres états* had presented an overly rosy picture of American race relations while refuting

Tocqueville's views on slavery. Unlike Tocqueville, Poussin saw no reason to fear "any struggle between the white and black population of the southern portion of the Union."[64]

Tocqueville disapproved of Poussin's conduct in the case at hand. But a comedy of errors ensued. Clayton, not sure whether Tocqueville would recall Poussin, dismissed him under instructions from President Zachary Taylor. This made it impossible for Tocqueville officially to receive the new American minister, who was none other than William Cabell Rives. Rives was the diplomat who had negotiated the 1831 indemnity treaty for Andrew Jackson while Tocqueville was visiting America; he was now returning for a second appointment in Paris. In the 1830s, Rives was a Jacksonian; by 1849, he had become a prominent member of the Whig Party. The dispute ended, and Rives was installed as minister, but only after Louis Napoléon's change of heart abruptly put an end to the second Barrot ministry and hence to Tocqueville's brief tenure as foreign minister. The irony of France's best-known advocate of American principles cutting off diplomatic relations with the United States was certainly not lost on him.

During his five months as foreign minister, Tocqueville tried hard to maintain his independence of action by strategically flattering the president as well as Thiers and Molé, who felt they had the stature to conduct their own foreign policy from their positions in the Assembly. He recruited Gobineau as his chief of staff and proceeded to put close friends on whom he could count in key diplomatic posts: Beaumont as ambassador to Vienna (Rémusat, Tocqueville's first choice, had declined[65]) and Lamoricière as ambassador to Saint Petersburg. Tocqueville developed his own vision of a France intent on recalibrating the balance of power between countries. He was focused on Europe. When writing his *Recollections*, Tocqueville did not deem his study of a protracted conflict between Uruguay and Argentina endangering the local French community worthy of mention.[66] Tocqueville took much more pride in that he helped Italy, yearning for unification and independence, negotiate favorable terms with commanding Austria. He had had a chance to train for that role earlier, during Cavaignac's transitional government, as Cavaignac had placed him in charge of preparing for possible peace negotiations between Piedmont-Sardinia and Austria. Although a planned conference never materialized, Tocqueville had become quite knowledgeable of the complexities of the conflict.[67] As minister, he obtained for Piedmont the integrity of the kingdom of Piedmont-Sardinia and a significantly reduced war indemnity to pay to Austria—far lower than the Piedmontese themselves would have secured, without his intervention, after their successive defeats at the hand of the Austrians at Custoza in November 1848 and Novara in March 1849 in the first Italian war of independence.[68]

Tocqueville wanted also to strengthen France's eastern border. His recent visit to Germany had made him contemplate a possible German unification not as a threat to France but instead as France's bulwark against the czars. "We must change our old precepts and be unafraid to strengthen our neighbors so that they might one day be prepared to join us in repelling the common master," he mused in *Recollections*.[69]

Tocqueville credited himself for standing up to Russian power. He protected Hungarian (and Polish) refugees of the 1848 revolution who had fled to Turkey from the wrath of czar and Austrian emperor alike. Although recognizing "Russia's right to ask the Porte to keep out and neutralize those men scheming to do her harm,"[70] Tocqueville defended the sultan's decision to shelter refugees from Russia on humanitarian grounds; he also convinced England to take in Hungarian leader Lajos Kossuth. All along, he worked closely with the English cabinet to dissuade Russia and Austria from declaring war on the Ottomans. At the same time, he worked to convince the Swiss not to grant asylum to revolutionaries indiscriminately.

The greatest affair that occurred during Tocqueville's tenure was the invasion of Rome, which the president had ordered just before forming the new ministry in hopes of restoring Pope Pius IX to temporal power. French troops were already camped at Civitavecchia when Tocqueville entered the cabinet.[71] As minister, he therefore had to implement a decision already made. He redefined the mission to suit his goal of liberalizing the church. He pushed Pius IX to make "real, substantive progress in the way of civil law and actual administrative powers, judicial control, local and regional institutions" and to create "an assembly that is at least somewhat representative, at least one that controls the budget," all this being "perfectly reconcilable with papal government."[72] He called on his British friends to have their government acknowledge that France was justified in intervening in Rome to serve the liberal cause in the spirit of modern civilization.[73] Tocqueville also had a message for French Catholics that he conveyed most directly to his devout colleague Falloux, minister of education and religious life. He maintained that the pope's illiberal behavior had heretofore contributed to the "profound weakening of the religious spirit in the world, a spirit that, even speaking on a purely human level we desperately need if we are to support our dysfunctional society."[74]

Tocqueville hoped that Louis Napoléon, suspected of having been a Carbonaro and of once fighting for Italian unification and independence, would insist on democratic reforms from Pius IX, but Tocqueville should have known that the president would be more interested in preventing Austria from meddling in Roman affairs than in constitutional and in-stitutional reforms to limit papal absolutism. Meanwhile, confusion regarding French goals prevailed among Roman revolutionaries. Giuseppe Mazzini, one of their leaders, who had read and admired *Democracy in America*, publicly denounced Tocqueville for betraying his ideals and lying about the purpose of the expedition.[75] Tocqueville was also criti-cized in Paris. The opposition claimed that France's new constitution had been violated, and Ledru-Rollin led a street demonstration on June 13, 1849. He attracted only a modest following—there was much greater violence in Lyon—but the government responded by declaring a state of siege in the capital. Members of the opposition were arrested or forced to escape abroad to avoid imprisonment.

As for Francisque de Corcelle, Tocqueville's friend and his hand-picked envoy to the Vatican, faith now trumped both geopolitics and social justice. Tocqueville entrusted Corcelle with securing concessions from the papacy, but Corcelle had become a devout Catholic; instead of following instructions, he submitted entirely to the pope. Tocque-ville's disappointment created great tension between the two friends and collaborators. Tocqueville rebuked his envoy, warning him that he was letting "the court of Rome amuse us with promises, as if we were

children, while it resumes all its old abuses through faits accomplis."
Tocqueville was dismayed at the restoration in Rome of inquisition and
"the law courts of the vicariate, the most disgraceful court in the roman
judicial system . . . and the persecution beneath our very eyes of former
members of the liberal party."[76] Although he maintained in the National
Assembly that the pope had promised adequate reform in the *Motu
proprio* he had issued, Tocqueville knew this not to be the case.[77] He
asked Corcelle, "Can our venture thus far be described as anything
other than a complete and glaring failure? Show me, I beg you, one sign,
one single sign of France's liberal hand, one thing that can be considered
with any apparent justification as evidence of our just influence, one act
that can be offered to the country as compensation for the blood spilled
and money spent? None exists. We cannot say: they refused us this but
gave us that. No, they have given us *absolutely* nothing."[78]

Tocqueville's responsibility ended abruptly when, on October 31,
Louis Napoléon dismissed the entire cabinet, with no warning, and
sent on the same day a message to the National Assembly expressing his
displeasure with his ministers' lack of personal loyalty. A vexed Tocqueville drafted the next day, but never sent, a letter expressing his surprise
that the president had not heretofore voiced any concerns about the
direction of the cabinet.[79] To Beaumont, he wrote of his suspicion that
Louis Napoléon was already planning to hold on to power illegally:
"The president became convinced that we not only would refrain from
assisting him in the final coup d'état but also would not allow him to
prepare for it so that he could do without us when that day came; and
second, his desire to govern and above all *appear* to govern by himself.
He believed we were allowing him to slip slowly into the shadows and
that in the end the country would forget about him. He wanted to
demonstrate his complete independence from us and the National Assembly. That is why he chose a moment when the majority was most
securely ours and, instead of bringing in the leaders of that majority as
ministers, turned to the lower party ranks in search of men he could
use. These men will not steal his glory or hide him from view. These are
the true causes of what happened."[80]

## The Tragedy of French History

Reflecting on his dismissal was painful. As Christmas 1849 approached and he had been out of power for almost two months, Tocqueville likened his time as minister to "a moonless night in December, thick with fog. Not only can you not see the horizon, you can't even see the path in front of you. The lawmakers leading society are as blind as the society they are driving through the bog."[81] Away from power, Tocqueville confided to Gobineau that he felt, once again, depressed. "What you will find hard to understand is the degree of apathy that has overtaken me. I am barely able to observe life as a spectator, because a spectator at least pays attention, whereas I do not even take the trouble to watch."[82] He kept old friends at bay. His only occupation early in the year was to proof the thirteenth printing of *Democracy in America* (4,000 copies), the last edition in Tocqueville's lifetime.[83]

One clear reason for Tocqueville's lethargy was his declining health. In early March 1850, he experienced an episode of coughing blood that was the first sign of the tuberculosis that would take his life nine years later. At the end of March, Tocqueville requested a six-month leave from the Assembly, the first five weeks of which he spent entirely in bed, nurses taking turns at his side.[84]

Life came to a standstill. Tocqueville, who had been so invested in the educational debate, did not attend the Assembly to vote on March 15, 1850 on the loi Falloux that institutionalized liberty of teaching and guaranteed an ex officio seat for a Catholic bishop in the university council of each department. Tocqueville left Paris in March as "red" victories in a few by-elections reignited fears of radicalism. He was no longer engaged when, on May 31, 1850, the conservative majority rescinded universal suffrage and adopted voting restrictions that reduced the electorate by a third. Karl Marx, writing for the *Neue Rheinische Zeitung*, denounced the law as an act of "bourgeois dictatorship."[85] For his part, Tocqueville considered the move self-defeating since universal suffrage brought conservatives to the Assembly. But he was out of the fray.

Only in late April 1850, Tocqueville told Eugène Stöffels, did he regain some strength and resume a modicum of political activity.[86] In June or July, he wrote the first part of his *Recollections* at his Normandy home. President of the Conseil général de la Manche, the governmental body administering the *département*,[87] Tocqueville officially received Louis Napoléon when the president came to Cherbourg as part of his tour of several regions in France. Tocqueville called forcefully for him to establish a rail connection between the Norman port town and Paris. Tocqueville's main argument rested on making the railroad line a natural extension of Cherbourg harbor, which already handled about a quarter of all French imports (including cotton for a growing number of French manufactures). The episode took all the recovered strength he could give.[88]

The medical reprieve did not last long. On the advice of his doctors, Tocqueville soon sought refuge from Normandy's cold and damp climate. Tocqueville and Marie left for Sicily on October 31, 1850 (Tocqueville had been there with Édouard in 1826), stopping in Naples on the way. After a rough voyage, they decided to stay in Sorrento, on the Bay of Naples. Tocqueville felt isolated there and begged his friends for political news. Senior and Ampère visited Sorrento during their friend's six-month convalescence, and Tocqueville shared in conversations with them fragments of his *Recollections*, to which he once again turned his attention. He could not reconcile himself with "vegetating"— that is, "spending all one's time looking at sky and sea, a beautiful coastline, and piles of old stones."[89] He devoted some thought to imagining life after politics and began to think of writing, he wrote Kergorlay, "another major work" of "political literature" on the "long drama of the French Revolution . . . that extends from 1789 to the present."[90]

Before returning to Paris in May 1851, Tocqueville arranged to rent a small house in Versailles from his friend Jean-Charles Rivet, intending to work there on the last part of his *Recollections* and to rest in bucolic surroundings while going to Paris occasionally for important sessions of the Assembly.[91] On May 15, Tocqueville met privately with the president to discuss the possibility of revising the constitution to legalize a second consecutive term and avoid a probable coup. Tocqueville thereafter led a failed effort to revise the constitution to keep Louis Napoléon within its bounds. It was his last chance to put his imprint on the constitution and at the same time save the Republic. He chaired the parliamentary committee that brought a constitutional amendment on this issue to the floor in July 1851, only to face opposition from members on the left who feared a less republican constitution and conservatives who opposed the right to work and welfare. Although the movement in favor of revision was strong, Tocqueville failed to obtain the required two-thirds majority to elect a new Constituent Assembly, which would be required for this change.[92]

It was commonly believed that Louis Napoléon would simply defy the existing constitution, run an illegal campaign, and get himself re-elected. Tocqueville, fearful of despotism, made it known that he would vote for the prince de Joinville, Louis Philippe's third son, even though many understood Joinville's candidacy to be a possible prelude to yet another restoration of the monarchy, perhaps even a fusion of the two branches of the royal family. Peasants would support Joinville, Tocqueville thought, because they had sold more cattle under the Orléans than under any other regime. A strong showing for Joinville would weaken Louis Napoléon's authority.[93] But the point was soon moot. There was no election. Instead, on December 2, 1851, the anniversary of the coronation of his uncle Napoleon, Louis Napoléon opted for the coup that had been widely anticipated. Tocqueville, along with fifty other members of the Assembly, was arrested and briefly jailed. The coup was, in Tocqueville's judgment, "one of the greatest crimes in history." Tocqueville gave a blow-by-blow account of the dramatic events of "force overturning law" and the brutal repression throughout France of those who resisted the new power, which was transmitted to the *Times* of London by Mrs. Grote and published there on December 8, 1851.[94]

At the same time, Tocqueville observed with great sadness that an overwhelming majority of the French people simply accepted what Marx labeled the Eighteenth Brumaire of Louis Bonaparte. He wrote to his brother Édouard,

What makes me regret not being in jail any longer, what would make me hide in the countryside tomorrow if only I could find a place with no Frenchmen or their business in sight, is contact with the so-called "honest" and "distinguished" classes. They accept the government of these wretches not only with resignation, as you say, but with pleasure. I see it in the eyes of those who talk to me. Yes, our souls are so base that it is not only peasants, bourgeois, or shopkeepers who readily trade freedom, dignity, and the country's honor for their peace and quiet, and the assurance they can continue sell their products or their merchandise. Every day I observe such vulgar feelings and depraved hearts among the men who call themselves the nation's elite. No need to go to Compiègne; the salons of Paris are full of them. They are full of so-called aristocrats and little cowardly women who were so scared of 1852, who trembled so much for their income, that they now rejoice at the recent and unfolding events, and the ignominy of the new regime.[95]

For Tocqueville, the curse of French history had redescended: the French had once more been unable to make a republic work. The radicals' passion for equality had made way for the bourgeoisie's greed to defeat democracy. Tocqueville quit politics rather than swear allegiance to the new regime. He felt that the French deserved the punishment a dictator brought because they had not stood up for their rights. Sadly, politics also took a toll on family relationships. The coup led to a major argument with Tocqueville's brother Édouard, who rallied behind Louis Napoléon, even loudly voicing his support for "a form of liberty that, while serious, is also contained by strong and respected authority."[96] The conflict became public when the newspaper L'Union mistakenly attributed Édouard's support of Louis Napoléon to Alexis, who required the paper to publish a correction.[97] The two brothers exchanged bitter letters expressing their diverging views, agreeing only to keep Hubert (Édouard's son) out of their conflict and protect his privileged relationship with his uncle and godfather. The always-inconsistent Hippolyte also rallied to the regime, which prompted Tocqueville to write him, "These actions are as foreign to me as the defining moments of your life in the past twenty years."[98] The family solidarity was broken again as in the days of Tocqueville's perceived misalliance with Marie. Except this time, there would be no real repair until the very end of Tocqueville's life. Only an aging Hervé de Tocqueville remained above the fray.

Under the circumstances Tocqueville joined with his National Assembly friends (Rivet, Barrot, Freslon, Vivien) in asking the comte de Chambord (the Bourbon heir who could become Henri V) to commit to a new *constitutional* monarchy that truly respected liberty now that the Republic had failed. Only a few years earlier, Tocqueville had chastised his brother Hippolyte for visiting Chambord in London (accompanying Chateaubriand). But circumstances were different. Now the Republican party had dramatically shrunk, even practically disappeared, said Rivet. Socialism was muted for a while. Tocqueville and his friends revived the idea of a fusion (or reconciliation) of the Bourbon and Orléans royal branches, with the crown going to Henri V and succession to the comte de Paris.[99] This seemed like a possibly viable means of saving constitutional government for France. The fusion might rally a good part of the provincial middle class against the regime. As Tocqueville explained to Rémusat, "The small-town middle class says to us, 'so long as the Princes are arguing, how do you expect us to make war on the government? Do you think we are trying to prepare the way for socialism?'"[100] Tocqueville wrote the count in mid-January 1852, asking him to make known "his firm and definitive intention" to reestablish in France, with appropriate steps, "a constitutional and representative monarchy with its chief characteristics, namely: 1) The guarantee of individual freedom; 2) A sincere national representation; 3) Freedom and complete publicity of parliamentary discussions; 4) Real freedom of the press."[101] Chambord not only ignored the proposal, but he made his case worse by defending feudal rights in a manifesto he published later that year.

Neither the Bourbon heir nor his supporters had any sympathy for Tocqueville's strategy. Hard-line Legitimists close to Tocqueville, such as the elder Kergorlays, were no longer even on speaking terms with Tocqueville. When Florian de Kergorlay died a few years later, Tocqueville decided against going to the funeral, concluding that his presence would be resented.[102] Still, the idea of a fusion lingered for a while; the duc de Nemours, Louis Philippe's second son, visited Chambord at Fröhsdorf the following year, but nothing came of it.

Tocqueville no longer saw a clear path to achieving his democratic aspirations. He had gone into politics with the hope of channeling his democratic convictions into political reforms aimed at balancing liberty and equality, but his hopes had been dashed. He ended his political life with the realization that political science and the art of governing were two very different things after all. His own attempt to blend political theory and real politics, begun with his first electoral campaign of 1837, had come to an end. He had hesitated in the face of an emerging revolution, decided to participate in a great historical event, experienced frustration in power, and in the end felt bitter disappointment and sheer anger at his failure. To Édouard, he admitted "finding life almost unbearable." "I feel like a foreigner in my own country, surrounded by people who do not share the ideas which, to my mind, are indispensable to human dignity; people who are cold to the feelings that constitute in my eyes my moral stature, and without which I would not want to exist."[103] The only possible escape for Tocqueville was to look the other way. This is what he did. He told Reeve, "I'm going back to work . . . in order to forget what has happened and to lose interest, as best I can, in my country and my times."[104] Eventually, at some distance from the dramatic events and having returned to his studies, Tocqueville reconciled himself with the idea that his true vocation was as a thinker and not a politician. He phlegmatically told his colleagues in the French Academy that even the great Montesquieu would have made a mediocre minister.[105]

# 10

# A Revolution "Fully Formed from the Society That It Was to Destroy"

DEFEATED IN POLITICS and battling declining health, Tocqueville immersed himself in the study of history during his political exile. He intended to shed light on France's troubling volatility and its repeated alternation between republican and despotic regimes, epitomized by the Revolution and its failure. The cycle was recurring before his own eyes as Louis Napoléon Bonaparte imposed the Second Empire rather than share power under the Second Republic. Tocqueville's idea, as he had expressed it in Sorrento, was to explain how the uncle half a century earlier had paved the way for the nephew in building the First Empire on the ashes of the First Republic.

## France as Police State

That democratic principles no longer applied after the coup, the prince-president made clear in adopting, in Tocqueville's words, "the most despotic constitution that France has ever had." The one Napoleon had promulgated to establish the consulate in December 1799 was, he thought, more liberal.[1] An alarmed Tocqueville told Henry Reeve, "We have to go back to the Terror and the Committee of Public Safety to find in our history something even remotely similar to what we are now seeing."[2] Tocqueville regularly updated his British friends, who had previously helped him publicize his narrative of the coup in the *Times of London*. He reported to Nassau Senior that "political deportees are to die of fever in Cayenne [and Algiers] if they survive the crossing."[3] He added to Harriet Grote that the empire's political adversaries were "convicted without a trial."[4] Tocqueville was also horrified by Louis Napoléon's gratuitous and vengeful acts of retaliation, such as the dispossession of the Orléans family. Tocqueville targeted his anger in this affair at Sébastien Boulatignier, a prominent jurist he had befriended and supported in local Normandy politics and now a conseiller d'état, who was endorsing this blatant disregard for property rights. Tocqueville cut off his relationship with him.[5]

Tocqueville's political circle shrank in the weeks following the coup. Close associates were sent into exile. Lamoricière and Bedeau, the expelled generals, sought refuge in Belgium.[6] Rémusat, Duvergier de Hauranne, and Chambolle went to London, as did Thiers, toward whom Tocqueville felt sympathy now that he had been banished.[7] Tocqueville's closest friends in the Chamber—associates of the Young Left including Barrot, Freslon, Dufaure, Lanjuinais, Vivien, and Rivet—all retired into domestic exile. Vivien lived on modest means at Saint-Germain-en-Laye. Dufaure withdrew to Saintonge for a while before returning to Paris as a barrister. Barrot, Freslon, and Lanjuinais also resumed their law practices, and Rivet now directed the Chemins de fer de l'ouest.[8] Running for office was unthinkable under a government that would not authorize any candidate to organize an electoral committee, print circulars, or even campaign. If elected, representatives could neither propose legislation nor exercise parliamentary interpellation.

Tocqueville likened his constrained circle of political friends, in a letter to Lanjuinais, to medieval Jews "who needed to live amongst themselves to rediscover their homeland"[9]—not a comparison you would expect a scion of aristocracy and member of the French Academy to make. Tocqueville used other images to describe his mood. To Lamoricière, exiled from France, Tocqueville wrote that living in France was like attempting to "pilot a ship on a dry riverbed. The water will return, but not for a long time."[10] Meanwhile, one must beware of "*le curieux*," as the people now nicknamed the nosy prosecutor, who could legally open mail and spy on unsuspecting citizens.[11]

Family provided little solace. Tocqueville distanced himself from his brothers who had both rallied to the regime.[12] He continued to draw intellectual and emotional support from his oldest friends, many of whom were also struggling. Kergorlay was in dire financial straits; fortunately, Chabrol, thanks to his banking family money, was able to come to Kergorlay's rescue and offer him a job. Beaumont, now without income from the Chamber, was broke, too. Hampered by an aristocratic resentment of commercial work, he retired to a diminished life in the country, yet remained devoted to helping Tocqueville achieve his goals, as did Ampère and Corcelle.[13] Sadly, Eugène Stöffels died in July 1852, the first from the Metz days to go.[14]

In his constricted circumstances, Tocqueville reflected on the prince-president's popularity, and he tried to understand why there was so little dissent in France and no channel for expressing it. On a general level, Tocqueville blamed Louis Napoléon's national appeal to the widespread fear of socialism that the radical republicans had inspired. As a result, he felt that the bulk of the nation supported the expansion of executive power to ensure that the ghost of socialism, that killjoy threatening its future, was seen no more. Tocqueville recognized, though, that different people supported the government for different reasons. He developed a political sociology of the nation, breaking down the country into distinct classes and assessing the reasons each one had for accepting the new authoritarian regime.

Tocqueville turned his attention first to the peasantry. He observed in Normandy that the president's political strategy of ensuring universal suffrage to legitimize his despotism served him well. To Rémusat, in London, he reported, "The peasant remains content with the new order of things. The idea that this government is the work of the people, created *by* and *for* him, is deeply rooted in the mind of this multitude."[15] But the belief was delusional, Tocqueville felt, so long as the government retained such tight control over the electoral process and the functioning of the Chamber. The peasantry remained loyal to the regime during the Crimean War in 1853, leading a disillusioned Tocqueville to sarcastically remark that peasants must "console themselves for the loss of their children by selling their cattle at a higher price."[16]

While the peasantry provided electoral support, the army guaranteed Louis Napoléon's authority. As a result, Tocqueville told both Corcelle and Lamoricière that "the true aristocracy of the country is now the army, the abusing and ruling class. . . . It dominates the nation alone in the absence of all political debates."[17]

With the economy doing well, business circles also rallied to the regime, which only reinforced Tocqueville's long-standing contempt for them. Tocqueville criticized the government for benefiting from a "frantic" climate of business speculation. He saw entrepreneurs as modern-day courtiers, seeking public works projects and other contracts by securing favors from the prince-president.[18] The "industrial aristocracy" whose arrival Tocqueville had foreseen in the second volume of Democracy in America was taking hold of vast segments of the economy. Industrialists and their wives, Tocqueville told Lamoricière, were becoming "the great lords and ladies of this new court. They engage in all manner of extravagances, which will no doubt get worse with the rising authority of their master."[19]

The government also succeeded in rallying the Catholic clergy. "These servile priests [plats-pieds de prêtres] who once cried, 'Long live the Republic!' now drive their master to boredom with their flattery," Tocqueville wrote his nephew Hubert, full of dismay.[20] The clergy supported Louis Napoléon because Philippe d'Orléans, comte de Paris, Louis Philippe's grandson, was still too young to govern, and they could not tolerate the prospect of his mother, the duchesse d'Orléans, who was a German Protestant, as regent.[21]

As for the Legitimists, Tocqueville recognized that they did not like the regime but still preferred it to that of the junior branch. To neutralize their opposition, prefects and local mayors effectively dispensed favors to the old nobility and held out the possibility of "gilding again their coats-of-arms."[22]

Everywhere Tocqueville turned, then, he saw the consolidation of the prince-president's rule. He had long predicted, he told Charles Stöffels, "that the madness of 1848 would bring about a government that the principles I had upheld all my life would forbid me from serving."[23] Tocqueville resigned in April 1852 from the last political office he held, that of serving his local constituency in the Conseil général of La Manche. He regretted doing so but felt he had no choice. He explained to Zacharie Gallemand, a wealthy landowner who had been his electoral agent in Valognes, "I return to private life out of a sense of self-respect that all men of taste and sound judgment should understand."[24] When the government unexpectedly authorized "canton" elections to fill these local positions again on July 31 and August 1, Tocqueville stood by his decision and resisted local pressure to return.[25]

Tocqueville gradually formed plans to write a book of political history relevant to the current political situation. He wanted not only to leave an intellectual mark but to also make a difference in how his compatriots judged the current state of French affairs. Tocqueville feared the French were reenacting a sequence of events he had diagnosed long ago: "Overthrow or coerce old powers" in the name of equality and liberty, then settle for a dictatorial regime while still laying a claim to "equality." As Tocqueville had put it in *Democracy in America*, the French "want equality in liberty, and if they cannot have it, they want it still in slavery."[26] When Tocqueville delivered his acceptance speech at the Académie française in 1842, he spoke of an immense French Revolution "taken up in the name of liberty but ending in despotism."[27] Tocqueville thought that exploring anew, and in depth, this cycle of freedom and dependence—a decidedly French malady—would be a fitting topic for a politician-philosopher fearing for the future of his country and yearning to be heard.

In the solitude of his convalescence in Sorrento, in December 1850, a full year before Louis Napoléon Bonaparte's coup and in anticipation of it, Tocqueville envisioned writing a book on the elder Bonaparte's illegal ascent to power. Tocqueville's idea was to show how Napoleon "discovered in the Revolution's most demagogic works everything which was apt to despotism, and made it come forth naturally." He would reveal how "this almost divine intelligence" became so "coarsely employed to restrain human freedom."[28]

Conversely, he would explain why the French "were ready to sacrifice this liberty that the Revolution had never more than promised them in order to finally obtain undisturbed enjoyment of the other goods that it had given them."[29] Tocqueville wrote Kergorlay that he wanted to give a "picture" of the society formed by the Revolution that facilitated Napoleon's ascent to power." However dramatic the actions leading to the 18 Brumaire were, he meant not to narrate them but determine what could have possibly make such a combination of events and outcome possible. He meant to select "an ensemble of reflections and judgments" on "the long drama of the French Revolution" to explain "how the Empire was able to establish itself amid the society created by the Revolution." He envisioned writing a "mixture of history properly so called with historical philosophy . . . the inimitable model of this genre" being Montesquieu's book on the grandeur and the decline of the Romans.[30]

Nothing, Tocqueville felt, could be more relevant to post-1848 politics than a book on the aftermath of 1789. Tocqueville conceived of this project while he was still writing his *Recollections* of the events he had just witnessed. After personally living through two revolutions, in 1830 and 1848, he questioned the explanatory power of the political theory to which he had up to now devoted so much of his time. He had learned how unpredictable political outcomes were. No longer trusting systemic explanations, he asserted, "I hate absolute systems that see all historical events as dependent on grand first causes linked together in ineluctable sequence, thus banishing individual human beings from the history of the human race. I find such theories narrow in their pretensions of grandeur and false beneath their air of mathematical truth." Still committed to political science, however, he added, "I also firmly believe that chance accomplishes nothing for which the groundwork has not been laid in advance. Prior facts, the nature of institutions, the cast of people's minds, and the state of mores are the materials out of which chance improvises the effects we find so surprising and terrible to behold."[31] Tocqueville therefore wanted to write a history shedding light on great complexity, more analytical than narrative—but not the kind recounting events mechanically following each other, such as Thiers wrote, and which he despised. He knew, he would someday tell Hubert, that "one cannot ever be sure of all the facts."[32]

Two years passed. In January 1852, after having failed to lead the assembly to revise the constitution and with Louis Napoléon Bonaparte's coup a fait accompli, Tocqueville returned to the question he had framed in Sorrento: How can the French so easily give up liberty gained through revolution and submit to a despot? Unbeknownst to him, Karl Marx was at that time drawing a similar parallel between November 9, 1799 and December 2, 1851, in a brilliant essay, *The 18 Brumaire of Louis Bonaparte*, published in 1852. Marx famously wrote that the coups of the two Napoleons, uncle and nephew, proved that history repeats itself, "first as tragedy, then as farce." Tocqueville would in due course put it this way: "History is a gallery of paintings in which there are few originals and many copies."[33]

Tocqueville followed a complex route to add his original voice to an ever-enlarging commentary on the French Revolution his contemporaries produced. A historian often changes direction during a large inquiry. Unearthed documentary evidence sheds light on unexpected yet critical actors and events; chance intellectual encounters open promising avenues of research; topics initially ignored take up an urgent significance. The paper trail of detailed notes and related correspondence Tocqueville left behind reveal his formidable intellectual journey in discovery and writing, bringing to the topic an intimate knowledge of aristocracy enriched by a lifetime of study and action committed to democracy.

Not unexpectedly, Tocqueville had to fight off discouragement after the coup to set his project in motion. Tocqueville complained to Beaumont that a *"maladie de l'âme"* prevented him from doing any work.[34] But as was so often the case, even as he declared himself unable to focus, he was making important inroads. This time, he undertook a regimen of reading for three to four hours every afternoon at the Bibliothèque nationale in Paris. Without a definite program, Tocqueville logically began by investigating the politics of the Directory.[35] He annotated young Benjamin Constant's first and influential 1796 pamphlet, *On the Strength of the Present Government of France, and upon the Necessity of Rallying Round It*, and a few subsequent ones. Constant argued for "a Republic established upon a firm basis" by "returning to the peaceable observance of the laws," with citizens acknowledging the same rights and protecting the same forms.[36] But the Directory instead degenerated into a bitter fight between political extremes that led to an initial coup of 18 Fructidor Year V (September 4, 1797). On that day, several members of the Directory called on the troops to purge royalists and counterrevolutionaries from the Corps législatif. Tocqueville saw in these dramatic events, carefully narrated in Antoine Thibaudeau's 1824 *Mémoires sur la Convention et le directoire*, a "perfect analogy" with the conflicts that preceded December 2, 1851. "It is as if you are reading the history of the last six months,"[37] Tocqueville noted. In each case, the Republican party had become an "honest third party running after an ideal and ever receding republic, caught between those who wanted the Terror and those who wanted the monarchy, laboriously trying to make the republic survive without Republicans."[38] Tocqueville then read Lafayette's memoirs, which his friend Corcelle had edited, to understand the attraction of a young General Bonaparte for the many Frenchmen who hoped he would return to France from his campaigns.[39]

Tocqueville reluctantly interrupted this reading to prepare an address to the Académie des sciences morales et politiques. As president in 1851, his was the honor of presenting the prizes that the Académie gave out each year. The award ceremony, originally scheduled for December 6, 1851, just four days after the coup, was postponed to early April 1852. Tocqueville complained of the distraction but produced a speech that was a turning point in his own intellectual program.[40] In it, he laid out the role of the intellectual in society.

Although Tocqueville no longer believed in the possibility of a coherent fusion of politics and political science in concrete policymaking, he argued that political scientists had a broader calling. After explaining the limited overlap between political science and politics in practical terms, he stressed their mutual enrichment in moral terms. He saw intellectuals as the thinkers who stood above action and provided the larger framework for political life. As he explained, "Political science generates, or at least shapes, those general ideas that make up the intellectual atmosphere of a society. The minds of both the governors and the governed breathe deeply from this source and draw the principles of their conduct from it, often unwittingly, and sometimes even unwillingly."[41]

In his rousing speech, Tocqueville declared it the mission of political theory to restore faith in democratic institutions, and he identified the Académie des sciences morales et politiques as the proper institutional home for its practitioners. Long gone were the days when Tocqueville looked at the Académie des sciences morales et politiques with disdain. He now saw the institution as a glimmer of hope. Tocqueville remained publicly prominent during these years only at the two academies of the Institut de France where he belonged, the Académie française and the Académie des sciences morales et politiques. Because these were centers of liberal thinking, the government attempted to silence their members. Most notably, it stripped the two great mandarins of academic philosophy and literature of the July Monarchy, academicians Victor Cousin and Abel-François Villemain (the latter had recovered from his nervous breakdown), from their university chairs after they refused to swear an oath of allegiance to the regime. For Cousin, this was a repeat scenario, as he had experienced the same fate early in the Bourbon Restoration (see chapter 1). The Académie des sciences morales et politiques's mission had been to serve the government in its social science inquiries, but the authoritarian populist government of Louis Napoléon had no use for it. Thus, Minister of Education Hippolyte Fortoul attempted in 1855 to block Barrot's election.[42] Unsuccessful in this, Fortoul turned to a packing scheme. He disregarded the rules governing the recruitment of new members by election to appoint a cohort of hand-picked pro-government members who would dilute the opposition. Villemain called the appointees "the garrison."[43] In Tocqueville's view, the government was depriving itself of "the influence of the most skilled, the wisest, and the most honest parts of the nation."[44]

## From Empire to Revolution

With spring, the time had come to leave for Normandy, where Tocqueville wanted to begin writing. The Tocquevilles left Paris in May 1852. On the way, they visited the Beaumonts at Beaumont la Chartre and the

Corcelles at Beaufossé.[45] Ampère joined them at Tocqueville. Tocqueville reported to Reeve that Ampère "works in the upper part of the tower, while I scribble down below, on the second floor."[46] He was eager to begin drafting the book on Napoleon's ascent that he had first sketched out at Sorrento. He readily admitted to Beaumont he did not yet have an argument for it but was looking for one "with energetic desperation."[47] Although not revealing exactly what he had in mind, Tocqueville acknowledged to his father—himself the author of one book on the reign of Louis XV and another on that of Louis XVI—that he was taking up writing again to remain engaged with the fate of the nation. "This too is politics," he wrote, "as you can well imagine I will not be dealing with the writings of the Medes or the Assyrians."[48]

Tocqueville utilized the notes he had compiled at the Bibliothèque nationale to draft two short chapters on Napoleon's meteoric rise: "How the Republic Was Ready to Accept a Master" and "How the Nation, while No Longer Republican, Had Remained Revolutionary." Tocqueville analyzed the political positions of opposing camps in the Directory. He highlighted how "the royalists, who saw that the nation had become disgusted with freedom, thought it was ready to return to the old regime." They failed, he noted, by making "the mistake the defeated people always make, believing they are loved because their successors are hated, without realizing that it is much easier for people to remain faithful in their hatreds than in their love. France, which no longer loved the Republic, remained deeply attached to the Revolution."[49] Tocqueville felt good about his progress. He told Kergorlay, "I got a taste for painting the period preceding 18 Brumaire, and the states of mind that led up to this coup d'état. I find . . . despite great divergences, numerous similarities between the period I am describing and the one we are going through." He added to Beaumont, "I wrote these two pieces with great enthusiasm, rendering emotions that struck me as almost contemporary."[50]

But Tocqueville wanted to do more than render emotions. He intended to determine what led the French to give up hard-won liberty and entrust a despot with their future. Positing that the people counted on Napoleon to protect their benefits, he asked what material advances the

people had really gained during the Revolution. Long before profes-
sional historians delved into quantitative methods for the study of economic trends and social change, Tocqueville set about trying to calculate
an answer to this difficult question.[51] He investigated several categories
of peasant financial gain, including the abolition of feudal rights and the
availability of cheap land confiscated during the Revolution. He attempted to "assess the value of the confiscated lands the people inherited, the feudal rights abrogated, the offensive, burdensome taxes that
were lifted, or even the debts and the rents that were satisfied by means
of entirely fictive new currencies."[52] He told Freslon, "What I want to
know is not the debts of the vanquished class [the émigrés], but those of
the victorious class, of the rural bourgeoisie, the peasantry, and the small
landowning class."[53]

Tocqueville undertook an ambitious survey of "old ledgers and other
dusty registers." He asked Gallemand for information about the change
in Valognes residents' financial standing before and after the Revolution. Gallemand was unable to find any local data but provided the useful feudalist Joseph Renauldon's *Traité historique et pratique des droits
seigneuriaux*, which helped Tocqueville trace the history of the abolition
of feudal dues.[54] Tocqueville also asked the local archivist in Saint-Lô
to extract relevant data from land surveys the Assemblée constituante
had required in 1790 to establish a land tax, but the archivist had no time
for such a difficult inquiry. Kergorlay gave his friend some preliminary
findings of his own for land around his family estate of Fosseuse, which
indicated an old subdivision of land, but told him it was difficult to calculate the exact material gain of the peasantry.[55] Still, at Kergorlay's suggestion, Tocqueville compared property maps made before and after
the Revolution within his own canton of Saint-Pierre-Église and found
both a large number of small property owners before the Revolution
and a subsequent increase. He came to the tentative conclusion that "in
a large part of France, the people owned more land than we commonly
imagine. These disgruntled small property holders, who today find a
home in socialism, were already a significant element of the Revolution."[56] This agreed with Necker's observation that "there was an *immense number* of small rural properties in France" before the Revolution

and confirmed the British Arthur Young's observation in his travels through France of "the great division of land among the peasants."[57]

This archival search was useful, yet inconclusive, regarding how much independence peasants actually gained during the eighteenth century. Several months later, Tocqueville had the good fortune to read an excellent entry submitted to the Académie des sciences morales et politiques's historical essay competition by a young Lyonnais professor, C. Dareste de la Chavanne, on the "condition of the agricultural classes in France from the thirteenth century up to the Revolution of 1789." Dareste documented a significant easing of feudal obligations in the eighteenth century, and this confirmed Tocqueville in his emerging sense that the Revolution arose in a period of relaxation of feudal abuses, greater recognition of individual rights, and increase in peasants' property ownership. These developments made their remaining feudal burden even more unacceptable and kindled their hatred for the old regime, a point Tocqueville would famously highlight in *The Ancien Régime and the French Revolution*: "It is not always going from bad to worse that leads to revolution. What happens most often is that a people that put up with the most oppressive laws without complaint, as if they did not feel them, rejects those laws violently when the burden is alleviated."[58]

By October 1852, with dampness filling the old Normandy manor, it was time to return to Paris. The Tocquevilles established their residence on place de la Madeleine, in Hervé de Tocqueville's apartment.[59] Tocqueville expected to continue his work at the Bibliothèque nationale while resuming a modest social life with an occasional dinner in town or visit to Madame de Circourt's salon. This was not to be, for he fell seriously ill. Pleurisy kept him bedridden for two full months. He recovered just as Louis Napoléon Bonaparte was being crowned Napoleon III on December 2, 1852, an event that he pointedly ignored. With the need for more sun and light than the father's apartment provided, the Tocquevilles moved to a "sunny little house" on rue de Courcelles, on the west side of Paris, in December, where the writer took stock of what he had accomplished so far.[60]

With the study of land ownership, Tocqueville had already begun to turn his gaze away from Napoleon toward the origins of the Revolution.

He began reading the works of Edmund Burke, which had the effect of interesting him even more in the prerevolutionary period. There is no indication from previous conversations with his British friends, which focused on the British aristocracy, that Tocqueville had ever intended to read Burke. Instead, he came across Burke accidentally while reading Ampère's diary of his time in New York and Boston in 1851, which Ampère published as the lead piece in the January 1853 issue of the *Revue des deux mondes*. Tocqueville was eager to read it. Among Ampère's hosts in Boston was Jared Sparks, who had been one of Tocqueville's most valuable American informants and was now Harvard president. By a happy coincidence, Sparks had just informed Tocqueville that Harvard was granting the Frenchman an honorary degree, a welcome renewal of an American friendship at a moment when Tocqueville objected to the US expansionist policy and its "spirit of conquest and plunder."[61]

However, it was not Ampère's essay but one Rémusat published in the same issue that pushed Tocqueville to make the Revolution, rather than Napoleon's rise to power, the focus of his study. Rémusat's essay was a survey of the literary career and thought of Edmund Burke, with particular attention to Burke's 1790 *Reflections on the French Revolution*. Burke had seen the Revolution as a catastrophic event digging "a void where there had been France." Rémusat pushed back, calling on Mirabeau to retort, "This void is a volcano."[62] An intensely curious Tocqueville began a critical intellectual engagement with Burke's ideas and consequently pursued his investigation of the French people's conditions at the moment "when the Revolution took the world by surprise."[63]

Burke's blanket condemnation of the Revolution drew a strong rebuke from Tocqueville who for many years in his legislative career had come not only to accept but to appreciate the principles of 1789 animating the French people, especially, as he would write in *The Ancien Régime*, "the Revolution's opening act . . . when love of equality coexisted in their bosoms with love of liberty; when they hoped to establish institutions that were not only democratic but also free; when they sought not only to destroy privileges but to recognize and consecrate rights. This was a time of youth, enthusiasm and pride, of generous and sincere passions, which will be eternally remembered despite its errors and which for many years to come will trouble the sleep of those who seek to corrupt and subjugate mankind."[64] Tocqueville felt that Burke missed the broader significance of the Revolution. "The character of general fact, the universality, the sense of finality and irreversibility in the Revolution escape him entirely. He remains buried in an ancient world—its English stratum—and cannot grasp the new and universal thing taking shape."[65]

But unlike other harsh critics of the Revolution, such as Mallet du Pan and Joseph de Maistre, whom Tocqueville read and dismissed,[66] Burke turned out to be a kindred spirit with whom Tocqueville shared several profound insights. A point that caught Tocqueville's special attention was Burke's assertion that the French were "not fit for liberty," just as Tocqueville had said repeatedly in heralding America as the example to follow. The French were, Burke argued, among the people who "must have a strong hand like that of their former masters to coerce them." Burke argued that the French were lacking what he called "a certain fund of natural moderation to qualify them for freedom" and instead misused their newfound liberty to illiberal ends.[67] Tocqueville could not agree more.

Another point of convergence between Tocqueville and Burke was in their judgment of the role of the philosophes in bringing about the French Revolution. In his presidential speech at the Académie des sciences morales et politiques in April 1852, Tocqueville endorsed the role of the political philosopher as advocate, expressing his ideas in a public forum, but he also worried about the political philosopher's lack of real political experience. Pointing to the eighteenth-century philosophes, Tocqueville noted then they were men "entirely removed from public life who nonetheless planted in the minds of our elders those seeds of novelty from which suddenly sprouted so many political institutions and civil laws that were unknown to their predecessors."[68] He agreed with Burke regarding the inexperience of the philosophes, their illiberal centralizing tendencies, and their advocacy of a total rebuilding of society rather than a policy of compromise and reform. Tocqueville also found himself of one mind with an irate Burke in condemning the confiscation of ecclesiastical property during the Revolution. He expressed deep concern about the corrupting influence of the "philosophical

revolution" that preceded the French Revolution in a follow-up correspondence with Corcelle. Tocqueville would eventually devote a whole
chapter of *The Ancien Régime* to that point.

Still, Tocqueville had no firm plan. It is fair to say that, by mid-1853,
he had made headway on different parts of his project but remained
without a clear sense of the nature of the book he would write and its
overarching argument. He had gained new insights on the state of society prior to 1789 and understood that the French people were freer and
more prosperous on the eve of revolution than ever before, but for that
reason less inclined to tolerate inequality. He also had a good grip on
the ending of his story in 1799, with the 18 Brumaire, because this is
where he had begun his investigations.

His progress, however, was hampered by his declining health. His
lungs were fragile, and he was suffering from recurring stomach ailments
that incapacitated him. On the advice of doctors, he and Marie began
planning for a long retreat to a more temperate part of France. The Tocquevilles sought the benefit of the Loire Valley. The devoted Beaumont went
scouting for a suitable house, which he found at Saint-Cyr-sur-Loire, a
village across the river from Tours. The house had all the Tocquevilles
wanted—sunlight, no dampness, an agreeable backyard—as well as a
few things the Tocquevilles did not want at all, such as the bedbugs they
found on arrival, which forced them to change all the mattresses and
draperies in short order. Pierre Bretonneau, a respected pulmonary spe-
cialist, lived nearby and kept an eye on the patient.[69] Save for the doctor
and a few visits from Archbishop (soon Cardinal) Morlot, there was no
contact with locals. But as in the Sorrento days, a few friends visited.
Beaumont and Corcelle were not far. Ampère and Dufaure came. Among
Tocqueville's immediate family, only eighty-one-year-old Hervé visited,
but his short stay was marred by an episode of gout.[70] The peripatetic
Senior arrived from England. He and Tocqueville visited Azay-le-Rideau
and Chenonceaux together (but not Chambord, where the exiled Bourbon heir still had his château!).[71]

Senior encouraged Tocqueville to reread Blackstone on the British
aristocracy. Tocqueville was far from satisfied with the result. He judged
Blackstone's purported genius "impoverished, displaying little freedom

of thought, and rather limited powers of discernment"[72] but accepted his views that the English nobility did not become a closed caste. In contrast to the French, the British did not abandon their country quarters and local obligations to live at the king's court, and they did not retain excessive privileges likely to inflame local sentiment. Senior followed through with additional information from British historian Thomas Macaulay on how a large body of untitled gentlemen kept enlarging the nobility. It was not that the British nobility was particularly open to newcomers but rather, as Tocqueville concluded in *The Ancien Régime*, that "its shape was ill-defined and its boundary unknown."[73]

Mrs. Grote spent ten days in February 1854 in a local inn. She recorded her daily conversation with Tocqueville, reporting that Tocqueville had misgivings about withdrawing from public life but now considered that he had a better chance of making an "indelible trace on the course of human progress" through his writings.[74] Tocqueville was working hard on his writings but still had no real road map for a major book. He needed time to read, and he wanted to perfect his style. He assembled a small library, "a volume for each of the great writers of our language." Returning to the advice Abbé Lesueur, his childhood tutor, had given very long ago, he studied the great seventeenth-century preachers and read for the first time Bourdaloue's 1684 *Sermon sur la fausse conscience.*[75]

All along, while mulling over what he had learned from both Burke and Dareste, Tocqueville began investigating the theories of the eighteenth-century *économistes* or physiocrats. He was going where the evidence was taking him. Starting with the assumption that the French people had gradually gained freedom from feudal rights, he wanted to understand more of the policies these influential reformers had advised the state to follow to replace an eroding feudal system. Tocqueville already knew something of the physiocrats' work from Jean Baptiste Say's *Cours complet d'économie politique pratique*, which he and Beaumont had read closely while crossing the Atlantic in 1831. He recalled that Say severely criticized the physiocrats' single-minded study of land as the main source of wealth and taxation as hopelessly limiting. Before moving to Tours, Tocqueville had annotated the six volumes of the collected works of Turgot, the physiocrat and minister to Louis XVI. They included the narrative of his 1761–74 intendancy as agent of the king to the Limousin province. He had found in Turgot "the father of the bureaucratic race that we know," and that meant "taste for order, for uniformity, for equality under the bureaucracy's thumb." But he balanced his assessment. He recognized in him "great qualities of heart and mind."[76] Tocqueville respected a few other Ancien Régime intendants. Among them, philanthropist Jean-Baptiste de Montyon had endowed the academic prizes Tocqueville had received and now oversaw distributing. Most, however, he judged harshly. At Saint-Cyr-sur-Loire, Tocqueville read a comprehensive collection of the *économistes'* writings, titled *Physiocrates*, compiled by Eugène Daire, Guillaume François Le Trosne's *De l'administration provinciale et de la réforme de l'impôt*, and the elder Mirabeau's *L'ami des hommes*. What struck him was these thinkers' disdain for popular participation hidden behind their zeal for equality.[77]

Reading the eighteenth-century economists was essential for understanding public policy, but Tocqueville was making little progress in understanding the organic connection between the Ancien Régime and the Revolution. All Tocqueville could tell Beaumont at this point is that he was hoping to write "a book worth reading."[78] Without any more definite plan, he informed Freslon he had perhaps reflected enough on the Ancien Régime to conceive only of "a little chapter of thirty pages" to introduce a book on the Revolution, but not enough to explain in what sense the Ancien Régime "guided the Revolution that destroyed it." He had, at least for now, abandoned Napoleon and wanted instead to highlight "what caused the Revolution to erupt in France rather than elsewhere," but he had not found his argument yet and was not sure how to proceed.[79]

## The Turning Point

Change came on the day Tocqueville strolled down a country road from his residence in the village to the city of Tours, crossed the bridge over the Loire River, entered the local archival repository in the prefecture, and encountered an enterprising young archivist. Charles de

Grandmaison was pleased to welcome a distinguished visitor he personally admired, having read *Democracy in America*. He had already crossed paths with Tocqueville in the reading rooms of the Bibliothèque nationale and Institut de France. The timing was right, as Grandmaison had just finished sorting through and cataloging the papers of the royal intendancy of Tours. Now, for the first time, Tocqueville would see for himself in intricate detail in the archival record, unfiltered by chroniclers' narratives, or philosophers' opinions, the daily interaction between the royal bureaucracy and the people under the Ancien Régime. Upon discovering the abundant and detailed manuscript files and voluminous correspondence, Tocqueville reported to Freslon, "In Tours I found not a rare treasure but precious raw material for my endeavor. (For that matter, I believe the same discoveries are to be had in all the archives of the old prefectures.) It is a patchwork of different elements that gives the attentive analyst a very clear notion of the way the different types of business were conducted, how they all combined to shape state bureaucracy, and even sheds light on the participants themselves. It makes for a very curious study. None other, I think, would have the courage to undertake such a project, nor the patience to complete it. There is an enormous amount of dust to uselessly inhale."[80] Tocqueville adopted a summer routine, walking to the Tours archives every day. Once there, Tocqueville allotted 1.5 hours for general conversation with the extremely knowledgeable Grandmaison; then he carefully studied the dossiers that Grandmaison brought out for him to study. He consulted them in Grandmaison's office, which the archivist made available to ensure privacy. Tocqueville compiled over 330 pages of reading notes between July and November 1853.[81]

Gaining a detailed understanding of the workings of the intendancy was critical to Tocqueville's epiphany that the profound transformation of France occurred before rather than after the Revolution. Nobody captured the depth of Tocqueville's insight and the spirit of his intellectual journey better than Rémusat in his review of Tocqueville's *L'ancien régime et la révolution*, published in *Revue des deux mondes* shortly after the book's publication: Tocqueville "knew very well, by the time he began his work, that the French of 1789 had worked harder than any other people to cut their destiny in half, so to speak, cleaving a deep chasm between what had been and what they wished to become. He never doubted that this chasm was a point of no return, and that it was impossible to revive what the Revolution had destroyed. Still, in attempting to prop up and assess the wrecked edifice with his intellect, he recognized in it what he had formerly only suspected, that the change undergone by our society was deeper than what appeared on the surface. Looking into the country's distant past, that change seemed the result of causes both ancient and permanent, less a revolutionary event than a historical effect. The Revolution had not so much transformed France as it had manifested the country to itself."[82]

Once engaged in the discovery of all this activity hidden in the archives, Tocqueville realized he had prepared for this special investigation into the workings of the French bureaucracy in the Ancien Régime one way or another all his life. Hervé de Tocqueville had been a prefect, the modern version of the Ancien Régime intendant, and the son had grown up watching the father at Metz and elsewhere representing royal authority under the Restoration. Bureaucratic centralization was an old bête noire for Tocqueville; one may even call it an obsession. From America, Tocqueville had written his father for details on the workings of the French centralized administration to contrast it with the American decentralization he was observing.

Tocqueville had attacked centralization as freedom's enemy. When Reeve translated the second volume of *Democracy in America*, Tocqueville insisted, "You can be certain that the great danger of democratic ages is the destruction or excessive weakening of *the parts* of society against the *whole*. . . . This is one of my *central* opinions; many of my ideas converge towards it. I have reached complete conviction on this point, and the main object of my book has been to convey this conviction to the reader."[83]

Back in 1836, in his essay titled "Political and Social Condition of France" (written at John Stuart Mill's request for the *London and Westminster Review*), Tocqueville had already critiqued the growth, during the old regime, of "administrative tyranny."[84] Yet at that time he still considered local liberty intact, at least as an ideal, in eighteenth-century

France. Nearly two decades later, in 1853, at the Paris Hôtel de Ville archives, Tocqueville dug through the prerevolutionary papers of the généralité de Paris and found evidence of a royal administration increasingly intruding into localities' affairs, with intendants gradually supplanting nobles in the second half of the eighteenth century. He began to sense that the "administrative regime of the Consulate and Empire is not a creation; it's a restoration."[85]

Despite this preparation, reading the papers of the intendancy of Tours in the summer and fall of 1853 was a shock. Tours revealed the profound penetration into the very details of daily life of ordinary people the bureaucratic intendants the royal administration dispatched throughout the so-called *pays d'élection* had achieved especially during the forty years preceding the Revolution. "France was governed by thirty intendants."[86]

The paper trail showed that intendants had total authority over taxes for local improvements such as roads. They, not farmers, created agricultural societies. They controlled so much of local life that local newspapers shrank in size for lack of activities to report. In other words, Tocqueville claimed he discovered the mechanisms the royal administration used to take the substance out of local life long before Napoleonic centralization. "Under the Ancien Régime the situation was just as it is today: no city, town, village, or hamlet however small, no hospital, factory, convent, or school anywhere in France, could manage its private affairs independently or administer its property as it saw fit. Then as now, all French citizens labored under government tutelage, and if the insolence of the word had yet to manifest itself, the thing itself already existed."[87]

This portrait was somewhat forced, as many readers have pointed out. Localities still had considerable latitude. Tocqueville himself admitted that many rules he uncovered were rigid only in theory. He characterized "the Ancien Régime in a nutshell" as "rigid rules" but "lax practice"—a point the reader may too easily lose sight of, so persuasively did Tocqueville sustain his argument.[88] Moreover, Tocqueville knew that bureaucracy spread its arms unevenly across the territory. He devoted an appendix to the few administratively independent pays d'état, such as Languedoc, and viewed them as a contrasting "lesson in political hope."[89]

Tocqueville saw government centralization as the primary mechanism the king used to diminish the French nobility's influence. "Because the lord had been deprived of his former powers, he shed his former obligations." Yet he kept his former privileges. These privileges had, in feudal times, been justifiable as payments for services rendered. "Nobles possessed irksome privileges and onerous prerogatives, but they maintained public order, administered justice, enforced the law, came to the aid of the weak, and took charge of common affairs." But intendants had ended this relationship of reciprocity. "To the extent that the nobility ceases to do these things, its privileges seem more burdensome, until ultimately it becomes impossible to understand why they even exist."[90]

Tocqueville therefore argued that already in the Ancien Régime, long before the Revolution, village residents had merely clung to "hollow forms" of a once-vibrant local community life. Tocqueville exposed French centralization not as consequence but cause of the French Revolution. In pointing to the loss of communal autonomy at the hands of ordinary intendants, Tocqueville recalled that he had once believed local liberties a trait "peculiar to the new world." But now he had discovered France had known them, too, prior to the centralizing turn. In drawing the contrast between free North American rural towns and French "subjugated communities," Tocqueville concluded their resemblance was as close as that "between a living individual and a corpse can be."[91]

Tocqueville made another important discovery in the same records: "the continual intervention of administrative power in the judicial sphere." He recognized that "any case in which the public authorities had an interest took place before an administrative tribunal."[92] In the United States, Tocqueville had seen the independence of judges from administrative power as a guarantee of liberty and had assumed that it had also been traditionally the case in France at least until Napoleon's reforms. But now he knew that "what we call administrative justice" (where the administration is both judge and party) was not Napoleon's creation but "the old regime preserved in aspic. As soon as we are speaking in terms of contracts, that is, a formal engagement between an individual and the State, the State decides its own case. Such an axiom, foreign to most modern nations, was held as sacred by an intendant of the Old Regime, just as it is by his latter-day incarnation, the prefect." He told Freslon, "Reading through the correspondence of Louis XV's ministers, one begins to discern a cluster of wiggling embryos, destined to grow up into professors of imperial administrative law, little Cormenin, Macarel, and Boulatignier when they were mere spermatazoa." Tocqueville quipped to Rivet that his studies had prepared him "to open a course on the study of administrative law under the Old Regime."[93]

After a few weeks in the archives, Tocqueville had settled the issue of Napoleonic bureaucratic innovation. He knew now that Napoleon had not imposed his restrictive administrative rule to repair the havoc caused by the Revolution. That theory of Napoleon as savior is what comte Molé invoked in his response to Tocqueville's acceptance speech at the Académie française in 1842. To the contrary, Napoleon's liberty-smothering bureaucratic rule was merely a reversion to the Ancien Régime. Toward the end of August, Tocqueville announced to the Tours archivist Grandmaison, whom he and Marie were hosting for dinner, that he had made up his mind to write a full-length book on the old regime. Tocqueville later credited Grandmaison for helping him connect "all that my previous studies had taught me was unconnected" and to find "the linking together of rules" that he was seeking.[94]

Tocqueville's next logical step was to see how the French people reacted to this bureaucratic despotism. To that end, he turned to the Cahiers de doléances (register of grievances) written for the convocation of the Estates General in 1789, or rather a *Résumé général, ou Extrait des cahiers* compiled by Louis-Marie Prudhomme (a source Tocqueville had already used to prepare for his April 1836 article for Mill's *London and Westminster Review*). In these books, local populations in multiple parishes recorded the complaints and wishes mediated by legists and other notables who could write that they wanted their representatives to the Estates General to convey for their eventual presentation to the king. Kings called such conventions occasionally in the Ancien Régime, and Louis XVI, at Finance Minister Loménie de Brienne's behest, had fatefully decided to conduct one such consultation in 1789, something not done in 175 years. In October 1853, Tocqueville began taking notes on thousands of grievances, a distillation of which became the chapter, "How the Writing of the Cahiers Made the Idea of a Radical Revolution Sink Deeply into the Minds of the Lower Classes."

Tocqueville found in the *Cahiers*, assembled separately by each order, nobility, clergy, and *tiers état*, what he was looking for. He did not record the numerous instances of peasants expressing their displeasure at the nobility.[95] He did not look for proof of the Revolution as the outcome of rebellion against hated aristocrats. Rather, he selectively extracted good evidence that all three orders recognized the oppressive power of centralization and all reacted against it. Tocqueville argued that "education and lifestyle had already created a thousand resemblances between the bourgeois and the noble" and that "Paris, which increasingly became France's sole tutor, ultimately imposed a common mold and style on all intellect."[96] Many *cahiers*, regardless of coming from the nobility, the clergy, or the *tiers état*, claimed inalienable human rights, called for due process, and asked for a "social compact" that held the government accountable to the people. What is more, Tocqueville realized that the three orders equally embraced centralizing mores in advocating for reforms. Instead of advocating for local liberties, they somehow all wanted to capture the center of power.

With his overall topic finally firmly in focus and much evidence at his disposal, Tocqueville began writing. In November 1853, Tocqueville told Ampère, "I am at the precipice. Pray God I find the strength to leap across."[97] On January 1, 1854, he added, "I have sketched the first chapter, on the goal of the Revolution, begun the second on 'the principal traits that characterize this revolution.'" Finding that his "mountain of notes crushes me, suffocates me,"[98] Tocqueville made the bold decision to ignore his reading notes entirely in writing the first drafts of books 2 (on the decline of feudal prerogatives) and 3 (on the influence of men of letters) at Tours.[99] Soon he told Beaumont, "I am well on my way, though I have ups and downs. I hope to have a few chapters to read to you by spring. Moreover, the overall shape of the book is becoming clearer to me."[100]

Tocqueville had long hoped to investigate whether Germany had experienced a similar evolution in the eighteenth century. He was naturally inclined toward comparison between nations and had engaged in multiple comparisons between France, England, and the United States but had never looked east except for his excursion to Frankfurt to observe the diet in 1849. In the fall of 1852, Tocqueville initiated a correspondence, on Harriet Grote's recommendation, with Charles von Bunsen, German ambassador to the Court of Saint James, for guidance in German sources.[101] He also began an extensive correspondence with diplomat Alphonse de Circourt, whom he would soon nickname his "dictionary" regarding German sources, and one with the equally knowledgeable Gobineau.[102] In Tours, Tocqueville studiously learned German, devoting as many as three hours a day to this task with the help of a tutor. He considered mastering this "diabolical language" with its guttural sounds a self-imposed misery but was intent on gaining direct access to German documents.[103] Tocqueville felt he had reached a reasonable reading level of the language and recovered enough physical strength to travel again by the time he and Marie (who herself spoke German[104]) left Tours to spend the summer of 1854 in Germany.

The Tocquevilles made a few stops on the way, first at Beaumont la Chartre, where Marie left the Beaumonts an envelope containing bonds for safekeeping.[105] They spent several days in Paris at Tocqueville's father's apartment on place de la Madeleine.[106] Molé, Cousin, Villemain, and Mignet had counted on Tocqueville to be on hand to elect to the Académie française the liberal bishop Félix Dupanloup against both the emperor's wishes and those of anticlerical members Mérimée (who boasted of not being baptized) and Sainte-Beuve. Tocqueville and his friends prevailed.[107] After a brief visit with Tocqueville's father at Clairoix (near Compiègne), the couple departed for Belgium. They had the pleasure of seeing Lamoricière in Brussels and Bedeau in Spa. They reached Bonn on June 17, where they had the additional satisfaction of a visit from British friend Henry Reeve, who had been in Aix, and another from George Cornewall Lewis and his wife Theresa.[108]

Circourt had provided several letters of introduction. One was to countess von Oriola, a local socialite, who could open doors for them in aristocratic circles. Another was to Friedrich Christoph Dahlmann, a historian at the University of Bonn, who had been a member of the diet in Frankfurt in 1848 and could serve as conduit to the scholarly world.[109] Tocqueville was frustrated that for all his efforts in Tours, he could not understand the Germans "any better than if they had spoken the language of the Iroquois." But he found "a large library, and even better for my purposes, a famous university" with professors who turned out to be solicitous.[110] Two law professors especially, Hugo Hälschner and Ferdinand Walter (the latter had served in the National Assembly in Berlin in 1848), proved especially forthcoming.[111] What pleased Tocqueville most is that they confirmed what he had guessed. He told Freslon, "What I am learning about the old institutions and the old social state of Germany is almost without exception that which I had imagined."[112] The nobility remained more powerful and maintained more of their credibility in Germany than in France. Unlike in France, ownership of land remained associated with governing the people. Lords' courts were also more resilient in Germany, where there were no administrative courts. And nobles were less resented, as they were still taxed in lieu of the military service they had once been bound to render.[113]

Tocqueville found what he came for. Because Germany had persisted in defending feudal rights, the country did not experience a revolution. Roman law, which had deeply penetrated Germany, served to keep serfdom in place through the centuries.[114] At the close of the eighteenth century, German peasants still formed part of the stock on the lands, as they had done during the Middle Ages. They were not allowed to leave the seigniory, were punished in court for idleness, could not change their calling or marry without permission from their master, and a great proportion of their time was given up to rigorously exacted three days of the week compulsory labor services.[115] Moreover, whereas irreligion had become a general and ardent passion in France, Germany remained quite religious, as Mirabeau had also noted.

Only the Rhenish provinces were comparable to France in terms of the erosion of the nobility. "From this fact arose sentiments and ideas which predisposed these people to a revolution to a far greater extent than the inhabitants of the other parts of Germany." Even there, however, only one-third of the soil belonged to the peasantry. This was additional evidence in support of Tocqueville's great theory that revolutions happen only when people already are faring reasonably well. Tocqueville put it most succinctly in *The Ancien Régime*: "The better the situation of the French became, the more unbearable they found it."[116]

On August 19, Tocqueville and Marie had to cut their stay in Bonn short and travel to Bad Wildbad, a town in the Black Forest known for its thermal baths. Marie was suffering from severe rheumatism in her right hand and needed treatment. At Wildbad, away from his sources of information, Tocqueville felt discouraged about his trip, but in fact, he had already reached the conclusions he needed. Moreover, loyal Ampère had joined the Tocquevilles after a long journey through cholera-infested northern Italy and Bavaria to keep the Tocquevilles company and provide companionship on their return trip.[117]

Tocqueville returned to France from Germany in October 1854. He collected all his papers and books from Paris to transport them to a small house he and Marie rented at Compiègne, near his father's home at Clairoix. In Compiègne, Tocqueville constructed an elaborate matrix of indices to his archival files to retrieve evidence he carefully selected. He made enough progress to write to Beaumont on January 11, "I hope to have finished in two or three months what will make up the first part of the book"[118]—that is, the solo part on the Ancien Régime that Tocqueville had intended to bring out separately.

By early 1855, then, Tocqueville had reflected on his stand-alone Ancien Régime volume extensively. In Tours, Tocqueville had conceived of a new kind of social/institutional history, at once removed from the great narrative of national politics and indispensable for understanding it. As he would proclaim in the published foreword, he had determined "the way in which public business was conducted, how institutions actually worked, how the various classes truly related to one another, the condition, and feelings of those segments of the population that still could be neither seen nor heard, and the true basis of opinions and customs." Then he had turned to comparisons with both England and Germany to explain why the Revolution erupted in France and not elsewhere. Tocqueville had most of his book done. But there remained what was arguably the biggest challenge: to make his sophisticated archival study of society and institutions on the eve of the Revolution relevant to revolutionary dynamics. Who acted on this social theater in such a way that revolution erupted? Why did "everyone [become] restless and dissatisfied with his situation and eager to change it"?[119]

While looking for a plausible answer, Tocqueville faced several distractions. In April–May 1855, the Tocquevilles moved again, relocating to Paris, where Tocqueville conducted some further research and handled affairs for the Académie française.[120] In June, they visited the Beaumonts and the Corcelles. Tocqueville read several chapters to the Beaumonts and received a favorable reception. At the end of the month, Tocqueville and Marie returned to Tocqueville for the first time in three years, where they caught up on neglected maintenance and worked to winterize the château for year-round habitation. Tocqueville managed affairs for his father, who still owned part of the land at Tocqueville. He wrote to him about maintenance and agricultural issues.[121] This took time.

When Tocqueville was finally able to take up his manuscript again, he did not return to the archives for signs of a burgeoning revolution. Rather, he stayed firmly within the realm of ideas. He had already decided when reading them at Tours that physiocrats were reformers who cared more about imposing their pet projects than the legitimate diverse wishes of the population. Tocqueville exposed in their work all of the ideas of centralization and tyranny to overthrow everything in the name of liberty. The physiocrats promoted the spirit of tyranny for the greatest good of society. No matter their good intentions, he explained they wanted to impose their views, which were often no more than "literary nonsense in place of true understanding of men."[122] The physiocrats argued that in the society they were to engineer, there was no need for countervailing powers because they would achieve a perfect symbiosis between general and private interest. Tocqueville cited Quesnay in saying, "The system of counter-forces in government is a fatal idea."[123] Tocqueville recognized in the physiocrats' proposals a dangerous authoritarian regime in the making. These reformers mean well, they want to help society, but they can think only of confiscating the state, appropriating its authority, and imposing one-size-fits-all reforms.

However judicious Tocqueville's opinion of the physiocrats was, he realized their actions alone could not account for the Revolution. There had to have been a much greater force at work. While in Tours, Tocqueville had annotated Necker's *De l'administration des finances de la France* (1784). He had been impressed by how Louis XVI's finance minister had described the "supreme power of public opinion at the approach of the Revolution." Necker spoke of that public opinion as an "invisible power."[124] Tocqueville was taken with this notion of invisible power, and he began speculating as to who really fueled it.

Consistent with his academic speech on political science and Burke's powerful analysis, Tocqueville argued without much evidence that eighteenth-century "men of letters"—there were many—with their "taste for abstract, general theories of government," became wildly influential in their relentless push for replacing "the complex traditional customs that governed the society in which they lived with certain simple, elementary rules, which could be deduced from reason and natural law." Their ideas did not remain "confined within a few philosophical heads." Instead, they filtered down to the masses and took on "the substance and warmth of a political passion." Philosophes, Tocqueville charged, had become capable of "inflaming the imaginations of even women and peasants."[125] Victor Hugo made much the same point later in *Les Misérables* when he had Gavroche sing on the barricades of 1830, "C'est la faute à Voltaire, c'est la faute à Rousseau." Even though Tocqueville took pains to acknowledge the great diversity of philosophical thought, he advanced a theory of hegemony, where some well-propagated ideas suddenly become widely accepted, and there is no return.

Tocqueville worked hard on these chapters at Tocqueville only to meet much criticism. Marie complained in August 1855 that she found the chapter on "How the Men of Letters Became Political Leaders" to be understated and languid.[126] Clémentine de Beaumont, too, was unconvinced. Tocqueville kept reworking the last part of the book. He told Beaumont that the section had cost him "the most reflection, work, and worry."[127] British friend George Cornewall Lewis criticized Tocqueville's rendering of the Voltairian spirit, and their exchange sheds much light on what Tocqueville had set out to prove. Lewis agreed with Tocqueville that Voltaire attacked "Christianity in every variety of form, and on every variety of occasion" but insisted that Voltaire limited his attacks to religion. Lewis rightly pointed out that Voltaire occupied himself little with politics, and he was not hostile to the established order of things. Tocqueville conceded that Voltaire "did not share definite views regarding government," but he maintained that Voltaire had "dishonored the foundation upon which society then stood" and "prepared minds for revolution" without ever formally stating a political position. Voltaire may not have called for a "revolution," but he wanted a "regeneration"—that is, "a radical and profound change in the civil and political laws that had informed his times." Only after several more letters were exchanged did Lewis recognize in Voltaire's writing "that tone of depreciation and vilipending" that Tocqueville wanted to expose.[128]

To the call for sweeping away the old and a wholesale new start that philosophes promoted and the people arguably embraced, Tocqueville explained, the government responded with some reforms but also immense condescension, thus only aggravating tensions. For instance, Louis XVI in fact created provincial assemblies of the kind Turgot had called for, where communities could share decisions regarding taxes and other local matters with intendants. But his government remained incapable of implementing reforms without conveying to ordinary people an unshakable sense of the government's superiority. The powerful showed their contempt to the powerless even when they listened to them. Tocqueville wrote that they somehow all behaved like Madame Duchâtelet, who, according to Voltaire's secretary, was "quite comfortable disrobing in front of her servants, in view of the absence of incontrovertible proof that valets were men."[129]

As he was finishing his manuscript, Tocqueville battled attacks of discouragement and occasionally disabling stomach ailments but nevertheless proceeded "obstinately, passionately, and sadly," as he told Ampère.[130] He was done with the entire manuscript, save for the foreword and the notes, by the end of January 1856. On February 5, Tocqueville returned to Paris to negotiate a publishing contract. He expected to experience "lots of disagreeable sensations and much mental agitation," but thanks to Louis de Loménie, a professor of literature and friend and colleague of Ampère's at the Collège de France, Tocqueville was able to sign a contract with publisher Michel Lévy, who gave him a first install-ment of 2,000 francs based on a minimum sale of 2,000 copies.[131] In late February, Tocqueville had to recopy the entire manuscript because printer Didot found the handwriting "indecipherable."[132]

Tocqueville, Lévy, and Beaumont went back and forth over a title for the book. Beaumont, seeing the continuity with *Democracy in America*, suggested *Democracy and Liberty in France*; Lévy proposed *The Ancien Régime and the Revolution*. Tocqueville hesitated, but Lévy settled the issue by printing his choice on a prospectus that he mailed to several thousand potential subscribers.[133] The Beaumonts helped with proofs. Tocqueville set up a relay system with them whereby they received proofs for all twenty-five chapters as well as the appendix, commented on their form and substance, and then sent them back to Tocqueville in Paris, where he finalized the corrections. This was all accomplished within six days of initial receipt to comply with the pub-lishing contract.[134]

Only after the proofs had been corrected did Tocqueville complete the preface (on which Loménie commented) and the endnotes, which were designed to provide the reader with an ample sense of the archival base Tocqueville had assembled. Publication was delayed by a week because of Tocqueville's grief at his father's sudden death.[135] But on June 19, 1856, the *Ancien Régime* was finally out. Readers would soon wrestle with Tocqueville's bold argument and significant, if partial, evi-dence that the Revolution had emerged "fully formed from the society that it was to destroy," only "adding the savagery of its spirit."[136]

# 11

# Catholicity and Liberty

TOCQUEVILLE BEGAN HIS STUDY of the Ancien Régime meaning only to prepare himself for a larger analysis of the French Revolution. Yet he found so much that captivated him that he set aside his initial project and wrote a highly original book delineating the elements of eighteenth-century France that set the stage for revolution. Although this book touched on the history of the French Revolution itself only indirectly and allusively, he had not abandoned his original project. In the concluding pages of *The Ancien Régime and the French Revolution*, he laid out the task awaiting him. He would study the unpredictable ways in which the two "equally sincere" and "equally vigorous" passions for equality and liberty the French felt "came together, briefly mingled and merged, each lending heat to the other, and ultimately inflamed the heart of France."[1] He was almost ready to turn to this challenging task—but first, he needed to recover from the final push of publishing *The Ancien Régime*, measure its reception in the larger public, and reorganize his own life to resume his work.

## Back at Tocqueville: A Needed Break

Tocqueville retired to Normandy after simultaneously burying his beloved father and publishing his much-anticipated book. As Gustave de Beaumont put it, the Tocquevilles were returning "to home port after terrible storms."[2] Tocqueville needed rest and a break from a noisy capital, much of it under construction as baron Haussmann was opening wide boulevards across the city. In Normandy, Tocqueville paused for a while. He told friends he had not been this lazy in twenty years and that he and Marie were counting on spending at least eight months a year at Tocqueville, now that he no longer had any political obligations keeping him in Paris.[3]

Tocqueville had many reasons to feel contented. For one thing, once-frigid family relationships were thawing. Tocqueville was optimistic about the possible development of a more amicable relationship between Marie and Émilie, Hippolyte's wife. Marie even agreed to spend four days at Nacqueville in October, a major event considering that although the brothers had remained in touch, the wives had not seen each other for ten years.[4] Marital discord briefly threatened when Rosalie Malye, the woman Tocqueville had loved in his teenage years in Metz (see chapter 1), unexpectedly resurfaced. Now Madame Begin, Rosalie had fallen on hard times and approached Tocqueville for money. Tocqueville seriously discussed with Kergorlay the possibility of helping Rosalie. Kergorlay would advance the money, which Tocqueville would reimburse in small installments, unbeknownst to his wife who kept the family books.[5] But Rosalie, not hearing back, did not renew her request, and Tocqueville managed to hide the incident from Marie, who was for once unsuspicious and busy supervising extensive renovations both inside and outside the château.[6]

Before Tocqueville left Paris, he and Beaumont had worked together to send out review copies of *The Ancien Régime* to both newspapers and friends. Tocqueville's friends returned effusive praise, and some, like Charles de Rémusat, also put their compliments into print. Only the hypercritical Kergorlay quibbled over style, underscoring a few passages that, in his view, reflected "overly complicated thought, leading only to impressions rather than distinct ideas." Tocqueville acknowledged the justness of this criticism, admitting to his childhood friend "a certain gap between my style and that of the great writers."[7] With others, however, he was sure his idiom was best. He wrote to Francis Lieber, who had in earlier days bungled the US translation of the prison report, to be sure to read *The Ancien Régime* in French because "the best translation is never anything but a cheap copy!"[8]

Tocqueville was especially anxious to hear back from John Stuart Mill. Their relationship had cooled after the Orient crisis (see chapter 8), compounded, presumably, by Harriet Mill's reservations about Tocqueville. Tocqueville asked Mrs. Grote to send *The Ancien Régime* to Mill and waited impatiently for a response.[9] When Mill at last turned to the book, he took the time to read it twice. Mill was among the few who recognized the unity of Tocqueville's work—how Tocqueville continued to investigate in *The Ancien Régime* the fundamental thesis of *Democracy in America*—the mutual overlapping of liberty and equality that was necessary for democracy to succeed. He delivered the affirmation Tocqueville hoped for. He saw that Tocqueville had taken his grand conceptual scheme to new heights: "If this work does not add new vistas to those that shine through your *Democracy* it perhaps does something better, reproducing the same images but with added light, and new applications." A relieved Tocqueville replied, "So long as I had not received your approval, I was never assured of having done right."[10]

Most French critics, however, did not think of *The Ancien Régime* as the continuation of *Democracy in America*, focused as they were on the heritage of the French Revolution. They welcomed *The Ancien Régime* as an attack against a regime returning France to the despotism the Revolution was supposed to have abolished. The duc d'Aumale, Louis Philippe's son, even commented that "one imbibes" in Tocqueville's book "a sincere horror of tyranny." Republicans joined Orléanists in this assessment while raising their own objections to the idea that the Ancien Régime gave birth to the Revolution. The only sustained criticism came, predictably, from principled defenders of authority—conservative ultramontane Catholics and of course Bonapartists. Most newspapers devoted substantial space to the book.[11]

Meanwhile, *The Ancien Régime* was selling briskly. By mid-September, the first printing of 2,200 copies as well as half of the second printing were sold out. This was better than Victor Hugo's sales in the same period and financially advantageous as well.[12] Tocqueville had clearly touched a chord with readers who, like him, were contemplating with anxiety an authoritarian regime in power yet again. Tocqueville told the liberal Catholic salonnière Sofia Swetchine, "Long practice has taught me that the success of a book is much more due to the ideas the reader already has in mind than to what the author writes."[13]

A rejuvenated Tocqueville could look forward to better days again. Five years earlier, the coup had made life miserable. Tocqueville convalesced in the Loire Valley, struggling for energy, with only dusty archives to stimulate his intellect. Now he had come out of domestic exile physically restored and enjoying a literary success that gave him renewed authority across a spectrum of opinions. Readers recognized in Tocqueville not only an opponent to the authoritarian regime but also a great defender of the spirit of 1789. In *The Ancien Régime*, Tocqueville unequivocally endorsed the early phase of the Revolution. He saw the Revolution's opening act as a rare, stirring moment of national unity. Tocqueville demonstrated in his book that the Revolution was not as revolutionary as the revolutionaries believed and that, on the night of August 4, 1789, the revolutionaries had not abolished the Ancien Régime but merely formally retired long-gone or drastically reduced feudal privileges. Yet at the same time, he conveyed the force of the revolutionary spirit that had overtaken the nation, a force so extraordinary that its causes "become incomprehensible by dint of their very success."[14]

## Personal Convictions

In writing *The Ancien Régime* and in the period of reflection and renewal that followed its publication, Tocqueville questioned his beliefs. He remained determined to explore his faith and simultaneously wished to see the Catholic Church open to liberal reforms. Tocqueville had thought his friend Francisque de Corcelle might serve as a spiritual guide. In 1850, Tocqueville urged Corcelle, "If you have the recipe for faith, for God's sake, give it to me! But how can the will affect the free motion of the spirit? If belief were a matter of will, I would long ago have become devout. Or rather, I would always have been so, for doubt has ever been the most unbearable of life's ills for me. I have always found it worse than death, and preferable only to disease."[15] But Corcelle lost his credibility as a mentor after he submitted uncritically to an authoritarian papal rule (see chapter 9) that was blind to the people's aspirations for freedom and equality. When Corcelle defended the pope's temporal power in a series of articles in 1856, he sought Tocqueville's approval. Tocqueville remained silent so as not to lose a friend to a quarrel he knew they could not resolve.[16]

Tocqueville also thought of turning to Louis Bouchitté for a serious exchange of views on religion. Bouchitté was an old friend from the Versailles days, a philosopher with a deep knowledge of theology, who had written with authority on Saint Anselm of Canterbury (see chapter 7) and who was currently working on the religious iconography of painter Nicolas Poussin. Tocqueville respected Bouchitté. He tried repeatedly to have Bouchitté elected corresponding member of the philosophy section of the Académie des sciences morales et politiques but each time failed to convince Victor Cousin, alias "Plato" and the section's "dictateur," to facilitate the election.[17] Tocqueville confided to Bouchitté how troubled he was by "the destiny of this singular being we call man, who was given just enough intelligence to see the misery of his condition, but not enough to change it." They might talk at Tocqueville, the perfect place "to take on metaphysical study: a deep restfulness amidst God's great creations, tall trees on the shore, the ocean up ahead, a noiseless abode whose inhabitants live like Benedictines."[18] In the end, though, Tocqueville, not well versed in philosophy, never engaged his friend in an ontological argument for which he did not feel fully equipped.[19]

Tocqueville unexpectedly found in the mid-1850s the spiritual guide he had been yearning for in the Russian Sofia Swetchine. A convert to Catholicism, Madame Swetchine settled in Paris in 1816 after having befriended Joseph de Maistre when he served as the king of Sardinia's ambassador to Saint Petersburg. In 1826, Madame Swetchine opened a salon for the liberal ultramontane Catholic elite. One quality that Tocqueville admired in Madame Swetchine was her support of a more liberal Catholicism that remained respectful of Catholic tradition. She had been one of the first subscribers to *L'Avenir*, Lamennais's journal attempting the reconciliation of "Catholicism and Liberty," as its masthead indicated. After the papal condemnation of *L'Avenir*, Madame Swetchine consoled Henri Lacordaire, the magnetic young priest at Notre Dame dismayed by the papal action. She supported his decision to join the Dominican order and reestablish it in France.[20] At the same time, she assisted Benedictine Dom Guéranger to rebuild Solesmes and promote Gregorian chant as a worthy substitute for Gallican liturgy. She even had to mend fences between Montalembert and Lacordaire when their personalities clashed. Her eclectic salon also attracted Catholics committed to social work, notably Frédéric Ozanam, who founded the Society of Saint Vincent de Paul, and Armand de Melun.[21] Madame Swetchine was instrumental politically in helping Minister Falloux write the loi Falloux for liberty of teaching, which was passed by the National Assembly in 1850.

Tocqueville probably met her in 1853. They began corresponding in 1855 and quickly grew in admiration for each other, and Madame Swetchine assumed the role of Tocqueville's spiritual confidante until her death in 1857. After failing to engage a dialogue on faith with two close friends, Corcelle and Bouchitté, Tocqueville finally found in Madame Swetchine a knowledgeable person willing to listen and take his beliefs and doubts seriously. Indeed, Tocqueville confided in her the circumstances in which he had lost his faith as a young adult (see chapter 1). Madame Swetchine strove to reassure Tocqueville, whose powerful intellect she deeply admired and whose search for faith she encouraged. She insisted that doubt was normal, not a pathology; in fact, it was a healthy path to belief.

Tocqueville had definite ideas about the place of church in society. He had realized while in America that it was necessary to draw a line between the kingdom of God and the kingdom on earth. Tocqueville had directly observed that "the less religion and its ministers are mixed up with government, the less they are involved in political debate, the more influential religious ideas will become."[22] In Democracy in America, he formalized this idea and presented the separation of church and state as the best way for the spirit of liberty to coexist with the spirit of religion in a democracy. In his work on the Ancien Régime, he had reflected on how much a wealthy church had been corrupted into an arm of absolute monarchy. At the same time, Tocqueville had always argued and continued to believe that the universality of the Catholic Church made it best suited for democracy.

Tocqueville welcomed the opportunity to probe current church affairs with kindred spirits at Madame Swetchine's salon. Tocqueville especially approved of the group's efforts to moderate, possibly even silence, Louis Veuillot. Veuillot had become the loudest voice of the Catholic faith, which he often presented as nothing more than submission to the pope's authority. His paper, *L'Univers*, made the Church the enemy of freedom. Tocqueville told Corcelle he thought of Veuillot as "one of the Church's most dangerous enemies in the world."[23] Unsurprisingly, though, Tocqueville was not without criticism for the other characters Madame Swetchine invited. Tocqueville was always on his guard with Montalembert, never sure they meant the same thing by reconciling church and democracy. He admired Falloux's political talents yet questioned his sincerity, he told Corcelle.[24] Tocqueville voted for Falloux's election to the Académie française, with Madame Swetchine's encouragement, but otherwise maintained his distance. Always his own man, Tocqueville similarly situated himself outside the ultramontane-Gallican debate that divided most French Catholics. He told Corcelle, "I never quite knew what exactly it meant to be a gallican or an ultramontane" simply because all reasonable Catholics should simultaneously demand that the church recognize national independence regarding temporal matters and accept papal control of church affairs.[25]

Madame Swetchine and Tocqueville agreed in advocating for Christianity as a form of individual liberation rather than as blind submission to papal authority. She believed in the power of faith to bring out catholicity and overcome the atomization of modern society. In her own words, "Christianity transformed the world through the transformation of consciousness. . . . It only seeks the salvation of souls, but by an admirable chain reaction—taking an approach that is both indirect and infallible—that which acts upon the individual later acts back upon the society as a whole." She insisted, "Christianity does not identify with any political regime, its character of universality will not allow it."[26] As Melun observed, Tocqueville "was becoming Christian again while listening to Madame Swetchine, someone in whom he found, as he said himself, saintliness and genius combined."[27]

While Tocqueville engaged Swetchine over spiritual matters and the political place of organized religion, he argued fiercely with his former secretary Arthur de Gobineau over the issue of the fundamental equality of all men. The debate, which began when Tocqueville was still at Saint-Cyr-sur-Loire, was both profound and painful, and it lasted a long time. Gobineau, Tocqueville's former protégé and chief of staff, was then serving as *premier secrétaire* in the French legation in Bern, which had recently become the capital of the Swiss confederation. Feeling isolated there and at odds with other embassy personnel, Gobineau immersed himself in histories of civilization as well as scientific treatises regarding race. His studies culminated in the writing of an *Essay on the Inequality of Races*, which he printed at his own expense (in two installments of two volumes each) between 1853 and 1855.[28]

Tocqueville had always thought of Gobineau as a contrarian. He was grateful for his loyal services at both Académie des sciences morales et politiques and the ministry and had thus agreed to promote Gobineau's career and intellectual ambitions. But Tocqueville could not possibly endorse Gobineau's newfound views of race. The dispute began innocently enough. In 1852, Gobineau asked Tocqueville his opinion regarding naturalist Buffon's interpretation as recorded by biologist Pierre Flourens (secrétaire perpétuel de l'Académie des sciences and colleague of Tocqueville at Académie française). After reading the referenced section, Tocqueville concluded that Flourens, like Buffon, believed in "the unity of the human species." Flourens's proof was the one Buffon already presented—that is, the different races "mix and perpetually generate offspring." The many diverse traits among men are the consequences not of different origins but of climate, food, and ways of living.[29] Buffon and Flourens contrasted the unity of species among men with the diversity of species among animals. Buffon had famously emphasized that a jackass and a mare, although looking strikingly alike and therefore appearing to be of the same species, could produce only an infertile mule, and that was evidence they belonged to different species.

Tocqueville believed the matter settled until he received in Tours the first two volumes of Gobineau's ponderous treatise in which Gobineau posited that "black, yellow, and white races" had distinct origins and unequal native abilities and were constantly degenerating through their unfortunate mixing. Gobineau thus was predicting "decadence without a cure"[30] in which humans regressed through the infusion of inferior blood, with no hope of recovering primitive purity, traces of which one found only among some groups of "Aryans." Migration and race mixing were thus the prime cause of the decline and eventual collapse of civilizations, "the day that the primordial ethnic element will find itself so drowned and subdivided under the contributions of strange races its potentiality will lack sufficient power [to manifest itself]."[31]

How much of Gobineau's book Tocqueville had the patience to read is unclear. He told Beaumont he could not finish it.[32] With Alphonse de Circourt and Corcelle, he labeled Gobineau's thought "horse breeder's philosophy" and judged the book to be (fortunately!) unreadable.[33] But Gobineau insisted on a response from Tocqueville, who was then busy in the Tours archives. Gobineau was also counting on his former mentor to advocate for him in his bid to enter the Académie des sciences morales et politiques.

Tocqueville was upset and did not mince words when he finally wrote back in November 1853 to Gobineau. He admitted that "surely among the different families which compose the human race there exist certain tendencies, certain proper aptitudes resulting from thousands of different causes. But that these tendencies, that these capacities should be insuperable has not only never been proven but no one will ever be able to prove it." To make his point clear, Tocqueville imagined that "Julius Caesar, had he had the time, would have willingly written a book to prove that the savages he had met in Britain did not belong to the same race as the Romans and that the latter were destined thus by nature to rule the world while the former were destined to vegetate in one of its corners."

Tocqueville viewed Gobineau's doctrine as "a sort of fatalism, of predestination." Tocqueville countered Gobineau with his diametrically opposite belief that "the destiny of men, whether of individuals or of nations, depends on what they want to be." Tocqueville rejected Gobineau's philosophical doctrines because they amounted to "a vast limitation, if not complete abolition, of human liberty." He concluded,

"There is an entire world between our beliefs."[34] Tocqueville had made similar comments to Charles Stöffels, writing, "The classification of races by their physical traits is a materialist doctrine, and materialism, much like a dead corpse, will never produce more than a bunch of earthworms."[35] A study of the rise of decline of civilizations would not change that.

Tocqueville was not done. He felt Gobineau was a fool if he did not know that his theories were dangerous, that words had consequences. He added a stern warning that proved remarkably accurate: "Be assured," he wrote Gobineau, "that [if] the masses, whose reasoning always follows the most beaten tracks, accept your doctrines, it would lead them straight from races to individuals and from social capacities to all sorts of potentialities." Gobineau's theories were not only "quite false," but they were also "very pernicious."[36] Specifically, Tocqueville predicted that the book would appeal to slave owners in the United States and to Germans in their exaltation of the Aryan race. Both predictions proved dramatically true.

As Tocqueville had anticipated, Gobineau soon learned of an American translation of his work. That was in January 1855, as Gobineau's last two volumes were about to appear, and Gobineau himself was about to leave for Persia as the newly appointed secretary of a French mission, after a checkered tenure at Bern. Josiah Nott, a skilled surgeon and expert on yellow fever from Mobile, Alabama, had authored a study, with George Gliddon, titled *Types of Mankind* in 1854. They argued for separate creations of the different human races, or *polygenesis*. Nott called on all the existing branches of knowledge, physiology, craniology, biology, and so forth to present his view and even brought in the Harvard zoologist Louis Agassiz who, without endorsing polygenesis, contributed to the volume an essay on distinct human types inhabiting distinct "zoological provinces."[37] Like Gobineau, Nott emphasized the destructive effects of race mixing. But to Nott, this was no aesthetic intellectual exercise for the admiration of erudites at Académie des sciences morales et politiques. Nott attempted to present instrumental evidence that mixed-race "mulattoes" were less capable of endurance and lived shorter lives than either Blacks or whites, and multiracial women were often incapable of conception. Nott hired a young protégé, Swiss-born twenty-one-year-old Henry Hotze, to translate Gobineau's book, which he welcomed as an opportunity to claim the authority of a French savant "who could not be charged with sectional prejudice."[38]

Gobineau complained, correctly, that the translation was highly selective. He was bothered that Nott and Hotze had twisted passages and added notes to turn his book into "a war machine against the negrophiles"—that is, abolitionists, and he told his friend Anton von Prokesch-Osten, the Austrian representative to the Frankfurt diet, that Americans "believe that I am encouraging them to bludgeon their Negroes."[39] This was exactly what Tocqueville had warned, and it was only the beginning of a long history of instrumentalization of Gobineau's theories, including by the Nazis, a sad destiny for an isolated aesthete, who naively wanted others to believe he was just making an interesting historical argument.

Gobineau persisted in asking Tocqueville to support his candidacy to the Académie des sciences morales et politiques, a request Tocqueville kept deflecting by creating obstacles. Tocqueville asked Gobineau to submit a report on Persia to the Académie, which Gobineau did, as he had learned Persian and, Tocqueville noted, become the only French diplomat "capable of speaking the tongue of Zoroaster while representing France."[40] Tired of Gobineau's pressure, Tocqueville in January 1857 sent to Rémusat, who knew Gobineau, a lukewarm endorsement of a possible Gobineau candidacy, suggesting that the new politics section, which Minister Fortoul had created by fiat in hopes of weakening political opposition in the institution (see chapter 10), would not object. Gobineau was never elected to the Académie des sciences morales et politiques, and Tocqueville asked him no longer to broach the topic of race relations with him.

Tocqueville was increasingly aware of the dangers of racial prejudice. In 1856, he welcomed a request from the abolitionist Maria Chapman to endorse the Female Anti-Slavery Society of Boston and contributed to its annual publication, *Liberty Bell*, a stinging denunciation of slavery on the grounds that "God grants freedom of the will, without distinction, to all who dwell upon this earth."[41] Tocqueville worried that the election of James Buchanan signaled the triumph of proslavery forces, while noting with pleasure in a letter to his friend abolitionist Senator Charles Sumner the victory of Free-Soil candidates for the Kansas territorial legislature. He welcomed Sumner in Paris, and at Tocqueville in May 1857 when the senator was touring Europe, still recovering from the caning that almost killed him inside the US Senate after he had denounced slavery.[42]

In June 1857, Tocqueville traveled to London to conduct research on the Revolution, which meant he was there for the outbreak of the Indian Rebellion. Tocqueville was having dinner at the home of Lord Granville, lord president of the Council, "when news of the Indian revolt came in via telegraph." As Tocqueville later related, "The noise of India broke out like thunder amidst all this stillness." Of the Sepoy rebels killing the local British population, Tocqueville commented, "I do not know that there has been such a tragedy in history since Mithridates' massacre of the Romans in Asia."[43] Marie remained deeply concerned for months about the Indian situation, and this led Tocqueville to quip he had never realized his wife had remained so profoundly British![44]

Tocqueville had been quiet about colonial issues for almost ten years, but this shook him. In his last commentary in 1847 on Algeria, he had finally voiced some concern about the violence the army continued to perpetrate on the Algerians, though he remained a strong advocate for French civilian settlement and for granting settlers significant administrative autonomy (see chapter 8). Now, surrounded by British friends worrying about the future of their empire, Tocqueville returned to the theme of colonialism and shared his thoughts on what options the British had in India. These thoughts were shaded by his concurrent exploration of Christian universalism and human equality.

Tocqueville had a long-standing interest in India. He had once thought of writing an essay on the British colonization of India, and only the difficulty of making the trip and visiting the country had forced him to drop the project.[45] To his British friends confronting the rebellion, Tocqueville expressed unequivocal support. They should not hesitate to assert British domination, he insisted. Any relaxation of control in India would be a sign of national decline. He told Lady Theresa Lewis,

"The loss of India would diminish England's place among the nations of the world. . . . There has been nothing so extraordinary under the sun as the conquest and especially the government of India by the English. No other place on earth invites men to gaze on this tiny island of which the Greeks did not even know the name. Do you think, Madam, that a people, having occupied such an immense place in the imagination of the human race, can suddenly withdraw itself with impunity?"[46]

But Tocqueville was no longer so enthusiastic about the Western colonial project. Although Tocqueville had tolerated French army brutality in the Algerian conquest, he advocated that the British show restraint in their response to the rebellion. He advised them (in vain, considering the brutal repression the British enforced) not to exceed "legitimate" reprisals. Appealing to the British sense of superiority, he told Lady Theresa, whose husband was in the cabinet, "you have the right to be the master of these merciless savages only because you are better than they."[47]

Recalling his study of Indian customs and law, Tocqueville expressed an empathy for local culture that was largely lacking in his views on Algeria. He chastised his British friends for their contempt of manners other than British. Even with good intentions, he observed, the British had a way of "exasperating by their *manners* even those subjects whom their *laws* favor."[48] Tocqueville interpreted the mutiny as a "revolt of barbarism against pride."[49] Contempt had bred negligence. Tocqueville judged that his British friends had not done enough for local populations. He wrote to Lord Hatherton that "for over a century, the English failed to provide for the Hindu people what one might have expected of their enlightenment and their institutions."[50]

Most importantly, Tocqueville revisited his lifelong commitment to colonies of settlement (Canada, Algeria). In the case of Algeria, he had always favored a policy of French settlement and wanted to make Algeria a part of France. He fought with marshal Bugeaud to shift authority from a military to a civilian government and grant much local autonomy to settlers. But in this instance, he drew a sharp distinction between governing a colony and settling it. When Henry Reeve suggested in the *Edinburgh Review* that more British citizens should settle in India because hostility was aroused by the army, not the local British population or even the princes, Tocqueville surprisingly demurred. He even suggested that the British be prevented from buying land in India.[51]

Tocqueville could be persuaded that the British provided more effective government than local leaders and even that Indians preferred British rule to that of their princes, but he did not think the local population would see individual settlers the same way. If "the foreign government only harms a weak national sentiment, the foreign settler harms, or seems to harm, in a thousand different ways the particular interests common to all men." Tocqueville said this based on the French experience in colonizing Algeria. Betraying a significant change of heart regarding colonization—which may be the reason for his long silence on the topic—he added, "I have no doubt that the Arabs and Kabyles of Algeria are more irritated by the presence of our settlers there than by that of our soldiers."[52] Tocqueville now believed that geopolitical domination was one thing, colonization another. He still supported the one but was expressing serious reservations about the other.

## The French Revolution

With questions of universal equality at the forefront of his mind, Tocqueville resumed his larger project. He had announced in *The Ancien Régime and the Revolution* that he would explain in a sequel "how a government more powerful, and far more absolute, than the one the Revolution overthrew then seized and concentrated all power, suppressed all the liberties for which such a high price had been paid, and put useless imitations in their place."[53] Tocqueville wanted to determine why and how the remarkable unity produced by the Revolution could have shattered so quickly, and how it was possible that the French, after defeating absolutism and creating a republic consecrated to liberty and equality, had so easily given up on their vision. How could they have submitted, in the name of their newfound version of equality, to a reborn absolutism under Napoleon? Tocqueville had already drafted short chapters on the 18 Brumaire (see chapter 10); now, in the summer of 1856, he got his feet wet again with a study of German publisher Friedrich Perthes. Perthes, after embracing the universal ideals of the French Revolution, had strenuously resisted Napoleonic invasion and rule. Editor François Buloz wanted an essay on Perthes for the *Revue des deux mondes*, but Tocqueville ultimately abandoned the project after taking detailed notes.[54] Decidedly, Buloz had no luck extracting copy from Tocqueville, who had never finished the essay on India he had once promised either.

Tocqueville wanted to respect the chronology of events that led to the Revolution and to its initial phase; he decided to write the immediate follow-up to the book he had just published. Tocqueville wrote the librarian at the Institut de France that he needed to compile sources covering the period beginning on January 1, 1787 ("to choose an exact date").[55] He wanted to investigate in chronological order the struggle of the royal court with the *parlements* (courts of law); the assemblies of notables; the reforms of all kinds attempted by the crown; the convocation of the Estates General; the meeting of the Estates General on May 5, 1789; their transformation into a National Assembly (June 17—renamed Constituent Assembly on July 9); and the dramatic Tennis Court Oath of June 20, 1789, in which participants vowed not to dissolve their assembly until a constitution was established.

As an academician and former minister, he received the preferential treatment he expected from librarians. Both the Institut de France librarian and the Bibliothèque impériale librarian obliged Tocqueville by shipping hundreds of revolutionary pamphlets to Normandy so that he could immerse himself in the arguments of the early Revolution in the comfort of his home. That fall, Tocqueville also acquired the Acts of the Constituent Assembly, a record he considered "the most productive and authentic of documents" to gain an understanding of the period.[56] Tocqueville drafted in November–December 1856 a "chapter zero" in which he highlighted the questions he longed to answer: "Why did Reform turn so quickly into Revolution? How could the lower classes have suddenly become so furious, and the leading power [in the struggle]?" He resolved to read the evidence in strict chronological order. Perhaps by looking methodically at the details, "the fundamental ideas will be born."[57]

Tocqueville soon realized that the librarians, obliging though they were, could not send all the material he needed. He decided to spend four months in the capital to further explore its libraries and archives.

The Tocquevilles left Normandy in late March 1857. They established their residence at Chamarande, in Essonne, near Vaux-le-Vicomte, south of Paris, to be close to the aging Mrs. Belam, Marie's aunt. They rented an apartment in a castle François Mansard had built (and for which Le Nôtre had designed the grounds). Interior Minister duc de Persigny, one of the plotters of Louis Napoléon Bonaparte's coup, had purchased the property in disrepair and was rehabilitating it. Tocqueville noted the irony of Persigny now becoming his landlord after having been his jailer. From Chamarande, Tocqueville traveled to Paris to work several days each week.[58]

Tocqueville's visit to England in June to explore an extensive collection of Revolutionary pamphlets in the British Museum made it possible for him to see the friends who had welcomed his book with a deluge of personal congratulations and published praise. Combining leisure and work, Tocqueville spent time with the Seniors, the Grotes, the Reeves, and the Lewises, all of whom had visited the Tocquevilles during previous trips to Paris, Normandy, Sorrento, Tours, and Germany. Tocqueville made several short visits to the countryside, to the homes of the Grotes and Lord Radnor, with whom he had struck up a friendship on his very first visit to England, as well as to the estate of Lord Hatherton, a recent acquaintance who made a point of taking his visitor on a detailed tour of his model farm of Teddesley in Staffordshire. These social visits went splendidly. Only one evening did Tocqueville cancel a dinner engagement with Nassau Senior because of a painful gastric episode.[59]

Tocqueville's good friend George Cornewall Lewis, chancellor of the exchequer, arranged for meetings with high officials. At the same dinner at Lord Granville's home where he first learned about the Indian Rebellion, Lord Clarendon, secretary of state for foreign affairs (and Lewis's brother-in-law) informed Tocqueville that Prince Albert wished to see him.[60] He proposed a date and time that had to be modified because Tocqueville had a previous engagement with the Orléans family, who were exiled in England. When the meeting finally took place, Tocqueville was deeply gratified to realize the prince consort had read *The Ancien Régime* carefully and accurately.

Mrs. Grote arranged a meeting with the historian Thomas Macaulay, whom Tocqueville was anxious to meet.[61] But the ostensible reason for Tocqueville's trip to England, the archives of the British Museum, turned out to be a disappointment. The museum's magnificent reading room, just completed in May, would become the favorite workplace of numerous great writers. Karl Marx—whose interests continued to intersect with Tocqueville's—renewed his ticket for the reading room in June 1857 and thus his time there is likely to have overlapped with Tocqueville's, though the two never met.[62] Yet the museum's collection of French revolutionary pamphlets was uncataloged and therefore proved too difficult to sort through. Lord Clarendon salvaged the research trip by giving Tocqueville special permission to read British closed diplomatic correspondence covering the years 1787 to 1793 and to have relevant sections copied and sent to him. Tocqueville could now put to rest the rumor circulated in France that the British had for years sought to create disarray in French affairs.[63]

Crossing the English Channel was a happy break in Tocqueville's routine. Tocqueville sent a letter almost daily to Marie to report on his activities and on how well he was treated. Tocqueville also had a rare opportunity in both London and Portsmouth to get better acquainted with Joe Mottley, one of Marie's brothers, and his family. To advance his brother-in-law's naval career, Tocqueville even put in a recommendation to the First Lord of the Admiralty, Sir Charles Wood. Sir Charles proved so eager to please Tocqueville that he also arranged for the Admiralty to provide a small naval ship to privately transport Tocqueville back to Cherbourg in early August, a unique honor that capped an appreciative reception.[64]

It is upon returning from England that Tocqueville began writing his history of the French Revolution. He brought to the project a generally optimistic outlook. Because illness ultimately prevented Tocqueville from ever completing the project, we can only appreciate what he achieved from the partial paper trail he left behind.

Tocqueville began indexing his notes in Normandy in September 1857. He worked steadily again, no longer distracted by house renovations, only sometimes worrying about money. In November, the financial panic in the United States alarmed him. Fearing the loss of railroad bonds he had purchased in 1848, he asked his friend Senator Sumner to inquire about the fate of the Central Michigan and the Galena-Chicago railroads.[65]

Mastering the narrative of the French Revolution did not come easily. Tocqueville had written to Pierre Freslon in February 1857 that "the Revolution (that immense movement that transported us from the Ancien Régime to where we are) is an as yet formless and indistinct object, but so vast that the mind expands and heats up at the sight of it."[66] He seemed to have made only slow progress fifteen months later, in May 1858, confiding into Kergorlay, "My mind exhausts itself trying to conceive this object clearly, and to find the means to faithfully depict it. Despite all the explanations for the French Revolution, there is something in its spirit and its actions that is inexplicable. I sense where the hidden object is, but try as I might, I cannot lift the veil that shrouds it."[67]

Tocqueville had few guides. He had concluded long before that historians provided too many facts and too few insights. Reading Thiers's history of the Revolution when it first appeared, he complained that Thiers documented a series of events but "in vain would we look from 1787 to 1789 for a guiding idea."[68] Moreover, in Thiers's narrative, he felt that events followed one after the other as if their succession were inevitable. In the second volume of *Democracy in America*, Tocqueville rejected this way of writing history. "Not content to show how things happened, [historians in democratic times] also like to show they could not have happened otherwise. They contemplate a nation that has reached a certain point in its history and contend that it was obliged to follow the path that took it there. This is easier than showing how it might have chosen a better route."[69] He was attacking not only Thiers but also Mignet, whose name Tocqueville mentioned in his working notes for the chapter. Tocqueville contrasted this idea of necessity, of fatality with his own search for explanations perfectly compatible with human freedom.[70]

To avoid this pitfall and elevate human agency, Tocqueville, encouraged by his experience with archives in Tours, insisted on working exclusively from primary sources, without referring to any interpretive guidance beyond his own judgment. He wanted to read as many original pamphlets and brochures as possible to capture the conversation between political actors as if he were in the room with them and to feel their changing mood, even at the risk of merely uncovering anew trends that others had described. He explained his method in 1856 in a note to Duvergier de Hauranne, one of the organizers of the banquet campaign in 1848, excusing himself for not reading the first installment of his *Histoire du gouvernement parlementaire en France*:

> When I have any kind of subject to discuss, it is almost impossible for me to read any of the books which have been written about the same issue; contact with other people's ideas agitates me and disturbs me to the point of making reading these works painful. . . . I take incredible pains to find the facts myself in the documents of the time; often I thus obtain, with immense labor, what I could have found easily by following another route. This harvest thus laboriously made, I shut myself up, as in a tight space, and examine with extreme care, in a general review, all these notions that I have acquired by myself. I compare them, I link them, and I then make it my rule to develop the ideas that have spontaneously come to me during this long labor, without any consideration whatsoever for the consequences that some persons might draw from them. It is not that I am not extremely sensitive to the opinion of different readers; but experience has taught me that as soon as I wanted to write from a preconceived perspective, to support a thesis, I lost absolutely all real talent, and I could do nothing worthwhile if I did not limit myself to trying to clearly render what was most personal and most real in my impressions and opinions.[71]

Tocqueville's claim is only partly credible. To begin with, his work was thesis-driven, following a scheme he had carefully developed in Sorrento. He conceived initially of the Revolution as a failed attempt to bring about equality and liberty sandwiched in between two absolutist regimes.

Moreover, Tocqueville did not live in a soundproof chamber in dialogue only with primary sources. He did not hesitate to consult people in the know, strewing his notes with comments of conversations he had or needed to have with (even) Thiers or Molé on given points.[72] Over the years he had become quite close to Mignet, with whom he frequently corresponded regarding Académie des sciences morales et politiques's matters, and despite some reservations, he was respectful of his work. He could safely ignore Lamartine's slapdash and inconsistent popular history of the Girondins, but he paid attention to the works of Michelet and Louis Blanc. Tocqueville was in conversation with Michelet at least since 1840. The two were colleagues at the Académie des sciences morales et politiques. At Michelet's prompting, Tocqueville had once urged Villemain to create a chair for Edgar Quinet at the Collège de France. Tocqueville acknowledged reading volume 4 of Michelet's *Histoire de France*, which the author had sent him. In return, Tocqueville sent him a copy of the second volume of *Democracy in America*.[73] Although they vigorously debated liberty of teaching, Tocqueville had partially supported Michelet and Quinet on certain aspects of the issue (see chapter 7). How much of Michelet's monumental history of the French Revolution, published between 1847 and 1853, much of it based on primary sources, Tocqueville was familiar with, is not possible to know, but Tocqueville was aware of the author's sensibilities and sympathies for *le peuple* in the making of the Revolution.

We can be sure, however, that Tocqueville was familiar with at least some of Blanc's history of the Revolution, written while the author was exiled in London and making use of the same British Museum pamphlets Tocqueville had hoped to exploit. Tocqueville discussed the work admiringly with Sumner in Paris in 1857, telling Sumner, "Thiers is not a good writer; in style, Louis Blanc is brilliant."[74] Tocqueville and Blanc observed each other from opposite sides of the Chamber during their entire political careers, but they were not without mutual regard. Blanc reviewed *Democracy in America* admiringly. Even though Tocqueville satirized Blanc's antics in *Recollections*, he bore him a measure of respect as well.

Briefly contrasting Tocqueville's work on the Revolution with Michelet's and Blanc's is an imperfect but useful means of highlighting the originality of Tocqueville's projected contribution. Despite long preliminary chapters, both Michelet and Blanc began their detailed narratives of the Revolution only in 1789 and ended them with the fall of Robespierre on Thermidor. They concerned themselves only modestly with early warning signs under the monarchy and not at all with the Napoleonic empire, which Tocqueville hoped to do. Michelet clearly had the broadest vision of the Revolution, claiming "that it was the very life of France that went into its preparation and gave meaning to the drama of its unfolding." Blanc offered a highly detailed but narrower political analysis of the Revolution. In his criticism of his rival, Michelet noted that Blanc attempted to "enclose this ocean within the narrow confines of the Jacobin cloister."[75]

In just two months in December 1857 and January 1858, Tocqueville sketched out preliminary versions of seven chapters that were to form the first book of the new volume. He narrated in broad strokes the years 1787 and 1788, briefly outlining chapters without inserting evidence and elaborating on themes already discussed in *The Ancien Régime*.[76] He wanted to detail the chronology of events and identify the prime movers. The first short chapter draft gave an overview of the situation in Europe, with a special focus on Germany, in 1787; draft Chapter Two described the popular state of mind in France in 1787. Tocqueville then narrated in draft Chapter Three the crown's struggle with the *parlements* (courts of law) in July 1787 and their subsequent dissolution and reestablishment in September 1788. Reading many of the debates the noble magistrates held in the *parlements*, Tocqueville was impressed by how intense their rhetoric against the crown had been *prior* to democratic revolt.[77] In draft Chapter Four, he highlighted the dramatic fall in popularity of the *parlements*. In draft Chapter Five, he turned to the writing of the Cahiers de doléances or grievance books and moved on to struggles around types of representation in draft Chapter Six. He then devoted draft Chapter Seven to "the sublime moment" of the meeting of the Estates General on May 5, 1789.

All three historians—Michelet, Blanc, and Tocqueville—agreed on the themes of this last chapter. The meeting of the Estates General was a sublime moment. Tocqueville spoke for all three when celebrating the moment's revolutionary clarity and consensus. When the Estates General opened, he explained:

> There was no Frenchman who did not believe he had in his hands, not the destiny of his country, but the very future of his species. . . . People made a supreme effort to agree. Instead of looking for where they differed, they tried to concentrate on what they wanted in common. . . . To destroy arbitrary power, to put the nation back in possession of itself, to assure the rights of every citizen, make the press free, individual liberty inviolable, soften the laws, strengthen the courts, guarantee religious toleration, destroy the hindrances to commerce and industry, this is what they all wanted. . . . This first spectacle was short, but it had incomparable beauty. It will never depart from human memory. . . . These first days of 1789 [left] an indelible mark.[78]

Michelet and Blanc had previously come to the same conclusion. Tocqueville was unique, however, in paying close attention to the very early political manifestations of revolution, and this is where he made a lasting if controversial mark in the historiography of the Revolution.

Tocqueville diagnosed an aristocratic revolution in 1787 and 1788 preceding the Revolution of 1789, an idea that historians have continued to argue about.[79] Tocqueville credited the nobility with being the initial engine of the Revolution. "It was the nobility that entered first and most boldly in the common struggle against the king's absolute power," he wrote. Moreover, Tocqueville saw the nobility as leading a unified resistance. The "writers who were most forceful against despotism" emerged from its midst because they were the ones most humiliated and oppressed by the *intendant*, that "obscure delegate of royal power" whom Tocqueville had described in detail in *The Ancien Régime*. Thus, "almost everywhere the new ideas had found their chief supporters among the nobles." The nobles led the resistance in their own interest, yes, but they also sincerely espoused—at least, at first—something like republican constitutional ideals and freedoms. In fact, with "prouder hearts" and "souls more used to looking directly and more carefully at the great ones of the earth" they were better equipped than the common people to take on despots in the name of liberty.[80]

Perhaps Tocqueville was taking a cue from his father's book on the reign of Louis XVI, in which Hervé de Tocqueville argued, "It was the upper classes that gave the signal for [the Revolution] without foreseeing that they would soon become the victims of the fire they had lit."[81] Perhaps Tocqueville was also settling a score with Guizot, who had offered faint praise for *The Ancien Régime*. Guizot wrote Tocqueville that he found *The Ancien Régime* "as true as it is useful and as useful as it is true; firmly of its own time yet independent of the spirit of the age." But he added that he also found it biased, just like *Democracy in America*. "I find in your book the same character that struck me in your great work about the United States of America. You describe and judge modern democracy as a vanquished aristocrat convinced that his vanquisher is right."[82] What better response to Guizot than to credit the "vanquished" with initiating the great transformation?

Tocqueville thus argued that the Revolution was first in the hands of nobles largely because he could not find evidence of it anywhere else. Emerging from his intense reading of sources, he wrote, "No sign that I can see . . . shows me that the rural population was yet aroused. . . . This vast part of the nation was mute and seemingly invisible. In the towns themselves, the lower classes showed themselves little moved by the emotion of the upper classes and at first remained indifferent to the commotion going on over their heads." Tocqueville also emphasized the inexperience of the "third estate, which was to be represented in the Estates General, no longer composed of only the urban bourgeoisie as it had been at its last meeting in 1614, but of twenty million peasants spread over the entire surface of the kingdom. These peasants had never before been concerned in public affairs; political life for them was not even a particular memory."[83]

For Tocqueville, the bourgeoisie became emboldened only progressively as the struggle went on, but in the first period, there were no traces of class war. "At the beginning, people spoke only of better balancing powers, better adjusting class relations"; "soon they walked, they ran, they threw themselves into the idea of pure democracy."[84]

While Tocqueville saw a progression to a popular revolution, Michelet assigned the principal role to ordinary people from the very beginning. In contrast to Tocqueville, Michelet argued that the people—despite having so little experience of democracy—rose to the occasion immediately. Michelet conveyed an almost mystical admiration for the people. "This people, though so unprepared, showed very reliable instincts. . . . They knew, in the presence of their lords, without shedding their patterns of deference, or attitudes of humility, how to nominate suitable electors, who in turn appointed trusted and dependable representatives." In addition, many of the deputies elected to the other two orders were parish priests, very hostile to their bishops. Meanwhile, city dwellers were "vividly aware of their rights" and were eager to exercise them. . . . It is an admirable phenomenon."[85]

Blanc, interestingly, recognized the nobility's role in resisting the crown, noting that the people deferred to them, but he denounced the nobles for rejecting measures supported by the people that would have reduced privileges and equalized the tax burden. Blanc took this apparent passivity of the third estate as evidence of early popular embrace of reform, when "morality trumped material and vulgar desires in the hearts of the people." For Blanc, the people sitting on the sidelines respected the "majesty of the principles invoked."[86] Tocqueville was not buying that argument from the left. In his notes, he expressed puzzlement "at the naïveté of some present-day revolutionaries" who believe "that it is easy to make a very civilized people patiently bear the discomfort inseparable from great political change" in the name of high-minded ideals.[87] Tocqueville believed it more likely that the people simply applauded anyone who had the determination to oppose the monarchy.

Tocqueville left only reading notes, not a preliminary narrative, for a second part covering the period "*From the taking of the Bastille on July 14, 1789, to uprisings in the countryside, to the End of the Constituent Assembly*" in September 1791. Most of these notes date from March to May 1858; Tocqueville stayed in Paris to work while Marie remained at Tocqueville. Tocqueville wrote every other day to his wife to narrate his time spent in the library and the archives, telling her of occasional meetings at the Institut and of suppers with his inner circle of friends, Beaumont, Circourt, Corcelle, Rivet, Dufaure, Lanjuinais, Freslon, and Senior. On good days, he could examine up to seventy pamphlets in a morning's work. On bad ones, he felt ready to give up, "lost in an ocean of papers with no sign of the shoreline in sight."[88]

One can follow in the notes how Tocqueville saw the full intensity of the revolutionary spirit emerge from the third estate in this second period. He recognized the developing of "general theories closely linked with each other and forming a single body of doctrine, a sort of political gospel where each principle resembled a dogma . . . ardently preached, an entirely new thing in history."[89] This is where Tocqueville acknowledged the true radicalism of 1789 as embodied not only in the effective dissolution of the monarchy but in the declaration of the rights of man. To Tocqueville, the key document to understanding this revolutionary spirit was the pamphlet Abbé Sieyès published before the meeting of the Estates General, in January 1789. Titled *Qu'est-ce que le tiers-état?*, the pamphlet that radically excluded from the nation a socially useless nobility.[90] Tocqueville highlighted Sieyès's main points as emblematic of the coming new radicalism. "The third estate forms a complete nation," wrote Sieyès. "Not only are the nobility and clergy useless, but they are also harmful." They therefore "ought to let themselves be exterminated," for the nobility is "a caste without function, without utility," "a barbarous enemy people in the heart of the French nation." It followed that "only the third estate should be forming a National Assembly."[91]

Tocqueville considered the union of the bourgeoisie and the lower classes a fait accompli by the Fête de la Fédération, July 14, 1790. In the process, he saw moderates embrace Rousseau's radical ideas and oppose Montesquieu's system of intermediary powers. Rousseau "became and he was to remain the sole teacher of the Revolution in its youth." Even the centrist Monarchien leader Jean-Joseph Mounier, although versed in British institutions, supported a single assembly.[92] Tocqueville noted Girondin Brissot de Warville as a rare exception pushing for bicameralism, and this was only because he had not only lived in England but also toured America. All others who claimed to follow an American model, Tocqueville observed, were merely "the worst imitators who had taken from the United States the abstract principles of their constitution without having understood the necessity of certain conservative applications of these principles that had been made in America." In his notes on the Revolution, Tocqueville kept returning to a counterintuitive point he had made repeatedly in *Democracy in America* regarding the necessity of limiting liberty to protect it.[93] But the Revolution followed instead the cult of absolute sovereignty.

This is most of what Tocqueville was able to cover in his notes before sickness returned. How Tocqueville would have connected the radicalism of 1789, which he captured so well, with the radicalism of 1793, "a virus of a new and unknown kind," to which he never turned, is impossible to know.[94] His reflections on the Terror are fragmentary and unoriginal, even though that episode of the Revolution evoked the most tragic of family memories (see Prologue). Tocqueville treasured the memory of his guillotined great-grandfather; he wrote to his cousin Eugénie de Grancey in 1857 that he had "always regretted not having a portrait of M. de Malesherbes" because he would have "put it in the most beautiful spot in the house."[95] Yet Tocqueville scarcely mentioned Malesherbes in his notes on the Revolution.[96] Neither do we know how Tocqueville might have reworked his early drafts on Napoleon Bonaparte's seizing power on 18 Brumaire.

## Cannes: The End

In late July 1858, Tocqueville wrote to Harriet Grote, "I coughed up blood a month ago. Eight years previously, a terrible disease started in this same way."[97] Tuberculosis had returned, and Tocqueville quickly felt its debilitating effects. Summer 1858 was quiet, the only excitement being the opening, in August, of the Paris-Cherbourg railroad and the large new docks of the Cherbourg Harbor. Tocqueville had promoted the railroad line and likely would have enjoyed meeting Queen Victoria and conversing again with Prince Albert, both of whom were in attendance. However, because the emperor was present, he boycotted the festivities. Hippolyte and Émilie, having no such qualms, were prominently present among the local guests at Cherbourg while Tocqueville took the Beaumonts and the Rivets to the top of his brother and sister-in-law's Tourlaville château to observe the ceremonies from a distance.[98] Afterward, Tocqueville was quite annoyed when the local newspaper mistook Émilie for Marie among the leading dancers at the opening ball![99]

This was a small vexation compared to what was to come. The disease progressed quickly. Tocqueville spent much of the fall traveling from Tocqueville to Paris to seek medical advice and receive treatment.[100] By October, the couple followed medical orders to move south. They traveled to Cannes, which was becoming a fashionable resort on the Riviera. Unfortunately, a cold snap, high winds, and related travel delays turned the journey into an exhausting trek. Tocqueville was dangerously frail on arrival while Marie could not shake off a bad cold.[101]

Once settled at Villa Montfleury in Cannes, Marie secured help from three local nuns, Sisters of Mercy, to care for Tocqueville while a young and shy seminarian came to the house in the evening to read out loud to them. During the five weeks from late December to early February, Tocqueville became progressively incapacitated. He was in constant pain, had great difficulty sleeping, and was ever more unable to read, write, or even speak.[102] Hippolyte, learning that his younger brother was seriously ill, took up residence at Villa Montfleury to help. Tocqueville did not overlook that his brother, when not at his bedside, associated with local Bonapartists; he characterized him as having a "weak character but a heart of gold."[103] Hippolyte was indispensable; Marie, still unable to shake off her cold, lost much of her own voice and could do little to help.

Tocqueville experienced a short reprieve in February and March 1859. Immediately upon its publication, John Stuart Mill sent him a copy of his *On Liberty* in which he acknowledged the large influence Tocqueville's theory of the tyranny of the majority had on his own thought. Tocqueville, who had resumed some correspondence, wrote back the next day, clear-headed about their intellectual companionship in a common search. "I have no doubt that at every moment in this field of liberty, we would have been unable to advance without each giving the other a hand." He added he had heard a rumor that Harriet had died, but he was not sure.[104] Had Tocqueville had the energy to open *On Liberty*, he would have seen Mill's moving dedication to his deceased wife, a woman of "unrivaled wisdom."

For a few weeks, Tocqueville took daily walks.[105] He read again, had some visitors, among them Lord Brougham who lived in Cannes when not in parliament in London. Tocqueville and Brougham had once argued over control of the slave trade and national sovereignty (see chapter 8), but that was forgotten. At Senior's request, Brougham made his personal library available to the patient.[106] Former German ambassador to the Court of Saint James, Charles von Bunsen, also staying in Cannes, visited in late February.[107] Tocqueville had once consulted with him on German history; they talked about the danger of war between France and Austria as the unpredictable and adventurous Napoleon III allied with Piedmont to liberate Venetian Lombardy.

In these last moments of intellectual and social activity, Tocqueville resumed a correspondence with Duvergier de Hauranne and complimented him on his volume covering the Restoration. He reported to Freslon in late February that he was reading Edward Gibbon's autobiography in English (likely from Brougham's library!). He advised his friend Corcelle to accept his daughter's engagement, and his cousin Eugénie de Grancey on how to guide her son in negotiating difficulties with his superior officers during the battle of Cochinchine, and he gave some marital advice to dear nephew Hubert.[108]

With Tocqueville seemingly recovering, Hippolyte left Cannes on February 28. But without a relative in the home, the Tocquevilles panicked. Tocqueville literally begged Beaumont to come: "VENEZ, VENEZ, VENEZ," he wrote him in capital letters on March 4, 1859.[109] Marie supported this request with an equally pressing letter to Clémentine. Beaumont of course immediately arrived and stayed through March, but he left on April 5, not knowing how close his friend was to the end.

In his last weeks of life, Tocqueville gave strong signals that he wanted to depart this world as a Catholic. They were consistent with the many attempts he had made over the years to recover the faith he had known in youth. Bishop Dupanloup paid a visit in March while he was in the region and celebrated mass privately in Tocqueville's bedroom. Dupanloup then advised the local priest, Abbé Gabriel, to make regular visits to Villa Montfleury. The nuns encouraged their patient to get to know Father Gabriel and trust him.[110]

On April 6, the day after Beaumont's departure, at Marie's prodding, Tocqueville confessed to Father Gabriel, and a few days later he and Marie together received communion from him. Beaumont, not present to witness the moment, later maintained privately that Tocqueville most likely yielded to Marie's pressure, that his confession and communion were not proof that Tocqueville had recovered his faith.[111] Whether Tocqueville had a full reconciliation with his Catholic faith need not be resolved. But there is no reason to doubt, at least, the sincerity of a gesture so completely consistent with his aspirations.

Alexis chose to be in total agreement with Marie in the last hours they shared together. He had repeatedly and consistently told her she was the one woman he loved, and he reaffirmed it now. His childhood friend and confidant Kergorlay, who had arrived in Cannes after Beaumont's departure, was at Tocqueville's bedside. Brother Édouard and nephew and protégé Hubert reached Villa Montfleury just in time. Jean-Jacques Ampère was still on his way from Italy when Tocqueville died on April 16, 1859.

# Epilogue

THE LAST YEARS of Tocqueville's life were shadowed by his fear that the democratic experiment might be failing. France was in the grip of an authoritarian regime. And in America, torn apart by the slavery question, democracy seemed inadequate to the challenges the country faced. To be sure, Tocqueville had voiced fears about the long-term viability of the American democratic experiment from the beginning. In *Democracy in America*, he expressed doubts about the ability of American democracy to contain economic conflicts between the North and the South that led to the nullification crisis, abolish slavery, and address lawlessness in the territories. But these fears resurfaced with greater intensity in the 1850s as the political crisis brewed.

Some American friends tried to assuage Tocqueville's fears. One of them, Edward Vernon Childe, a Harvard graduate, had been a longtime Paris correspondent for New York newspapers. Tocqueville admired his wife, Catherine Mildred, Robert E. Lee's younger sister, who held a salon in Paris he liked to attend, and he also developed much affection for their son.[1] In January 1857, a few months after returning to the United States, Childe wrote to Tocqueville from Boston that he had dutifully conveyed the latter's messages of friendship to Jared Sparks and Edward Everett. Turning to the state of the nation, Childe assured Tocqueville that the secessionists were fanatics who posed no threat. He felt "no apprehension of a dismemberment of the Union," reporting instead that the free states regarded "the frantic contortions of southern demagogues as grown men look on the freaks of a child."[2]

But abolitionist Massachusetts senator Charles Sumner, who had visited Tocqueville in Normandy, saw battle lines being drawn. Sumner wrote to Tocqueville in 1858 that slavery "has demoralized our government and introduced everywhere the vulgar principles of force. . . . And now, my dear friend, if you hear the American Republic abused, pray charge its evil deeds to slavery, and say that there are good people here who are determined that this source of our woes shall cease."[3]

Of course, Sumner was right and Childe was wrong. By 1861, only two years after Tocqueville's death, eleven Southern states had seceded from the Union. In their new confederation, whites could cling to their belief that liberty rested on being able to keep Black people enslaved. Indeed, they hoped to extend slavery even farther west. Inequality, not equality, was the keystone of their brand of liberty.

The impending war made Northerners, especially abolitionists from New England, turn to Tocqueville with intense interest. Tocqueville's proposition that all people are equally responsible for organizing society came into sharper focus. When Tocqueville was touring the United States in 1831–32, it had seemed to him that the two principles of liberty and equality could be congruent in America, if not in France. Now the Civil War was calling all this into question, and the importance of Tocqueville's essential theory was finally being grasped by his American readership.

In 1861, Gustave de Beaumont issued *Œuvres et correspondance inédites d'Alexis de Tocqueville*, two volumes of letters from Tocqueville, and never-before-seen essays; they reached a receptive audience.[4] Upon publication in Paris, respected literary critic Sainte-Beuve, who had not always seen eye to eye with Tocqueville, wrote an appreciative advance review recognizing that Tocqueville had hit on a few fundamental insights while still young. As Sainte-Beuve put it, grudgingly but largely accurately, Tocqueville had "begun to think before he knew anything."[5] Much of what Tocqueville had understood about democracy early in his adult life, he did by observing Americans.

The edited volumes of correspondence and essays quickly reached the desk of Charles Eliot Norton, an antislavery radical, Boston Brahmin, art historian, and translator of Dante. Much younger than Tocqueville, he had met him once while touring Europe. Norton wrote a detailed review in *The Atlantic* with a recapitulation of Tocqueville's life and works and a deep appreciation for Tocqueville's formulation of how a democracy should work.

Norton seized on Tocqueville's essential proposition and rephrased it as a simple question for Americans to ponder: "Can equality, which, by dividing men and reducing the mass to a common level, smooths the way for the establishment of a despotism, either of an individual or of the mob, be made to promote and secure liberty?" To leave no doubt in the minds of *The Atlantic*'s subscribers that he was talking about events unfolding in the United States, Norton stressed that "Tocqueville's services to liberty did not end with his life." Rather, "whenever men are striving in thought or in action to support the cause of freedom and of law, to strengthen institutions founded on principles of equal justice, to secure established liberties by defending the government in which they are embodied, his teachings will be prized, and his memory be honored."[6] Tocqueville's ideas needed the emergence of a real threat to win acknowledgment of their full force.

Norton's efforts to revive Tocqueville were immediately echoed in several New England journals during the Civil War years. *Democracy in America* became a lens through which the causes of secession and the future of the Union could be viewed and explained. In the hands of New Englanders, the chapter on race finally took on the meaning Tocqueville had intended: as a warning of the danger slavery presented to the Union.[7]

The lifelong friends Tocqueville had made in Boston were defenders of the Union and firm supporters of President Lincoln. The tragedy of war affected them poignantly. Francis Lieber, for example, rescued his oldest son, who lost an arm fighting for the Union, from the battlefield only to learn that another son had died defending the Confederacy.[8] The cost of preserving the Union and expanding democracy was on display at the dedication of the cemetery for the Union dead at the Gettysburg battlefield in November 1863. It is a symbolic coincidence that Tocqueville's friend Edward Everett was the main orator for the event. Although a so-called doughface before the war (a Northerner supporting Southern politics), Everett had emerged as a passionate defender of

the Union. He was the unanimous choice of speaker the seventeen
Union state governors recommended to the organizing committee for
the ceremony.[9] Everett spoke for two hours on the historical significance of the heroic battle of Gettysburg before the president, who had
been invited only as second speaker. When Lincoln's turn came, he reaffirmed in an address made immortal through its eloquent brevity the
United States as a "new nation, conceived in liberty, and dedicated to
the proposition that all men are created equal." After the bloodiest car-
nage of the war, with the Union still in grave peril, Lincoln reaffirmed
what Tocqueville saw as the purpose of democracy.

In the years following the Civil War, Sumner did much to cement
Tocqueville's reputation as a visionary. He included a section on Tocqueville in his last book, *Prophetic Voices Concerning America* (1874). Sumner saluted Tocqueville for recognizing the unity of the American
people as "something entirely new in the world, the implications of
which imagination can hardly seize the extent" while at the same time
predicting "peril" to the Union would come "from slavery and from the
pretensions of the states."[10]

Tocqueville lived his short life, dying at age fifty-three, between two
great national tragedies he did not personally witness—the Revolutionary Terror in France that decimated his aristocratic family and the
American Civil War that came close to razing the American Republic
he had taken as his model for democracy. Had Tocqueville lived a dozen
more years, he would have witnessed, like Marx, the class war of 1871,
which he had so feared could devastate France in 1848. The event would
most likely have aggravated his doubts about ever reconciling democracy (or equality, in his vocabulary) and liberty.

Yet Tocqueville's doubts never weakened his resolve. As a writer, he
developed his ideas partly for their beauty but mostly as tools of human
improvement. As a politician, Tocqueville strove to turn his complex
theories into concrete policy. His thinking was radical in its attempt to
overcome, rather than reconcile, conflicting ideals and purposes. Tocqueville had exacting standards that he applied most stringently to himself,
constantly deepening his judgments. His method was intrinsically comparative, drawing him to various parts of the world to formulate and test

his ideas against different systems. He understood America so well that his work has helped Americans make sense of their democratic experiment. Although Tocqueville never ceased to complain that doubt crippled him, he channeled his anxiety into a creative force and translated his passion for liberty into a deep and demanding appreciation of democracy.

# NOTE ON SOURCES

## English-Language Translations of Tocqueville's Writings

*On the Penitentiary System in the United States and Its Application in France*, with Gustave de Beaumont, trans. Francis Lieber (Philadelphia, 1833). Reprinted with an introduction by Thorstein Sellin and a foreword by Herman R. Lantz (Carbondale: Southern Illinois University Press, 1964). New translation by Emily Katherine Ferkaluk (Cham, Switzerland: Palgrave Macmillan, 2018).

*Democracy in America*, ed. Olivier Zunz, trans. Arthur Goldhammer, 2 vols. (New York: Library of America, 2004), abbreviated in the notes as **DA I** for the 1835 volume and **DA II** for the 1840 volume.

*Democracy in America*, augmented with the author's surviving drafts and manuscript notes, ed. Eduardo Nolla, trans. James T. Schleifer, 4 vols. (Indianapolis: Liberty Fund, 2010).

*Recollections: The French Revolution of 1848 and Its Aftermath*, ed. Olivier Zunz, trans. Arthur Goldhammer (Charlottesville: University of Virginia Press, 2016).

*The Ancien Régime and the French Revolution*, ed. Jon Elster, trans. Arthur Goldhammer (Cambridge: Cambridge University Press, 2011), abbreviated in the notes as **AR**.

*The Old Regime and the Revolution*, ed. François Furet and Françoise Mélonio, trans. Alan Kahan, vol. 2 (Chicago: University of Chicago Press, 1998), abbreviated in the notes as **OR**.

*Alexis de Tocqueville and Gustave de Beaumont in America: Their Friendship and Their Travels*, ed. Olivier Zunz, trans. Arthur

Goldhammer (Charlottesville: University of Virginia Press, 2010), abbreviated in the notes as *Tocqueville and Beaumont*.

*Tocqueville on America after 1840: Letters and Other Writings*, trans. and ed. Aurelian Craiutu and Jeremy Jennings (New York: Cambridge University Press, 2009).

*The Tocqueville Reader: A Life in Letters and Politics*, ed. Olivier Zunz and Alan S. Kahan (Oxford: Blackwell, 2002).

*Memoir on Pauperism*, trans. Seymour Drescher, with an introduction by Gertrude Himmelfarb (Chicago: Ivan R. Dee, 1997).

*Journeys to England and Ireland*, ed. J. P. Mayer, trans. George Lawrence and K. P. Mayer (1958; reprint, New Brunswick, NJ: Transaction Books, 1988).

*Alexis de Tocqueville's Journey in Ireland, July–August, 1835*, trans. and ed. Emmet Larkin (Washington, DC: Catholic University of America Press, 1990).

*Writings on Empire and Slavery*, trans. and ed. Jennifer Pitts (Baltimore: Johns Hopkins University Press, 2001).

## French Editions of Tocqueville's Works

In 1951, a French National Commission (Commission nationale pour la publication des œuvres d'Alexis de Tocqueville) began to collect Tocqueville's complete works and publish them under the Gallimard imprint. The project took seventy years of editorial work, with the last volumes released in spring 2021. It might never have come to fruition had the Cherbourg Fire Department not been able to extinguish, after a long battle full of mishaps, a fire that engulfed the family château in 1954 and destroyed most of its interior. Miraculously, the manor's central stone staircase protected Tocqueville's study and the archival *chartrier* above the study in the main tower just long enough for them to be saved. Also saved during that fateful night were some of the papers of Tocqueville's maternal great-grandfather, Malesherbes, the director of the book trade under Louis XV and friend of the philosophes. The correspondence from Louis XIV to Vauban, his master of military fortifications and another Tocqueville ancestor, escaped the flames as well.

The Gallimard *Œuvres complètes* comprise thirty-two volumes in eighteen tomes. *Œuvres complètes* is abbreviated in the notes as **OC**:

Tome I, *De la démocratie en Amérique*, 2 vols., 1951, ed. J.-P. Mayer (**OC I:1; OC I:2**).

Tome II, *L'ancien régime et la révolution*, 2 vols., 1952, 1953, ed. J.-P. Mayer (**OC II:1**) and André Jardin (**OC II:2**).

Tome III, *Écrits et discours politiques*, 3 vols., 1962, 1985, 1990, ed. André Jardin (**OC III:1; OC III:2; OC III:3**).

Tome IV, *Écrits sur le système pénitentiaire en France et à l'étranger*, 2 vols., 1984, ed. Michelle Perrot (**OC IV:1; OC IV:2**).

Tome V, *Voyages*, 2 vols., 1957, 1958, ed. J.-P. Mayer (**OC V:1**, *en Sicile et aux États-Unis*) and J.-P. Mayer and André Jardin (**OC V:2**, *en Angleterre, Irlande, Suisse, et Algérie*).

Tome VI, *Correspondance anglaise*, 3 vols., 1954, 1991, 2003, ed. J.-P. Mayer and Gustave Rudler (**OC VI:1**, *Correspondance d'Alexis de Tocqueville avec Henry Reeve et John Stuart Mill*); Hugh Brogan, A. P. Kerr, and Lola Mayer (**OC VI:2**, *Correspondance et conversations d'Alexis de Tocqueville et de Nassau William Senior*); and A. P. Kerr (**OC VI:3**, *Correspondance anglaise*).

Tome VII, *Correspondance étrangère, Amérique-Europe continentale*, 1 vol., 1986, ed. Françoise Mélonio, Lise Queffélec, and Anthony Pleasance, **OC VII**).

Tome VIII, *Correspondance d'Alexis de Tocqueville et de Gustave de Beaumont*, 3 vols., 1967, ed. André Jardin (**OC VIII:1; OC VIII:2; OC VIII:3**).

Tome IX, *Correspondance d'Alexis de Tocqueville et d'Arthur de Gobineau*, 1 vol., 1959, ed. M. Degros (**OC IX**).

Tome X, *Correspondance et écrits locaux*, 1 vol., 1995, ed. Lise Queffélec-Dumasy (**OC X**).

Tome XI, *Correspondance d'Alexis de Tocqueville avec P.-P. Royer-Collard et avec J.-J. Ampère*, 1 vol., 1970, ed. André Jardin (**OC XI**).

Tome XII, *Souvenirs*, 1 vol., 1964, ed. Luc Monnier (**OC XII**).

Tome XIII, *Correspondance d'Alexis de Tocqueville et de Louis de Kergorlay*, 2 vols., 1977, ed. André Jardin (**OC XIII:1; OC XIII:2**).

Tome XIV, *Correspondance familiale*, 1 vol., 1998, ed. Jean-Louis Benoît and André Jardin (**OC XIV**).

Tome XV, *Correspondance d'Alexis de Tocqueville et de Francisque de Corcelle; correspondance d'Alexis de Tocqueville et de Madame Swetchine*, 2 vols., 1983, ed. Pierre Gibert (**OC XV:1; OC XV:2**).

Tome XVI, *Mélanges*, 1 vol., 1989, ed. Françoise Mélonio (**OC XVI**).

Tome XVII, *Correspondance à divers*, 3 vols., 2021, ed. Françoise Mélonio and Anne Vibert (**OC XVII:1; OC XVII:2; OC XVII:3**).

Tome XVIII, *Correspondance d'Alexis de Tocqueville avec Adolphe de Circourt et avec Madame de Circourt*, 1 vol., 1983, ed. A. P. Kerr (**OC XVIII**).

The Bibliothèque de la Pléiade (Paris: Gallimard) has published three volumes of Tocqueville's **Œuvres**, or **OP** in the notes (for *Œuvres Pléiade*). Editors of the Pléiade volumes have selectively revised texts published earlier in the OC.

Tome I, *Voyages et écrits académiques et politiques*, 1991, ed. André Jardin, Françoise Mélonio, and Lise Queffélec.

Tome II, *De la démocratie en Amérique*, 1992, ed. André Jardin, Jean-Claude Lamberti, and James T. Schleifer.

Tome III, *État social et politique de la France avant et depuis 1789, L'ancien régime et la révolution, Esquisses de* L'ancien régime et la révolution, [*Considérations sur la révolution,*] *Souvenirs*, 2004, ed. François Furet and Françoise Mélonio.

One can read a large selection of Tocqueville's letters in *Tocqueville: Lettres choisies, Souvenirs*, ed. Françoise Mélonio and Laurence Guellec (Paris: Gallimard, 2003), abbreviated in the notes as **LC**.

Beaumont's letters from the United States are available in *Gustave de Beaumont: Lettres d'Amérique*, ed. André Jardin and G. W. Pierson (Paris: Presses Universitaires de France, 1973).

Gustave de Beaumont himself published a two-volume selection of his friend's works as *Œuvres et correspondance inédites d'Alexis de Tocqueville* (Paris, 1861), followed by a nine-volume selection as *Œuvres complètes d'Alexis de Tocqueville publiées par Madame de Tocqueville* (Paris, 1865–67). The two-volume set became Tomes V and VI of the nine-volume set. The abbreviation in the notes for an occasional use of this older edition is **OCB**.

To facilitate the reader's access to Tocqueville's writings, the notes provide both English and French references whenever possible.

Names recurring in the notes have been abbreviated as follows:

AG   Arthur de Gobineau
AT   Alexis de Tocqueville
ET   Édouard de Tocqueville
GB   Gustave de Beaumont
HT   Hervé de Tocqueville
JSM  John Stuart Mill
LK   Louis de Kergorlay
LNB  Louis Napoléon Bonaparte
RC   Pierre-Paul Royer-Collard

The Archives de la Manche in Saint-Lô maintain a large, digitized collection of Tocqueville's personal archives, accessible at https://www .archives-manche.fr, and the Beinecke Manuscript and Rare Book Library at Yale University has an extensive collection of Tocqueville and Beaumont papers.

# NOTES

## Prologue

1. Thomas Paine, *Rights of Man: Being an Answer to Mr. Burke's Attack on the French Revolution* (London, 1791), 71.

2. "Mon instinct, mes opinions," in *The Tocqueville Reader: A Life in Letters and Politics,* ed. Olivier Zunz and Alan S. Kahan (Oxford: Blackwell, 2002), 219; *Œuvres complètes* (hereafter OC) III:2, 87.

3. Alexis de Tocqueville (hereafter AT), *Democracy in America,* ed. Olivier Zunz, trans. Arthur Goldhammer (New York: Library of America, 2004) (hereafter DA I [1835] or DA II [1840]), II, 586; *Œuvres* Pléaide (hereafter OP) II:613–14.

4. DA II, 581; OP II:607.

5. AT to Chateaubriand, January 1835, OC XVII:1, 216. On Malesherbes, see Françoise Mélonio, "Tocqueville: Aux origines de la démocratie française," in *The French Revolution and the Creation of Modern Political Culture,* ed. François Furet and Mona Ozouf (Oxford: Pergamon, 1987), 3:596; and David A. Bell, "Malesherbes et Tocqueville: Les origines parlementaires du libéralisme français," *The Tocqueville Review / La revue Tocqueville* 37, no. 2 (2006): 273–82.

6. *Mémoires d'Hervé Clérel, comte de Tocqueville, 1772–1856,* ed. Jean-Louis Benoît, Nicolas Fréret, and Christian Lippi (Saint-Lô: Archives départementales, Maison de l'histoire de la Manche, Conseil départemental de la Manche, 2019), 172.

7. DA I, 3; OP II:3.

8. AT to Reeve, compare June 5, 1836, OC VI:1, 34 to November 15, 1839, OC VI:1, 48. Some scholars argue against overwhelming evidence to the contrary that Tocqueville liked neither America nor democracy. According to Arthur Kaledin, Tocqueville saw in America "an inert society . . . a culture without any sense of order and limits . . . a democratic Hell": *Tocqueville and His America: A Darker Vision* (New Haven, CT: Yale University Press, 2011), 71; Hugh Brogan, more moderately, was satisfied to label Tocqueville "a fellow traveller of legitimism": *Alexis de Tocqueville: A Life* (New Haven, CT: Yale University Press, 2006), 264.

9. AT to Orglandes, November 29, 1834, in *Alexis de Tocqueville and Gustave de Beaumont in America: Their Friendship and Their Travels,* ed. Olivier Zunz, trans. Arthur Goldhammer (Charlottesville: University of Virginia Press, 2010), 563; the letter was initially thought to have been written to Louis de Kergorlay and published in OC XIII:1, 373–75; new attribution in OC XVII:1, 213; *Tocqueville: Lettres choisies, Souvenirs,* ed. Françoise Mélonio and Laurence Guellec (Paris: Gallimard, 2003), 311.

10. AT to Louis Le Peletier de Rosanbo, March 13, 1839, OC XIV, 209.

11. AT to Chateaubriand, January 1835, OC XVII:1, 216.

## Chapter 1

1. Alexis de Tocqueville (hereafter AT), *Democracy in America*, ed. Olivier Zunz, trans. Arthur Goldhammer (New York: Library of America, 2004) (hereafter DA I [1835] or DA II [1840]), I, 31; *Œuvres* Pléaide (hereafter OP) II:29.

2. Chateaubriand, *Mémoires d'outre-tombe*, Bibliothèque de la Pléiade (Paris: Gallimard, 1951), 1:576.

3. Chartrier, Château de Tocqueville, 154 AP III (Sénozan).

4. *Mémoires d'Hervé Clérel, comte de Tocqueville, 1772–1856*, ed. Jean-Louis Benoît, Nicolas Fréret, and Christian Lippi (Saint-Lô: Archives départementales, Maison de l'histoire de la Manche, Conseil départemental de la Manche, 2019), 167.

5. Chartrier, Château de Tocqueville, 154 AP I B, 154 AP III.

6. *Mémoires d'Hervé de Tocqueville*, 175n97, citing official registry at Verneuil.

7. Estimates vary: 2.4 million men were recruited between 1804 and 1814. See *Napoléon et l'empire*, ed. Jean Misler (Paris, 1968), 2:175.

8. *Mémoires d'Hervé de Tocqueville*, 177.

9. Nassau Senior, "Conversations," May 2, 1857, *Œuvres complètes* (hereafter OC) VI:2, 470.

10. Nassau Senior, "Conversations," August 24, 1850, OC VI:2, 301.

11. Chateaubriand, *Mémoires d'outre-tombe*, 576.

12. AT to Lady Lewis, May 6, 1857, OC VI:3, 237; see also AT to Corcelle, December 3, 1853, OC XV:2, 87.

13. A priest who refused to swear an oath of allegiance to the state under the 1790 Civil Constitution of the Clergy. See David A. Selby, *Tocqueville, Jansenism, and the Necessity of the Political in a Democratic Age: Building a Republic for the Moderns* (Amsterdam: Amsterdam University Press, 2015), 63–65.

14. AT to Grancey, December 28, 1856, OC XVII:3, 362; *Tocqueville: Lettres choisies, Souvenirs*, ed. Françoise Mélonio and Laurence Guellec (Paris: Gallimard, 2003) (hereafter LC), 1226.

15. Lesueur to AT, September 8, 1824 (1821?) in Jean-Louis Benoît, *Tocqueville moraliste* (Paris: Honoré Champion, 2004), 571.

16. AT to Sofia Swetchine, September 10, 1856, OC XV:2, 293.

17. AT to Hubert, March 7, 1854, OC XIV, 296.

18. AT to Lesueur, April 4, 1814, OC XIV, 40.

19. See Édouard's and Hippolyte's military records in OC XIII:1, 46.

20. AT to Lesueur, July 6, 1816 [1817], OC XIV, 42.

21. André Jardin, *Tocqueville: A Biography*, trans. Lydia Davis with Robert Hemenway (Baltimore: Johns Hopkins University Press, 1998), 16.

22. Guillaume Bertier de Sauvigny, *La restauration* (Paris: Flammarion, 1955), 156–65.

23. AT to Freslon, July 8, 1858, OC XVII:3, 501–4; LC, 1310–12.

24. Pierre Karila-Cohen, *L'état des esprits: L'invention de l'enquête politique en France (1814–1848)* (Rennes: Presses Universitaires de Rennes, 2008), 141–44.

25. François Guizot, *Mémoires pour servir à l'histoire de mon temps* (Paris, 1860), 3:14; Karila-Cohen, *L'état des esprits*, 139.

26. Chartrier, Château de Tocqueville, 154 AP I C (Tocqueville C) Préfecture de la Moselle.

27. Chartrier, Château de Tocqueville.

28. Chartrier, Château de Tocqueville.

29. See Jardin, *Tocqueville*, 59.

30. Lesueur to AT, July 27, 1820 [1821?] in Benoît, *Tocqueville moraliste*, 587–88.

31. Louis de Kergorlay (hereafter LK), "Étude littéraire sur AT," OC XIII:2, 360; and AT ms. note in DA II, part 3, chap. 2 in Eduardo Nolla's critical edition of DA, trans. James Schleifer (Indianapolis: Liberty Fund, 2009), 4:996.

32. AT to Alexis Stöffels, January 4, 1856, OC XVII:3, 230; LC, 1142.

33. LK to AT, May 16, 1823, OC XIII:1, 62.

34. Lesueur to AT, September 8, 1824, in Benoît, *Tocqueville moraliste*, 573. The date may be inaccurate as AT had already admitted his loss of faith to Lesueur in 1821 or 1822; see OC XIV, 43–44.

35. AT to Charles Stöffels, October 22, 1831, OC XVII:1, 126; LC, 239.

36. AT to Swetchine, February 26, 1857, OC XV:2, 313–16.

37. OC XIV, 43n3; see Jardin, *Tocqueville*, 57–58.

38. Save for her name, Louise Charlotte Meyer, see LC, 102.

39. OC XIII:1, 79n2.

40. LK to AT, May 16, 1823, OC XIII:1, 60.

41. Lesueur to AT, February 12, February 13, April 24, and May 3, 1823, in Benoît, *Tocqueville moraliste*, 566–67.

42. Lesueur to Édouard, September 14, 1822, in Benoît, *Tocqueville moraliste*, 54.

43. AT to Hubert, January 12, 1854, OC XIV, 291–92.

44. Jean-Louis Benoît, *Tocqueville: Un destin paradoxal* (Paris: Bayard, 2005), 40.

45. LK to AT, June 4, 1825, OC XIII:1, 84.

46. Louis Liard, *L'enseignement supérieur en France, 1789–1893* (Paris, 1894), 2:147.

47. LK to AT, March 14, 1822, OC XIII:1, 43.

48. Not in charge of a diocese.

49. Liard, *L'enseignement supérieur*, 158.

50. Paul Gerbod, "La vie universitaire à Paris sous la restauration, de 1820 à 1830," *Revue d'histoire moderne et contemporaine* 13 (January–March 1966): 31, 35.

51. Liard, *L'enseignement supérieur*, 162.

52. OC XVI, 33–37.

53. OC V:1, 37–54.

54. AT to Édouard and Alexandrine, April 6, 1830, OC XIV, 62.

55. *Mémoires d'Hervé de Tocqueville*, 358.

56. R. M. Milnes, *Commonplace Books*, OC VI:3, 320.

57. Hugh Brogan, *Alexis de Tocqueville: A Life* (New Haven, CT: Yale University Press, 2006), 77.

58. OP I:26.

59. AT to LK, July 23, 1827, OC XIII:1, 106–7.

60. AT to Gustave de Beaumont (hereafter GB), 1828 or 1829, OC VIII:1, 75.

61. AT to GB, March 18, 1829, OC VIII:1, 76; October 25, 1829, OC VIII:1, 91–93.

62. Louis Passy, *Le marquis de Blosseville: Souvenirs* (Evreux, 1898), 70.

63. Jardin, *Tocqueville*, 83.

64. AT to LK, March 30, 1828, OC XIII:1, 133.

65. AT to LK, July 28, 1827, OC XIII:1, 107–8.

66. OC XVI, 67, 72.

67. OC XVI, 54, 63.

68. OC XVI, 77–84.

69. Karila-Cohen, *L'état des esprits*, 281.

70. LK to AT, July 28, 1828, OC XIII:1, 140–41.

71. One can follow several episodes of the melodrama in the correspondence between AT and LK, OC XIII:1, 91–151.

72. Ross Carroll, "The Hidden Labors of Mary Mottley, Madame de Tocqueville," *Hypatia* 33 (Fall 2018): 645.

73. AT to GB, October 5, 1828, OC VIII:1, 48–49.

74. AT to GB, December 7, 1828, OC VIII:1, 72.

75. AT to GB, September 19, 1829, OC VIII:1, 86.

76. AT to GB, October 5, 1828, OC VIII:1, 62, 50.

77. AT to GB, October 5, 1828, OC VIII:1, 63, 69.

78. AT, *État social et politique de la France avant et depuis 1789* (1836), OP III:28.

79. AT to GB, October 5, 1828, OC VIII:1, 50; François Guizot, *The History of Civilization in Europe* (1846), ed. Larry Siedentrop, trans. William Hazlitt (Indianapolis: Liberty Fund, 1997), 62.

80. AT to GB, August 20, 1829, OC VIII:1, 80; see Robert T. Gannett Jr., *Tocqueville Unveiled: The Historian and His Sources for the Old Regime and the Revolution* (Chicago: University of Chicago Press, 2003), 19.

81. OC XVI, 482–83, trans. Hugh Brogan, *Tocqueville*, 93.

82. OC XVI, 494.

83. Brogan, *Tocqueville*, 116; "séance du 8 mai 1830," OC XVI, 516.

84. AT to Charles Stöffels, April 21, 1830, in Robert T. Gannett Jr., "Tocqueville and the Local Frontiers of Democracy," in *Tocqueville and Local Frontiers of Democracy*, ed. Ewa Atanassow and Richard Boyd (Cambridge: Cambridge University Press, 2013), 323; OC XVII:1, 60–61; LC, 145.

85. OC XVI, 534.

86. Brogan, *Tocqueville*, 104.

87. Passy, *Blosseville*, 108.

88. AT to Édouard and Alexandrine, May 6, 1830, OC XIV, 67–68.

89. Bertier de Sauvigny, *Restauration*, 437.

90. AT to Édouard and Alexandrine, May 6, 1830, OC XIV, 68.

91. Bertier de Sauvigny, *Restauration*, 443–45.

92. Passy, *Blosseville*, 123.

93. Passy, *Blosseville*, 124.

94. AT to Mary Mottley, July 29, 1830, OC XIV, 375.

95. Passy, *Blosseville*, 130; AT to Eugène Stöffels, October 18, 1831, in GB, *Œuvres complètes d'Alexis de Tocqueville publiées par Madame de Tocqueville* (Paris, 1865–67) (hereafter OCB), V:420–21. George W. Pierson, *Tocqueville in America* (1938; repr., Baltimore: Johns Hopkins University Press, 1996), 26.

96. AT to Mary Mottley, July 30, 1830, OC XIV, 375.

97. *Récits d'une tante: Mémoires de la comtesse de Boigne née d'Osmond*, ed. Charles Nicoullaud, 3rd ed. (Paris, 1908), 4:6.

98. Passy, *Blosseville*, 130.

99. AT had to repeat the oath in October when the position of *auditeur* was replaced with that of *suppléant*, a still-unpaid position, not a promotion.

100. AT to Mary Mottley, August 17, 1830, OC XIV, 376.

101. AT to Auguste Henrion, October 17, 1830, OC XVII:1, 68.

102. GB, "Notice," in OCB V:8.

103. Benoît, *Destin paradoxal*, 44–45.

104. AT to GB, October 4, 1829, OC VIII:1, 88–89; October 25, 1829, OC VIII:1, 95.

105. AT to Charles Stöffels, November 4, 1830, in *Alexis de Tocqueville and Gustave de Beaumont in America: Their Friendship and Their Travels*, ed. Olivier Zunz, trans. Arthur Goldhammer (Charlottesville: University of Virginia Press, 2010) (hereafter *Tocqueville and Beaumont*), 34; OC XVII:1, 69–70; LC, 158–60.

106. Benjamin Franklin, as quoted in René Rémond, *Les États-Unis devant l'opinion française: 1815–1852* (Paris: Librairie Armand Colin, 1962), 2:532.

107. Chateaubriand, *Œuvres romanesques et voyages*, Bibliothèque de la Pléiade (Paris: Gallimard, 1969), 1:681; Marc Fumaroli, *Chateaubriand: Poésie et terreur* (Paris: Éditions de Fallois, 2003), 621.

108. See *Plaidoyer prononcé par M. Mérilhou, avocat, à l'audience du Tribunal de police correctionnelle de Paris, le 17 Janvier 1818: pour M. Charles-Arnold Scheffer, auteur de l'ouvrage intitulé de l'état de la liberté en France, prévenu d'écrits séditieux; suivi de la défense prononcée par l'accusé* (Paris, 1818); and Arnold Scheffer, *Histoire des États-Unis de l'Amérique septentrionale* (Paris, 1825), 228.

109. Catherine Duprat, "Punir et guérir," in *L'impossible prison: Recherches sur le système pénitentiaire au XIXe siècle*, ed. Michelle Perrot (Paris: Éditions du Seuil, 1980), 65–122.

110. André Normandeau, "Pioneers in Criminology: Charles Lucas, Opponent of Capital Punishment," *Journal of Criminal Law, Criminology, and Political Science* 61 (1970): 218–28.

111. Brogan, *Tocqueville*, 143–44.

112. Passy, *Blosseville*, 160.

113. Guillaume Tusseau, "Sur le panoptisme de Jeremy Bentham," *Revue française d'histoire des idées politiques* 19 (2004): 3–38; on Howard, see Thorsten Sellin, "Introduction," in *On the Penitentiary System in the United States and Its Application in France*, foreword by Herman R. Lantz (Carbondale: Southern Illinois University Press, 1964), xv–xl.

114. Michelle Perrot, "Introduction," OC IV:1, 10–12.

115. AT to GB, March 14, 1831, in *Tocqueville and Beaumont*, 5; OC VIII:1, 104–7; Pierson, *Tocqueville in America*, 36.

116. AT to Eugène Stöffels, July [June] 28, 1831, in *Tocqueville and Beaumont*, 47; OC XVII:1, 94.

117. AT to GB, October 29, 1829, OC VIII:1, 93.

## Chapter 2

Chapter title quote from Alexis de Tocqueville (hereafter AT), *Democracy in America*, ed. Olivier Zunz, trans. Arthur Goldhammer (New York: Library of America, 2004) (hereafter DA I [1835] or DA II [1840]), I, 323; *Œuvres* Pléiade (hereafter OP) II:322.

1. Gustave de Beaumont (hereafter GB) to Father, April 25, 1831, in *Alexis de Tocqueville and Gustave de Beaumont in America: Their Friendship and Their Travels*, ed. Olivier Zunz, trans. Arthur Goldhammer (Charlottesville: University of Virginia Press, 2010) (hereafter *Tocqueville and Beaumont*), 6; GB, *Lettres d'Amérique, 1831–1832*, ed. André Jardin and George W. Pierson (Paris: Presses Universitaires de France, 1973), 28.

2. Alexis de Tocqueville (hereafter AT) to Mother, October 24, 1831, in *Tocqueville and Beaumont*, 151; *Œuvres complètes* (hereafter OC) XIV, 144; AT to Louis de Kergorlay (hereafter LK), June 29, 1831, in *Tocqueville and Beaumont*, 57; OC XIII:1, 236. Only a few fragments of Beaumont's notebooks have survived.

3. AT, DA I, 349; OP II:350.

4. AT, DA I, 7; OP II:8. See Raymond Aron, "Tocqueville retrouvé," *The Tocqueville Review / La revue Tocqueville* 1, no. 1 (1979): 8–23; Raymond Boudon, "L'exigence de Tocqueville: La 'science politique nouvelle,'" *The Tocqueville Review / La revue Tocqueville* 37, no. 2 (2006): 14–34; Harvey C. Mansfield Jr. and Delba Winthrop, "Tocqueville's New Political Science," in *The Cambridge Companion to Tocqueville*, ed. Cheryl B. Welch (Cambridge: Cambridge University Press, 2006), 81–107.

5. James Fenimore Cooper, *Notions of the Americans: Picked Up by a Travelling Bachelor* (Philadelphia, 1828), 72.

6. AT to Mother, May 14, 1831, in *Tocqueville and Beaumont*, 8; OC XIV, 81.

7. GB to Mother, May 14, 1831, in *Tocqueville and Beaumont*, 13; GB, *Lettres d'Amérique*, 36.

8. AT to Mother, May 15, 1831, in *Tocqueville and Beaumont*, 11; OC XIV, 85.

9. See Gibbons v. Ogden, 22 US 1, 1824. See also DA I, 427; OP II:430, for Tocqueville's fears that the states would adopt internal customs were they to disunite.

10. Sean Wilentz, *The Rise of American Democracy: Jefferson to Lincoln* (New York: Norton, 2005), 529; AT to Mother, May 14, 1831, in *Tocqueville and Beaumont*, 9; OC XIV, 82.

11. AT, DA II, 534; OP II:563.

12. AT to Mother, May 15, 1831, in *Tocqueville and Beaumont*, 9; OC XIV, 82.

13. See biographical notes in *The Encyclopedia of New York City*, ed. Kenneth T. Jackson (New Haven, CT: Yale University Press, 1995).

14. George W. Pierson, *Tocqueville in America* (1938; repr., Baltimore: Johns Hopkins University Press, 1996), Appendix B, 782–83.

15. GB to Father, May 16, 1831, in *Tocqueville and Beaumont*, 18–19; GB, *Lettres d'Amérique*, 44; Edwin G. Burrows and Mike Wallace, *Gotham: A History of New York City to 1898* (New York: Oxford University Press, 1999), 445.

16. GB to Father, May 16, 1831, in *Tocqueville and Beaumont*, 15; GB, *Lettres d'Amérique*, 39.

17. GB to Father, May 16, 1831, in *Tocqueville and Beaumont*, 15; GB, *Lettres d'Amérique*, 39–40; Pierson, *Tocqueville in America*, 63.

18. GB to Father, May 16, 1831, in *Tocqueville and Beaumont*, 18; GB, *Lettres d'Amérique*, 44.

19. "Conversation with Mr. Livingston," Non-alphabetic Notebook 1, in *Tocqueville and Beaumont*, 211; OP I:32.

20. Burrows and Wallace, *Gotham*, 475.

21. Formerly Castle Clinton, a fort built between 1808 and 1810 on an artificial stone island in the port of New York, converted in the 1820s into a center for popular entertainment, until it became an immigration processing center in 1855.

22. AT to Lesueur, May 28, 1831, in *Tocqueville and Beaumont*, 26; OC XIV, 95.

23. "Reforms Schools (Maisons de refuge)," chapter 1 of part 3 of GB and AT, *On the Penitentiary System in the United States and Its Application in France*, trans. Francis Lieber (Philadelphia, 1833), in *Tocqueville and Beaumont*, 471; OC IV:1, 253.

24. GB and AT, *Le système pénitentiaire aux États-Unis et son application en France et à l'Étranger* (Paris, 1833), OC IV:1, 167n1.

25. Pierson, *Tocqueville in America*, 86.

26. AT to Le Peletier d'Aunay, June 7, 1831, in *Tocqueville and Beaumont*, 443; OC XVII:1, 80; *Tocqueville: Lettres choisies, Souvenirs*, ed. Françoise Mélonio and Laurence Guellec (Paris: Gallimard, 2003) (hereafter LC), 178.

27. AT, "Pénitentiaries," Alphabetic notebook A, in *Tocqueville and Beaumont*, 330; OP I:223.

28. AT to Lesueur, May 28, 1831, in *Tocqueville and Beaumont*, 27; OC XIV, 97.

29. Founded in 1783 by officers of the Continental Army who served in the Revolutionary War.

30. GB to his brother Achille, June 18, 1831, in *Tocqueville and Beaumont*, 42; GB, *Lettres d'Amérique*, 66.

31. AT to Lesueur, May 28, 1831, in *Tocqueville and Beaumont*, 25; OC XIV, 95.

32. GB to Mother, June 7, 1831, in *Tocqueville and Beaumont*, 34; GB, *Lettres d'Amérique*, 60.

33. GB to Achille, June 18, 1831, in *Tocqueville and Beaumont*, 42; GB, *Lettres d'Amérique*, 66.

34. AT to Chabrol, July 16, 1831, in *Tocqueville and Beaumont*, 80; OC XVII:1, 100; LC, 206.

35. On Livingston, see Burrows and Wallace, *Gotham*, 484.

36. AT to Chabrol, May 18, 1831, in *Tocqueville and Beaumont*, 23; OC XVII:1, 77.

37. AT to Chabrol, October 7, 1831, in *Tocqueville and Beaumont*, 139; OC XVII:1, 109.

38. Pierre Manent, "Guizot et Tocqueville devant l'ancien et le nouveau," in *François Guizot et la culture politique de son temps*, ed. Marina Valensise (Paris: Gallimard, 1991), 146.

39. AT to Orglandes, November 29, 1834, in *Tocqueville and Beaumont*, 563; OC XVII:1, 213; LC, 311.

40. AT to Chabrol, June 20, 1831, in *Tocqueville and Beaumont*, 46; OC XVII:1, 93; LC, 190.

41. The New York court of appeals had overturned Kent's judgment to protect unfair monetary agreements, provided they were freely entered into.

42. "Conversation with Mr. Gallatin," June 10, 1831, Non-alphabetic Notebook 1, in *Tocqueville and Beaumont*, 213; OP I:34.

43. AT to Mother, May 15, 1831, in *Tocqueville and Beaumont*, 10–11; OC XIV, 83–84.

44. AT to LK, June 29, 1831, in *Tocqueville and Beaumont*, 52; OC XIII:1, 229.

45. Burrows and Wallace, *Gotham*, 531; Mark A. Noll, "Tocqueville's America, Beaumont's Slavery, and the United States in 1831–32," *American Political Thought* 3 (Fall 2014): 273–302.

46. AT to LK, June 29, 1831, in *Tocqueville and Beaumont*, 50; OC XIII:1, 227.

47. AT, "Conversation with Mr. Wainwright, Anglican Minister," in *Tocqueville and Beaumont*, 331; OP I:225.

48. AT to LK, June 29, 1831, in *Tocqueville and Beaumont*, 50; OC XIII:1, 227.

49. AT to LK, May 18, 1831, in *Tocqueville and Beaumont*, 20; OC XIII:1, 224.

50. AT to Chabrol, June 9, 1831, in *Tocqueville and Beaumont*, 38; OC XVII:1, 88; LC, 185.

51. AT to Eugène Stöffels, June 28, 1831, in *Tocqueville and Beaumont*, 49; OC XVII:1, 96.

52. GB to Mother, June 7, 1831, in *Tocqueville and Beaumont*, 33–34; GB, *Lettres d'Amérique*, 59–60.

53. AT to LK, May 18, 1831, in *Tocqueville and Beaumont*, 21; OC XIII:1, 224.

54. AT to LK, June 29, 1831, in *Tocqueville and Beaumont*, 49; OC XIII:1, 225–26.

55. AT to Édouard, May 28, 1831, in *Tocqueville and Beaumont*, 24; OC XIV, 92.

56. AT to LK, June 29, 1831, in *Tocqueville and Beaumont*, 55; OC XIII:1, 233–34.

57. GB to his brother Jules, July 4, 1831, in *Tocqueville and Beaumont*, 60–61; GB, *Lettres d'Amérique*, 76–77.

58. John Niven, *Martin Van Buren: The Romantic Age of American Politics* (Newtown, CT: American Political Biography Press, 1983), 109–10; Herbert D. A. Donovan, *The Barnburners: A Study of the Internal Movements in the Political History of New York State and of the Resulting Changes in Political Affiliation, 1830–1852* (New York: New York University Press, 1925), 7–25; on the political economy of distribution, see L. Ray Gunn, *The Decline of Authority: Public Economic Policy and Political Development in New York, 1800–1860* (Ithaca, NY: Cornell University Press, 1988), 99–143.

59. GB to Jules, July 4, 1831, in *Tocqueville and Beaumont*, 62–63; GB, *Lettres d'Amérique*, 79.

60. GB to his sister Eugénie, July 14, 1831, in *Tocqueville and Beaumont*, 72–73; GB, *Lettres d'Amérique*, 90–91.

61. AT to Chabrol, July 16, 1831, in *Tocqueville and Beaumont*, 78–79; OC XVII:1, 98–99; LC, 205.

62. GB to Jules, July 4, 1831, in *Tocqueville and Beaumont*, 62; GB, *Lettres d'Amérique*, 79.

63. Daniel Walker Howe, *What Hath God Wrought: The Transformation of America, 1815–1848* (New York: Oxford University Press, 2007), 382.

64. Beaumont eventually wrote a note on the case in *Marie*; see *Tocqueville and Beaumont*, 545–46. AT remained silent on the movement. On the antimasonic fervor of this era, see Kevin Butterfield, *The Making of Tocqueville's America: Law and Association in the Early United States* (Chicago: University of Chicago Press, 2015), 171–82.

65. GB to Jules, July 4, 1831, in *Tocqueville and Beaumont*, 62; GB, *Lettres d'Amérique*, 78.

66. Nathan Miller, *The Enterprise of a Free People: Aspects of Economic Development in New York State during the Canal Period, 1792–1838* (Ithaca, NY: Cornell University Press, 1962), 77–91.

67. GB to Eugénie, July 14, 1831, in *Tocqueville and Beaumont*, 77; GB, *Lettres d'Amérique*, 95.

68. AT to Chabrol, July 16, 1831, in *Tocqueville and Beaumont*, 79; OC XVII:1, 99; LC, 205.

69. GB to Eugénie, July 14, 1831, in *Tocqueville and Beaumont*, 73; GB, *Lettres d'Amérique*, 92.

70. Whitney R. Cross, *The Burned-Over District: The Social and Intellectual History of Enthusiastic Religion in Western New York, 1800–1850* (Ithaca, NY: Cornell University Press, 2015); see also Paul E. Johnson, *A Shopkeeper's Millennium: Society and Revivals in Rochester, NY: 1815–1837*

(New York: Hill & Wang, 1978); and Mary P. Ryan, *Cradle of the Middle Class: The Family in Oneida County, New York, 1790–1865* (New York: Cambridge University Press, 1981).

71. GB to Eugénie, July 14, 1831, in *Tocqueville and Beaumont*, 69; GB, *Lettres d'Amérique*, 87.

72. AT realized the influence of evangelical religion only much later. It is only in a draft of DA II, part 2, chapter 12, that he described a scene of evangelical zeal, not a camp meeting but an imagined indoor scene in a Methodist chapel, yet did not incorporate it in the final text; see OP II, 1123–24 (in part translated in Leo Damrosch, *Tocqueville's Discovery of America* [New York: Farrar, Straus and Giroux, 2010], 52). AT most likely took at his model the Shaker meeting he had witnessed outside Albany.

73. GB to Jules, July 4, 1831, in *Tocqueville and Beaumont*, 67; GB, *Lettres d'Amérique*, 84.

74. Cooper, *Notions of the Americans*, 247.

75. GB to Eugénie, July 14, 1831, in *Tocqueville and Beaumont*, 75; GB, *Lettres d'Amérique*, 94.

76. AT, "Two Weeks in the Wilderness" (hereafter "Two Weeks"), in *Tocqueville and Beaumont*, 402; OP I:361.

77. German novelist Sophie von La Roche had first narrated a fictionalized account; see Victor Lange, "Visitors to Lake Oneida: An Account of the Background of Sophie von La Roche's Novel *Erscheinungen am See Oneida*," *Symposium: A Quarterly Journal in Modern Literature* 2, no. 1 (1948): 48–78. As a child, AT read the French translation of Campe's adaptation "Voyage au Lac Oneida" in the Bibliothèque géographique et instructive des jeunes gens, ou Recueil de voyages intéressants dans toutes les parties du monde. Pour l'instruction et l'amusement de la jeunesse (Paris: J.-E.-G. Dufour, 1802–3).

78. AT, "The Journey to Oneida Lake," in *Tocqueville and Beaumont*, 399; OP I:355–56, 358–59.

79. AT to Émilie, July 25, 1831, in *Tocqueville and Beaumont*, 87; OC XIV, 121.

80. AT to Mother, July 17, 1831, in *Tocqueville and Beaumont*, 82; OC XIV, 118.

81. AT, "Conversation with Mr. Elam Lynds, in Syracuse," July 7, 1831, Non-alphabetic Notebook 1, in *Tocqueville and Beaumont*, 214; OP I:35–36.

82. Solitary cells in Auburn were initially only three and a half feet eight inches by seven feet six inches, but soon thought way too small; see New York Writers' Project, *New York: A Guide to the Empire State* (New York: Oxford University Press, 1940), 199.

83. AT and GB to the French Interior Minister, July 14, 1831, in *Tocqueville and Beaumont*, 449; OC IV:2, 22.

84. AT, "Conversation with Mr. Elam Lynds, in Syracuse," July 7, 1831, Non-alphabetic Notebook 1, in *Tocqueville and Beaumont*, 216; OP I:38.

85. AT and GB to the French Interior Minister, July 14, 1831, in *Tocqueville and Beaumont*, 451; OC IV:2, 23.

86. AT, "Second Conversation with Elam Lynds," Non-alphabetic Notebook 1, in *Tocqueville and Beaumont*, 217–18; OP I:39–40.

87. Edward Livingston, *Code of Procedure: For Giving Effect to the Penal Code of the State of Louisiana* (New-Orleans, 1825) and *Code of Reform and Prison Discipline: Being the Third Part of the System of Penal Law Prepared for the State of Louisiana* (New-Orleans, 1826).

88. AT would meet Edward Livingston in Washington, DC, toward the end of the trip, but it is not clear that AT associated him with the Livingstons he had befriended in New York, as

AT referred to him only as coming from Louisiana. Early in his career, Livingston had experienced political difficulties in New York and moved to Louisiana.

89. OC IV:1, 202, 204–5.

90. AT to Émilie, July 25, 1831, in *Tocqueville and Beaumont*, 88; OC XIV, 122.

91. AT, "Conversation with Mr. Spencer, Canandaigua," July 17 and 18, 1831, Non-alphabetic Notebook 1, in *Tocqueville and Beaumont*, 219; OP I:43. Spencer was a Jacksonian before moving over to the National Republicans. In September 1831, the antimason party tried to establish itself on a permanent basis; see Lee Benson, *The Concept of Jacksonian Democracy: New York as a Test Case* (Princeton, NJ: Princeton University Press, 1961), 57. Beaumont's single surviving page of his diary, dated September 1831, mentions a great division between Jackson and National Republican Clay only mistakenly to add that their political differences did not affect local politics and assert again these American political debates had no relevance for Europe, in *Tocqueville and Beaumont*, 133.

92. AT, "Conversation with Mr. Spencer, Canandaigua," July 17 and 18, 1831, Non-alphabetic Notebook 1, in *Tocqueville and Beaumont*, 218; OP I:41–42.

93. AT, "Two Weeks," in *Tocqueville and Beaumont*, 403; OP I:361.

94. AT, "Indians," July 19, 1831, Alphabetic Notebook A, in *Tocqueville and Beaumont*, 325–26; OP I:215–17.

95. AT, "Two Weeks," in *Tocqueville and Beaumont*, 403–4; OP I:362–64.

96. AT, July 22, 1831, Travel Notebook 2, in *Tocqueville and Beaumont*, 295; OP I:152.

97. John T. Fierst, "Return to 'Civilization': John Tanner's Troubled Years at Sault Ste. Marie," *Minnesota History* 50 (Spring 1986): 23–36.

98. *A Narrative of the Captivity and Adventures of John Tanner (U.S. Interpreter at the Sault de Ste. Marie): During Thirty Years Residence among the Indians in the Interior of North America*, prepared for the press by Edwin James (New York, 1830); *Mémoires de John Tanner ou trente années dans les déserts de l'Amérique du Nord*, trans. Ernest de Blosseville (Paris, 1835).

99. AT to Chabrol, August 17, 1831, in *Tocqueville and Beaumont*, 112; OC XVII:1, 101; LC, 216.

100. AT to Grancey, October 10, 1831, in *Tocqueville and Beaumont*, 142; OC XVII:1, 112; LC, 232.

101. AT, July 23, 1831, Travel Notebook 2, in *Tocqueville and Beaumont*, 296; OP I:153. AT would later, in Philadelphia, meet his older brother, Nicholas, president of the Second Bank of the United States who was about to engage in a major fight with Andrew Jackson.

102. Without mentioning either the Land Ordinance of 1785 or the Northwest Ordinance of 1787.

103. GB to Chabrol, August 2, 1831, in *Tocqueville and Beaumont*, 92; GB, *Lettres d'Amérique*, 112.

104. AT, "Two Weeks," in *Tocqueville and Beaumont*, 407; OP I:368.

105. AT to Chabrol, August 17, 1831, in *Tocqueville and Beaumont*, 112; OC XVII:1, 101; LC, 216.

106. AT to Chabrol, August 17, 1831, in *Tocqueville and Beaumont*, 113; OC XVII:1, 102; LC, 217.

107. AT, "Two Weeks," in *Tocqueville and Beaumont*, 408; OP I:369.

108. AT, "Two Weeks," in *Tocqueville and Beaumont*, 412; OP I:375.

109. GB to Chabrol, August 2, 1831, in *Tocqueville and Beaumont*, 93–94; GB, *Lettres d'Amérique*, 109; "Two Weeks," in *Tocqueville and Beaumont*, 416–47; OP I:381. AT drew of a portrait of courageous wives on the frontier and the spread of literacy, with Shakespeare and Milton on the shelves inside log cabins. In Tennessee, they drew a similar portrait in poor southern country, slavery added. Moreover, "the philosophical, argumentative spirit of the English exists here as it does

throughout America," and there is "an astonishing circulation of letters and newspapers." AT, "Kentucky, Tennessee," Notebook E, in *Tocqueville and Beaumont*, 361; OP I:286.

110. AT, "Two Weeks," in *Tocqueville and Beaumont*, 418; OP I:383.

111. GB to Chabrol, August 2, 1831, in *Tocqueville and Beaumont*, 94; GB, *Lettres d'Amérique*, 113.

112. AT, "Two Weeks," in *Tocqueville and Beaumont*, 412, 422, 425; OP I:375, 388–89, 392.

113. AT, "Two Weeks," in *Tocqueville and Beaumont*, 429; OP I:398.

114. AT, "Two Weeks," in *Tocqueville and Beaumont*, 432; OP I:401.

115. AT, "Two Weeks," in *Tocqueville and Beaumont*, 432–33; OP I:401–3.

116. AT, July 22, 1831, Travel Notebook 2, in *Tocqueville and Beaumont*, 295–96; OP I:152.

117. AT, "Two Weeks," in *Tocqueville and Beaumont*, 434–35; OP I:404–6.

118. AT, "Two Weeks," in *Tocqueville and Beaumont*, 440; OP I:413. AT uses the same language in a letter to Eugène Stöffels, October 18, 1831, in *Œuvres complètes d'Alexis de Tocqueville publiées par Madame de Tocqueville* (Paris, 1865–67), V: 420–21, and OC XVII: 1, 123–24.

119. GB to Achille, August 11, 1831, in *Tocqueville and Beaumont*, 101–2; GB, *Lettres d'Amérique*, 120.

120. A beautiful text full of romantic imagery in a style reminiscent of Chateaubriand's, not the classical restraint of DA, published posthumously by Beaumont in 1861.

121. GB to Achille, August 11, 1831, in *Tocqueville and Beaumont*, 104; GB, *Lettres d'Amérique*, 121–22. AT's and GB's notes of the excursion are corroborated by the journal of an English tourist on board, Godfrey T. Vigne, who wrote two accounts in the *Detroit Courier* of August 18 and September 1, 1831, as well as in his *Six Months in America* (Philadelphia, 1833), 137–49.

122. See Keith R. Widder, *Battle for the Soul: Métis Children Encounter Evangelical Protestants at Mackinaw Mission, 1823–1837* (Lansing: Michigan State University Press, 1999), 91–93.

123. "Conversation with Mr. Mullon," Non-alphabetic Notebook 1, in *Tocqueville and Beaumont*, 222; OP I:46.

124. In the winter of 1780, transporting its buildings on ice across the lake. Current Mackinaw city on mainland was not platted until 1857; today's Michilimackinac did not exist during AT and GB's visit.

125. GB to Achille, August 11, 1831, in *Tocqueville and Beaumont*, 100; GB, *Lettres d'Amérique*, 119–20.

126. AT, "Conversation with Major Lamard," August 12, 1831, Non-alphabetic Notebook 1, in *Tocqueville and Beaumont*, 225; OP I:50.

127. GB to Achille, August 11, 1831, in *Tocqueville and Beaumont*, 108; GB, *Lettres d'Amérique*, 126.

128. AT, August 12, 1831, Travel Notebook 2, in *Tocqueville and Beaumont*, 306; OP I:165.

129. AT to Émilie, September 7, 1831, in *Tocqueville and Beaumont*, 125–26; OC XIV, 131–32.

130. AT to Mother, August 21, 1831, in *Tocqueville and Beaumont*, 114–15; OC XIV, 126–27.

131. AT to Dalmassy, another young magistrate at Versailles, late August 1831, in *Tocqueville and Beaumont*, 118; OC XVII:1, 104.

132. GB to Father, September 5, 1831, in *Tocqueville and Beaumont*, 120; GB, *Lettres d'Amérique*, 141.

133. AT, August 27, 1831, Alphabetic Notebook A, in *Tocqueville and Beaumont*, 316; OP I:202.

134. AT, August 31, 1831 and "General Remarks," September 1, 1831, Alphabetic Notebook A, in *Tocqueville and Beaumont*, 321–22; OP I:202, 207, 209–10. For an overview of Tocqueville's

exploration of Canada, see Simon Langlois, "Alexis de Tocqueville, un sociologue au Bas-Canada," *The Tocqueville Review / La revue Tocqueville* 27, no. 2 (2006): 553–73; Claude Corbo, "Présentation," Alexis de Tocqueville, *Regards sur le Bas-Canada* (Montréal: Typo, 2003), 7–46; and Corbo, *Tocqueville chez les perdants* (Montreal: Del Busso, 2016).

135. AT, "Conversation with Mr. Neilson," August 27, 1831, Non-alphabetic Notebook 1, in *Tocqueville and Beaumont*, 229; OP I:54.

136. GB to Father, September 5, 1831, in *Tocqueville and Beaumont*, 121–22; GB, *Lettres d'Amérique*, 142.

137. AT, August 29, 1831, Alphabetic Notebook A, in *Tocqueville and Beaumont*, 321; OP I:209.

138. AT, August 27, 1831, Alphabetic Notebook A, in *Tocqueville and Beaumont*, 317; OP I:204.

139. AT to Émilie, September 7, 1831, in *Tocqueville and Beaumont*, 126; OC XIV, 132.

140. AT to Lesueur, September 7, 1831, in *Tocqueville and Beaumont*, 124; OC XIV, 129.

141. GB to Father, September 5, 1831, in *Tocqueville and Beaumont*, 119; GB, *Lettres d'Amérique*, 140.

142. AT, "Conversation with Mr. Neilson," August 27, 1831, Non-alphabetic Notebook 1, in *Tocqueville and Beaumont*, 231; OP I:58.

143. GB to Father, September 5, 1831, in *Tocqueville and Beaumont*, 120; GB, *Lettres d'Amérique*, 140.

144. AT to Hervé de Tocqueville, August 14, 1831, in *Tocqueville and Beaumont*, 110; OC XIV, 124.

145. AT, August 27, 1831, Alphabetic Notebook A, in *Tocqueville and Beaumont*, 319; OP I:205.

# Chapter 3

1. Alexis de Tocqueville (hereafter AT) to Freslon, July 30, 1854, *Œuvres complètes* (hereaffer OC) XVII:3, 164–66; and *Tocqueville: Lettres choisies, Souvenirs*, ed. Françoise Mélonio and Laurence Guellec (Paris: Gallimard, 2003) (hereafter LC), 1107.

2. AT, September 20, 1831, "Massachusetts," Alphabetic Notebook A, in *Alexis de Tocqueville and Gustave de Beaumont in America: Their Friendship and Their Travels*, ed. Olivier Zunz, trans. Arthur Goldhammer (Charlottesville: University of Virginia Press, 2010) (hereafter *Tocqueville and Beaumont*), 6, 329; *Œuvres* Pléiade (hereafter OP) I:221.

3. Gustave de Beaumont (hereafter GB) to Jules, September 16, 1831, in *Tocqueville and Beaumont*, 128; GB, *Lettres d'Amérique, 1831–1832*, ed. André Jardin and George W. Pierson (Paris: Presses Universitaires de France, 1973), 46.

4. AT to Grancey, October 10, 1831, in *Tocqueville and Beaumont*, 140; OC XVII:1, 110; LC, 230.

5. GB to Jules, September 16, 1831, in *Tocqueville and Beaumont*, 128; GB, *Lettres d'Amérique*, 146.

6. AT to Chabrol, October 7, 1831, in *Tocqueville and Beaumont*, 138; OC XVII:1, 108.

7. AT, "General Remarks," September 18, 1831, Non-alphabetic Notebook 1, Boston, in *Tocqueville and Beaumont*, 234; OP I:61.

8. GB to Jules, September 16, 1831, in *Tocqueville and Beaumont*, 130; GB, *Lettres d'Amérique*, 148.

9. George W. Pierson, *Tocqueville in America* (1938; repr., Baltimore: Johns Hopkins University Press, 1996), 362; Robert A. McCauchey, *Josiah Quincy, 1772–1864: The Last Federalist* (Cambridge, MA: Harvard University Press, 1974); Samuel Eliot Morison, *Harrison Gray Otis, 1765–1848: The Urbane Federalist* (Boston: Houghton Mifflin, 1969).

10. Morison, *Harrison Gray Otis*, 219–21.

11. David B. Tyack, *George Ticknor and the Boston Brahmins* (Cambridge, MA: Harvard University Press, 1967), 90–128.

12. Frank Freidel, *Francis Lieber: Nineteenth Century Liberal* (Baton Rouge: Louisiana State University Press, 1947).

13. AT, September 22, 1831, Non-alphabetic Notebooks 2 and 3, in *Tocqueville and Beaumont*, 240; OP I:70.

14. GB to Jules, September 16, 1831; and GB diary fragments, in *Tocqueville and Beaumont*, 129, 132; GB, *Lettres d'Amérique*, 147, 151.

15. "Second Reply to Hayne," January 1830, in *American Speeches: Political Oratory from the Revolution to the Civil War* (New York: Library of America, 2006), 233.

16. AT, October 1, 1831, Non-alphabetic Notebooks 2 and 3, in *Tocqueville and Beaumont*, 243; OP I:75.

17. Van Wyck Brooks, *The Flowering of New England*, rev. ed. (New York: E. P. Dutton, 1940), 122.

18. AT, September 29, 1831, Non-alphabetic Notebooks 2 and 3, in *Tocqueville and Beaumont*, 241–42; OP I:72–73; Alexander Everett, a former US ambassador to Spain, concurred.

19. AT to Hervé de Tocqueville (hereafter HT), October 7, 1831, in *Tocqueville and Beaumont*, 138; AT, September 29, 1831, Non-alphabetic Notebooks 2 and 3, in *Tocqueville and Beaumont*, 242; OP I:73.

20. AT, *Democracy in America*, trans. Arthur Goldhammer, ed. Olivier Zunz (New York: Library of America, 2004), (hereafter DA I [1835] or DA II [1840]), I, 45; OP II:44.

21. "Observations by Jared Sparks on the Government of Towns in Massachusetts," in Herbert B. Adams, "Jared Sparks and Alexis de Tocqueville," *Johns Hopkins University Studies in Historical and Political Science* 16, no. 12 (1898): 22–23.

22. AT to HT, October 7, 1831, in *Tocqueville and Beaumont*, 137–38; OC XIV, 138.

23. Samuel Freeman, *The Town Officer; or, The Power and Duty of Selectmen, Town Clerks . . . and Other Town Officers, as Contained in the Laws of the Commonwealth of Massachusetts*, 7th ed. (Boston, 1808).

24. AT to Sparks, December 2, 1831, in *Tocqueville and Beaumont*, 182; OC VII, 36–37.

25. DA I, 42–43.

26. Sparks to AT, January 11, 1832, in "Observations by Jared Sparks," 17.

27. "Observations by Jared Sparks," 7.

28. DA I, 68; OP II:65.

29. AT to Sparks, December 2, 1831, in *Tocqueville and Beaumont*, 182–84; OC VII, 37.

30. See Johann N. Neem, *Creating a Nation of Joiners: Democracy and Civil Society in Early National Massachusetts* (Cambridge, MA: Harvard University Press, 2008), 21–22, 67–68, 154–55, 186n15.

31. "Observations by Jared Sparks," 25; Barnes v. First Parish in Falmouth, 6 Mass, 400 (1810).

32. In 1819, in a famous sermon given on the occasion of Sparks's ordination in Baltimore, see Daniel Walker Howe, *The Unitarian Conscience: Harvard Moral Philosophy, 1805–1861*, with a new introduction (Middletown, CT: Wesleyan University Press, 1988), 100–101; Paul K. Conkin, *American Originals: Homemade Varieties of Christianity* (Chapel Hill: University of North Carolina Press, 1997), 67–73.

33. Dwight to AT, Boston, September 16, 1831, Non-alphabetic Notebook 1, in *Tocqueville and Beaumont*, 233; OP I:61.

34. October 2, 1831, Non-alphabetic Notebooks 2 and 3, in *Tocqueville and Beaumont*, 245; OP I:78.

35. AT to Chabrol, October 26, 1831, in *Tocqueville and Beaumont*, 157; OC XVII:1, 130; LC, 243–44; GB said the same to his father on June 29, 1831; *Tocqueville and Beaumont*, 57; GB, *Lettres d'Amérique*, 72.

36. See H. Richard Niebuhr, *The Social Sources of Denominationalism* (New York, 1929), and *The Kingdom of God in America* (New York: Willett, Clark & Co., 1937); Nathan O. Hatch, *The Democratization of American Christianity* (New Haven, CT: Yale University Press, 1989).

37. Pierson, *Tocqueville in America*, 428–30; *Reports of the Prison Discipline Society, Boston*, vol. 1, *1826–1835* (Boston, 1855); on separating inmates, 11–12.

38. GB to Jules, September 16, 1831, in *Tocqueville and Beaumont*, 131; GB, *Lettres d'Amérique*, 149; AT, September 21 and 28, 1831, Non-alphabetic Notebooks 2 and 3, in *Tocqueville and Beaumont*, 237–38, 240–41; OP I:66–68, 71; Marjorie B. Cohn, *Francis Calley Gray and Art Collecting in America* (Cambridge, MA: Harvard University Art Museums, 1986), 82–93.

39. GB and AT, *On the Penitentiary System in the United States and Its Application in France*, trans. Francis Lieber (Philadelphia, 1833), in OC IV:1, 360–65.

40. DA I, 314–15; OP II:313–15.

41. GB, Diary fragments, September 1831, in *Tocqueville and Beaumont*, 132; GB, *Lettres d'Amérique*, 150.

42. AT, "Mores," September 21, 1831, Alphabetic Notebook B, in *Tocqueville and Beaumont*, 337; OP I:242.

43. GB to Mother, June 7, 1831, in *Tocqueville and Beaumont*, 35; GB, *Lettres d'Amérique*, 61. AT and GB, *On the Penitentiary System in the United States and Its Application in France* (1833), in OC IV:1, 245.

44. AT to Alexandrine, October 18, 1831, in *Tocqueville and Beaumont*, 147–48; OC XIV, 141.

45. AT to unknown, November 8, 1831, in *Tocqueville and Beaumont*, 166; OC XVII:1, 142–43.

46. AT to Chabrol, November 19, 1831, in *Tocqueville and Beaumont*, 168; OC XVII:1, 144–45.

47. AT to Mother, October 24, 1831, in *Tocqueville and Beaumont*, 150; OC XIV, 143.

48. GB to Father, October 16, 1831, in *Tocqueville and Beaumont*, 147; GB, *Lettres d'Amérique*, 165.

49. GB to Father, October 16, 1831, in *Tocqueville and Beaumont*, 146; GB, *Lettres d'Amérique*, 164.

50. AT to Chabrol, October 26, 1831, in *Tocqueville and Beaumont*, 156–57; OC XVII:1, 129–30; LC, 242.

51. AT, November 6, 1831, Travel Notebook 3, in *Tocqueville and Beaumont*, 310; OP I:177.

52. GB to Jules, September 16, 1831, in *Tocqueville and Beaumont*, 126; GB, *Lettres d'Amérique*, 143; AT, "Convention," October 14, 1831, Alphabetic Notebook B, in *Tocqueville and Beaumont*, 334; OP I:233–34.

53. "Convention," October 14, 1831, Alphabetic Notebook B, in *Tocqueville and Beaumont*, 334; OP I:233–34; Daniel Peart, *Lobbyists and the Making of US Tariff Policy, 1816–1861* (Baltimore: Johns Hopkins University Press, 2018), 102.

54. On the Force Bill and military preparations, Sean Wilentz, *The Rise of American Democracy: Jefferson to Lincoln* (New York: Norton, 2005), 384.

55. AT, Boston, October 1, 1831, Non-alphabetic Notebooks 2 and 3, in *Tocqueville and Beaumont*, 243; OP I:74. Peart, *Lobbyists*, 105.

56. Peart, *Lobbyists*, 104.

57. AT, "Convention, Id.," October 14, 1831, Alphabetic Notebook B, in *Tocqueville and Beaumont*, 335; OP I:234.

58. AT, "Association," October 10, 1831, Alphabetic Notebook B, in *Tocqueville and Beaumont*, 333; OP I:232.

59. AT, November 3, 1831, Non-alphabetic Notebooks 2 and 3, in *Tocqueville and Beaumont*, 262; OP I:101.

60. AT had met John Biddle, Nicholas's brother, in Detroit where he was the land agent, but it is not clear whether AT made the connection between these two informants.

61. November 18, 1831, Non-alphabetic Notebooks 2 and 3, in *Tocqueville and Beaumont*, 265; OP I:104.

62. John Quincy Adams, "January 28, 1832," *Diaries, 1821–1848* (New York: Library of America, 2017), 287.

63. AT, "Great and Minor Parties," January 14, 1832, Notebook E, in *Tocqueville and Beaumont*, 342; OP I:257–58; DA I, 199; OP II:195–96.

64. On Biddle's complex negotiations with the Whigs, see Thomas Payne Govan, *Nicholas Biddle: Nationalist and Public Banker, 1786–1844* (Chicago: University of Chicago Press, 1959), 260–74.

65. An Anti-Masonic Party convention was held in Baltimore, Maryland on September 26, 1831, and was attended by ninety-six delegates from ten states, who for the first time nominated a candidate for president, a practice soon to be followed by National Republicans, then Democrats.

66. AT, November 3, 1831, Non-alphabetic Notebooks 2 and 3, in *Tocqueville and Beaumont*, 260–61; OP I:98–99.

67. AT, October 27, 1831, Non-alphabetic Notebooks 2 and 3, in *Tocqueville and Beaumont*, 250; OP I:84.

68. AT, November 5, 1831, Non-alphabetic Notebooks 2 and 3, in *Tocqueville and Beaumont*, 263; OP I:102.

69. AT, October 16, 1831, Non-alphabetic Notebooks 2 and 3, in *Tocqueville and Beaumont*, 249; OP I:82.

70. AT, November 5, 1831, Non-alphabetic Notebooks 2 and 3, in *Tocqueville and Beaumont*, 263–64; OP I:103.

71. AT, November 2, 1831, Non-alphabetic Notebooks 2 and 3, in *Tocqueville and Beaumont*, 260; OP I:97.

72. AT, November 1, 1831, Non-alphabetic Notebooks 2 and 3, in *Tocqueville and Beaumont*, 257; OP I:94.

73. AT, October 28, 1831, Non-alphabetic Notebooks 2 and 3, in *Tocqueville and Beaumont*, 251; OP I:86.

74. AT to LK, June 29, 1831, in *Tocqueville and Beaumont*, 50; OC XIII:1, 227.

75. AT to Chabrol, October 26, 1831, in *Tocqueville and Beaumont*, 159–60; OC XVII:1, 133; LC, 246.

76. GB to sister-in-law Félicie, October 26, 1831, in *Tocqueville and Beaumont*, 152; GB, *Lettres d'Amérique*, 169.

77. François-Alexandre-Frédéric, duc de La Rochefoucauld-Liancourt, *Des prisons de Philadelphie: Par un Européen* (Paris, 1796); J. P. Brissot, *Nouveau voyage dans les États-Unis de l'Amérique septentrionale* (Paris, 1791), 2:161–89.

78. *Acts of the General Assembly Relating to the New Eastern State Penitentiary: And to the New Prisons of the City and County of Philadelphia* (Philadelphia: J. W. Allen, 1831), 3.

79. Norman Johnston, *Eastern State Penitentiary: Crucible of Good Intentions* (Philadelphia: Philadelphia Museum of Arts, 1994), 35.

80. AT and GB to the French Minister of the Interior, November 10, 1831, in *Tocqueville and Beaumont*, 463; OC IV:2, 38.

81. AT and GB, Excerpts from Beaumont and Tocqueville, *On the Penitentiary System and Its Application in France*, Appendix 7: Study of the Philadelphia Penitentiary (October 1831), in *Tocqueville and Beaumont*, 490; OC IV:1, 339. The prison housed only male inmates at the time of the visit, but two African American women were incarcerated only two months later; see Leslie Patrick, "Ann Hinson: A Little-Known Woman in the Country's Premier Prison, Eastern State Penitentiary, 1831," *Pennsylvania History: A Journal of Mid-Atlantic Studies* 67 (Summer 2000): 361–75.

82. See Roger Boesche, "The Prison: Tocqueville's Model for Despotism," in *The Western Political Quarterly* 33 (December 1980): 552; Jane Brox, *Silence: A Social History of One of the Last Understood Elements of Our Lives* (Boston: Houghton Mifflin Harcourt, 2019), 8–9, on Charles Williams, an eighteen-year-old Black farmer taken hooded to his cell in 1829.

83. AT and GB, Excerpts from Beaumont and Tocqueville, *On the Penitentiary System and Its Application in France*, Appendix 7: Study of the Philadelphia Penitentiary (October 1831), in *Tocqueville and Beaumont*, 490; OC IV:1, 339.

84. AT and GB to the French Minister of the Interior, November 10, 1831, in *Tocqueville and Beaumont*, 461–62; OC IV:2, 36–37.

85. AT and GB, Excerpts from Beaumont and Tocqueville, *On the Penitentiary System and Its Application in France*, Appendix 7: Study of the Philadelphia Penitentiary (October 1831), in *Tocqueville and Beaumont*, 482, 483, 486; OC IV:1, 328, 330–31, 334.

86. AT and GB to the French Minister of the Interior, November 10, 1831, in *Tocqueville and Beaumont*, 456; OC IV:2, 30.

87. Thomas B. McElwee, *A Concise History of the Eastern State Penitentiary of Pennsylvania Together with a Detailed Statement of the Proceedings of the Committee Appointed by the Legislature* (Philadelphia, 1835), 18, 143.

88. GB to Félicie, October 26, 1831, in *Tocqueville and Beaumont*, 153; GB, *Lettres d'Amérique*, 169.

89. AT, October 29, 1831, Travel Notebook 3, in *Tocqueville and Beaumont*, 308; OP I:173–74.

90. AT, October 27, 1831, Non-alphabetic Notebooks 2 and 3, in *Tocqueville and Beaumont*, 250; OP I:85.

91. GB to Achille, November 8, 1831, in *Tocqueville and Beaumont*, 163; GB, *Lettres d'Amérique*, 175–76.

92. AT to Mother, October 24, 1831, in *Tocqueville and Beaumont*, 151; OC XIV, 144.

93. GB to Achille, November 8, 1831, in *Tocqueville and Beaumont*, 161; GB, *Lettres d'Amérique*, 173.

94. GB to Achille, November 8, 1831, in *Tocqueville and Beaumont*, 161; GB, *Lettres d'Amérique*, 173.

95. AT, November 5, 1831, Non-alphabetic Notebooks 2 and 3, in *Tocqueville and Beaumont*, 263; OP I:102.

96. November 25, 1831, Travel Notebook 3, in *Tocqueville and Beaumont*, 310; OP I:178.

97. Opened in 1826, *Tocqueville and Beaumont*, 464n6; and Pierson, *Tocqueville in America*, 543–44.

98. GB, Diary fragments, December 1831, in *Tocqueville and Beaumont*, 175; GB, *Lettres d'Amérique*, 200.

99. Ohio, Notebook E, in *Tocqueville and Beaumont*, 356; OP I:279.

100. Cincinnati, Notebook E, in *Tocqueville and Beaumont*, 359; OP I:283.

101. Frances Trollope, *Domestic Manners of the Americans* (1839; New York: Dodd, Mead, 1901), 2:64. She also complained that the absence of Blacks made it hard to find servants.

102. Ohio, Notebook E, in *Tocqueville and Beaumont*, 357; OP I:279–80.

103. Second conversation with Mr. Walker, Non-alphabetic Notebooks 2 and 3, in *Tocqueville and Beaumont*, 270; OP I:110. Thus, William Henry Harrison (1773–1841) had earned notoriety as an Indian fighter in the Northwest and solidified his fame with his victory at Tippecanoe in 1811, served as the governor of the Indiana Territory, a representative and senator in the US Congress, and a minister to Colombia, was defeated locally in a bid for the Senate in 1831 after he returned to his Ohio farm in 1829.

104. Non-alphabetic Notebooks 2 and 3, in *Tocqueville and Beaumont*, 267, 273; OP I:107, 114.

105. DA I, 398n35; OP II:400n.

106. AT to HT, December 20, 1831, OC XIV, 156; DA I, 399; OP I:401.

107. October 14, 1821, Travel Notebook 3, in *Tocqueville and Beaumont*, 307; OP I:171.

108. "Alexis de Tocqueville at Sandy Bridge," The Historical Marker Database, https://www .hmdb.org/m.asp?m=52647, accessed July 16, 2021.

109. Except for a brief visit, off the boat. "Report on the Plantations of Louisiana." "Today, December 31, 1831, I visited a beautiful sugar plantation situated on the Mississippi 50 leagues from New Orleans. It employs 70 slaves. Its revenue, I was told, is approximately 5 or 6,000 dollars per year, net of all expenses, or 25 to 30,000 francs." Notebook E, in *Tocqueville and Beaumont*, 342; OP I:258.

110. AT to HT, in *Tocqueville and Beaumont*, 191; OC XIV, 156–57.

111. Kentucky, Notebook E, in *Tocqueville and Beaumont*, 362; OP I:287–88.

112. On this hard reality, see Edmund S. Morgan, *American Slavery, American Freedom* (New York: Norton, 1975).

113. AT to Mother, December 25, 1831, in *Tocqueville and Beaumont*, 193; OC XIV, 158.

114. Elections, Notebook E, in *Tocqueville and Beaumont*, 351–52; OP I:272.

115. AT to Mother, December 25, 1831, OC XIV, 160–61; and DA I, 374–75; OP II:377.

116. Indians, Notebook E, in *Tocqueville and Beaumont*, 343; OP I:259.

117. Marquis James, *The Raven: A Biography of Sam Houston* (Austin: University of Texas Press, 2016).

118. Indians, Notebook E, in *Tocqueville and Beaumont*, 345, OP I:261–62.

119. Conversation with M. Guillemin, Non-alphabetic Notebooks 2 and 3, in *Tocqueville and Beaumont*, 278; OP I:120.

120. Conversation with M. Mazureau, Non-alphabetic Notebooks 2 and 3, in *Tocqueville and Beaumont*, 276–77; OP I:117–19.

121. Pierson, *Tocqueville in America*, 628, see also Conversation with M. Guillemin, in *Tocqueville and Beaumont*, 277–80; OP I:180.

122. Conversation with Mr. Brown, Non-alphabetic Notebooks 2 and 3, in *Tocqueville and Beaumont*, 251–52; OP I:85–87.

123. AT to Chabrol, January 16, 1832, in *Tocqueville and Beaumont*, 200; OC XVII:1, 157.

124. Conversation with M. Guillemin, Non-alphabetic Notebooks 2 and 3, in *Tocqueville and Beaumont*, 279; OP I:121.

125. Conversation with Gilpin, Notebook F, in *Tocqueville and Beaumont*, 366; OP I:297.

126. Joseph McIlvaine, lawyer and city recorder, sent three memoranda to AT in February 1832, one on penal codes, one on the judicial system in Pennsylvania, and one on Louisiana, described in Pierson, *Tocqueville in America*, 530–35; see also *Tocqueville and Beaumont*, 366–67.

127. Mark Fernandez, "Edward Livingston, America, and France: Making Law," in *Empires of the Imagination: Transatlantic Histories of the Louisiana Purchase*, ed. Peter J. Kastor and François Weil (Charlottesville: University of Virginia Press, 2009), 239–67; "Common Law," Notebook F, in *Tocqueville and Beaumont*, 381.

128. Travel Notebook 3, January 2, 1832, OP I:182.

129. AT to Édouard, January 20, 1832, in *Tocqueville and Beaumont*, 204; OC XIV, 165.

130. Conversation with Lawyer from Montgomery, Non-alphabetic Notebooks 2 and 3, in *Tocqueville and Beaumont*, 282; OP I:124–26.

131. Conversation with Mr. Poinsett, Non-alphabetic Notebooks 2 and 3, in *Tocqueville and Beaumont*, 283–90; OP I:126–36.

132. December 29, 1831, Notebook E, in *Tocqueville and Beaumont*, 349; OP I:266.

133. Knoxville, January 8, 1832, Travel Notebooks 4 and 5, in *Tocqueville and Beaumont*, 312; OP I:184–85; DA I, 370; OP II:372.

134. Conversation with Mr. Poinsett, Non-alphabetic Notebooks 2 and 3, in *Tocqueville and Beaumont*, 288; OP I:133.

135. GB to Mother, January 22, in *Tocqueville and Beaumont*, 203; GB, *Lettres d'Amérique*, 212.

136. John Quincy Adams, "January 28, 1832," *Diaries*, 287; and January 24, 1832, in *Tocqueville and Beaumont*, 290–91; OP I, 136–37.

137. GB to Mother, January 20, 1832, in *Tocqueville and Beaumont*, 201–2; GB, *Lettres d'Amérique*, 210.

138. AT to GB, April 1832, OC VIII:1, 111; AT to Édouard, January 20, 1831, in *Tocqueville and Beaumont*, 204; OC XIV, 165.

# Chapter 4

1. Alexis de Tocqueville (hereafter AT) to Chabrol, January 24, 1832, in *Alexis de Tocqueville and Gustave de Beaumont in America: Their Friendship and Their Travels*, ed. Olivier Zunz, trans. Arthur Goldhammer (Charlottesville: University of Virginia Press, 2010) (hereafter *Tocqueville and Beaumont*), 207; *Œuvres complètes* (hereafter OC) XVII:1, 159.

2. AT had joined them by April 10. OC VIII:1, 113 (visiting on April 6 but definitely there by April 10).

3. See H. A. C. Collingham, *The July Monarchy: A Political History of France, 1830–1848* (London: Longman, 1988), 67–68, and OC VIII:1, 111n16.

4. AT to Blanche de Kergorlay, April 10, 1832, OC XIII:1, 249.

5. Collingham, *The July Monarchy*, 68.

6. James T. Schleifer, *The Making of Tocqueville's* Democracy in America, 2nd ed. (Indianapolis: Liberty Fund, 200), 13.

7. If only Beaumont could join them in Saint-Germain, but this proved impractical. AT to Gustave de Beaumont (hereafter GB), April 10, 1832, OC VIII:1, 115.

8. His depression began in the United States, where he described himself as feeling "beset with a kind of heavy stupidity during the last month I spent in America"; AT to GB, April 4, 1832, OC VIII:1, 111.

9. AT to GB, April 4, 1832, OC VIII:1, 112.

10. AT to Eugène Stöffels, April 22, 1832, OC XVII:1, 171.

11. Chateaubriand, *Mémoires d'outre-tombe*, Bibliothèque de la Pléiade (Paris: Gallimard, 1951), 2:520.

12. Louis Blanc devoted a large part of his study of the decade to the never-resolved affair; see his *Histoire de dix ans, 1830–1840* (Paris, 1882), 182–202.

13. Some speculated the duke might have died because of an erotic exercise gone wrong. See Émile Lesueur, *Le dernier Condé: Louis-Henri-Joseph de Bourbon* (Paris: Librairie Félix Alcan, 1937), 253, 267; Emmanuel Maury, *Le dernier des Condé: La vie romanesque d'un prince de France* (Paris: Tallandier, 2019), 315–17.

14. Lesueur, *Le dernier Condé*, 261.

15. GB to AT, May 17, 1832, OC VIII:1, 116–18; GB's Legitimist father would soon help his son financially.

16. AT to procureur général, May 21, 1832, in Gustave de Beaumont, *Œuvres complètes d'Alexis de Tocqueville publiées par Madame de Tocqueville* (Paris, 1865–67), V:36.

17. AT to Chabrol, January 24, 1832, OC XVII:1, 159.

18. GB to AT, May 17, 1832, OC VIII:1, 117.

19. Introductory note, OC XIII:1, 247–48.

20. J. Lucas-Dubreton, *La princesse captive: La duchesse de Berry, 1832–1833* (Paris: Librairie académique Perrin, 1925).

21. André Jardin, *Tocqueville: A Biography*, trans. Lydia Davis and Robert Hemenway (Baltimore: Johns Hopkins University Press, 1998), 188–89.

22. Introductory note, OC XIII:1, 247–48.

23. GB to AT, September 3, 1837, OC VIII:1, 224–25.

24. Second of three letters. Copy in AT's library at Tocqueville.

25. AT, "Note préparée et non publiée à l'occasion de l'élection du 10 juillet 1842," OC III:2, 71.

26. AT, "Discours prononcé en faveur de M. Louis de Kergorlay, le 9 mars 1833," OC XIII:1, 325, 26.

27. AT to GB, April 4, 1832, OC VIII:1, 113.

28. GB to AT, May 17, 1832, OC VIII:1, 118.

29. GB and AT, Penitentiary Report, OC IV:2, 56.

30. AT to Blanche de Kergorlay, n.d., OC XIII:1, 251–54.

31. AT, "Examen du livre de M. de Blosseville *De la question des colonies pénales*," OC IV:2, 62–63; GB and AT, *On the Penitentiary System in the United States and Its Application in France, 1833*, trans. Emily Katherine Ferkaluk (Cham, Switzerland: Palgrave Macmillan, 2018), xliin17; OC IV:1, 153n3. In the penitentiary report, however, AT and GB suggested that following Holland's model of establishing agricultural colonies within France would provide an outlet for released prisoners: *On the Penitentiary System*, 114 and Appendix 4: Agricultural Colonies, 197–200; OC IV:1, 244 and appendix I, 309–12.

32. "Notes sur les prisons de Genève et de Lausanne, 1832," OC IV:2, 65, 70.

33. "Notes sur les prisons de Genève et de Lausanne, 1832," OC IV:2, 64–66.

34. AT to Blanche de Kergorlay, June 16, 1832, OC XIII:1, 255.

35. GB, "Visite de la Prison de la Roquette," August 7, 1832, OC IV:1, 464–65.

36. "Maison de refuge de la rue de l'Oursine," OC IV:2, 76–77.

37. "Maison de Saint Lazare"; "Maison de correction de l'hôtel de Bazencourt," OC IV:1, 79, 83.

38. AT, *Tocqueville and Beaumont in America*, 474–75; OC IV:1, 257.

39. AT to Chabrol, November 19, 1831, in *Tocqueville and Beaumont*, 167–68; OC XVII:1, 144.

40. AT used the word "*rédacteur*"; AT to Droz, June 26, 1841, OC XVII:2, 131 (Michelle Perrot attributes Mignet as the recipient; see OC IV:1, 23).

41. These "*pièces justificatives*" have been lost.

42. Michelle Perrot, "Introduction," OC IV:1, 21.

43. GB and AT, *On the Penitentiary System*, 66; OC IV:1, 206.

44. Louis de Kergorlay (hereafter LK) to AT, January 17, 1833, OC XIII:1, 316.

45. AT to GB, April 12, 1832, OC VIII:1, 113.

46. GB and AT, *On the Penitentiary System*, 67; OC IV:1, 207.

47. GB and AT, *On the Penitentiary System*, 104; OC IV:1, 234.

48. GB and AT, *On the Penitentiary System*, 102, 113; OC IV:1, 232–33, 243.

49. GB and AT, *On the Penitentiary System*, 105; OC IV:1, 235–36.

50. GB and AT, *On the Penitentiary System*, 111; OC IV:1, 241.

51. "Useful for the improvement of mores" was also AT's phrase in describing the work when submitting his candidacy to the Académie française; AT to Pierre-Antoine Lebrun, June 29, 1841, OC XVII:2, 133.

52. AT, *Democracy in America*, ed. Olivier Zunz, trans. Arthur Goldhammer (New York: Library of America, 2004), (hereafter DA I [1835] or DA II [1840]), I, 60; *Œuvres* Pléiade (hereafter OP) II:58.

53. GB and AT, *On the Penitentiary System*, 36; OC IV:1, 183.

54. Richard Avramenko and Robert Gingerich, "Democratic Dystopia: Tocqueville and the American Penitentiary System," *Polity* 46 (January 2014): 56–80; Sheldon S. Wolin, *Tocqueville between Two Worlds: The Making of a Political and Theoretical Life* (Princeton, NJ: Princeton University Press, 2001), 384.

55. DA I, 50; OP II:49.

56. GB and AT, *On the Penitentiary System*, 48; OC IV:1, 196.

57. GB and AT, *On the Penitentiary System*, trans. Francis Lieber (Philadelphia, 1833), 47–48; OC IV:1, 196.

58. AT to LK, 1824, OC XIII:1, 69–74.

59. Jardin, *Tocqueville*, 176.

60. GB to AT, August 7, 1833, OC VIII:1, 119; respectively personification of England and New England.

61. Seymour Drescher, *Tocqueville and England* (Cambridge, MA: Harvard University Press, 1964), 23; Regina Pozzi, "Guizot et Tocqueville face à l'histoire anglaise," *The Tocqueville Review / La revue Tocqueville* 22, no. 2 (2001): 155–67.

62. AT to LK, October 18, 1847, OC XIII:2, 209.

63. As quoted in George W. Pierson, "Le 'second voyage' de Tocqueville en Amérique," in *Alexis de Tocqueville, Livre du Centenaire, 1859–1959* (Paris: CNRS, 1960), 71; Seymour Drescher's translation in *Tocqueville and England* (Cambridge, MA: Harvard University Press, 1964), 36.

64. AT to Mary Mottley, July 1833, OC XIV, 385.

65. GB and AT, *On the Penitentiary System*, xxxix; OC IV:1, 152.

66. Say traced the word *pauperism* to the pauperization British Poor Laws presumably generated by making alms broadly available. *Cours complet d'économie politique pratique* (Paris, 1829), 5:352, 388; AT did not annotate this section in his reading notes; OC XVI, 425–34. See also Seymour Drescher, *Dilemmas of Democracy: Tocqueville and Modernization* (Pittsburgh: University of Pittsburgh Press, 1968), 103, 104, 109; Michael Drolet, "Democracy and Political Economy: Tocqueville's Thoughts on J.-B. Say and T. R. Malthus," *History of European Ideas* 29, no. 2 (2003): 159–81.

67. AT to Mother, August 7, 1833, OC XIV, 172.

68. AT to GB, August 13, 1833, OC VIII:1, 124.

69. AT to Hervé de Tocqueville (hereafter HT), August 24, 1833, OC XIV, 173–74; AT to Pisieux, July 5, 1833, OC XVII:1, 190–91.

70. AT to HT, August 24, 1833, OC XIV, 173–74.

71. AT to Charles Stöffels, July 31, 1834, OC XVII:1, 204; *Tocqueville: Lettres choisies, Souvenirs*, ed. Françoise Mélonio and Laurence Guellec (Paris: Gallimard, 2003) (hereafter LC), 301.

72. AT, *Journeys to England and Ireland*, ed. J. P. Mayer, trans. George Lawrence and J. P. Mayer (1979; reprint, New Brunswick, NJ: Transaction Books, 1988), 43; OP I, 420.

73. AT, *Journeys to England and Ireland*, 44–45; OP I, 421–23.

74. AT to Mary Mottley, August 27, 1833, OC XIV, 389.

75. Drescher, *Tocqueville and England*, 38, 49.

76. AT to HT, August 24, 1833, OC XIV, 174; AT to Senior, March 24, 1834, OC VI:2, 65. See also S. Leon Levy, *Nassau W. Senior, 1790–1864: Critical Essayist, Classical Economist and Adviser of Governments* (Newton Abbot, UK: David & Charles, 1970); Richard Swedberg, *Tocqueville's Political Economy* (Princeton, NJ: Princeton University Press, 2009), 87–91.

77. Karl Marx "La dernière heure de Senior," *Le Capital*, in *Œuvres, Économie I*, Bibliothèque de la Pléiade (Paris: Gallimard, 1965), 778–84.

78. AT to Mary Mottley, OC XIV, 392.

79. AT, "Voyage en Angleterre de 1833," OP I, 429–31; AT to Mary Mottley, August 30, 1833, OC XIV, 391–94.

80. AT to HT, August 24, 1833, OC XIV, 174.

81. AT, *Journeys to England and Ireland*, 71–72; OP I, 455.

82. Thomas Jefferson to James Madison, September 6, 1789, in *The Papers of Thomas Jefferson*, vol. 15 (Princeton, NJ: Princeton University Press, 1958). See also Joyce Appleby, "Jefferson and His Complex Legacy," in *Jeffersonian Legacies*, ed. Peter S. Onuf (Charlottesville: University Press of Virginia, 1993), 13.

83. These were local administrators and judges whom the king selected from among the local aristocracy. See Drescher, *Tocqueville and England*, 42.

84. AT, *Journeys to England and Ireland*, 51–54; OP I, 431–33, and *Mémoire sur le paupérisme*, OC XVI, 134. See also Ronald K. Huch, *The Radical Lord Radnor: The Public Life of Viscount Folkestone, Third Earl of Radnor (1779–1869)* (Minneapolis: University of Minnesota Press, 1977), 137–38.

85. AT, *Journeys to England and Ireland*, 61–62; OP I, 444.

86. AT, *Journeys to England and Ireland*, 59–61; OP I, 441–42.

87. AT, *Journeys to England and Ireland*, 67; OP I, 449–50.

88. AT to GB, August 13, 1833, OC VIII:1, 124–26; Jardin, *Tocqueville*, 192–93.

89. AT, "Les desseins d'une nouvelle revue," OC III:2, 35–39.

90. AT to LK, September 28, 1834, OC XIII:1, 361–62.

91. Lise Queffélec, Notice de la Pléiade, L'Irlande, OP I, 1407.

92. AT to Mary, April 18, 1858, OC XIV, 638.

93. Eduardo Nolla's critical edition of *Democracy in America*, trans. James T. Schleifer (Indianapolis: Liberty Fund, 2010), 1:14u.

94. DA I, 6–7; OP II:7; DA II, 525; OP II:554.

95. DA I, 6; OP II:7; see also Pierre Gibert, "Tocqueville et la religion: Entre réflexion politique et confidences épistolaires," *The Tocqueville Review / La revue Tocqueville* 27, no. 2 (2006): 133–48; David A. Selby, "Tocqueville's Politics of Providence: Pascal, Jansenism and the Author's Introduction to *Democracy in America*," *The Tocqueville Review / La revue Tocqueville* 32, no, 2 (2012): 168–90.

96. AT, "Mon instinct, mes opinions," OC III:2, 87.

97. DA I, 15; OP II:15.

98. Schleifer, *The Making of Tocqueville's* Democracy in America, 7–9, 13, 17.

99. AT to Mary Mottley, April 18, 1858, OC XIV, 638.

100. AT to LK, November 1833, OC XIII:1, 344.

101. LK to AT, October 1834, OC XIII:1, 366; see also Daniel Gordon, "Tocqueville and Linguistic Innovation," in *The Anthem Companion to Alexis de Tocqueville*, ed. Daniel Gordon (London: Anthem Press, 2019), 65–87.

102. AT to LK, November 10, 1836, OC XIII:1, 418.

103. AT to Eugène Stöffels, July 31, 1834, OC XVII:1, 205; LC, 302.

104. GB to Senior, August 26, 1860, OC VI:2, 503; see also Laurence Guellec, "Tocqueville écrivain," in *Tocqueville et la littérature*, ed. Françoise Mélonio and José-Luis Diaz (Paris: Presses de l'Université Paris-Sorbonne), 110.

105. AT to GB, October 24, 1834, OC VIII:1, 144.

106. Senior, "Conversations," August 25, 1850, OC VI:2, 303.

107. Pierre Rosanvallon, *Le moment Guizot* (Paris: Gallimard, 1985), 255–62. On AT's independence from Chateaubriand in writing DA I, see Françoise Mélonio, "Tocqueville and the

French," in *The Cambridge Companion to Tocqueville* (Cambridge: Cambridge University Press, 2006), 343.

108. Nolla, *Democracy in America*, 2:348h.

109. Nolla, *Democracy in America*, 2:508y.

110. AT to Chabrol, November 19, 1831, OC XVII:1, 144.

111. C. A. Sainte-Beuve, "Nouvelle correspondance inédite de M. de Tocqueville, lundi 18 décembre 1865," in *Nouveaux lundis*, 2nd ed. (Paris, 1874), 320–21.

112. DA I, 29; OP II:28.

113. DA I, 31; OP II:30. Montesquieu, "l'esprit général de la nation," *Esprit des lois* 19, nos. 4 and 5 (1748); LK to AT, August 5, 1832, OC XIII:1, 274–75.

114. DA I, 52; OP II:50. Montesquieu said, "Laws, customs, and various usages of all peoples"; see Melvin Richter, "The Uses of Theory: Tocqueville's Adaptation of Montesquieu," in *Essays in Theory and History* (Cambridge, MA: Harvard University Press, 1970), 79; Montesquieu, "Essai sur les causes qui peuvent affecter les esprits et les caractères," in *Œuvres* (Paris: Bibliothèque de la Pléiade, 1951), 2:39–68. On Guizot's fourth lecture, see Nolla, *Democracy in America*, 1:18a.

115. DA I, 36, 35; OP II:34, 33.

116. Nolla, *Democracy in America*, 1:58.

117. DA I, 48; OP II:46. For Isaiah Berlin's "positive liberty," see *Two Concepts of Liberty: An Inaugural Lecture Delivered before the University of Oxford on 31 October 1958* (Oxford: Clarendon Press, 1958).

118. Possibly as a reaction to the writings of Pascal; for AT, the angel is stronger than the beast. See Alan S. Kahan, "Democratic Grandeur: How Tocqueville Constructed His New Moral Science in America," in *Tocqueville's Voyages: The Evolution of His Ideas and Their Journey beyond His Time*, ed. Christine Dunn Henderson (Indianapolis: Liberty Fund, 2014), 186–87.

119. DA II, 105 ("touch and become one"); OP II:607 ("se touchent et se confondent").

120. DA I, 275; OP II:275.

121. DA I, 60; OP II:59.

122. DA I, 63; OP II:61.

123. DA I, 68; OP II:65.

124. AT to Senior, March 24, 1834, OC VI:2, 66.

125. James W. Ceaser, "Alexis de Tocqueville and the Two-Founding Thesis," *The Review of Politics* 73 (Spring 2011): 219–43.

126. DA I, 96; OP II:94.

127. DA I, 133; OP II:131.

128. DA I, 177; OP II:176.

129. On the difference between government and administration, see "centralization" in "Fragment," *La Nouvelle Revue Française* 13 (1959): 762–64.

130. DA I, 185; OP II:184.

131. DA I, 180; OP II:180–81.

132. DA I, 172; OP II:171.

133. DA I 152; OP II:151.

134. Publius, "The Federalist X," November 22, 1787, in *The Debate on the Constitution, Part One* (New York: Library of America, 1993), 405.

135. DA I, 215; OP II:213.

136. DA I, 220; OP II:217.

137. DA I, 107; OP II:106.

138. DA I, 363; OP II:365; see also Arthur Goldhammer, "Tocqueville, Associations, and the Law of 1834," *Historical Reflections* 35 (Winter 2009): 74–84.

139. DA I, 362–63; OP II:364.

140. DA I, 220; OP II:217.

141. DA I, 316; OP II:315–16.

142. DA I, 331, 315; OP II:331, 314.

143. DA I 323; OP II:322

144. DA I, 328; OP II:327.

145. DA I, 280–81; OP II:281.

146. DA I, 16; OP II:17.

147. We may add John Tanner, who appears in a footnote, as having given Tocqueville his memoir of life among Native Americans; DA I, 16, 382n18; OP II:16, 384n.

148. DA I, 293; OP II:292.

149. DA I, 271; OP II:272.

150. DA I, 288; OP II:288.

151. DA I, 391; OP II:393.

152. DA I, 376; OP II:379.

153. DA I, 403; OP II:405.

154. DA I, 416; OP II:418.

155. DA I, 218–19, 441n, 450–52; OP II:215–16, 453–55.

156. Schleifer, *The Making of Tocqueville's* Democracy in America, 146.

157. DA I, 440; OP II:443.

158. AT admitted his error on this point in an 1838 note. Schleifer, *The Making of Tocqueville's* Democracy in America, 37.

159. DA I, 431; OP II:433–34.

160. DA I, 364; OP II:366.

161. On mores over laws, see "Fragment," 762; but especially DA I, 315, 331; OP II:314, 331.

162. DA I, 460; OP II:463; DA I, 471; OP II:475; DA I, 444; OP II:447.

163. DA I, 323; OP II:322; on liberty and servitude, DA I, 476; OP II:480—a much-discussed comparison at the time, see Nolla, *Democracy in America*, 2:656h.

# Chapter 5

1. Alexis de Tocqueville (hereafter AT) to Orglandes, November 29, 1834, in *Alexis de Tocqueville and Gustave de Beaumont in America: Their Friendship and Their Travels*, ed. Olivier Zunz, trans. Arthur Goldhammer (Charlottesville: University of Virginia Press, 2010) (hereafter *Tocqueville and Beaumont*), 563; *Œuvres complètes* (hereafter OC) XVII:1, 213; *Tocqueville: Lettres choisies, Souvenirs*, ed. Françoise Mélonio and Laurence Guellec (Paris: Gallimard, 2003) (hereafter LC), 311.

2. AT to Eugène Stöffels, February 16, 1835, OC XVII:1, 224; LC, 313.

3. René Rémond, *Les États-Unis devant l'opinion française, 1815–1852* (Paris: Librairie Armand Colin, 1962), 2:795–96.

4. AT, "Note sur les pouvoirs du président des États-Unis," OC XVI, 85–87.

5. John M. Belohlavek, *Let the Eagle Soar! The Foreign Policy of Andrew Jackson* (Lincoln: University of Nebraska Press, 1985), 90–126.

6. AT to Chateaubriand, January 1835; Chateaubriand to AT, January 11, 1835, OC XVII:1, 215–17.

7. Chateaubriand, *Mémoires d'outre-tombe*, Bibliothèque de la Pléiade (Paris: Gallimard, 1951), 2:921.

8. AT to Charles Stöffels, October 22, 1831, OC XVII:1, 125–27; LC, 238–40.

9. DA I, 345; *Œuvres* Pléiade (hereafter OP) II:346.

10. AT to Grancey, October 4, 1835, OC XVII:1, 259. He used the word "*mécreant.*"

11. AT to Lamennais, January 24, 1835, OC XVII:1, 220. For an overview of liberal ultramontanism, see Austin Gough, *Paris and Rome: The Gallican Church and the Ultramontane Campaign, 1848–1853* (Oxford: Clarendon Press, 1986), 64–66. On Lamennais's liberal Catholicism, see Émile Perreau-Saussine, *Catholicism and Democracy: An Essay in the History of Political Thought*, trans. Richard Rex (Princeton, NJ: Princeton University Press, 2012), 59–60, 69–70.

12. AT to Freslon, July 8, 1858, OC XVII:3. 501–4; LC, 1309–12.

13. Jean-Claude Lamberti, *Tocqueville and the Two Democracies*, trans. Arthur Goldhammer (Cambridge, MA: Harvard University Press, 1989), 122, 133, 283n59.

14. AT to John Stuart Mill, 1841, OC VI:1, 334.

15. For a good capsule biography, see Lamberti, *Tocqueville and the Two Democracies*, 131; Aurelian Craiutu, *Liberalism under Siege: The Political Thought of the French Doctrinaires* (Lanham, MD: Lexington Books, 2003), 89–90.

16. October 13, 1836, OC XI, 24; On Royer-Collard (hereafter RC) breaking up with Guizot, and Guizot holding on to the policy of resistance, see Lamberti, *Tocqueville and the Two Democracies*, 127.

17. AT to RC, August 28, 1835, OC XI, 11.

18. Charles de Rémusat, "De l'esprit de réaction: Royer-Collard et Tocqueville," *Revue des deux mondes* 35 (October 15, 1861): 777–813.

19. Pamela Law, "Mary Clarke and the Nineteenth-Century Salon," *Sydney Studies* (2008): 65; Kathleen O'Meara, *Madame Mohl: Her Salon and Her Friends; A Study of Social Life in Paris* (Boston, 1891); Anne Martin-Fugier, *La vie élégante ou la formation du Tout-Paris, 1815–1848* (Paris: Fayard, 1990); Steven D. Kale, *French Salons: High Society and Political Sociability from the Old Regime to the Revolution of 1848* (Baltimore: Johns Hopkins University Press, 2004).

20. Marc Fumaroli, "La conversation," in *Trois institutions littéraires* (Paris: Gallimard, 1994), 111–210.

21. AT to Senior, August 24, 1850, OC VI:2, 301.

22. Pierre-Simon Ballanche, *Essai de palingénésie sociale* (Paris, 1827); see also Lucien Jaume's *Tocqueville: The Aristocratic Sources of Liberty*, trans. Arthur Goldhammer (Princeton, NJ: Princeton University Press, 2013), 214. Ampère read his Hilda at Madame Récamier's; Ampère to AT, October 15, 1839, OC XI, 132–33.

23. This was a small circle; Mary Clarke married Julius Mohl, a German orientalist, disciple of Silvestre de Sacy, who became Ampère's colleague at the Collège de France. On the Mohls, see OC XI, 135n7. Victor Cousin was Royer-Collard's successor as philosophy chair of the Sorbonne.

24. Abel Villemain, "Rapport sur les concours de l'Académie française en 1836," in *Discours et mélanges littéraires*, nouvelle edition (Paris, 1860), 278; AT had already won once with Beaumont; RC to AT, June 10, 1836, OC XI, 16–17; Beaumont, second prize ex aequo; AT to Reeve, June 5, 1836, OC VI:1, 34; André Jardin, *Tocqueville: A Biography*, trans. Lydia Davis with Robert Hemenway (Baltimore: Johns Hopkins University Press, 1988), 227.

25. *Memoirs of the Duchesse de Dino (afterwards Duchesse de Talleyrand et de Sagan) 1836–1840*, ed. Princesse Radziwill, née Castellane (London: Heinemann, 1910), 2:23.

26. Jacques-Alain de Sédouy, *Le comte Molé ou la séduction du pouvoir* (Paris: Librairie Académique Perrin, 1994).

27. Mérimée said of her that she could not do anything simply, much like a crab cannot walk straight; quoted in OC VIII:1, 219n5.

28. Sophie Marchal, "Une correspondance inédite de Balzac autour d'une amitié de Salon: Virginie Ancelot," *L'Année balzacienne* 2 (2001): 269–82; AT to Ancelot, December 8, 1857, OC XVII:3, 446–47.

29. Madame Ancelot, *Un salon de Paris, 1824 à 1864* (Paris, 1866), 79.

30. Jonathan Beecher, *Victor Considerant and the Rise and Fall of French Romantic Socialism* (Berkeley: University of California Press, 2001), 84, 86; see also Lise Queffélec and Françoise Mélonio, "Introduction: Tocqueville et l'Europe," in OC VII, 265; OC XV:1, 62n8.

31. George Ticknor, *Life, Letters, and Journals of George Ticknor* (1876; reprint, Boston: Houghton Mifflin, 1909), 2:366–67.

32. AT to Gustave de Beaumont (hereafter GB), July 14, 1834, OC VIII:1, 141–42; AT approaches Bouchitté for a review in *Le Temps*, see OC XVII:1, 218, January 15, 1835.

33. AT to Eugène Stöffels, February 21, 1835, OC XVII:1, 225–26; LC, 315.

34. AT to Eugène Stöffels, October 5, 1836, OC XVII:1, 309; LC, 366.

35. A strong polemic regarding solitary confinement will erupt in 1843.

36. Léon Faucher, *Le courrier français*, December 24, 1834, no. 358.

37. AT to Sainte-Beuve, April 8, 1835, OC XVII:1, 231; see also Lucien Jaume, *Tocqueville: The Aristocratic Sources of Liberty*, trans. Arthur Goldhammer (Princeton, NJ: Princeton University Press, 2008), 190–91.

38. Pierre Gibert, "Introduction," OC XV:1, 21.

39. Francisque de Corcelle, "De la démocratie américaine," *Revue des deux mondes*, 4th ser., 2 (1835): 739–61.

40. The French Carbonari borrowed their name from the Neapolitan society but had no connection to them; see Guillaume Bertier de Sauvigny, *La restauration* (Paris: Flammarion, 1955), 179–82.

41. Cousin was introducing Hegel to the French readership to justify the *juste milieu*'s policy of pragmatism and compromise.

42. François de Corcelle, *Documents pour servir à l'histoire des conspirations* (Paris, 1831), 53, 84.

43. Corcelle, "De la démocratie américaine," 742.

44. Louis Blanc, "De la démocratie en Amérique," *Revue républicaine: Journal des doctrines et des intérêts démocratiques* 5 (1835): 115, 153.

45. Louis de Kergorlay (hereafter LK) to AT, September 10, 1834, OC XIII:1, 353–54.

46. Blanc, "De la démocratie en Amérique," 161; see also Stephen W. Sawyer, *Demos Assembled: Democracy and the International Origins of the Modern State, 1840–1880* (Chicago: University of Chicago Press, 2018), 159–84.

47. Françoise Mélonio, *Tocqueville and the French*, trans. Beth G. Reps (Charlottesville: University Press of Virginia, 1998), 41–43.

48. AT to Hervé de Tocqueville (hereafter HT), May 7, 1835, OC XIV, 177–78.

49. Abel Villemain, "Rapport sur les concours de l'Académie française en 1836," 280; Mélonio, *Tocqueville and the French*, 31.

50. Alphonse de Custine, *L'Espagne sous Ferdinand VII* (Paris, 1838), 2:355; Mélonio, *Tocqueville and the French*, 38.

51. See Mélonio, *Tocqueville and the French*, 44.

52. AT to GB, December 14, 1846, OC VIII:1, 603.

53. Reprinted as a chapter in Louis Joseph Marie de Carné, *Des interêts nouveaux en Europe depuis la révolution de 1830* (Paris: F. Bonnaire, 1838), 97, 103, 159.

54. Pierre Rosanvallon, *Le moment Guizot* (Paris: Gallimard, 1985), 105–40.

55. Édouard Alletz, *De la démocratie nouvelle, ou des moeurs et de la puissance des classes moyennes en France* (Paris, 1837); Auguste Billiard, *Essai sur l'organisation démocratique de la France* (Paris, 1837).

56. François Guizot, "De la démocratie dans les sociétés modernes," *Revue française* 3 (October 15, 1837): 195–96.

57. AT to LK, October 4, 1837, OC, XIII:1, 479.

58. AT to Le Peletier d'Aunay, mid-January 1835, OC XVII:1, 219.

59. AT to Lamartine, 1835, OC XVII:1, 222.

60. AT to Édouard, June 13, 1837, OC XIV, 196.

61. AT to Marie, June 12, 1841, OC XIV, 435. A constant complaint—see AT to Corcelle, June 10, 1837, OC XV:1, 77–78.

62. GB to AT, January 28, 1838, OC VIII:1, 280.

63. *Memoir on Pauperism*, trans. Seymour Drescher, with an introduction by Gertrude Himmelfarb (Chicago: Ivan R. Dee, 1997); OC XVI, 17–39.

64. AT to GB, December 7, 1828, OC VIII:1, 72.

65. *Tocqueville and Beaumont*, 220–21; OP I:44–45.

66. OC IV:1, appendix 3, 319–22, and notes on 574–75.

67. AT, *Journeys to England and Ireland*, ed. J. P. Mayer, trans. George Lawrence and J. P. Mayer (1979; reprint, New Brunswick, NJ: Transaction Books, 1988), 51–54; OP I:431–33; drawn from AT, *Memoir on Pauperism*, 64; OC XVI, 134.

68. AT, *Journeys to England and Ireland*, 72; OP I:455.

69. DA I, 240; OP II:238–39. Sensing something awkward in this choice of words, Tocqueville noted by asterisk that he was using the term *poor* only in a "relative" sense.

70. AT, *Memoir on Pauperism*, 37–38; OC XVI, 117–18; Michael Drolet, *Tocqueville, Democracy and Social Reform* (London: Palgrave Macmillan, 2003), 95–111; Eric Keslassy, *Le libéralisme de*

*Tocqueville à l'épreuve du paupérisme* (Paris: L'Harmattan, 2000), 95; Françoise Mélonio, "Introduction," OC XVI, 21.

71. Alban de Villeneuve-Bargemont, *Économie politique chrétienne, ou, Recherches sur la nature et les causes du paupérisme, en France et en Europe, et sur les moyens de le soulager et de le prévenir* (Paris, 1834), 1:7, 23.

72. AT to de Thun, February 2, 1835, OC VII, 283.

73. AT to LK, September 28, 1834, OC XIII:1, 361–62.

74. AT had already asked Senior for that report (completed in February 1844) as early as March 1844, but it is unclear whether Senior had sent it.

75. Joseph Persky, "Classical Family Values: Ending the Poor Laws as They Knew Them," *Journal of Economic Perspectives* 11 (Winter 1997): 185–86.

76. AT, *Memoir on Pauperism*, 46; OC XVI, 123, 119n.

77. AT, *Journeys to England and Ireland*, 208; OP I:599.

78. AT, *Memoir on Pauperism*, 68, 60; OC XVI, 136, 131.

79. AT to Duvergier de Hauranne, May 4, 1837, OC XVII:1, 320.

80. AT to Nassau Senior, May 1835, OC VI:2, 75.

81. AT to Eugène Stöffels, July 24, 1836, OC XVII:1, 296; LC, 354.

82. David Cannadine, *Victorious Century: The United Kingdom, 1800–1906* (New York: Viking, 2017), 153.

83. Richard Reeves, *John Stuart Mill, Victorian Firebrand* (London: Atlantic Books, 2007), 88, 513n20; George Macaulay Trevelyan, *British History in the Nineteenth Century* (London: Longmans, Green, 1922), 244.

84. AT to Le Peletier d'Aunay, June 7, 1835, OC XVII:1, 246.

85. AT, *Journeys to England and Ireland*, 80; OP I:466.

86. AT to Molé, April 19, 1835, OC XVII:1, 232.

87. Senior to AT, February 17, 1835, OC VI:2, 66.

88. AT in turn pressured Senior to push the book at the *Edinburgh Review*, the *Quarterly*, and the *Westminster Review*. OC VI:2, 66–67.

89. AT to Ancelot, April 28, 1835, OC XVII:1, 233; LC, 320; AT to HT, April 29, 1835, OC XIV, 175.

90. AT to HT, May 1, 1835, OC XIV, 176.

91. AT to Marie, May 5, 1835, OC XIV, 397.

92. Seymour Drescher, *Tocqueville and England* (Cambridge, MA: Harvard University Press, 1964), 55–56.

93. AT to HT, May 1, 1835, OC XIV, 176.

94. AT to Marie, May 5, 1835, OC XIV, 397.

95. AT to HT, May 1, 1835, OC XIV, 176.

96. AT, *Journeys to England and Ireland*, 82; OP I:468.

97. AT to Ancelot, April 28 and May 27, 1835, OC XVII:1, 234, 241 LC, 320–21.

98. AT to Ancelot, June 19, 1835, OC XVII:1, 249.

99. AT to HT, April 29, 1835, OC XIV, 175.

100. AT to Senior, May 10, 1835, OC XVII:1, 235.

101. John Knox Laughton, *Memoirs of the Life and Correspondence of Henry Reeve, 1813–1895* (London: Longmans, Green and Co., 1898).

102. AT to Alexandrine, May 22, 1835, OC XIV, 179–80.

103. AT, *Journeys to England and Ireland*, 81–82; OP I:466–67; Byung-Hoon Suh, "Mill and Tocqueville: A Friendship Bruised," *History of European Ideas* 42 (2016): 55–72.

104. John Stuart Mill, *Autobiography* (1873), ed. John M. Robson (London: Penguin Books, 1989), 149; see OC VI:2, 72n2.

105. Mill in concluding "De Tocqueville on Democracy in America," *London Review* 1 (October 1835) (equivalent to *Westminster Review*, no. 30).

106. Drescher, *Tocqueville and England*, 56.

107. AT, *Journeys to England and Ireland*, 86–87; OP I:472–73.

108. AT had read Charles Cottu, *De l'administration de la justice criminelle en Angleterre et de l'esprit du gouvernement* (Paris, 1820), while in the United States; see Notebook F in *Tocqueville and Beaumont in America*, 391.

109. AT, *Journeys to England and Ireland*, 205–9; OP I:596–600.

110. AT, *Journeys to England and Ireland*, 81–82; OP I:466–67.

111. AT, *Journeys to England and Ireland*, 77–78; OP I:463–64.

112. AT, *Journeys to England and Ireland*, 83–84, 210–32; Drescher, *Tocqueville and England*, 55, 82n22; May 29, 1835, conversation on bribery with Mr. Hallam, OP I:469–70; Testimony in the Commons, William Henry Ord leads the interview, June 22, 1835, OC XVI, 88–111.

113. AT to HT, May 7, 1835, OC XIV, 178.

114. AT to Molé, August 1835, in Gustave de Beaumont, *Œuvres complètes d'Alexis de Tocqueville publiées par Madame de Tocqueville* (Paris, 1865–67), VII:135, dated September 1835, in OC XVII:1, 253; see also DA II, 723–24; OP II:744.

115. AT to Molé, May 19, 1835, OC XVII:1, 236; LC 326–27.

116. AT, *Journeys to England and Ireland*, 90–92; OP I:478–79.

117. AT to Le Peletier d'Aunay, June 7, 1835, OC XVII:1, 248.

118. AT to Marie, May 5, 1835, OC XIV, 397.

119. Arthur James White, *The Early Life and Letters of Cavour, 1810–1848* (Oxford: Oxford University Press, 1925), 116.

120. AT, "Voyage en Angleterre et en Irlande de 1835," OP I:480.

121. Doris Gunnell, *Sutton Sharpe et ses amis français* (Paris: Champion, 1925), 15.

122. White, *Early Life and Letters of Cavour*, 130.

123. AT, *Journeys to England and Ireland*, 92; OP I:480.

124. AT to Molé, May 19, 1835, OC XVII:1, 238; LC, 328.

125. AT, *Journeys to England and Ireland*, 104; OP I:500.

126. AT, *Journeys to England and Ireland*, 95; OP I:491.

127. AT, *Journeys to England and Ireland*, 98–99; OP I:495; on labor leaders such as Richard Carlile, William Cobbett, or Henry Hunt, see E. P. Thompson, *The Making of the English Working Class*, with revisions (London: Pelican Books, 1963).

128. Drescher, *Tocqueville and England*, 67.

129. AT to Marie, July 1, 1835, OC XIV, 398.

130. AT, *Journeys to England and Ireland*, 107–8; OP I:504.

131. AT, *Journeys to England and Ireland*, 110; OP I:507.

132. Charles de Montalembert, "Lettre sur le Catholicisme en Irlande," January 1831, in Marie-Hélène Pauly, *Les voyageurs français en Irlande au temps du romantisme* (Paris: Librairie Gabriel Enault, 1939), 87.

133. AT to Sparks, September 11, 1835, OC VII, 62–63.

134. AT, *Journeys to England and Ireland*, 26; OP I:518.

135. *Alexis de Tocqueville's Journey in Ireland. July–August 1835*, trans. and ed. Emmet Larkin (Washington, DC: Catholic University of America Press, 1990), 24–25; OP I:517–18.

136. *Journey in Ireland*, 62; OP I:538.

137. *Journey in Ireland*, 29; OP I:522.

138. *Journey in Ireland*, 79; OP I:551.

139. *Journey in Ireland*, 22–23; OP I:515.

140. *Journey in Ireland*, 29; OP I:521.

141. AT to Grancey, July 26, 1835, OC XVII:1, 251–52; LC, 339.

142. *Journey in Ireland*, 29; OP I:521.

143. *Journey in Ireland*, 59; OP I:543.

144. *Journey in Ireland*, 121; OP I:567.

145. On August 10–13; OC XIV, 189n2; see Michael Drolet, "Tocqueville's Interest in the Social," *History of European Ideas* 31, no. 4 (2005): 451–71.

146. AT to HT, May 7, 1835, OC XIV, 178–79; Jardin, *Tocqueville*, 239.

147. On AT aware of Michel Chevalier's visit to Lowell and his own omission in DA I, see GB to AT, May 17, 1837, OC VIII:1, 189.

148. AT, "Political and Social Condition of France," *The London and Westminster Review* (April–July 1836): 137–69.

149. Edward Everett, "De Tocqueville's Democracy in America," *North American Review* 43, no. 92 (July 1836): 198–99; AT to Reeve, November 21, 1836, OC VI:1, 36; AT to GB, November 22, 1836, OC VIII:1, 175.

150. Herbert Baxter Adams, "Jared Sparks and Alexis de Tocqueville," *Johns Hopkins University Studies in Historical and Political Science* 16, no. 12 (December 1898): 601; AT to Sparks, February 14, 1837, OC VII, 63–64.

151. AT to Marie, May 5, 1835, OC XIV, 397–98.

152. "From Mr. Everett, March 29, 1837," in *Sir Robert Peel from His Private Papers*, ed. Charles Stuart Parker (London, 1899), 2:333–35. Peel would continue to describe AT's work as a Tory book, as Mill wrote to AT on May 11, 1840, regarding DA II, see OC VI:1, 328.

153. An initial effort to negotiate a royalty agreement with Tocqueville failed; see AT to Spencer, September 20, 1838, and September 12, 1839, in OC VII, 70–72, 77–80.

154. Alexis de Tocqueville, *Democracy in America*, ed. John C. Spencer, trans. Henry Reeve (New York, 1838), 452.

155. Thomas Hart Benton, *Thirty Years' View; or, A History of the Working of the American Government for Thirty Years, from 1820–1850* (New York: Appleton, 1854), 1:227–28.

# Chapter 6

1. In *Alexis de Tocqueville and Gustave de Beaumont in America: Their Friendship and Their Travels*, ed. Olivier Zunz, trans. Arthur Goldhammer (Charlottesville: University of Virginia Press, 2010) (hereafter *Tocqueville and Beaumont*), 573; Alexis de Tocqueville (hereafter AT) to Henry Reeve, March 22, 1837, *Œuvres complètes* (hereafter OC) VI:1, 37–38.

2. AT to Greg, October 1, 1858; OC VI:3, 307.

3. AT to Austin, November 26, 1835, OC VI:3, 49 (text known only in English).

4. *Democracy in America* (hereafter DA) I, 336; *Œuvres* Pléiade (hereafter OP) II:337.

5. AT to Hubert, February 23, 1857, OC XIV, 329.

6. André Jardin, *Tocqueville: A Biography*, trans. Lydia Davis with Robert Hemenway (Baltimore: Johns Hopkins University Press, 1998), 232.

7. AT to Louis de Kergorlay (hereafter LK), July 6, 1835, OC XIII:1, 377.

8. LK to AT, August 18, 1833, OC XIII:1, 333–34.

9. AT to Camille d'Orglandes, October 14, 1835, OC XVII:1, 261; *Tocqueville: Lettres choisies, Souvenirs*, ed. Françoise Mélonio and Laurence Guellec (Paris: Gallimard, 2003) (hereafter LC), 343; AT to Charles Stöffels, October 16, 1835, OC XVII:1, 262–63, only a few days before the wedding.

10. AT to Édouard and Alexandrine, July 12, 1835, OC XIV, 181–82.

11. AT to Gustave de Beaumont (hereafter GB), August 26, 1835, OC VIII:1, 155.

12. OC XIII, 377n5.

13. AT to Grancey, January 11, 1836, OC XVII:1, 266.

14. AT to Marie, late July 1833, OC XIV, 384–85.

15. Jardin, *Tocqueville*, 5.

16. AT to Édouard, October 3, 1836, OC XIV, 193.

17. AT to GB, June 14, 1836, OC VIII:1, 160.

18. AT to Corcelle, July 27, 1836, OC XV:1, 70; AT, *Voyages en Suisse*, OP I:622n2.

19. AT to GB, July 30, 1836, VIII:1. 163.

20. James T. Schleifer, *The Making of Tocqueville's* Democracy in America, 2nd ed. (Indianapolis: Liberty Fund, 2000), 33.

21. GB, "Notice," in *Œuvres complètes d'Alexis de Tocqueville publiées par Madame de Tocqueville* (Paris, 1865–67) (hereafter OCB), V:52.

22. Pierre-Paul Royer-Collard (hereafter RC) to AT, September 18, 1836, OC XI, 23.

23. Michel Auguste (aka François-Adolphe) Chambolle, *Retours sur la vie: Appréciations et confidences sur les hommes de mon temps* (Paris: Plon-Nourrit, 1912), 143; AT to LK, August 5, 1836, OC XIII:1, 390; AT to RC, August 25, 1836, OC XI, 19; AT to RC, December 6, 1836, OC XI, 29; AT, early reading notes on Thiers, OC XVI, 537–40.

24. AT to LK, August 5, 1836, OC XIII:1, 389. AT elaborated in his draft for DA II: see Eduardo Nolla's critical edition of *Democracy in America*, trans. James T. Schleifer (Indianapolis: Liberty Fund, 2009), 3:960; Agnès Antoine, *L'impensé de la démocratie: Tocqueville, la citoyenneté et la religion* (Paris: Fayard, 2003), 160; Alan Kahan, "Tocqueville and Religion: Beyond the Frontier of Christendom," in *Tocqueville and the Frontiers of Democracy*, ed. Ewa Atanassow and Richard Boyd (Cambridge: Cambridge University Press, 2013), 93.

25. AT to LK, October 10, 1836, OC XIII:1, 410.

26. See AT to LK, November 1833, OC XIII:1, 345; AT to Corcelle, October 9, 1838, OC XV:1, 102; AT to Édouard, September 2, 1840, OC XIV, 214.

27. AT to Corcelle, September 2, 1837, OC XV:1, 85; AT to Ampère, September 27, 1840, OC XI:145.

28. AT to Corcelle, June 25, 1838, OC XV:1, 100.

388   NOTES TO CHAPTER 6

29. Charles H. Pouthas, "A. de Tocqueville, représentant de la Manche," in *Alexis de Tocqueville: Livre du Centenaire, 1859–1959* (Paris: Editions du Centre national de la recherche scientifique, 1960), 25; Nassau Senior, "Conversations," OC VI:2, 285.

30. AT to Édouard, October 3, 1836, OC XIV, 195.

31. Pierre Rosanvallon, *Le moment Guizot* (Paris: Gallimard, 1985), 125–26.

32. AT to electors of the cantons of Beaumont and des Pieux, 1836, OC X, 729–30.

33. Even though not a formal candidate anywhere, fifty-two electors voted for AT in Cherbourg for Conseil général; AT to a journalist, December 1836, OC X, 56–57.

34. AT to Noël-Agnès, Fall 1836, OC X, 54.

35. Laurent Theis, *François Guizot* (Paris: Fayard, 2008), 59; Karl Marx, *Le 18 Brumaire de Louis Bonaparte* (1852), in *Œuvres* (Paris: Bibliothèque de la Pléiade, 1994), 4:457.

36. Aurelian Craiutu, *Liberalism under Siege: The Political Thought of the French Doctrinaires* (Lanham, MD: Lexington Books, 2003), 113.

37. "Discours de M. Odilon Barrot," in *Chefs-d'œuvre de l'éloquence française et de la tribune anglaise*, 5th ed., ed. Abbé Marcel (Paris, 1844), 360; *Mémoires posthumes de Odilon Barrot*, 3rd ed. (Paris, 1875), 1:316–17.

38. "Discours de M. Guizot," in Marcel, *Chefs-d'œuvre de l'éloquence française*, 365–66.

39. GB to AT, May 11, 1837; AT to GB, May 14, 1837, OC VIII:1, 179–80, 183–86. See also Melvin Richter, "Tocqueville and Guizot on Democracy: From a Type of Society to a Political Regime," *History of European Ideas* 30 (2004): 61–82.

40. As quoted by André Jardin, "La chute du régime de juillet," in *François Guizot et la culture de son temps*, ed. Marina Valensise (Paris: Hautes Études, Gallimard, Le Seuil, 1991).

41. AT to RC, June 29, 1837; RC to AT, July 21 and November 21, 1837, OC XI, 35, 38, 54.

42. AT to GB, May 26, 1837, VIII:1, 192.

43. AT to Hervieu, May 17, 1837, OC X, 60.

44. AT to Édouard, June 13, 1837, OC XIV, 196; AT to GB, July 9, 1837, OC VIII:1, 205.

45. AT to RC, June 8, 1837, OC XI, 31–33; AT to GB, December 24, 1837, OC VIII:1, 274.

46. AT to GB, May 14, 1837; GB to AT, June 15, 1837, OC VIII:1, 184–85, 198–200.

47. AT to Corcelle, June 5, 1837, OC XV, 82–83.

48. Eugène Stöffels to AT, July 16, 1836, OC XVII:1, 290–94; AT to Eugène Stöffels, July 24, 1836, OC XVII:1, 296; LC 352–55.

49. AT to GB, October 16, 1836, OC VIII:1, 170–71.

50. AT to GB, October 16, 1836, OC VIII:1, 169–70.

51. Jardin, *Tocqueville*, 286–88.

52. Jean Quellien, "Un milieu ouvrier réformiste: Syndicalisme et réformisme à Cherbourg à la 'Belle Époque,'" *Le mouvement social* 127 (1984): 65–88; on Flora Tristan, see Maurice Agulhon, *Une ville ouvrière au temps du socialisme utopique: Toulon de 1815 à 1851* (Paris: Mouton, 1970), 154–64.

53. AT to GB, May 16, 1837, OC VIII:1, 185.

54. Draft of the second memoir on pauperism in OC XVI, 140–57; related brochures kept and bound in Tocqueville's library at Tocqueville. See also Eric Keslassy, *Le libéralisme de Tocqueville à l'épreuve du paupérisme* (Paris: L'Harmattan, 2000), 196; Michael Drolet, *Tocqueville, Democracy and Social Reform* (Houndsville, UK: Palgrave Macmillan, 2003), 144–46, 157.

55. AT to Édouard, June 13, 1837, OC XIV, 197; AT to GB, November 15, 1841, OC VIII:1, 452–53.

56. GB to AT, September 3 and 22, and October 15, 1837, OC VIII:1, 218, 232, 243.

57. AT to GB, May 26, 1837, OC VIII:1, 192; AT to Bouchitté, January 15, 1835, OC XVII:1, 218.

58. François Guizot, *Mémoires pour servir à l'histoire de mon temps* (Paris, 1865), 7:126; Louis Blanc, *Histoire de dix ans, 1830–1840* (Paris, 1844), 45.

59. AT, "Second Letter on Algeria," August 22, 1837, in Alexis de Tocqueville, *Writings on Empire and Slavery*, trans. Jennifer Pitts (Baltimore: Johns Hopkins University Press, 2001) (hereafter Pitts), 24; OC III:1, 151.

60. LK to AT, September 20, 1833, OC XIII:1, 340; Jean-Jacques Chevallier and André Jardin, "Introduction," OC III:1, 12–13.

61. Amédée Desjobert, *La question d'Alger: Politique, colonisation, commerce* (Paris: Dufaure, 1837).

62. AT, "Second Letter on Algeria," August 23, 1837, Pitts, 23–24; OC III:1, 149–51.

63. AT to RC, October 19, 1837, OC XI, 44–49.

64. Cens estimates from André-Jean Tudesq, "Preface," OC X, 18–20. Tudesq gives 457 voters in 1837 (247 voted for Le Marois), 12.

65. AT to Lesdos, December 5 and 15, 1836, OC X, 55.

66. AT to Lelut, November 3, 1837, OC X, 79.

67. AT to Moulin, September 1837, OC X, 72; AT to Clamorgan, October 9, 1847, OC X, 431.

68. AT, "À MM. les électeurs de l'arrondissement de Valognes," October 14, 1837, OC III:2, 41–44.

69. AT to GB, November 12, 1837, OC VIII:1, 262. Le Marois wore the title of comte that Napoleon had granted his father; Ancien Régime nobility kept its distance from the so-called *noblesse d'empire* Napoleon created.

70. AT to Molé, September 18, 1837, OC XVII:1, 346–47; LC, 392–93; GB to AT, September 22, 1837, OC VIII:1, 230–31.

71. AT to Corcelle, January 17, 1838, OC XV:1, 95.

72. Molé to AT, September 14, 1837, in OCB, 1861, 2:76; also in Sainte-Beuve, *Les causeries du lundi* (January 7, 1861) (Paris, 1885), 110. Later, AT also rejected Lamartine's overture to join his *parti social*; see GB to AT, June 10, 1838, OC VIII:1, 299–300n3.

73. AT, "Réponse à un anonyme se disant électeur et qui a adressé une lettre à messieurs les électeurs, le 31 octobre 1837," OC III:2, 46.

74. AT to RC, November 14, 1837, OC XI, 51–52.

75. Alphonse de Lamartine, in the Chamber, on January 10, 1839, *Journal de la France et des Français* (Paris: Gallimard, 2001).

76. AT to GB, January 31, 1839, OC VIII:1, 337–38.

77. AT to GB, January 6, 1839, OC VIII:1, 332.

78. AT to GB, February 1, 1839, OC VIII:1, 339.

79. AT, "À messieurs les électeurs de l'arrondissement de Valognes," OC III:2, 51.

80. AT to Clamorgan, January 1, 1839, OC X, 106.

81. GB to AT, February 16, 1839, OC VIII:1, 352.

82. AT, "À messieurs les électeurs de l'arrondissement de Valognes," OC III:2, 52; see Jean-Claude Lamberti, *Tocqueville and the Two Democracies*, trans. Arthur Goldhammer (Cambridge, MA: Harvard University Press, 1989), 137–38.

83. GB to AT, February 9 and 11, 1839, OC VIII:1, 341, 347.

84. Jean-Louis Benoît, *Tocqueville: Un destin paradoxal* (Paris: Bayard, 2005), 199.

85. AT to Corcelle, October 9, 1838, OC XV:1, 102; AT to GB, September 30, 1838, OC VIII:1, 316.

86. AT, "Allocution à la suite de son élection le 2 mars, 1839," OC III:2, 56–57.

87. AT to GB, March 11, 1839, OC VIII:1, 364.

88. AT to Rosanbo, March 13, 1839, OC XIV, 207.

89. AT to GB, October 8, 1839, OC VIII:1, 380.

90. AT, "Political and Social Condition of France," trans. John Stuart Mill and John Bowring, *The London and Westminster Review* 3 (April–July 1836), 155, 157, 159, 166; OP III:24, 25, 28, 36. See also François Furet, "Tocqueville et le problème de la révolution française," in *Penser la révolution française*, rev. ed. (Paris: Gallimard, 1983), 173–211.

91. OC IV:1, 466–70.

92. AT to Faucher, April–July 1836, OC XVII:1, 283–84.

93. AT to "Un membre de la Société des sciences morales de Seine-et-Oise," March 29, 1836, OC XVII:1, 277–82.

94. OC IV:1, 95, 111.

95. AT to GB, May 26, 1837, in *Tocqueville and Beaumont*, 492–93; OC VIII:1, 194–95.

96. Montalivet sent his circular out in August 1838 to Conseils généraux. OC IV:1, 529, note pertaining to p. 115**.

97. OC IV:2, 93–100.

98. AT to GB, October 19, 1838, OC VIII:1, 318–21; GB to AT, October 25, 1838, OC VIII:1, 324.

99. Michelle Perrot, "Introduction," OC IV:1, 27.

100. AT to GB, December 11, 1837, OC VIII:1, 271.

101. Rosanvallon, *Moment Guizot*, 226.

102. Françoise Mélonio, "Introduction," OC XVI, 16.

103. *Memoirs of the Duchesse de Dino, 1836–1840*, ed. Princesse Radziwill (née Castellane) (London, 1910), 28.

104. AT to RC, October 21, 1839, OC XI, 87–88.

105. AT to Mignet, January 8, 1838, OC XVII:1, 369–70; AT to GB, OC VIII:1, 294–95.

106. DA II, 822; OP II:841.

107. AT to RC, December 6, 1836, OC XI, 29.

108. AT to RC, August 30, 1838, in *Tocqueville and Beaumont*, 578; OC XI, 71.

109. AT to John Stuart Mill, November 9, 1836, OC VI:1, 314.

110. AT to Reeve, November 21, 1836, in *Tocqueville and Beaumont*, 571–72; OC VI:1, 35.

111. AT to Castellane, December 1837 or January 1838, OC XVII:1, 366.

112. AT to Salvandy, January 2, 1838, OC XVII:1, 369.

113. AT to GB, November 22, 1836, OC VIII:1, 174.

114. AT to GB, April 1838, OC VIII:1, 291.

115. AT to LK, November 10, 1836, OC XIII:1, 418.

116. AT, "Mon instinct, mes opinions," circa 1841, in *The Tocqueville Reader: A Life in Letters and Politics*, ed. Olivier Zunz and Alan S. Kahan (Oxford: Blackwell, 2002), 219; OC III:2, 87; Roger Boesche, *The Strange Liberalism of Alexis de Tocqueville* (Ithaca, NY: Cornell University Press, 1987), 264–66.

117. DA II, 658; OP II:679.

118. AT to Reeve, February 3, 1840, in *Tocqueville Reader*, 158; OC VI:1, 52.

119. DA I, 15; OP II:16.

120. Fragment quoted in James T. Schleifer, *The Making of Tocqueville's* Democracy in America, 2nd ed. (Indianapolis: Liberty Fund, 2000), 36n.

121. DA II, 581; OP II:607.

122. Alexis de Tocqueville, *Democracy in America*, ed. Eduardo Nolla, trans. James T. Schleifer (Indianapolis: Liberty Fund, 2010), 3:709u; see also Jean-Claude Lamberti, *La notion d'individualisme chez Tocqueville* (Paris: Presses Universitaires de France, 1970).

123. See Pierre Manent, *Tocqueville and the Nature of Democracy*, trans. John Waggoner (Lanham, MD: Rowman & Littlefield, 1996), 68; Peter Augustine Lawler, *The Restless Mind: Alexis de Tocqueville on the Origin and Perpetuation of Human Liberty* (Lanham, MD, Rowman & Littlefield, 1993), 77.

124. DA II, 587; OP II:614.

125. DA II, 599; OP II:625.

126. DA II, 709; OP II:729.

127. DA II, 610; OP II:635.

128. DA II, 611; OP II:636.

129. Michel Chevalier, *Lettres sur l'Amérique du Nord* (Paris, 1836), letters XII and XIII; AT to GB, December 3, 1836, OC VIII:1, 176.

130. DA II, 559; OP II:589. See also Claude Lefort, *Ecrire à l'épreuve du politique* (Paris: Calmann-Lévy, 1992), 55.

131. See Laurence Guellec, *Tocqueville et les langages de la démocratie* (Paris: Honoré Champion, 2004), 202.

132. DA II, 552; OP II:582.

133. DA II, 705; OP II:725.

134. On August 12, 1837, see Nolla, *Democracy in America*, 4:1060k.

135. AT to Corcelle, August 1837, OC XV:1, 86.

136. DA II, 708; OP II:729. See also Lisa Pace Vetter, "Sympathy, Equality, and Consent: Tocqueville and Harriet Martineau on Women and Democracy in America," and Delba Winthrop, "Tocqueville's American Woman and 'The True Conception of Democratic Progress,'" in *Feminist Interpretations of Alexis de Tocqueville*, ed. Jill Locke and Eileen Hunt Botting (University Park: Pennsylvania State University Press, 2009), 151–76 and 177–97, respectively.

137. AT to Corcelle, September 2, 1837, OC XV:I, 86.

138. AT to GB, January 18, 1838, OC VIII:1, 279.

139. DA II, 3, 21, written in March 1838, according to date on manuscript; see Lamberti, *Tocqueville and the Two Democracies*, 143; AT to Corcelle, June 25, 1838, OC XV:1, 100–101.

140. AT to Corcelle, June 25, 1838, OC XV:1, 100–101.

141. AT to RC, OC XI, 67, 71.

142. DA II, 814; OP II:833.

143. DA II, 797; OP II:816.

144. DA II, 834; OP II:854.

145. DA II, 818; OP II:837; see also Steven B. Smith, "Tocqueville's Two Despotisms," *The Tocqueville Review / La revue Tocqueville* 27, no. 2 (2006): 44–63.

146. DA II, 526; OP II:555.

147. DA II, 525; OP II:554.

148. AT to GB, November 5, 1838, OC VIII:1, 325; AT to Corcelle, December 20, 1838, OC XV:1, 105.

149. AT to Ampère, September 17, 1839, OC XI, 128–29, 134–35.

150. DA II, 833; OP II:852.

# Chapter 7

1. Lamartine to Alexis de Tocqueville (hereafter AT), 1840 (not dated but after April), *Œuvres complètes* (hereafter OC) XVII:2, 102.

2. AT to Édouard, August 21, 1842, OC XIV, 228.

3. AT to Pierre-Paul Royer-Collard (hereafter RC), September 27, 1841, OC XI, 107–8.

4. AT to Corcelle, March 10, 1839, OC XV:1, 125.

5. Jean-Claude Lamberti, *Tocqueville and the Two Democracies*, trans. Arthur Goldhammer (Cambridge, MA: Harvard University Press, 1989), 281n39.

6. AT to Gustave de Beaumont (hereafter GB), August 4, 1839, OC VIII:1, 370.

7. A. (Michel Auguste, aka François-Adolphe) Chambolle, *Retours sur la vie: Appréciations et confidences sur les hommes de mon temps* (Paris: Plon-Nourrit, 1912), 130.

8. Charles de Rémusat, "Rapport, 20 juillet 1839, Proposition Gauguier relative aux fonctionnaires députés," *Annales du Parlement Français* (Paris, 1841), 2:232.

9. Le Peletier d'Aunay, "Rapport, 6 janvier 1840, Proposition Gauguier relative aux fonctionnaires députés," *Annales du Parlement Français* 2 (Paris, 1841): 244.

10. Prosper Duvergier de Hauranne, *De la réforme parlementaire et de la réforme électorale*, 2nd ed. (Paris, 1837), 198.

11. Quoted in Pierre Rosanvallon, *Le moment Guizot* (Paris: Gallimard, 1985), 130–31n3.

12. AT, "Notes pour un discours," 1842, OC III:2, 208.

13. AT, "À Messieurs les électeurs de l'arrondissement de Valognes," OC III:2, 52.

14. AT to RC, August 8, 1839, OC XI, 80–81; AT to GB, August 4, 1839, OC VIII:1, 370.

15. OC VIII:1, 373n2.

16. AT to GB, August 4, 1839, OC VIII:1, 371; AT to Corcelle, September 4, 1839, OC XV:1, 135.

17. AT quoted in R. Pierre Marcel, *Essai politique sur Alexis de Tocqueville* (Paris, 1910), 211.

18. Tocqueville quoting Guizot, "Discussion sur les fonds secrets," March 2, 1843, OC III:2, 385.

19. Louis Girard, William Serman, Édouard Cadet, and Rémi Gossez, *La Chambre des députés en 1837–1839* (Paris: Publications de la Sorbonne, 1976), 14–17, 23–26.

20. Duvergier de Hauranne, *De la réforme parlementaire*, 153.

21. AT, "Discussion de l'adresse," January 18, 1842, OC III:2, 201.

22. AT, "La proposition Gauguier sur les incompatibilités parlementaires," February 7, 1840, OC III:2, 243.

23. Chambolle, *Retours sur la vie*, 195.

24. AT to Louis de Kergorlay (hereafter LK), August 12, 1839, OC XIII:2, 64.

25. AT to Eugène Stöffels, July 14, 1840, OC XVII:2, 89; and *Tocqueville: Lettres choisies, Souvenirs*, ed. Françoise Mélonio and Laurence Guellec (Paris: Gallimard, 2003) (hereafter LC), 458.

26. Nassau Senior, "Conversations," August 21, 1850, OC VI:2, 293–94.

27. AT to Ampère, January 18, 1842, OC XI, 157.

28. AT to John Stuart Mill (hereafter JSM), November 14, 1839, OC VI:1, 326.

29. JSM, *The Edinburgh Review* 145 (October 1840): 3–5.

30. RC to AT, August 29, 1840, OC XI, 93.

31. Ampère to AT, OC XI: 136; verses, OC XI, 141–42. ("To counter the negative effects of equality, be sure to love, you tell us, to love liberty.")

32. AT, *Journeys to England and Ireland*, ed. J. P. Mayer, trans. George Lawrence and J. P. Mayer (New Brunswick, NJ: Transaction Books, 1988), 117; *Œuvres* Pléiade (hereafter OP) I, 514.

33. See OC XI, 137n5.

34. AT to JSM, December 18, 1840, OC VI:1: 330.

35. Nassau Senior to AT, February 27, 1841, OC VI:2, 89–90.

36. GB to AT, August 25, 1840, OC VIII:1, 426.

37. Silvestre de Sacy's review of the second volume of *Democracy in America*, in Lucien Jaume, *Tocqueville: The Aristocratic Sources of Liberty*, trans. Arthur Goldhammer (Princeton, NJ: Princeton University Press, 2008), 332.

38. AT to Sacy, October 18, 1840, in Jaume, *Tocqueville*, 336.

39. See Helena Rosenblatt, *The Lost History of Liberalism: From Ancient Rome to the Twenty-First Century* (Princeton, NJ: Princeton University Press, 2018), 108–10.

40. AT to Eugène Stöffels, July 14, 1840, OC XVII:2, 90; LC 459.

41. AT to Guiraud, January 8, 1842, OC XVII:2, 167.

42. RC to AT, October 28, 1839, OC XI, 88–89; Ampère to AT, October 15, 1839, OC XI, 131; AT to Ampère, December 21 and 24, 1841, OC XI, 155–57; Guizot to AT, October 28, 1839, OC XVII:2, 82.

43. AT to GB, October 8, 1839, OC VIII:1, 379–80.

44. GB to AT, October 26, 1839, OC VIII:1, 394; see also OC XI, 146n1.

45. GB to AT, August 5, 1841, OC VIII:1, 441; AT to GB, October 23, 1839, OC VIII:1, 388.

46. AT to Cousin, [early] February, 1841, OC XVII:2, 122; AT to Charles Stöffels, August 17 and November 16, 1841, OC XVII:2, 139, 158–59.

47. AT to Blosseville, December 25, 1841, OC XVII:2, 162; see also Hugh Brogan, *Alexis de Tocqueville: A Life* (New Haven, CT: Yale University Press, 2006), 402–6.

48. AT to Charles Stöffels, July 13, 1842, OC XVII:2, 182 (Henri V, aka comte de Chambord and duc de Bordeaux); see also AT to Corcelle, June 9, 1842, OC XV:1, 153.

49. AT, "À M.M. les électeurs de l'arrondissement de Valognes," June 1842, OC III:2, 59.

50. AT to Corcelle, July 16, 1840, OC XV:1, 146.

51. AT to marquise de Leusse, August 29, 1842, OC XVII:2, 187.

52. AT to Marie, July 24, 1842, OC XIV, 456.

53. AT, "À M.M. les électeurs de l'arrondissement de Valognes," July 8, 1842, OC III:2, 74.

54. AT, "À M.M. les électeurs de l'arrondissement de Valognes," June 1842, OC III:2, 61.

55. André Jardin, *Tocqueville: A Biography*, trans. Lydia Davis with Robert Hemenway (Baltimore: Johns Hopkins University Press, 1998), 315.

56. AT to Corcelle, October 19, 1842, OC XV:1, 161.

57. AT, "Discussion de la loi de régence," August 18, 1842, OC III:2, 137–47; AT to Marie, August 19, 1842, OC XIV, 471.

58. AT to GB, November–December 1842, in Marcel, *Essai politique*, 339.

59. AT to Corcelle, September 1, 1842, OC XV:1, 160.

60. AT to Barrot, September 16, 1842, OC XVII:2, 192; LC, 500.

61. Charles de Rémusat, *Mémoires de ma vie*, ed. Charles H. Pouthas (Paris: Plon, 1962), 4:46–47; on Rémusat being a profound thinker of democracy, see Aurelian Craiutu, *Liberalism under Siege: The Political Thought of the French Doctrinaires* (Lanham, MD: Lexington Books, 2003), 115; Rosanvallon, *Le moment Guizot*, 54.

62. The Société républicaine des saisons, under Barbès and Blanqui's leadership, stormed the Hôtel de Ville and police headquarters in Paris in a failed and violently repressed attempt to establish a republic on May 12, 1839.

63. AT, "Lettres sur la situation intérieure de la France," OC III:2, 119; see also AT to GB, December 15, 1842, OC VIII:1, 488.

64. AT to Barrot, September 16, 1842, OC XVII:2, 195; LC 504.

65. September (1835) laws, after Giuseppe Fieschi's attempt to assassinate King Louis Philippe; Barrot to AT, October 11, 1842, in Marcel, *Essai politique*, 482–86.

66. AT, "Lettres sur la situation intérieure de la France," OC III:2, 100–101.

67. AT, "Lettres sur la situation intérieure de la France," OC III:2, 107–8.

68. AT to Reeve, July 16, 1844, OC VI:1, 75.

69. AT, "Manifeste pour la Nouvelle équipe du Commerce," July 24, 1844, OC III:2, 124.

70. AT to GB, October 3, 1845, OC VIII:1, 564–65.

71. AT to Corcelle, August 13, 1844, OC XV:1, 183.

72. AT to Corcelle, October 19, 1842, OC XV:1, 162.

73. AT to Corcelle, August 13, 1844, OC XV:1, 185; see also Françoise Mélonio, "Préface," in *Tocqueville et la littérature*, ed. Françoise Mélonio and José-Luis Diaz (Paris: Presses de l'Université Paris-Sorbonne, 2005), 7.

74. Jardin, *Tocqueville*, 392.

75. AT to Corcelle, September 17, 1844, OC XV:1, 195.

76. AT to Corcelle, November 15, 1843, OC XV:1, 173; AT to Édouard, December 6, 1843, OC XIV, 236. See also David A. Selby, "The Path Not Taken: Tocqueville, the Freedom of Education, and Alfred Stepan's 'Twin Tolerations' in France, 1843–50," *Journal of Church and State* 55 (2012): 640–68.

77. Prison report prepared for June 20, 1840 (printed in 1841). Not in OC IV:2; a copy is held at the Archives de la Manche.

78. AT, "Observations sur le mémoire de M. Ch. Lucas relatif au régime parlementaire," Académie des sciences morales et politiques, February 1844, OC IV:2, 185, 189.

79. Abbé Crozes to AT, May 13, 1844, OC IV:2, 305–7.

80. AT, "Rapport fait au nom de la Commission chargée d'examiner le projet de loi sur les prisons, session de 1843," OC IV:2, 119.

81. AT, "Observations sur le mémoire de M. Ch. Lucas," OC IV:2, 135.

82. AT, "Projet de discours sur les affaires religieuses," 1844, OC III:2, 593.

83. GB, Four articles, September 7, 9, 22, and October 2, 1843, in *Le Siècle*, OC IV:1, 473–89.

84. AT to Corcelle, December 11, 1843, OC XV:1, 175. Mont-Saint-Michel Abbey was used as a prison at the time.

85. GB to AT, December 9, 1843, OC VIII:1, 516–17.

86. AT, "Observations sur le mémoire de M. Ch. Lucas," OC IV:2, 184; AT to Bouchitté, April 13, 1844, OC XVII :2, 257; see also Michelle Perrot's note **, OC IV:2, 338; Jean-Louis Benoît, *Tocqueville moraliste* (Paris: Honoré Champion, 2004), 582.

87. AT, "Interventions en qualité de rapporteur de la loi sur la réforme des prisons," April 24, 1844, OC IV:2, 223, 226.

88. AT, "Projet de discours sur les affaires religieuses," OC III:2, 593.

89. Alexis de Tocqueville, *Democracy in America*, ed. Olivier Zunz, trans. Arthur Goldhammer (New York: Library of America, 2004) (hereafter DA I [1835] or DA II [1840]), I, 47; OP II:45.

90. DA II, 501; OP II:530.

91. AT, "Idées de discours," October 1844, OC III:2, 551.

92. AT to Savoye, April 25, 1841, OC XVII:2, 128–29.

93. Jean-Jacques Chevallier, "Introduction," OC IX, 9.

94. AT to Arthur de Gobineau (hereafter AG), October 22, 1843, OC IX, 67–69.

95. AT to AG, October 2, 1843, OC IX, 57.

96. AT to AG, August 8, 1843 and October 4, 1844, OC IX, 43 and 74, respectively.

97. AT relied on AG for summaries of works by Kant, Saint-Simon, Godwin, and Darwin and reports on their respective roles in the evolution of moral thinking. Despite JSM's prodding to read the English Utilitarians as the most important contributors to the modern conversation on ethics, AT had not mastered them and was still asking AG for summaries of Bentham's work in 1843. AG to AT, October 2, 1843, OC IX, 56–57.

98. *Democracy in America* as part of the "rubish [*sic*]," the fragments Tocqueville threw away. See Eduardo Nolla's critical edition, trans. James Schleifer (Indianapolis: Liberty Fund, 2009), 3:961.

99. AT to AG, September 5, 1843, OC IX, 46.

100. Sonia Chabot, "Education civique, instruction publique et liberté de l'enseignement dans l'œuvre d'Alexis de Tocqueville," *The Tocqueville Review / La revue Tocqueville* 17, no. 1 (1996): 211–49.

101. R. P. Lecanuet, *Montalembert: La liberté d'enseignement* (Paris, 1909), 2:198.

102. AT to Lord Radnor, May 3, 1835, OC VI:3, 42.

103. Rémusat, *Mémoires*, 4:59.

104. On March 29, 1837, Guizot unsuccessfully proposed a bill favoring liberty of education at the secondary school level, thoroughly analyzed in a series of draft articles for *Le Commerce* AT wrote in October 1844; see AT, "Articles sur la liberté d'enseignement," OC III:2, 527–49.

105. OC XIV, 238n3.

106. AT to Clamorgan, March 7, 1840, OC X, 155n4.

107. Rémusat, *Mémoires*, 4:69.

108. LK to Marie, October 9, 1844, OC XIII:2, 151–52. LK had recognized AT's prose in *Le Commerce*.

109. Lecanuet, *Montalembert*, 2:153.

110. Jardin, *Tocqueville*, 363.

111. Abbé Desgarets, *La charte et la liberté de l'enseignement* (Lyon: Librairie chrétienne, 1843), 12.

112. Jules Michelet and Edgar Quinet, *Des Jésuites*, 6th ed. (Paris, 1844), 69, 13. See also Joan Wallach Scott, *Sex and Secularism* (Princeton, NJ: Princeton University Press, 2018), 38–39.

113. Michelet and Quinet, *Des Jésuites*, 264.

114. AT to Quinet, June 19 or July 3, 1843, OC XVII:2, 222.

115. A History of Proofs of God's Existence, Considered in their Most General Principles, from the Most Ancient Times to Anselm of Canterbury's *Monologium*.

116. AT to Cousin, March 21, 1842, OC XVII:2, 171. Later, AT will also promote Bouchitté's book on Poussin also for the Montyon Prize, again unsuccessfully.

117. Rémusat, *Mémoires*, 4:60.

118. "Nihil magis diligit Deus in hoc mundo quam libertatem Ecclessiae suae."

119. AT to Édouard, December 6, 1843, OC XIV, 237.

120. AT, "Discussion de l'adresse," January 17, 1844, OC III:2, 487.

121. AT, Notes on "Liberté d'enseignement," OC III:2, 558.

122. *L'Univers*, January 18, 1844; *Le Siècle*, January 18, 1844; *Le Constitutionnel*, January 18, 1844.

123. AT to Bouchitté, February 4, 1844, OC XVII:2, 246–47.

124. M. H. Corne, *De l'éducation publique dans ses rapports avec la famille et avec l'état* (Paris, 1844), vii, an opinion AT fully shared; see his "Discussion dans un bureau de la Chambre," OC III:2, 510.

125. Abbé Dupanloup, second letter to M. le duc de Broglie, 1844, 18, 21 (brochure in Tocqueville's library).

126. *Procès de M. L'Abbé Combalot, précédé d'une introduction par M. Louis Veuillot* (Paris, March 1844), VI; AT to Édouard, December 6, 1843, OC XIV, 238. See also Waldemar Gurian, "Louis Veuillot," *The Catholic Historical Review* 36 (January 1951): 385–414.

127. Lecanuet, *Montalembert*, 2:190.

128. See Mgr. Dupanloup, *Défense de la liberté de l'église* (Paris, 1861), 168; AT, "Annexe du 2ème article," OC III:2, 537n1.

129. AT, draft article "Sur la liberté d'enseignement," written for *Le Commerce* but unpublished, OC III:2, 534.

130. AT, "La liberté d'enseignement," *Le Commerce*, July 28, 1844, OC III:2, 514.

131. AT to Corcelle, November 15, 1843, OC XV:1, 173.

132. AT, "Polémiques à propos de la liberté d'enseignement," *Le Commerce*, November 28, 1844, OC III:2, 564.

133. AT, still on good terms with Chambolle, visited with him during the latter's recovery; see Chambolle, *Retours sur la vie*, 205.

134. AT, "Polémiques à propos de la liberté d'enseignement," November 28, 1844, OC III:2, 560–61n2; see also Jean-Louis Benoît, *Tocqueville: Un destin paradoxal* (Paris: Bayard, 2005), 247–48.

135. See OC III:2, 562n2.

136. See OC VIII:1, 543n1.

137. GB to AT, December 10, 1844, OC VIII:1, 553.

138. AT to GB, December 9, 1844, OC VIII:1, 548–49.

139. AT to AG, September 5, 1843, OC IX, 47; AT to AG, October 2, 1843, OC IX, 61.

140. AT, "Rapport sur les enfants trouvés, 1843. Rapport fait au nom de la Commission d'administration générale," August 28, 1843, OC X, 593–607.

141. The Constituent Assembly was in session from July 9, 1789 to September 30, 1791; OC IX, appendix 4, 352.

142. Corcelle, "De l'impôt progressif," *Revue des deux mondes* (April 1833): 63–87.

143. AT, "Note sur l'affaire du recensement et en général sur les impôts directs. Incident sur l'appel aux conseils généraux," September 1841, OC III:2, 187–93.

144. Roger Boesche, *Tocqueville's Road Map* (Lanham, MD: Lexington Books, 2006), 193.

145. Jardin, *Tocqueville*, 390; AT to Marie, 1846, OC XIV, 502. In the fall of 1845, Tocqueville joined two other attemps to launch other newspapers, first *Le Soleil* and then *Le Pays*. He helped define ambitious goals for them, with in each case an impassioned defense of freedom of the press, freedom of association, and freedom of teaching, and the setting of concrete goals for various ministries, but both attemps aborted. See "Prospectus du *Soleil*, supplement au *Commerce* du 16 Septembre 1845," and "*Le Pays*, journal des intérêts nationaux, prospectus du 14 octobre 1845," OC XVII:2, 17, 323–34.

146. AT, "Rapport sur les enfants trouvés," September 19, 1846, OC X, 691.

147. Michael Drolet, *Tocqueville, Democracy and Social Reform* (Houndmills, UK: Palgrave Macmillan, 2003), 171; OC XVI, 286n4.

148. Drolet, *Tocqueville*, 161; Edmond L'Hommedé, *Un département français sous la monarchie de juillet: Le Conseil Général de la Manche et Alexis de Tocqueville* (Paris: Boivin, 1933), 138–45.

149. AT to GB, July 20, 1846, OC VIII:1, 577.

150. AT to Jules Dufaure, September 2, 1846, OC XVII:2, 374; Jardin, *Tocqueville*, 398.

151. AT to Corcelle, September 25, 1846, OC XV:1, 216.

152. AT to GB, October 28, 1846, OC VIII:1, 592–94; GB to AT, November 16, 1846, OC VIII:1, 596–600; AT to GB, December 14, 1846, OC VIII:1, 601–6.

153. AT, "Fragments pour une politique sociale" and "Question financière," October 1847, OC III:2, 737, 744.

154. *Bulletin des Amis de la société d'Ismaÿl Urbain* 6 (December 1994).

155. AT to Enfantin, November 10, 1847, OC XVII:2, 422–23; LC 592.

156. Eric Keslassy, *Le libéralisme de Tocqueville à l'épreuve du paupérisme* (Paris: L'Harmattan, 2000), 213.

157. AT, "Question financière," October 1847, OC III:2, 737.

158. AT, "De la responsabilité des agents du pouvoir," February 16 and 27, 1845, OC III:2, 156, 162–67; "Discussion du budget de la marine," June 28, 1843, OC III:2, 227–35.

159. AT, "De la classe moyenne et du peuple," October 1847, OC III:2, 740.

## Chapter 8

1. See Lawrence C. Jennings, *French Anti-slavery: The Movement for the Abolition of Slavery in France, 1802–1848* (Cambridge: Cambridge University Press, 2000), 56–58 for the list of society members.

2. Alexis de Tocqueville (hereafter AT) to Corcelle, February 9, 1836, *Œuvres complètes* (hereafter OC) XV:1, 59.

3. AT, "L'émancipation des esclaves," OC III:1, 100–101.

4. Jennings, *French Anti-slavery*, 124–26.

5. AT to Eckstein, March 8, 1838, OC XVII:1, 377.

6. AT, Discours improvisé, Académie des sciences morales et politiques, in *Le phare de la Manche*, May 26, 1839, OC XVI, 167.

7. AT, "Intervention dans la discussion de la loi sur le régime des esclaves dans les colonies," April 1845, OC III:1, 124–25.

8. AT to Louis de Kergorlay (hereafter LK), July 3, 1839, in R. Pierre Marcel, *Essai politique sur Alexis de Tocqueville* (Paris, 1910), 315.

9. "L'émancipation des esclaves," *Le Siècle*, October 22, 1843, OC III:1, 81.

10. AT, "Rapport fait au nom de la commission chargée d'examiner la proposition de M. de Tracy, relative aux esclaves des colonies," July 23, 1839, OC III:1, 81, 87.

11. AT to Royer-Collard, October 21, 1839, OC XI, 87–88.

12. Senior to AT, June 25 and 26, 1839, OC VI:2, 86–89.

13. Comte de Mauny, *Appel à l'honneur national* (Paris, 1839), 97, 99, from AT, *Democracy in America*, ed. Olivier Zunz, trans. Arthur Goldhammer (New York: Library of America, 2004) (hereafter DA) I, 473–74; *Œuvres* Pléiade (hereafter OP) II:478.

14. AT to Sparks, October 13, 1840, in *Tocqueville and Beaumont in America: Their Friendship and Their Travels*, ed. Olivier Zunz, trans. Arthur Goldhammer (Charlottesville: University of Virginia Press, 2010), 593.

15. *Tocqueville and Beaumont on Social Reform*, ed. and trans. Seymour Drescher (New York: Harper & Row, 1968), 98–99n; Seymour Drescher, *Dilemmas of Democracy: Tocqueville and Modernization* (Pittsburgh: University of Pittsburgh Press, 1968), 184n50.

16. AT to Gustave de Beaumont (hereafter GB), August 9, 1843, OC VIII:1, 506.

17. AT, "L'émancipation des esclaves," *Le Siècle*, December 14, 1843, OC III:1, 106, 106n1.

18. AT, "L'émancipation des esclaves," *Le Siècle*, December 6, 1843, OC III:1, 104–5.

19. AT, "Intervention dans la discussion de la loi sur le régime des esclaves dans les colonies," May 30, 1845, OC III:1, 116.

20. AT, address to the Chamber in the "Discussion du budget," May 20, 1842, OC III:2, 328.

21. The French had been active in the slave trade for a long time, illegally transporting almost 80,000 slaves to the Caribbean between 1814 and 1831, but Franco-British treaties for the mutual right to search suspected slavers had reduced some of this traffic in the early days of the July Monarchy. Jennings, *French Anti-slavery*, 32.

22. AT, address to the Chamber in the "Discussion du budget," May 20, 1842, OC III:2, 326–27, 332.

23. AT, "Discours prononcé à la Chambre des députés, le 28 janvier 1843, dans la discussion du projet d'adresse au roi," January 28, 1843, OC III:2, 338–52, especially 345.

24. He had inquired with his friend Nassau Senior whether an English minister could technically retain his position if Parliament disavowed him. AT to Senior, December 14, 1842; Senior to AT, December 20, 1842, OC VI:2, 93–96.

25. AT, "Discours prononcé à la Chambre des députés, le 28 janvier 1843, dans la discussion du projet d'adresse au roi," January 28, 1843, OC III:2, 345.

26. AT to Spencer, November 10, 1841, in *Tocqueville on America after 1840: Letters and Other Writings*, ed. Aurelian Craiutu and Jeremy Jennings (Cambridge: Cambridge University Press, 2009), 58–60; OC VII:85.

27. *Le Constitutionnel* published AT's letter to Brougham on February 18–19, 1843; see AT to Reeve, February 20, 1843, OC VI:1, 70–71. See also AT's February 1843 letters to Brougham and John Stuart Mill (hereafter JSM), OC VI:1, 339–44.

28. John Knox Laughton, *Memoirs of the Life and Correspondence of Henry Reeve* (London: Longmans, Green and Co., 1898), 118.

29. AT, "Premier discours sur la question d'Orient," July 2, 1839, OC III:2, 265; "Ordre des idées," 1840, OC III:2, 279.

30. AT, "Projet du discours sur l'alliance anglaise, ordre général des idées," OC III:2, 436; conversation with M. Thiers, June 2, 1839, OC III:2, 269–71; James Brophy, "The Rhine Crisis of 1840 and German Nationalism," *Journal of Modern History* 85, no. 1 (March 2013): 1–35.

31. AT supported the idea but abstained, objecting to the vagueness of the law; "Fortifications de Paris" (1841), OC III:2, 665–66.

32. François de Corcelle, *Documens pour server à l'histoire des conspirations, des partis et des sectes* (Paris, 1831), 28, 50.

33. AT to Thiers, July 31, 1840, OC XVII:2, 94.

34. The incident took place in Châtillon, a suburb of Paris, on August 31, 1840. See *Journal de la France et des Français* (Paris: Gallimard, 2001), 1520; see also Paul Thureau-Dangin, *Histoire de la monarchie de juillet* (Paris, 1912), 4:232.

35. Thureau-Dangin, *Histoire de la monarchie de juillet*, 4:247.

36. Laughton, *Memoirs*, 1:125, 130, 132.

37. *Journal de la France et des Français*, 1522.

38. AT to Reeve, November 7, 1840, OC VI:1, 62–63; see also A. P. Kerr, "Introduction," in OC VI:3, 8–9.

39. Laughton, *Memoirs*, 1:140–41.

40. AT, "Second discours sur la question d'Orient," November 30, 1840, OC III:2, 290, 300.

41. Laughton, *Memoirs*, 1:137.

42. AT to Reeve, November 7, 1840, OC VI:1, 64.

43. JSM to AT, December 30, 1840, OC VI:1, 332; Senior to AT, February 27, 1841, OC VI:2, 90.

44. JSM to AT, December 30, 1840, OC VI:1, 333.

45. AT to JSM, March 18, 1841, OC VI:1, 334–36.

46. F. A. de Chateaubriand, *De Buonaparte, des Bourbons et de la nécessité de se rallier à nos princes légitimes, pour le bonheur de la France et celui de l'Europe* (Paris: Mame frères, 1814), 24.

47. "Discours de M. de Tocqueville prononcé dans la séance publique du 21 avril 1842 en venant prendre séance à la place de M. Le comte de Cessac," OC XVI, 256–57.

48. "Discours de M. de Tocqueville," OC XVI, 259, 267.

49. "Réponse de M. Molé," OC XVI, 270–80.

50. JSM to AT, August 9, 1842, OC VI:1, 338.

51. Richard Boyd, "Tocqueville and the Napoleonic Legend," in *Tocqueville and the Frontiers of Democracy*, ed. Ewa Atanassow and Richard Boyd (Cambridge: Cambridge University Press, 2013), 265.

52. AT, "Quatre articles sur Tahiti," *Le Commerce* (Summer 1844), OC III:2, 403–20.

53. AT, "Projet de discours sur l'affaire de l'Oregon," OC III:2, 441–48.

54. AT, "Discussion sur l'amendement Dufaure-Billault à l'adresse enjoignant par un paragraphe additionnel de ne rien céder aux anglais en compensation des mariages espagnols," February 2, 1847, OC III:2, 459–61.

55. John Stuart Mill, "On Liberty," in *On Liberty and Other Writings*, ed. Stefan Collini (Cambridge: Cambridge University Press, 1989), 13. See also Jennifer Pitts, *A Turn to Empire: The Rise of Imperialism in Britain and France* (Princeton, NJ: Princeton University Press, 2005), 200; and Prata Bahnu Mehta, "Liberalism, Nation, and Empire, the Case of J. S. Mill," in *Empire and Modern Political Thought*, ed. Sankar Muthu (Cambridge: Cambridge University Press, 2012), 232–60. For the French, see Tzvetan Todorov, *On Human Diversity: Nationalism, Racism, and Exoticism in French Thought*, trans. Catherine Porter (Cambridge, MA: Harvard University Press, 1993), 195; Cheryl B. Welch, "Out of Africa: Tocqueville's Imperial Voyages," in *Tocqueville's Voyages: The Evolution of His Ideas and Their Journey beyond His Time*, ed. Christine Dunn Henderson (Indianapolis: Liberty Fund, 2014), 304–34.

56. An overly rosy picture; see Jennifer Sessions, *By Sword and Plow: France and the Conquest of Algeria* (Ithaca, NY: Cornell University Press), 208–11.

57. Louis Blanc, *Histoire de dix ans, 1830–1840* (Paris, 1882), 2:893.

58. A position he shared with Saint-Simonians; see Michel Chevalier, *Lettres sur l'Amérique du Nord* (Paris, 1836), letter XIII.

59. AT to Lamoricière, April 5, 1846, OC XVII:2, 358; *Tocqueville: Lettres choisies, Souvenirs*, ed. Françoise Mélonio and Laurence Guellec (Paris: Gallimard, 2003) (hereafter LC), 567.

60. LK to AT, July 8, 1830, OC XIII:1, 199.

61. AT, "Essay on Algeria, October 1841," in Alexis de Tocqueville, *Writings on Empire and Slavery*, trans. Jennifer Pitts (Baltimore: Johns Hopkins University Press, 2001), 111 (hereafter Pitts, *Writings*); OP I:752.

62. AT to Gobineau, October 22, 1843, OC IX, 69.

63. AT, "Notes prises avant le voyage d'Algérie et dans le courant de 1840," OC III:1, 174, 181–83.

64. AT, "Essay on Algeria, October 1841," in Pitts, *Writings*, 111; OP I:752.

65. AT, "First Report on Algeria, 1847," in Pitts, *Writings*, 144; OP I:818.

66. LK to AT, June 28, 1830, OC XIII:1, 197.

67. AT to Lamoricière, December 20, 1840, OC XVII:2, 113.

68. "Notes prises sur le livre de l'Abbé Dubois," OP I:1019–36.

69. AT, "Essay on Algeria, October 1841," 83; OP I:718–19.

70. AT, "Intervention in the Debate over the Appropriation of Special Funding (1846)," in Pitts, *Writings*, 127; OC III:1, 305.

71. AT to Lamoricière, December 20, 1840 and March 30, 1841, OC XVII:2, 113, 125.

72. AT, "Notes to the Voyage to Algeria in 1841," in Pitts, *Writings*, 36; OP I: 659.

73. AT to Lanjuinais, May 16, 1841, OC XVII:2, 130.

74. AT to Hervé de Tocqueville (hereafter HT), May 12, 1841, OC XIV, 216.

75. AT to Marie, May 23, 1841, OC XIV, 428.

76. AT to Marie, August 1843, OC XIV, 479; LK to Marie, August 30, 1843, OC XIII:2, 115.

77. AT to Lanjuinais, May 16, 1841, OC XVII:2, 130.

78. AT to Faucher, July 5, 1841, OC XVII:2, 134–35.

79. AT, "Notes to the Voyage to Algeria in 1841," 54–55; OP I:682–83.

80. AT, "Notes to the Voyage to Algeria in 1841," 43; OP I:667.

81. AT, "Notes to the Voyage to Algeria in 1841," 54; OP I:683.

82. AT to Marie, June 12, 1841, OC XIV, 435.

83. "Opinion de M. François de Corcelle, député de l'Orne, sur les crédits supplémentaires et extraordinaires de 1841–1842," Chambre des députés, séance du 4 avril 1842, brochure in AT's library.

84. AT, "Essay on Algeria, October 1841," 59; OP I:691.

85. See some debates on the issue: Jean-Louis Benoît responded in Res Publica to Olivier Le Cour Grandmaison's June 2001 essay in Le monde diplomatique, "Quand Tocqueville justiifiait les boucheries," reprinted in Jean-Louis Benoît, Tocqueville moraliste (Paris: Honoré Champion, 2004), 553–61. Françoise Mélonio took on Michel Onfray's Tocqueville et les Apaches: Indiens, Nègres, Ouvriers, Arabes et autres hors-la loi (Paris: Autrement, 2017) in "Tocqueville sous le signe du ressentiment," Commentaire 1 (2018): 236–40.

86. AT, "Notes to the Voyage to Algeria in 1841," 57; OP I:687.

87. AT to HT, May 23, 1841, OC XIV, 219; AT, "Essay on Algeria, October 1841," 64; OP I:697; AT, "Notes to the Voyage to Algeria in 1841," 56; OP I:686.

88. AT, "Essay on Algeria, October 1841," 70–71; OP I:704. For a discussion of violence in Algeria in the larger context of French history, see Kevin Duong, The Virtues of Violence: Democracy against Disintegration in Modern France (New York: Oxford University Press, 2020), 53–82.

89. AT, "Essay on Algeria, October 1841," 85; OP I:721.

90. AT, "Intervention in the Debate over the Appropriation of Special Funding (1846)," 118; OC III:1, 294.

91. OP I:1519n1.

92. AT, "Essay on Algeria, October 1841," 111, 113; OP I:752, 755.

93. AT, "Notes prises avant le voyage d'Algérie et dans le courant de 1840," OC III:1, 206.

94. AT, "Essay on Algeria, October 1841," 98; OP I:736.

95. Henri de Saint-Simon famously argued that France could easily afford to lose powerful people but not productive workers, for people who benefit from the work of others are parasitic and can easily be dispensed with, but people engaged in productive work are indispensable to society.

96. AT to Faucher, July 5 and 15, 1841, OC XVII:2, 134, 136.

97. AT, "Notes prises avant le voyage d'Algérie et dans le courant de 1840," OC III:1, 197.

98. AT, "Essay on Algeria, October 1841," 78; OP I:713.

99. AT, "Essay on Algeria, October 1841," 108; OP I:748.

100. AT, "Notes to the Voyage to Algeria in 1841," 37; OP I:660.

101. AT, "Essay on Algeria, October 1841," 89, 96–97; OP I:726, 734–35.

102. AT, "Essay on Algeria, October 1841," 78, 96; OP I:712, 734.

103. GB, *Le Siècle*, November 26 and 30, and December 3, 7, and 11, 1842.

104. AT, "Intervention in the Debate over the Appropriation of Special Funding (1846)," 117–28; OC III:1, 292–307.

105. AT to Dufaure, November 6, 1846, OC XVII:2, 379; LC, 568.

106. AT, "Intervention in the Debate over the Appropriation of Special Funding (1846)," 119, 123; OC III:1, 295, 300.

107. AT to Lamoricière, April 5, 1846, OC XVII:2, 358; LC, 566.

108. AT to Marie, August 19, 1846, OC XIV, 496–97.

109. Auguste Bussière, "Le Maréchal Bugeaud et la colonisation de l'Algérie: Souvenirs et récits de la vie coloniale en Algérie," OP I:907–53.

110. See Françoise Mélonio, "Le choc des civilisations: Chassériau et Tocqueville en Algérie," in *Chassériau: Un autre romantisme* (Paris: La Documentation Française; Musée du Louvre, 2002), 171–91; Valbert Chevillard, *Un peintre romantique: Théodore Chassériau* (La Rochelle: Rumeur des ages, 2002).

111. AT, "Voyage en Algérie (novembre–décembre, 1846)," OP I:766, 768, 773; AT to Lamoricière, April 5, 1846, OC XVII:2, 358; LC 566.

112. AT to Corcelle, March 4, 1847, OC XV:1, 228.

113. AT, "First Report on Algeria, 1847," 132; OP I:801.

114. AT, "First Report on Algeria, 1847," 148; OP I:822.

115. AT, "First Report on Algeria, 1847," 145–46; OP I:819–20.

116. AT, "First Report on Algeria, 1847,"138; OP I:810.

117. AT, "First Report on Algeria, 1847," 142; OP I:815.

118. AT, "Report by M. de Tocqueville on the Bill Requesting a Credit of Three Million Francs for Algerian Agricultural Camps," in Pitts, *Writings*, 174–98; OP I:874–905.

119. Philippe Vigier, *La monarchie de juillet* (Paris: Presses Universitaires de France, 1962), 106.

# Chapter 9

1. Alexis de Tocqueville (hereafter AT) to Eugène Stöffels, July 21, 1848, in AT, *Recollections: The French Revolution of 1848 and Its Aftermath*, ed. Olivier Zunz, trans. Arthur Goldhammer (Charlottesville: University of Virginia Press, 2016) (hereafter *Recollections*), 245–46; *Œuvres complètes* (hereafter OC) XVII:2, 463; *Tocqueville: Lettres choisies, Souvenirs*, ed. Françoise Mélonio and Laurence Guellec (Paris: Gallimard, 2003) (hereafter LC), 635.

2. *Recollections*, 4; *Souvenirs (1850–1851)*, in *Œuvres* Pléiade (hereafter OP), III:728. See Arthur Goldhammer, "Tocqueville's Literary Style," in *Recollections*, xxix–xxxvi; see also L. E. Shiner, *The Secret Mirror: Literary Form and History in Tocqueville's Recollections* (Ithaca, NY: Cornell University Press, 1988).

3. *Recollections*, 47, OP III:779.

4. *Recollections*, 5, OP III:730.

5. *Recollections*, 23, OP III:750.

6. *Recollections*, 12, OP III:736.

7. *Recollections*, 14, OP III:739.

8. *Recollections*, 49, OP III:781–82; see another discussion of this event as reported by Nassau Senior on February 11, 1851, OC VI:2, 347.

9. AT to Eugène Stöffels, March 7, 1848, OC XVII:2, 451.

10. AT, "On Socialism," in *Recollections*, 242; OC III:3, 195.

11. AT, Foreword to the twelfth edition of *Democracy in America*, in *Alexis de Tocqueville and Gustave de Beaumont in America: Their Friendship and Their Travels*, ed. Olivier Zunz, trans. Arthur Goldhammer (Charlottesville: University of Virginia Press, 2010) (hereafter *Tocqueville and Beaumont*), 652.

12. *Recollections*, 225–26; OC III:2, 44–46.

13. *Recollections*, 77, OP III:816.

14. AT to Marie, March 23, 1848, in *Recollections*, 229; OC XIV, 519.

15. AT to Marie, March 30, 1848, in *Recollections*, 230; OC XIV, 530.

16. "Circulaire électorale," in *Recollections*, 225–26; OC III:3, 40.

17. AT to Gustave de Beaumont (hereafter GB), April 22, 1848, in *Recollections*, 231; OC VIII:2, 13.

18. AT to Marie, March 30, 1848, in *Recollections*, 230; OC XIV, 529.

19. *Recollections*, 69; OP III:807.

20. AT to William Rathbone Greg, July 27, 1853, in *Recollections*, 232; OC VI:3, 155.

21. The two were commisaires de la République; see Jean-Patrice Lacam, *Tocqueville et la république: Récit d'un ralliement et de combats* (Paris: L'Harmattan, 2020), 82; Sharon B. Watkins, *Alexis de Tocqueville and the Second Republic, 1848–1852: A Study in Political Practice and Principles* (Lanham, MD: University Press of America, 2003), 37.

22. Gareth Stedman Jones, *Karl Marx: Greatness and Illusion* (Cambridge, MA: Belknap Press of Harvard University Press, 2016), 269.

23. Jones, *Karl Marx*, 310.

24. Richard Rush noted this on April 16, 1848, in *Recollections of a Residence at the English and French Courts* (London, 1872), 463.

25. AT to Senior, April 17, 1848, OC VI:2, 103. See also narrative of this episode in AT's Le Peletier necrology, April 6, 1855, OC XVI, 418, and *Recollections*, 109–10; OP III:858.

26. *Recollections*, 93–94; OP III:838.

27. *Recollections*, 86–87; OP III:829.

28. *Recollections*, 91–92; OP III:834.

29. *Recollections*, 95–96; OP III:841.

30. AT agreed with the favorable portrait Corcelle drew later of Cavaignac (AT to Corcelle, January 1, 1858, OC XV:2, 214–15), but GB dissented (GB to AT, January 11, 1858, OC VIII:3, 533).

31. *Recollections*, 96–97; OP III:842.

32. *Recollections*, 243; OC X, 468–69.

33. Karl Marx, *The Class Struggles in France (1848–1850)* (London, 1895), 60.

34. Marx, *Class Struggles in France*, 50.

35. AT to Eugène Stöffels, July 21, 1848, OC XVII:2, 463; LC, 635–36. See also Roger Boesche, "Tocqueville and Marx: Not Opposites," *The Tocqueville Review / La revue Tocqueville* 35, no. 2 (2014): 167–96.

36. AT to Zacharie Gallemand, June 25, 1848, in *Recollections*, 244; OC X, 469–70.

37. AT to Eugène Stöffels, July 21, 1848, OC XVII:2, 463–64; LC, 636. For a contrast with Marx, see Leonard Krieger, "Marx and Engels as Historians," in Krieger, *Ideas and Events: Professing History*, ed. M. L. Brick (Chicago: University of Chicago Press, 1992), 305–6.

38. AT to Claude Raudot, July 15, 1848, OC XVII:2, 461.

39. AT to Senior, April 10, 1848, OC VI:2, 101.

40. AT to Eugène Stöffels, March 7, 1848, OC XVII:2, 452.

41. *Recollections*, 12; OP III:736; AT, "On Socialism," in *Recollections*, 242; OC III:3, 195.

42. *Recollections*, 236–38; OC III:3, 170–71.

43. Claudia Elzey, "Shifting Landscapes of Association: Tocqueville and the Utopian Socialists," seminar paper, University of Virginia, 2015.

44. AT, "On Cherbuliez's *Democracy in Switzerland*," from *Séances et travaux de l'Académie des sciences morales et politiques*, January 15, 1848, in *Tocqueville and Beaumont*, 645; OC XVI, 217.

45. *Tocqueville and Beaumont*, 640–41; OC XVI, 212–13.

46. Spencer to AT, June 10, 1848, in *Tocqueville on America after 1840: Letters and Other Writings*, ed. and trans. Aurelian Craiutu and Jeremy Jennings (Cambridge: Cambridge University Press, 2009), 93–96.

47. See OC VII, 122n.

48. Duer to AT, July 1, 1848, in Craiutu and Jennings, *Tocqueville on America after 1840*, 97.

49. AT, *Democracy in America*, ed. Olivier Zunz, trans. Arthur Goldhammer (New York: Library of America, 2004) (hereafter DA I [1835] or DA II [1840]), I, 172; OP II:171.

50. *Recollections*, 119–21; OP III:870–72.

51. AT to Adolphe Billault, July 8, 1848, OC XVII:2, 458.

52. *Recollections*, 234; OC III:3, 84. Prior to the Seventeenth Amendment to the US Constitution, which instituted the direct election of US senators, state senators and representatives in State Houses elected US senators; DA I, 173, 229–30; OC II:171–72, 227.

53. *Recollections*, 242; OC III:3, 217.

54. DA I, 153–54; OP II, 152.

55. "Procès-verbaux-de la Commission de la Constitution de 1848," in *Recollections*, 235; OC III:3, 99.

56. AT to Freslon, December 9, 1857, OC XVII:3, 449.

57. On November 15, 1848; *Recollections*, 194; OP III:962.

58. *Recollections*, 215; OP III:984.

59. AT to Clamorgan, OC X, 503–4.

60. AT to Eugène Stöffels, March 9, 1849, OC XVII:2, 489; LC, 649.

61. AT to Rivet, from Frankfurt, May 17, 1849, OC XVII:2, 500.

62. The Montagne had also gained seats; see Hugh Brogan, *Alexis de Tocqueville: A Life* (New Haven, CT: Yale University Press, 2006), 477–78. AT returned to Paris on May 25, 1849, four days before the opening of the legislative session.

63. Mary Wilhelmine Williams, "John Middleton Clayton," in *The American Secretaries of State and Their Diplomacy*, ed. Samuel Flagg Bemis (New York: Alfred A. Knopf, 1928), 19–31.

64. Guillaume Tell Poussin, *The United States: Its Power and Progress* (Philadelphia: Lippincott, Grambo and Co., 1851), 424; *Considérations sur le principe démocratique qui régit l'union*

*américaine et de la possibilité de son application à d'autres états* (Paris, 1841), 173. On the Poussin affair, see Craiutu and Jennings, *Tocqueville on America after 1840*, 409–54.

65. AT to Rémusat, July 4, 1849, OC XVII:2, 517.

66. OC III:2, 31–32, 369–93; see also André Jardin, *Tocqueville: A Biography*, trans. Lydia Davis with Robert Hemenway (Baltimore: Johns Hopkins University Press, 1998), 446–48.

67. AT to GB, October 19, 1848, OC VIII:2, 69.

68. AT to d'Azeglio, July 19, 1849, and AT to Bois le Comte, July 23, 1849, OC XVII:2, 530, 536.

69. *Recollections*, 173; OP III:937.

70. AT to Lamoricière, October 1, 1849, OC XVII:2, 629.

71. Senior, "Conversations," February 15, 1851, OC VI:2, 352.

72. AT to Alphonse de Rayneval, who had been with the pope in Gaëte, July 2, 1849, OC XVII:2, 509.

73. AT to Reeve, June 30 and July 5, 1848, OC VI:1, 102–5; Reeve to AT, July 6, 1849, OC VI:3, 334–35.

74. AT to Falloux, July 22, 1849, OC XVII:2, 534.

75. Giuseppe Mazzini, *A Letter to Messrs. de Tocqueville and de Falloux, Ministers of France* (London, 1849).

76. AT to Corcelle, August 4, 1849, OC XV:1, 34.

77. "Déclaration sur le *Motu proprio* et l'amnistie décrétés par le gouvernement pontifical," *Moniteur universel*, October 19, 1849, OC III:3, 345–65.

78. AT to Corcelle, September 2, 1849, OC XV:1, 374.

79. AT to Louis Napoléon Bonaparte, November 1, 1849, OC III:3, 411–12.

80. AT to GB, November 4, 1849, OC VIII:2, 232.

81. AT to Pauline de Leusse, December 22, 1849, OC XVII:2, 662.

82. AT to Gobineau, January 7, 1850, OC IX, 101.

83. AT to Laurent-Antoine Pagnerre, March 6, 1850, OC XVII:2, 670.

84. AT to Barrot, April 3, 1850; AT to Mignet, April 17, 1850, OC XVII, 2: 670–71.

85. In the articles Marx published in the *Neue Rheinische Zeitung* in March 1850. Marx collected these chronicles under the title *The Class Struggles in France, 1848–1850*.

86. AT to Eugène Stöffels, April 28, 1850, OC XVII:2, 673–74.

87. OC XV:2, 182n.

88. AT to Lanjuinais, September 13, 1850, OC XVII:2, 690–91; AT reported that the rural population had received the president coldly by shouting, "Vive la République." See AT's speech of September 6, 1850, to address the president in OC X, 709–11, OC III:3, 191–92, and AT's initial "Rapport sur le projet de chemin de fer de Paris à Cherbourg, 1844," in OC X, 622–47.

89. AT to Rivet, December 3, 1850, OC XVII:2, 700.

90. AT to Louis de Kergorlay (hereafter LK), December 13, 1850, OC XIII:2, 231.

91. AT to Rivet, December 3, 1850, OC XVII:2, 700.

92. Nassau Senior, "Conversations," OC VI:2, 346, 366; AT to Senior, July 27, 1851, OC VI:2, 132–35.

93. AT to Dufaure, October 4, 1851, OC XVII:2, 729; LC, 724–25.

94. OC VI:1, 119–29.

95. AT to Édouard de Tocqueville (hereafter ET), December 7, 1851, in *The Tocqueville Reader: A Life in Letters and Politics*, ed. Olivier Zunz and Alan S. Kahan (Oxford: Blackwell, 2002), 261–62; OC XIV, 272; Compiègne was the site of Napoleon III's court.

96. ET was candidate to legislative elections in 1852; see Jardin, *Tocqueville*, 49; ET to AT, OC XIV, 275.

97. Jardin, *Tocqueville*, 445; AT to Rédacteur de *L'Écho de L'Oise*, February 13, 1852, OC XVII:3, 28.

98. AT to Hippolyte, December 1852, OC XIV, 287–88.

99. The junior branch remained hesitant; see Alphonse de Circourt to AT, December 9, 1853, OC XVIII, 124.

100. AT to Rémusat, March 22, 1852, OC XVII:3, 33; LC, 1033.

101. Zunz and Kahan, *The Tocqueville Reader*, 263–64; OC III:3, 469.

102. AT to LK, June 1856, OC XIII:2, 297.

103. AT to ET, December 7, 1851, 261–62; OC XIV, 272.

104. AT to Reeve, January 9, 1852, OC VI:1, 133–34.

105. "Discours prononcé à la séance publique annuelle de l'Académie des sciences morales et politiques du 3 avril 1852," OC XVI, 231.

## Chapter 10

1. Alexis de Tocqueville (hereafter AT) to Gustave de Beaumont (hereafter GB), February 1, 1852, *Œuvres complètes* (hereafter OC) VIII:3, 18.

2. AT to Reeve, January 9, 1852, OC VI:1, 132.

3. Senior, "Conversations," January 8, 1852, OC VI:2, 390.

4. AT to Grote, October 30, 1856, OC VI:3, 225.

5. AT to Boulatignier, November 8, 1852, OC XVII:3, 68–69.

6. AT to Lamoricière, May 12, 1832, OC XVII:3, 45–48.

7. AT to Rémusat, March 22, 1852, OC XVII:3, 30–36; *Tocqueville: Lettres choisies, Souvenirs*, ed. Françoise Mélonio and Laurence Guellec (Paris: Gallimard, 2003) (hereafter LC), 1030–36.

8. AT to Lanjuinais, April 18, 1852, OC XVII:3, 45; AT to Montalembert, December 1, 1852, OC XVII:3, 75–76; AT to Rivet, June 19, 1853, OC XVII:3, 95.

9. AT to Lanjuinais, June 11, 1852, OC XVII:3, 50–51.

10. AT to Lamoricière, April 2, 1852, OC XVII:3, 38.

11. AT to Corcelle, November 21, 1852, OC XV:2, 61.

12. AT to Hippolyte, OC XIV, end of December 1852, 288; AT to Édouard de Tocqueville, February 14, 1852, OC XIV, 277.

13. AT's and GB's correspondence between April 15 and 29, 1853, OC VIII:3, 105–16.

14. AT to Charles Stöffels, July 30, 1852, OC XVII:3, 59.

15. AT to Rémusat, March 22, 1852, OC XVII:3, 31; LC, 1031.

16. AT to Lavergne, early July 1855, OC XVII:3, 203.

17. AT to Corcelle, May 13, 1852, in *The Tocqueville Reader: A Life in Letters and Politics*, ed. Olivier Zunz and Alan S. Kahan (Oxford: Blackwell, 2002); OC XV:2, 54; AT to Lamoricière, May 12, 1852, OC XVII:3, 46.

18. AT to Corcelle, January 1, 1853, OC XV:2, 71.

19. AT to Lamoricière, November 24, 1852, OC XVII:3, 73; LC, 1060.

20. AT to Hubert, 1854, OC XIV, 290.

21. AT to Rémusat, March 22, 1852, OC XVII:3, 33–34; LC, 1033–34.

22. AT to Hubert, OC XIV, 1854, 290.

23. AT to Charles Stöffels, July 30, 1852, OC XVII:3, 60.

24. AT to Gallemand, July 19, 1852, OC X, 565.

25. AT to GB, August 4, 1852, OC VIII:3, 66.

26. AT, *Democracy in America*, ed. Olivier Zunz, trans. Arthur Goldhammer (New York: Library of America, 2004) (hereafter DA I [1835] or DA II [1840]), II, 584; *Œuvres* Pléiade (hereafter OP) OP II:611.

27. "Discours de M. de Tocqueville prononcé dans la séance publique du 21 avril 1842, en venant prendre séance à la place de M. le comte de Cessac," OC XVI, 267.

28. AT, "Notes on the French Revolution and Napoleon," in *The Old Regime and the Revolution*, ed. François Furet and Françoise Mélonio, trans. Alan Kahan (Chicago: University of Chicago Press, 1998) (hereafter OR), II:185; OP III: 635.

29. OR II:206; OP III:658.

30. AT to Louis de Kergorlay (hereafter LK), December 15, 1850, OC XIII:2, 231; see also Melvin Richter, "Tocqueville, Napoleon, and Bonapartism," in *Reconsidering Tocqueville's Democracy in America*, ed. Abraham S. Eisenstadt (New Brunswick, NJ: Rutgers University Press, 1988), 110–45.

31. AT, *Recollections*, 44–45; OP III:776.

32. AT to Hubert, February 23, 1857, OC XIV, 329.

33. Marx, in the opening sentence of *The 18th Brumaire of Louis Bonaparte* (1852); AT, *The Ancien Régime and the French Revolution*, ed. Jon Elster, trans. Arthur Goldhammer (Cambridge: Cambridge University Press, 2011) (hereafter AR), 65, OP III:107.

34. AT to GB, January 13, 1852, OC VIII:3, 12.

35. AT to GB, March 7, 1852, OC VIII:3, 32; AT, "Notes Taken on the Register of Deliberations of the Directory at the National Archives. May 1852; Transcripts of the Directory," in OR II, 232–37; OP III:685–90.

36. Robert T. Gannett Jr., *Tocqueville Unveiled: The Historian and His Sources for* The Old Regime and the Revolution (Chicago: University of Chicago Press, 2003), 32–33; Benjamin Constant, *Observations on the Strength of the Present Government of France and upon the Necessity of Rallying Round It* (London, 1797), 7. Constant attempted to separate the Revolution from the Terror; see Dennis Wood, "Benjamin Constant: Life and Work," in *The Cambridge Companion to Constant*, ed. Helena Rosenblatt (Cambridge: Cambridge University Press, 2009), 7. On fortuitous similarities between Constant and Tocqueville, see Olivier Meuly, *Liberté et société: Constant et Tocqueville face aux limites du libéralisme moderne* (Geneva: Librairie Droz, 2002), 120.

37. OR II: 214; OP III:667.

38. OR II:209; OP III:661–62.

39. Gannett, *Tocqueville Unveiled*, 32.

40. AT to GB, April 7, 1852, OC VIII:3, 39.

41. "Discours prononcé à la séance publique annuelle de l'Académie des sciences morales et politiques du 3 avril 1852 par M. de Tocqueville, président de l'Académie," April 3, 1852, OC XVI, 233.

42. AT to Mignet, January 31, 1855, OC XVII:3, 187.

43. AT to Gobineau, January 24, 1857, OC IX, 278.

44. AT to Lamoricière, November 24, 1852, OC XVII:3, 74; LC, 1062.

45. AT to Corcelle, May 30, 1852, OC XV:2, 57.

46. AT to Reeve, August 8, 1852, OC VI:1, 134.

47. AT to GB, July 1, 1852, OC VIII:3, 58.

48. AT to Hervé de Tocqueville (hereafter HT), July 24, 1852, OC XIV, 283.

49. OR II:200–201; OP III:652.

50. AT to LK, July 22, 1852, OC XIII:2, 244; AT to GB, August 24, 1852, OC VIII:3, 71.

51. AT to LK, July 22, 1852, OC XIII:2, 244.

52. LK to AT, August 2, 1852, OC XIII:2, 246–47.

53. AT to Freslon, September 7, 1852, OC XVII:3, 64.

54. AT to Gallemand, August 28, 1852, OC X, 569–70; Gannett, *Tocqueville Unveiled*, 45.

55. LK to AT, August 2, 1852, OC XIII:2, 246–47.

56. AT to LK, July 22, 1852, OC XIII:2, 244.

57. AR, 32–33; OP III:72–73.

58. Gannett, *Tocqueville Unveiled*, 48; AR, 157; OP III:202.

59. AT to Charles Stöffels, July 30, 1852, OC XVII:3, 60; AT to Theodore Sedgwick, December 4, 1852, OC VII, 147.

60. AT to Madame de Circourt, September 18, 1852, OC XVIII, 85–86; AT to Corcelle, December 17, 1852, OC XV:2, 65.

61. AT to Sparks, December 11, 1852, in *Alexis de Tocqueville and Gustave de Beaumont in America: Their Friendship and Their Travels*, ed. Olivier Zunz, trans. Arthur Goldhammer (Charlottesville: University of Virginia Press, 2010) (hereafter *Tocqueville and Beaumont*), 602–3; OC VII, 148–49.

62. Charles de Rémusat, "Burke: Sa vie, ses écrits," *Revue des deux mondes* 32, no. 1 (1853): 490.

63. AR, 27; OP III:69. See also Ralph Lerner, "Tocqueville's Burke, or Story as History," in *Tocqueville and the Frontiers of Democracy*, ed. Ewa Atanassow and Richard Boyd (Cambridge: Cambridge University Press, 2013), 74.

64. AR, 4; OP III:46.

65. OC II:2, 340–41.

66. Gannett, *Tocqueville Unveiled*, 66.

67. Edmund Burke to the Earl of Claremont, August 9, 1789, in *Selected Letters of Edmund Burke*, ed. Harvey C. Mansfield (Chicago: University of Chicago Press, 1984), 251.

68. "Discours prononcé à la séance publique annuelle de l'Académie des sciences morales et politiques du 3 avril 1852 par M. de Tocqueville, président de l'Académie," April 3, 1852, OC XVI, 233.

69. GB to AT, April 19, 1853, OC VIII:3, 110; AT to GB, June 4, 1853, OC VIII:3, 128.

70. Gannett, *Tocqueville Unveiled*, 80; AT to GB, August 6, August 26, September 6, October 3, and October 10, 1853, OC VIII:3, 138, 144, 147, 153, and 156, respectively; AT to Jules Dufaure, October 12, 1853, OC XVII:3, 111; AT to Corcelle, February 20, 1854, OC XV:2, 96.

71. AT to GB, March 23, 1854, OC VIII:3, 199; Nassau Senior, "Conversations," April 6, 1854, OC VI:2, 422–23.

72. AT to Senior, July 2, 1853, OC VI:2, 160–61.

73. AR, 86; OP III:128.

74. AT to GB, February 16, 1854, OC VIII:3, 188–89; Harriet Grote in OC VI:2, 415.

75. AT to Corcelle, December 31, 1853, OC XV:2, 89.

76. OC II:2, 383–84; OR II:305; AT to Corcelle, December 31, 1853, OC XV:2, 88–89.

77. AT to GB, July 1, 1853, OC VIII:3, 132–33; Gannett, *Tocqueville Unveiled*, 101–4.

78. AT to GB, December 28, 1853, OC VIII:3, 178.

79. AT to Freslon, July 30, 1854, OC XVII:3, 165; LC, 1108.

80. AT to Freslon, June 9, 1853, OC XVII:3, 92; LC, 1066.

81. Gannett, *Tocqueville Unveiled*, 83.

82. Charles de Rémusat, "L'ancien régime et la révolution par M. de Tocqueville," *Revue des deux mondes* (August 1, 1856): 652–70.

83. AT to Reeve, February 3, 1840, OC VI:1, 52–53.

84. AT, "Political and Social Condition of France," *London and Westminster Review*, April 1, 1836, 163; OP III:33. See also François Furet, *Penser la révolution française* (Paris: Gallimard, 1983), 173–211.

85. Gannett, *Tocqueville Unveiled*, 59.

86. AR, 42; OP III:83.

87. AR, 54; OP III:96.

88. AR, 66; AT, OP III:109.

89. François Furet and Françoise Mélonio, "Introduction," OR I:74; OP III:1011.

90. AR, 45, 37; OP III:87, 78.

91. AR, 52; OP III:93.

92. AR, 56; OP III:98.

93. AT to Freslon, August 10, 1853, OC XVII:3, 105; AT to Rivet, October 23, 1853, OC XVII:3, 113.

94. AT to Charles de Grandmaison, quoted in Charles de Grandmaison, *Alexis de Tocqueville en Touraine: Préparation du livre sur l'ancien régime, Juin 1853–Avril 1854; Notes et souvenirs intimes* (Paris, 1893), 29.

95. François Furet, *La révolution, 1770–1814*, Collection "Pluriel" (Paris: Hachette, 1988), 1:123; Pierre Goubert and Michel Denis, *Les Français ont la parole*, Collection "Archives" (Paris: Julliard, 1964).

96. AR, 79; OP III:120.

97. AT to Ampère, November 18, 1853, OC XI, 227.

98. AT to Ampère, January 1, 1854, OC XI, 232.

99. These two book parts were combined in a single part when the AR was first published in 1856; they were only separated in later editions.

100. AT to GB, January 29, 1854, OC VIII:3, 186.

101. AT to von Bunsen, January 2, 1853, OC VII, 328.

102. Senior, "Conversations," May 1, 1857, OC VI:2, 466.

103. AT to Lavergne, October 31, 1853, OC XVII:3, 118.

104. Alphonse de Circourt on AT, August 1859, OC XVIII, 560.

105. AT to GB, May 12, 1854, OC VIII:3, 213.

106. AT to HT, May 12, 1854, OC XIV, 298.

107. Austin Gough, *Paris and Rome: The Gallican Church and the Ultramontane Campaign, 1848–1853* (Oxford: Clarendon Press, 1986), 231; AT to Gobineau, July 30, 1856, OC IX, 267.

108. AT to Corcelle, June 10, 1854, OC XV:2, 102; AT to Lanjuinais, June 30, 1854, OC XVII:3, 161; AT to GB, August 6, 1854, OC VIII:3, 229.

109. Circourt to AT, June 4, 1853, OC XVIII, 170–71.

110. AT to Rivet, June 25, 1854, OC XVII:3, 160; AT to Freslon, July 30, 1854, OC XVII:3, 164.

111. AT to Ampère, June 21, 1854, OC XI, 246–47; Circourt to AT, July 15, 1856, OC XVIII, 318n.

112. AT to Freslon, July 30, 1854, OC XVII:3, 165; LC, 1108.

113. AR, 35, 85; OP III:75–76, 127.

114. Gannett, *Tocqueville Unveiled*, 207n106.

115. AR, 31–32; OP III:71–72.

116. AR, 157; OP III:202. See also Jon Elster, *France before 1789: The Unraveling of an Absolutist Regime* (Princeton, NJ: Princeton University Press, 2020), 6.

117. AT to Senior, September 19, 1854, OC VI:2, 172–73; Ampère to AT, July 27, 1854, OC XI, 248; AT to Ampère, August 24, 1854, OC XI, 251.

118. AT to GB. January 11, 1855, OC VIII:2, 262.

119. AR, 153; OP III:197.

120. Gannett, *Tocqueville Unveiled*, 140.

121. AT to HT, August 18 and 23, and October 6, 1855, OC XIV, 309–13.

122. OR II:371; OP III:445.

123. AR, 144; OP III:188.

124. Gannett, *Tocqueville Unveiled*, 106.

125. AR, 128–29; OP III:170–71.

126. OP III:1060n.

127. AT to GB, April 24, 1856, OC VIII:3, 394.

128. Lewis to AT, July 31, 1856, OC VI:3, 203; AT to Lewis; August 13, 1856, OC VI:3, 210; Lewis to AT, November 3, 1856, OC VI:3, 226; Mona Ozouf, "Régénération," in *Dictionnaire critique de la révolution française*, ed. François Furet and Mona Ozouf (Paris: Flammarion, 1988), 821–31.

129. AR, 16; OP III:207.

130. AT to Ampère, November 25, 1855, OC XI, 302.

131. AT to GB, January 31 and February 17, 1856, OC VIII:3, 360, 370.

132. AT to GB, February 22, 1856, OC VIII:3, 373.

133. GB to AT, March 8, 156, OC VIII:3, 377–78; AT to GB, March 17, 1856, OC VIII:3, 379.

134. Gannett, *Tocqueville Unveiled*, 142.

135. AT to Lieber, September 1, 1856, OC VII, 178.

136. AR, 4, 169; OP III:46, 215.

# Chapter 11

1. Alexis de Tocqueville (hereafter AT), *The Ancien Régime and the French Revolution*, ed. Jon Elster, trans. Arthur Goldhammer (Cambridge: Cambridge University Press, 2011) (hereafter AR), 182; *L'ancien régime et la révolution*, in *Œuvres* Pléaide (hereafter OP), III:228–29.

2. Gustave de Beaumont (hereafter GB) to AT, June 25, 1856, *Œuvres complètes* (hereafter OC) VIII:3, 417.

3. AT to Rivet, January 20, 1857, OC XVII:3, 367.

4. AT to GB, October 19, 1856, OC VIII:3, 440.

5. AT to Louis de Kergorlay (hereafter LK), August 28, 1856, OC XIII:2, 307–10.

6. AT to Hubert, February 23, 1857, OC XIV, 328.

7. AT to LK, August 28, 1856, OC XIII:2, 308–9.

8. AT to Lieber, September 1, 1856, OC VII, 178.

9. AT to Grote, October 30, 1856, OC VI:3, 223; Suh Byung-Hoon, "Mill and Tocqueville: A Friendship Bruised," *History of European Ideas* 42 (2016): 55–72.

10. John Stuart Mill (hereafter JSM) to AT, December 15, 1856; AT to JSM, December 19, 1856, OC VI:1, 350–51.

11. Françoise Mélonio, *Tocqueville and the French*, trans. Beth G. Raps (Charlottesville: University of Virginia Press, 1998), 98–99.

12. GB to AT, July 8, 1856, OC VIII:3, 423; AT to Corcelle, November 15, 1856, OC XV:2, 186; AT to Freslon, August 20, 1856, OC XVII:3, 305; *Tocqueville: Lettres choisies, Souvenirs*, ed. Françoise Mélonio and Laurence Guellec (Paris: Gallimard, 2003) (hereafter LC), 1189.

13. AT to Swetchine, January 7, 1856, OC XV:2, 269. On the indictment of the Second Empire, see Richard Herr, *Tocqueville and the Old Regime* (Princeton, NJ: Princeton University Press, 1962), 118–19.

14. AR, 14; OP III:56.

15. AT to Corcelle, August 1, 1850, OC XV:2, 29. AT had recorded the same thoughts years earlier in Philadelphia; see chapter 3.

16. AT to GB, September 5, 1856, OC VIII:3, 435.

17. GB to AT, July 8, 1856, OC VIII:3, 423; AT to Ampère, September 18, 1856, OC XI, 346.

18. AT to Bouchitté, January 8, 1858; October 21, 1855, OC XVII:3, 461, 220.

19. Agnès Antoine, *L'impensé de la démocratie: Tocqueville, la citoyenneté et la religion* (Paris: Fayard, 2003), 176.

20. Tatyana V. Bakhmetyeva, *Mother of the Church: Sofia Svechina, the Salon, and the Politics of Catholicism in Nineteen-Century Russia and France* (DeKalb: Northern Illinois University Press, 2016), 177, 184.

21. George Armstrong Kelly, *The Humane Comedy: Constant, Tocqueville, and French Liberalism* (Cambridge: Cambridge University Press, 1992), 114–33.

22. Alexis de Tocqueville, "Conversation with Mr. Mullon," Non-alphabetic Notebook 1, in *Alexis de Tocqueville and Gustave de Beaumont in America: Their Friendship and Their Travels*, ed. Olivier Zunz, trans. Arthur Goldhammer (Charlottesville: University of Virginia Press, 2010), 221–22; OP I:46.

23. AT to Corcelle, November 13, 1856, OC XV:2, 183.

24. AT to Corcelle, October 23, 1854, OC XV:2, 121.

25. AT to Corcelle, March 10, 1857, OC XV:2, 199–200; see also Austin Gough, *Paris and Rome: The Gallican Church and the Ultramontane Campaign, 1848–1853* (Oxford: Clarendon Press, 1986), 61–79; Emile Perreau-Saussine, *Catholicism and Democracy: An Essay in the History of Political Thought*, trans. Richard Rex (Princeton, NJ: Princeton University Press, 2012), 69–80.

26. Alfred de Falloux, *Madame Swetchine: Sa vie et ses œuvres*, 10th ed. (Paris, 1869), 229–30.

27. *Mémoires du vicomte Armand de Melun*, ed. comte Le Camus (Paris, 1891), 1:174.

28. Jean Gaulmier, "Introduction," in Arthur de Gobineau, *Œuvres*, Bibliothèque de la Pléaide (Paris: Gallimard, 1983), 1:ix–lvii.

29. AT to AG, May 15, 1852, OC IX, 197.

30. Gaulmier, "Introduction," 1:xi.

31. AG, *Essai sur l'inégalité des races humaines* (Paris, 1853), in *Œuvres*, 162–63.

32. AT to GB, January 29, 1854, OC VIII:3, 186.

33. AT to Corcelle, June 10, 1854, OC XV:2, 104–5; AT to Adolphe de Circourt, October 15, 1853, OC XVIII, 110.

34. AT to AG, November 17, 1853, in Alexis de Tocqueville, *The European Revolution and Correspondence with Gobineau*, ed. and trans. John Lukacs (Garden City, NY: Doubleday, 1959), 226–30; OC IX, 202–3.

35. AT to Charles Stöffels, April 14, 1842, OC XVII:2, 176.

36. AT to AG, November 17, 1853, OC IX, 202.

37. Edward Lurie, *Louis Agassiz: A Life in Science* (Baltimore: Johns Hopkins University Press, 1988), 264.

38. Reginald Horseman, *Josiah Nott of Mobile: Southerner, Physician, and Racial Theorist* (Baton Rouge: Louisiana State University Press, 1987), 87, 207.

39. Michael D. Bidiss, *Father of Racist Ideology: The Social and Political Thought of Count Gobineau* (New York: Weybright and Talley, 1970), 147.

40. AT to Rémusat, January 28, 1857, OC XVII:3, 373.

41. Alexis de Tocqueville, "Testimony against Slavery," *The Liberty Bell: By Friends of Freedom* 14 (1856): 29–30.

42. AT to Charles Sumner, November 14, 1857, OC VII:198; Edward L. Pierce, *Memoir and Letters of Charles Sumner* (Boston, 1893), 3:548–49.

43. AT to Pisieux, September 21, 1857, OC XVII:3, 428; LC 1263.

44. AT to Reeve, September 22, 1857, OC VI:1, 236; AT to Lady Theresa Lewis, August 5, 1857, OC VI:3, 259–60.

45. AT to Hatherton, November 27, 1857, OC VI:3, 281.

46. AT to Theresa Lewis, October 18, 1857, OC VI:3, 275.

47. AT to Theresa Lewis, October 18, 1857, OC VI:3, 275–76.

48. AT to Grancey, October 8, 1857, OC XVII:3, 431; LC, 1268.

49. AT to Reeve, January 30, 1858, OC VI:1, 255.

50. AT to Hatherton, November 27, 1857, OC VI:3, 281.

51. AT to Reeve, January 30, 1858, OC VI:1, 253–54.

52. AT to Hatherton, March 6, 1858, OC VI:3, 288–90.

53. AR, 4, OP III:47.

54. AT to GB, August 6, 1856, OC VIII:3, 428n; Alexis de Tocqueville, *The Old Regime and the Revolution*, ed. François Furet and Françoise Mélonio, trans. Alan Kahan, 2 vols. (Chicago: University of Chicago Press, 1998) (hereafter OR), II:168–77; OP III:618–30.

55. François Furet and Françoise Mélonio, "Introduction," OR II:5–6; OP III:1121.

56. AT to Duvergier de Hauranne, September 1, 1856, OC XVII:3, 316; LC, 1201.

57. OR II:28; OP III:456.

58. AT to Lanjuinais, February 11, 1857; AT to Rémusat, March 14, 1857; AT to Freslon, December 9, 1857; AT to Rivet, December 24, 1857, OC XVII:3, 377, 389, 448–49, 456.

59. Senior, "Conversations," 1857, OC VI:2, 481–86; AT to Senior, July 10, 1857, OC V:2, 201.

60. AT to Marie, June 27, 1857, OC XIV, 607.

61. AT to Marie, June 25, 1857, OC XIV, 605; AT to Senior, July 2, 1853, OC VI:2, 161.

62. Colin Higgins, "'Seeing Sights That Don't Exist': Karl Marx in the British Museum Round Reading Room," *Library and Information History* 33, no. 2 (2017): 81–96.

63. AT to Reeve, August 8, 1857, OC VI:1, 232–45; AT to Pisieux, September 21, 1857, OC XVII:3, 427; LC, 1262.

64. AT to Marie, July 22, 1857, OC XIV, 625.

65. AT to Sumner, November 14, 1857, OC VII, 217–18.

66. AT to Freslon, February 3, 1857, OC XVII:3, 374.

67. AT to LK, May 16, 1858, OC XIII:2, 338.

68. AT, "Notes sur la révolution française de Thiers," OC XVI, 537.

69. AT, *Democracy in America*, trans. Arthur Goldhammer, ed. Olivier Zunz (New York: Library of America, 2004) (hereafter DA I [1835] or DA II [1840]), II, 572; OP II:600.

70. AT, *Recollections: The French Revolution of 1848 and Its Aftermath*, ed. Olivier Zunz, trans. Arthur Goldhammer (Charlottesville: University of Virginia Press, 2016), 45; OP III:776.

71. AT to Duvergier de Hauranne, September 1, 1856, in *The Tocqueville Reader: A Life in Letters and Politics*, ed. Olivier Zunz and Alan S. Kahan (Oxford: Blackwell, 2002), 273–74; OC XVII:3, 315–16; LC, 1200–201.

72. OR II:237–29; OP III:690–92.

73. AT to Michelet, February 1840 and April 27, 1840, OC XVII:2, 68–69, 71–72.

74. Pierce, *Memoir and Letters of Charles Sumner* 3:531–32.

75. Jules Michelet, "Préface," October 1868, in *Histoire de la révolution française*, Bibliothèque de la Pléiade (Paris: Gallimard, 2019), 2:1109–10.

76. Furet and Mélonio, "Introduction," OR II:8–9; OP III:1124.

77. Keith Baker, "Tocqueville's Blind Spot? Political Contestations under the Old Regime," *The Tocqueville Review / La revue Tocqueville* 27 (2006): 265–66.

78. OR 67–68; OP III:504–6.

79. R. R. Palmer, "Introduction," in *The Two Tocquevilles: Father and Son; Hervé and Alexis de Tocqueville on the Coming of the French Revolution* (Princeton, NJ: Princeton University Press, 1987), 31. Historians have debated whether an "aristocratic reaction" against royal absolutism recurred during the Ancien Régime.

80. OR II:46; OP III:479–80.

81. Hervé de Tocqueville, *Survey of the Reign of Louis XVI*, in Palmer, *The Two Tocquevilles*, 92; *Coup d'œil sur le règne de Louis XVI: Depuis son avènement à la couronne jusqu'à la séance du 23 juin 1789: Pour faire suite à l'histoire philosophique du règne de Louis XV* (Paris, 1850), 277.

82. François Guizot to AT, June 30, 1856, partially reproduced in OC XVI, 343n; also in Lucien Jaume's *Tocqueville: The Aristocratic Sources of Liberty*, trans. Arthur Goldhammer (Princeton, NJ: Princeton University Press, 2013), 285–86.

83. OR II:49, 64; OP III:482, 500.

84. OR II:57; OP III:492.

85. Michelet, *Histoire de la révolution française*, 72–73.

86. Louis Blanc, *Histoire de la révolution française*, 12 vols. (Brussels, 1847–62), 2:179.

87. OR II:203; OP III:655.

88. AT to Marie, April 18, 1858, OC XIV, 637.

89. OR II:162; OR III, 610–11.

90. David Bien, "Aristocratie," in *Dictionnaire critique de la révolution française*, ed. François Furet and Mona Ozouf (Paris: Flammarion, 1988), 639–52.

91. OR II:98–99, 103; OP III:537–38, 542.

92. OR II:57, 108; OP III:492, 548.

93. DA I, 172; OP II:171.

94. AT to LK, May 16, 1858, OC XIII:2, 337.

95. AT to Grancey, November 18, 1857, OC XVII:3, 444.

96. With the notable exception of his 1836 essay "Political and Social Condition of France," written at JSM's request for the *London and Westminster Review*; OP III:1–40.

97. AT to Grote, July 23, 1858, OC VI:3, 294–95.

98. AT to Milnes, July 22, 1858, OC VI:3, 293–94; AT to Hubert, July 28, 1858, OC XIV, 349; AT to GB, May 21, 1858, OC VIII:3, 569–70.

99. AT to Ampère, August 30, 1858, OC XI, 408–9.

100. AT to Édouard, September 16, 1858, OC XIV, 351–52.

101. André Jardin, *Tocqueville: A Biography* (Baltimore: Johns Hopkins University Press, 1998), 525.

102. AT to Lanjuinais, February 7, 1859, OC XVII:3, 551; LC, 1327–28.

103. AT to GB, December 24, 1858, OC VIII:3, 613.

104. AT to JSM, February 9, 1839, OC VI:1, 351–52.

105. AT to Lanjuinais, March 10, 1859, OC XVII:3, 561.

106. AT to Brougham, March 1859, OC VI:1, 283–84.

107. AT to Duvergier de Hauranne, February 25, 1859, OC XVII:3, 558.

108. AT to Corcelle, February 23, 1859, OC XV:2, 242–43; AT to Grancey, December 3, 1858, OC XVII:3, 536–37; AT to Hubert, March 17, 1859, OC XIV, 369–70.

109. AT to GB, March 4, 1869, OC VIII:3, 616.

110. John Lukacs, "The Last Days of Alexis de Tocqueville," *The Catholic Historical Review* 50 (July 1964): 155–70.

111. Senior, "Conversations," 1860, with GB and Mignet, OC VI:2, 502–3.

## Epilogue

1. "Portrait de Mme Childe née Lee par M. de Tocqueville," OC VII, 249–51.

2. Childe to Alexis de Tocqueville (hereafter AT), January 13, 1857, in *Tocqueville on America after 1840: Letters and Other Writings*, ed. Aurelian Craiutu and Jeremy Jennings (Cambridge: Cambridge University Press, 2009), 199.

3. Sumner to AT, May 7, 1858, in Craiutu and Jennings, *Tocqueville on America after 1840*, 289.

4. *Œuvres et correspondance inédites d'Alexis de Tocqueville*, ed. Gustave de Beaumont, 2 vols. (Paris, 1861) [became vols. 5 and 6 of the nine-volume OCB, 1864–66].

5. Charles-Augustin Sainte-Beuve, "Œuvres et correspondance inédites de M. de Tocqueville," December 31, 1860, in *Causeries du lundi*, 3rd ed. (Paris, 1885), 15:105.

6. Charles Eliot Norton, "Alexis de Tocqueville," *Atlantic Monthly* 8 (1861): 551–57; see James Turner, *The Liberal Education of Charles Eliot Norton* (Baltimore: Johns Hopkins University Press), 87.

7. Olivier Zunz, "Tocqueville and the Americans: *Democracy in America* as Read in Nineteenth-Century America," in *The Cambridge Companion to Tocqueville*, ed. Cheryl B. Welch (Cambridge: Cambridge University Press, 2006), 374–78.

8. Frank Freidel, *Francis Lieber: Nineteenth-Century Liberal* (Baton Rouge: Louisiana State University Press, 1947), 325–26.

9. Matthew Mason, *Apostle of Union: A Political Biography of Edward Everett* (Chapel Hill: University of North Carolina Press, 2016), 301–6.

10. Charles Sumner, *Prophetic Voices Concerning America* (Boston, 1874), 160–64.

# ACKNOWLEDGMENTS

LONG BEFORE I EVER ENVISIONED narrating the life of Alexis de Tocqueville, I was introduced to his writings on the French Revolution by the late François Furet—the surest of guides—whom I met in the ebullient Paris of 1968. Nineteen years my senior, François exerted a deep influence on my development as a historian. Ten years later I joined the history faculty of the University of Virginia and had another significant encounter with Tocqueville, helping sociologist Theodore Caplow form a Tocqueville Society, for the comparative study of social change, and launch *The Tocqueville Review/La revue Tocqueville*, now in its forty-fourth year. In 1985, Ted and I organized a symposium at the Library of Congress to mark the 150th anniversary of the publication of Tocqueville's *Democracy in America*, where Furet joined us.

I kept my research focused on the social, intellectual, and institutional history of the modern United States during these years, content to be a "Sunday Tocquevillean." But through a series of fortunate collaborations, I eventually became more involved in Tocquevillean studies. Each new project was a learning experience. Alan S. Kahan and I coedited *The Tocqueville Reader* (Blackwell, 2002). Arthur Goldhammer, translator *extraordinaire*, asked me in 2002 to review his in-progress translation of *Democracy in America* (Library of America, 2004). This important assignment forced me to penetrate Tocqueville's thought process in a new way. Then, as president of the Tocqueville Society in 2005, I collaborated with Françoise Mélonio, in Paris, and Frank M. Turner, at Yale, to organize scholarly meetings marking the bicentennial of Tocqueville's birth. We held these meetings in Normandy, at the Centre culturel de Cerisy and the Archives départementales de la Manche at Saint-Lô, near Tocqueville's ancestral home; in Paris at the

Académie des sciences morales et politiques; and in New Haven at Yale University's Beinecke Manuscript and Rare Book Library. Each meeting offered me the opportunity to exchange ideas with Tocqueville scholars from around the world; several of these dialogues blossomed into lasting friendships.

Art Goldhammer and I continued to work together on critical editions of Tocqueville's writings: *Alexis de Tocqueville and Gustave de Beaumont in America: Their Friendship and Their Travels* (University of Virginia Press, 2010) and *Recollections: The French Revolution of 1848 and Its Aftermath* (University of Virginia Press, 2016). We codirected a National Endowment for the Humanities Summer Seminar for College Teachers in 2016. By then, numerous friends were remarking that the time had come for me to bring all this preparation to fruition and write a biography, a genre of history I had never attempted before. Jean-Guillaume and Stéphanie de Tocqueville invited me to stay in their home, which was once Tocqueville's, explore freely its archival treasures, and develop a special feel for Tocqueville's Normandy surroundings.

I have worked on this biography with the full support of my longtime academic home, the University of Virginia, where I have read Tocqueville with cohorts of students, who have borne witness to Tocqueville's ability never to age and inspire readers to think anew. The history department, which combines collegiality with the search for academic excellence, has facilitated my research in numerous ways. The university's Institute for Advanced Studies in Culture generously welcomed me as one of its senior fellows and made its wonderful facilities available to me as I was drafting and redrafting the manuscript. I extend heartfelt thanks to James Davison Hunter and Ryan S. Olson for their unfailing hospitality at the institute.

A few special people have generously helped me: Claudia Elzey-Aiken, who had already worked with me on the edition of Tocqueville's *Recollections*, diligently researched many parts of this book, and she commented on draft chapters, all the while pursuing a distinguished career in urban planning. I have been very fortunate to have her at my side. Maxwell Pingeon, doctoral student in religious studies, has been an outstanding research assistant, and he proved especially adept at translating some of Tocqueville's unpublished letters. Françoise Mélo-nio, who heads the French commission for the publication of Tocque-ville's complete works (see the Note on Sources), shared with me unpublished material when I needed it. Maurice Kriegel and Eric Cra-han commented on early drafts. As with previous books, my old friend Charlie Feigenoff read the entire manuscript with critical care, as have Art Goldhammer, Jay Tolson, and Priya Nelson. Alexia Blin, who has translated this book into French, has also suggested improvements. I owe all of them an immense debt, while I take full responsibility for the deficiencies of fact or judgment that remain.

My wife, Christine, my children, Emmanuel and Sophie, and Sophie's husband, LaDale, and their children, Henry, Lila, and Ernest, have helped me far more than they know.

*Olivier Zunz*
*Charlottesville, Virginia*

# INDEX

*Note*: In the index, AT is Alexis de Tocqueville, GB is Gustave de Beaumont, DA I is
*Democracy in America* (1835), DA II is *Democracy in America* (1840), and *ARFR* is
*The Ancien Régime and the French Revolution*. Page numbers in *italics* indicate maps.

Abd El Kader, 176, 243, 246, 247, 248, 254.
    *See also* Algeria
abolition by Great Britain, 227, 228, 231–34.
    *See also* slavery
abolitionists: and Algeria, 242; America, 47,
    327–28, 347–48; for French Caribbean
    islands, 226–32. *See also* slavery
Académie des sciences morales et poli-
    tiques: AT's election to, 184–85; AT's
    essay on Cherbuliez, 271–72; AT's
    speech on intellectual in society, 294–95,
    300–301; AT's speech on slavery, 228;
    Bouchitté's lectures, 216; Dareste's
    essay, 298; Gobineau's attempt to enter,
    325, 327; under Louis Napoléon, 295;
    moral doctrines and policy research,
    211–13; nominations, 321; voting
    politics, 137
Académie française: AT's acceptance
    speech, 240, 291, 308; AT's aspirations
    to, 185; AT's colleagues at, 324; AT's
    communication with colleagues, 286;
    AT's election to, 202–3, 208; AT's
    handling of affairs for, 313; elections
    to, 310, 323; under Louis Napoléon,
    295; Montyon Prize, 33, 111, 136–37, 168;
    Montyon Prize nominations, 217, 218;
    *prix de vertu*, 168; reviews of DA I, 140;
    voting politics, 137

Adams, John Quincy: on factions, 81, 82,
    125–26; as host, 99; political career, 72–73;
    on slavery, 73, 92, 94, 95
Agassiz, Louis, 326
Aguessau, Marie Catherine Lamoignon,
    marquise d', 137
Albany, New York, 49–52
Albert (A. Martin, alias), 265
Albert, Prince Consort of England, 332, 342
Alcibiades, 219–20
Algeria: AT's views on colonization, 175–77,
    253–56, 329–30; AT's visit (1841), 245–47;
    AT's visit (1846), 252–53; coexistence
    with Arabs, 253–56; colonization, 242,
    249–56; colonization models, 244–45;
    conquest of, 28–29, 241–44, 246–49,
    252–54; land acquisition/ownership,
    249; letters on (1837), 175. See also
    *Travail sur l'Algérie* (AT)
America: abolitionist movement, 47,
    327–28, 347–48; class differences, 41–42;
    commerce, 37, 47, 50–51, 52, 78, 89–90;
    constitutional and legal principles, 57;
    constitution as model for France, 271–76;
    decentralization, 74–75; election choices,
    90; ethnic and racial diversity, 62; fear of
    disunion, 97, 98; federal-state relation-
    ship, 80–81, 131; free Blacks, 87, 90;
    freedom of press, 57; French residents,